THE END OF THE
SPANISH EMPIRE, 1898-1923

The End of the Spanish Empire
1898–1923

SEBASTIAN BALFOUR

CLARENDON PRESS · OXFORD

Oxford University Press, Great Clarendon Street, Oxford OX2 6DP
Oxford New York
Athens Auckland Bangkok Bogota Buenos Aires Calcutta
Cape Town Chennai Dar es Salaam Delhi Florence Hong Kong Istanbul
Karachi Kuala Lumpur Madrid Melbourne Mexico City Mumbai
Nairobi Paris São Paolo Singapore Taipei Tokyo Toronto Warsaw
and associated companies in
Berlin Ibadan

Oxford is a registered trade mark of Oxford University Press

Published in the United States by
Oxford University Press Inc., New York

British Library Cataloguing in Publication Data
Data available

Library of Congress Cataloging in Publication Data
Balfour, Sebastian.
The end of the Spanish empire, 1898-1923/Sebastian Balfour.
p. cm.
Includes bibliographical references.
1. Spain—Politics and government—1886-1931. 2. Spanish-American
war, 1898—influence. 3. Public opinion—Spain I. Title.
DP243.B28 1997
946'.071—dc20 96-26833
ISBN 0-19-820507-4

3 5 7 9 10 8 6 4

Printed in Great Britain
on acid-free paper by
Antony Rowe Ltd, Chippenham

Preface

Everything is broken in this unhappy country; there is no government, no electorate, no political parties; no army, no navy; all is fiction, all decadence, all ruins . . .

So wrote a mournful Spanish newspaper, *El Correo*, on 7 February 1901, two years after Spain lost the last of her old colonies in America following a catastrophic war with the United States. The Disaster of 1898, as the defeat was soon called, came as a profound shock to most Spaniards, many of whom had deluded themselves that America was no match for Spain. For some thereafter, it became the original sin from which derived the crisis of Spain in the first part of the twentieth century. For quite the opposite reason, the Spanish–American War of 1898 is a landmark in the history of the United States and of those Spanish colonies which broke away from the metropolis as a consequence. Yet while there is no shortage of American and Cuban histories of the war, there are hardly any global accounts based on Spanish sources. Still less are there any comprehensive studies of the consequences on Spain of the loss of Empire. None the less, 1898 looms almost as large in Spanish historiography as that other fateful and much more trumpeted year of 1492.

This book seeks to fill that gap. Its main focus is on the Disaster and its domestic repercussions yet it also locates these within the wider parameters of early nineteenth- and mid-twentieth-century Spanish history. Although touching on these chronological extremities, it is set almost entirely within the period of 1895 to 1923, that is from the outbreak of the last independence struggles in the Spanish colonies to the end of the liberal monarchy or Restoration system. It is axiomatic to the analysis which follows that the loss of the Empire contributed to the fall of this political system.

The book is framed on one hand by a prologue which sets out to paint the imperial background before this period and on the other by a short epilogue which describes the survival of a residue of imperial ideology until the middle of the twentieth century. The structure that has been adopted is mainly chronological; Chapter 1 is a largely narrative account of the colonial wars and the Spanish–American War. Chapter 2 deals with the immediate aftermath in Spain of the Disaster. Chapters 3 to 6, on the other hand, adopt a thematic approach, examining in turn the reactions of sections of Spanish society to war and disaster within the period of 1898 and 1909: the middle classes, the popular masses, the Catalans, and the military. The four themes play a crucial role in the subsequent analysis of the period between 1910 and 1923. The chronological narrative is resumed in the second half of Chapter 7 and the final chapter is a compressed analysis of the crisis of the Restoration state between 1913 and the military seizure of power in 1923.

One hundred years or so after the event, the passion and dismay that greeted the Disaster have long dissipated and historians can now more coolly evaluate its multiple meanings and legacies. The centenary of the Spanish–American War makes a reappraisal of the end of the Spanish Empire an even more urgent and exciting enterprise.

Acknowledgements

A number of friends, colleagues and relatives helped in the preparation of the book. My thanks go firstly to Paul Preston for suggesting the theme and urging me to undertake it. José Alvarez Junco generously agreed to read many of the chapters in draft form and gave warm encouragement. Frances Lannon and Martin Blinkhorn gave some valuable advice at an early stage. I am also indebted to Pep Benaul, Muriel Casals, Lola Elizalde, Enrique Moradiellos, Carlos Navajas, Inés Roldán and Paco Romero who read individual chapters or helped to locate sources or gave expert comments on specific issues or on the wider analysis contained in the book. I am also grateful to my stepfather, Sir William Glock, for reading through the whole manuscript as a layman and making his ever-incisive observations about sense and style, and to my daughter Rosa Balfour for so ably preparing the bibliography for publication. Above all, I want to thank my wife Gráinne for her unfailing support and patience throughout the enterprise and for her acute comments on parts of the original draft.

I owe a debt of gratitude to the British Council for enabling me to do research in Spain and to meet Spanish historians working on the same theme through a grant under the Acciones Integradas scheme. At the Oxford University Press, Tony Morris was, as always, encouraging and generous as History Editor, and Anna Illingworth guided the manuscript through the initial stages of publication with great efficiency.

There are many others, at work in libraries, archives and elsewhere, whom I have not mentioned but who helped in different ways in the preparation of this book. To all of them, I extend my warmest thanks.

Table of Contents

List of Figures

Acknowledgements to the illustrations Figures 1 to 7 inclusive are taken from *La Campana de Gracia*, a Catalan Republican periodical. Figure 8 is from *El Cardo* and Figure 10 is from *!Cu-Cut!*. The author would like to thank the Arxiu Històric de la Ciutat de Barcelona for permission to reproduce Figures 1 to 7 and 9 to 10, and the Biblioteca Nacional for permission to reproduce Figure 8.

Note The illustrations have been selected mainly for their dramatic and satirical qualities. While they depict attitudes widely held at the time, it is not intended by their inclusion to suggest that they represented a cross-section of public opinion.

List of Maps

Prologue

IT could be said that Spain lost her Empire twice over. In the early nineteenth century she lost her colonies on mainland America after protracted wars of independence. And at the end of the century, Spain lost the remnants of her old overseas empire after the Spanish–American War of 1898. The loss of all of Spain's mainland American Empire by the mid-1820s was the result of the fragility of her imperial system in a new age of national revolution. The paternalist bonds joining the Empire together were severely weakened by Napoleon's invasion of the Iberian peninsula in 1808 and after his defeat, by the domestic conflict in Spain between absolutism and liberalism. The imperial system, designed both for the glory of the monarch and the Church and for the economic benefit of the metropolis, disintegrated under the impact of war and civil war at its heart. Neither the monarchy nor its liberal opponents were able or even determined to retain the loyalty of their American subjects. At the same time, independence from Spain proved increasingly seductive to the creole élites of the different component parts of the Empire when they began to taste the benefits of free trade and as the new ideology of bourgeois nationalism penetrated their ranks.[1]

The loss of the continental American Empire was a devastating blow for Spain's economy. Denied the revenue from trade with mainland Spanish America, the treasury plunged at first into chronic deficit. The end of the special relationship with huge areas of America, which had provided Spain with a reserved market for her finished goods and a cheap source of raw materials, deprived the economy of its comparative advantage over others. In the absence of any restructuring of the state, the repatriation of the military and the colonial bureaucracy swelled the ranks of its employees, adding to the burden of the treasury.

Nevertheless, the loss of the mainland was not seen by Spain's élites as the end of the Empire. On the contrary, it was viewed as only a temporary setback. There was a widespread belief amongst them that the cultural and ideological ties binding Spain with Spanish America were so strong that their erstwhile American subjects would eventually return to the

---

[1] Timothy E. Anna, *Spain and the loss of America* (Nebraska, 1983).

fold.[2] Between 1840 and 1860, Spain made repeated attempts to reconquer parts of her old Empire. Above all, the retention of fragments of the Empire, in particular its richest colony, Cuba, sustained the illusion that Spain was still an imperial power of some rank. Indeed, after England and the Netherlands, Spain still had the third most populous seaborne Empire in the mid-nineteenth century. Its continued existence, however reduced, shored up the legitimacy of the monarchy and attendant nobility, helping to maintain the hegemony of aristocratic values amongst Spain's élites.[3]

The components of national culture in late nineteenth-century Spain, therefore, were made up of traditional icons of Spanish identity: the Reconquest of Spain in the Middle Ages, the Discovery of America, the Second of May uprising against the French, victories against rebellious Moroccans in the nineteenth century. 'A bath of romantic history,' wrote one writer in 1907 recalling the books of his childhood.

It was axiomatic that God, with inexhaustible largesse, had given us all that is magnificent and desirable on earth; riches, fertility, a delicious climate, the gift of fruit, illustrious talent, courage and beauty, everything except a good government . . .[4]

While the language may not have been that different from other imperialisms, Spanish nationalism took pride in asserting old-fashioned imperial values as opposed to those of the new colonial expansionism of other European powers. The 1859–60 war against rebellious tribesmen in Morocco was defined thus by a right-wing paper:

In the midst of a godless Europe . . . Spain, a nation reputed to be of third rank, is undertaking a chivalresque war of honour, civilization, of religious enthusiasm. Wars of this kind are a real anachronism in an era in which European soldiers seem to be commercial representatives who kill and let themselves be killed for the profits of their masters . . .[5]

Even in its attenuated form, the Empire provided a common purpose for disparate economic interests of Spain, above all in its main function as a captive market for a range of Spanish products from flour to footwear. So the Castilian wheat farmers, the Andalusian wine growers, the Levante

[2] Frederick B. Pike, *Hispanismo, 1898–1936* (Notre-Dame and London, 1971), 3.

[3] Martin Blinkhorn, 'Spain: the "Spanish Problem" and the Imperial Myth', *Journal of Contemporary History*, vol. 15 (1980), 5–25.

[4] Miquel S. Oliver, *La literature del Desastre*, 75–6.

[5] *El Pensamiento español*, 8 Feb. 1860, quoted in M. C. Lécuyer and C. Serrano, *La Guerre d'Afrique et ses répercussions en Espagne (1859–1904)*, (Paris, 1976), 97.

leather producers, the Catalan textile magnates, the banks, ports and shipping companies and many more, all shared in the benefits of this unequal trade. The preservation of this scattered Empire ensured the state the loyalty of economic élites such as the Catalan industrialists who were largely excluded from political power. The political subordination of the Spanish bourgeoisie within the dominant power bloc was compensated for by the preservation of a protected market overseas. But protectionism eroded the competitiveness of Spanish industry, making Spanish products ever more dependent on the colonial market.

As the new age of imperialist expansion dawned in the 1870s, Spain was singularly ill-placed to defend her colonial interests. The remnants of the Empire were dotted across the globe: Cuba and Puerto Rico in the Caribbean; the Philippine Islands and a sprinkling of other barely colonized islands in the Pacific, the Marianas, the Pelew islands, and Carolines. Spain retained her old historic possessions of Ceuta and Melilla on the northern coast of Morocco and the Canary Islands off the coast of northwest Africa. To these were added the fruits of mid-century Spanish exploration and trade, the protectorate of Ifni in Southern Morocco, the two small islands of Fernando Po and Annobon in the Gulf of Guinea off the west coast of Africa and the small coastal enclave of Rio Muni opposite them, through which trade with equatorial Africa passed. These fragments of Empire were scattered across a vast space, some 45 degrees East to West and 15 degrees North to South (see Maps 1 and 2).[6]

As the scramble for colonial possessions and spheres of influence began, it was Spanish policy to withdraw from international involvement in order to concentrate on domestic reconstruction after the traumas of the First Republic and the civil wars with the Carlists.[7] During this period of internal consolidation in Spain, however, the contours of the world order changed dramatically. From the early 1870s, the more economically dynamic societies, such as the United States, Britain, Germany, France and Japan, underwent an accelerated process of modernization. Economic development, demographic growth, urbanization, and social mobility combined to create mass societies permeated with the values of national-

---

[6] As the energetic journalist and agitator for neo-colonialism Gonzalo de Reparaz pointed out: *La Epoca*, 10 July 1898.

[7] *La Epoca*, the unofficial mouthpiece of the Conservatives, who formed the first government of the 1876 Restoration, declared on 2 Aug. that Spain's foreign policy should be 'modest', 'a policy of withdrawal', allowing 'a reconcentration of all our vital forces': Elena Hernández Sandoica, 'Pensamiento burgués y problemas coloniales en la España de la Restauración (1875–1887)', Ph.D. thesis, Universidad Complutense de Madrid, vol. 1, 565–6 n. 10.

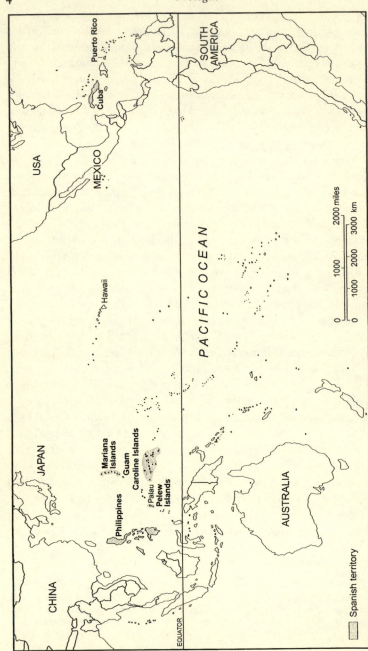

Map 1 The Spanish overseas Empire before the Disaster of 1898

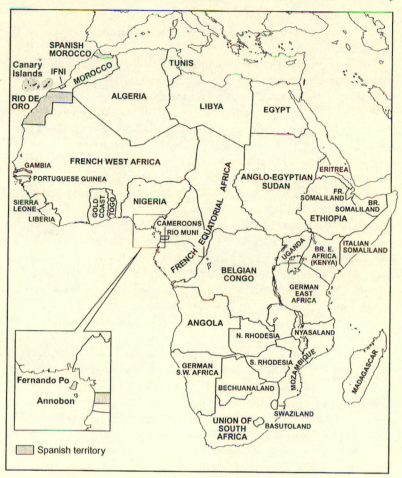

Map 2 Areas under Spanish colonial rule in 1912

ism and capitalism. Many parts of the world, hitherto on the margins of
the earlier process of modernization or untouched by it, began to be drawn
into a close relationship with the expanding economies through trade,
emigration, and conquest. Before 1879, for example, the European Powers had shown little interest in Africa; by the end of the century, they had
carved out most of the continent between them.[8] As the world shrank, the

[8] For a useful discussion of the complex issues around this question see G. N. Sanderson,
'The European Partition of Africa: Coincidence or Conjuncture?' in E. S. Penrose, *European
Imperialism and the Partition of Africa* (London, 1975), 1–54.

far-flung colonies of old but less dynamic powers such as Portugal and Spain, acquired during an earlier wave of imperialism, also began to be challenged.

This process of expansion profoundly altered the previous balance of international power, which had rested until the mid-1860s on the Concert of Europe. In the new multi-polar world, the foci of international tensions multiplied—Africa, the Mediterranean, the Balkans, the Middle East, the Far East, the Pacific and South America. During the 1890s, in particular, a global division of territory and influence took place, giving rise to confrontations and sometimes wars.[9] The tensions between the Great Powers were not only over the partition of previously uncolonized areas of the world but also about the freedom to trade, the concession of monopolies and commercial rights, and the demarcation of spheres of influence in nominally independent territories. What defined power was more the balance of technology than location within the shifting international alliances. The possession of swift fleets, strategically placed coaling stations, and a communications network via submarine cables, allowing control of strategic shipping lanes and canals, was more important for the defence of a realm and its colonies than dynastic connections or good international friends. But the level of technology, in turn, depended on industrial strength.

Spain's weakness in the new world order derived fundamentally from the relative slowness of her process of modernization in the nineteenth century. In relation to France and Britain, Spain's per capita income had fallen in the first part of the nineteenth century and remained stagnant in the second half.[10] Her relatively slow process of industrialization and low level of technology did not allow Spain to adopt a vigorous policy abroad nor attract the alliance of greater powers. As the conservative Carlist, Vázquez de Mella, declared in parliament, 'it is inappropriate to go begging from door to door for an alliance which we know already will not be granted'.[11]

Yet the foreign policy chosen by her governments also weakened

---

[9] Jesús Pabón, 'El 98, acontecimiento internacional', in *Días de ayer. Historias e historiadores contemporáneos* (Barcelona, 1963), 139–95; José María Jover Zamora '1898: Teoría y práctica de la redistribución colonial', *Fundación Universitaria Española* (Madrid, 1979).

[10] Gabriel Tortella, *El desarrollo de la España contemporánea. Historia económica de los siglos XIX y XX* (Madrid, 1994), 2–4. See also Leandro Prados de la Escosura, *De Imperio a Nación. Crecimiento y atraso económico en España (1780–1930)*, (Madrid, 1988).

[11] Quoted in Victor Morales Lezcano, *León y Castillo, Embajador (1887–1918). Un estudio sobre la política exterior de España* (Las Palmas, 1975), 24.

Spain's ability to defend the remnants of Empire. In a world whose frontiers were shrinking fast, her governments failed to develop policies to cope with potential challenges to the colonies. Instead, Spanish diplomats and politicians relied on a balance of international power that was beginning to crumble. Moreover, the Mediterranean and North Africa remained the axis of her foreign policy. It was significant that foreign and colonial policy were separated into two distinct Ministries; thus issues concerning Africa, the Mediterranean and Europe were dealt with by the Minister of State, or Foreign Affairs, while colonial matters were handled by the Overseas Ministry, or Colonial Office, as if the colonies were essentially an extension of domestic politics. This policy, as internal critics warned, was a recipe for disaster in an era when colonial power was being redefined.[12]

It is true that some attempts were made to break out of the semi-isolationist policies followed by the successive Spanish governments. In 1887 Spain entered a secret agreement with the Triple Alliance to maintain the balance of power in the Mediterranean. However, Spain's traditional allies showed little interest in extending this sort of agreement to areas such as the Pacific and the Caribbean where they would obtain no special advantage and where, on the contrary, some risk of upsetting the new regional Powers might increase from such an alliance.

While Spanish commercial interests in Africa were not taken seriously except by a small band of enthusiasts and entrepreneurs, the tiny residue of the old American Empire occupied a vital space in the Spanish psyche. It was seen as a sacred inheritance that Spain could not lose without undermining her national identity. Of these colonies, Cuba was by far the most important in both economic and psychological terms. Its retention was a matter of national prestige. 'Cuba is Spain's Alsace-Lorraine; the honour of Spain is at stake,' said the Prime Minister Antonio Cánovas in 1897 on the eve of the war with the United States. 'Spain without Cuba', wrote the semi-official Conservative paper *La Epoca* in the same year, 'would be as little valued amongst the nations of Europe as Portugal, and would enter a period of rapid and inevitable decadence.'[13] Besides, the Spanish élites felt a sense of duty, as leaders of a nation that had brought civilization to a large part of the world, to maintain their imperial role in

[12] Amongst these critics was the writer Rafael María de Labra; see his speech to the Madrid Atenco in February 1897 in his book, *Las relaciones internacionales de España* (Madrid, 1899), 13–42.

[13] From an interview with Cánovas in Routier, *L'Espagne en 1897*, 166–7; *La Epoca* quoted in Pablo de Alzola y Minondo, *El problema cubano* (Bilbao, 1898), 82.

order to prevent chaos developing amongst what they saw as the untutored and heterogeneous peoples they still ruled.[14]

Unlike the rest of Spanish America, Cuba, along with Puerto Rico, had remained in the metropolitan fold because it was a more conservative society resting on a slave economy whose predominantly sugar trade was largely controlled by Spaniards. The economy of both islands was locked into that of the metropolis. It provided a guaranteed market for Spanish goods and helped to balance Spain's chronic global trade deficit. So successful was its sugar industry that by 1855 Cuba was producing almost a third of the world's sugar. Indeed, the profits it generated fuelled the industrialization of Catalonia.[15]

However, the extraordinary economic growth experienced by Cuba, in particular, created deep contradictions. Spain could neither absorb all of its produce nor provide all the manufactured goods that the island needed. The natural outlet for Caribbean exports was the burgeoning American market, whence Cuba could also satisfy its demand for manufactured goods and technology more easily than from Spain. Yet Spain's colonial tariffs made trade with a third country prohibitively expensive. They also inhibited the diversification of Cuba's economy. The weakness of Spanish rule over Cuba rested not just on the grossly unequal terms of trade between the two countries but on the contrast between the feeble economic pull of the metropolis and the buoyancy of the colonial economy.[16]

Another contradiction arose from the structural crisis of the sugar industry in mid-nineteenth-century Cuba caused by mechanization and the development of the sugar-beet industry in Europe. The resulting intensification of competition led to a restructuring of the industry, driving numerous small farmers out of business, in particular those in the Eastern part of the island. The first independence movement was launched in the East in 1868 by the combined forces of planters, nationalist sections of the middle class and freed slaves. Its more radical charac-

---

[14] Replying to an American diplomatic Note, the Spanish government insisted, 'with the heterogeneous combination of races that exist there [Cuba] the disappearance of Spain would be the disappearance of the only bond of union which can keep them in balance and prevent an inevitable struggle among the men of different colour, contrary to the spirit of Christian civilization': French Ensor Chadwick, *The Relations of the United States and Spain* (New York, 1909–11), vol. 1, 461.

[15] Jordi Maluquer de Motes Bernet, 'El mercado colonial antillano en el siglo XIX', in J. Nadal and G. Tortella (eds.), *Agricultura, comercio colonial y crecimiento económico en la España contemporánea* (Barcelona, 1974), 322–57.

[16] 'Ultramar', *Liga Agraria*, 10 Apr., 1895, in Carlos Serrano, *Final del Imperio. España, 1895–1898* (Madrid, 1984), 159–61.

ter derived from this mix of economic grievance, national liberation and social struggle. The ensuing Ten Years War, a spasmodic guerrilla war between the Spanish army and Cuban insurgents across central and eastern Cuba, caused thousands of victims and devastated the economy.

The 1868–78 War and its brief sequel in 1879 led to a change in colonial policy towards Cuba. Indeed, one influential and knowledgeable Spaniard went as far as to advocate its independence; General Camilo Polavieja, a veteran of the war and Governor-General successively of various provinces after it, called for its abandonment in a letter that eventually reached the Minister of War, General Martínez Campos.

[I]nstead of wishing to prevent the independence of Cuba at all cost and for all time, which would be a vain task, we should prepare ourselves for it, stay on the island only as long as we can rationally remain, and take the necessary measures so as not to be thrown off it violently, against our interests and to the detriment of our honour, before the time when we should abandon it amicably.[17]

Although his advice was ignored, some serious attempts were made by the Spanish government to satisfy Cuban demands for freer trade and greater autonomy. As part of the peace settlement of Zanjón, slavery was abolished in 1880. Two years later, the Law of Commercial Relations was passed lifting duties on a range of lesser Cuban exports to Spain while allowing a progressive reduction in tariff duties on its most important exports to the metropolis. At the same time however, duties on non-Spanish imports into Cuba were raised by over 40 per cent while tariffs on Spanish exports to Cuba were lowered.[18] The effect was merely to strengthen Cuba's dependence on Spain. Colonial relations were put under further strain by a fitful tariff war between Spain and the US. Spain was forced to reduce customs duties for imports into Cuba, thereby plunging the Cuban budget into deficit.

The restoration of high tariffs on American imports, on the other hand, had the effect of raising prices in Cuba. This was combined with a fall in the price and the sales of sugar following the American depression of 1893. Together, these economic problems undid Spanish efforts to improve the balance of colonial trade. At the same time, the protectionist barriers that the Spanish government felt necessary to maintain in order to safeguard peninsular economic interests exacerbated the division in Cuba between sections of the bourgeoisie linked to the Spanish bureau-

---

[17] Letter to General Blanco in Marqués de Polavieja, *Mi política en Cuba. Lo que vi, lo que hice, lo que anuncié* (Madrid, 1898), 34–5.

[18] Alzola, *Relaciones Comerciales*, 36–7.

cracy and those more entrepreneurial sections seeking to expand their markets.

Attempts to concede greater political autonomy to the Caribbean colonies were even less successful. The efforts of the architect of the Zanjón Pact, General Martínez Campos, to use his brief term of office as Premier in 1879 to bring about lasting reform in Cuba foundered on internal political divisions.[19] Indeed, all reformist politicians of one kind or another were confronted with the problem that they might destabilize the fragile system of political alliances on which the Restoration system depended. As Overseas Minister in the Liberal Cabinet of 1893, Antonio Maura proposed a law on administrative reform in Cuba which would have doubled the island's representation in the Spanish parliament and strengthened its own devolved administration.[20] But his proposals were resisted fiercely by the powerful Spanish-linked community in Cuba, backed by their commercial partners and political patrons in Spain. Opponents of colonial reform argued that any concessions of this nature would lead eventually to the loss of Cuba. But their own vested interest in the *status quo* made them blind to the danger that Cuba might be lost much sooner because of their own intransigence.

The failure of Maura's White Paper cut the ground from under reformists such as the Cuban Autonomist Party, polarizing opinion, on one hand, around the Spanish colonial party, the Constitutional Union, whose objective was assimilation into Spain, and on the other, around the separatist movement, led by José Martí's Cuban Revolutionary Party in exile. After the fall of the Liberal government, new watered-down proposals for administrative devolution became law in February 1895 but they were too little and too late to satisfy demands for autonomy and, amongst growing numbers of Cubans, for independence.[21] Ten days later, though there was only a symbolic correlation between the two events, a new and, as it turned out, final insurrection broke out in Cuba.

[19] See Earl R. Beck, 'The Martínez Campos Government of 1879: Spain's Last Chance in Cuba', *Hispanic American Historical Review*, LVI, 1976, 268–89.
[20] J. Durnerin, *Maura et Cuba. Politique coloniale d'un ministre libéral* (Paris, 1978).
[21] Inés Roldán de Montaud, 'La Unión Constitucional y la política colonial de España en Cuba (1868–1898)', Ph.D. Thesis, Universidad Complutense de Madrid, 1991.

I

The Colonial Wars and the Disaster
of 1898

As the second Cuban War of Independence began in 1895, few Spaniards could have imagined that it would end with the loss of Spain's last colonies. Out of all the statements about the new rebellion, only a handful envisaged such a disastrous outcome. Three months before the insurrection began, for example, the ex-President of the First Republic, Nicolás Salmerón, warned parliament, 'What you do not concede to the colonies in a spontaneous gesture, recognising their right to liberty, they will take through revolutionary explosion.'[1] In retrospect such statements would appear prophetic but they were not said with any special knowledge or powers of analysis and they were drowned by voices expressing confidence in Spain's capacity to pacify or crush the insurrection.

Indeed, there were grounds for believing that the uprising stood little chance of success. It was easily and instantly suppressed in the western part of the island and appeared at first to be confined to the eastern part of the island from where the insurrectionists had failed to break out during the two previous wars. The Liberal government in power at the time promised to dedicate all the resources necessary to crush the rebellion, up to the 'last peseta' and the 'last drop of blood', as the Premier, Mateo Sagasta, declared. The new aggressive mood was exemplified by the smashing by officers of the printing presses of two newspapers which had suggested that some of them were shy of war. The Conservative government, which replaced the Liberal as a result of the ensuing crisis, redoubled efforts to bring the insurrection to an end under the leadership of the elder statesman of Spain, the man who had constructed the Restoration system in 1875, Antonio Cánovas. Reservists were called up and thousands of troops sent in rapid succession to Cuba.[2] The hero of the Ten

---

[1] Luis Morote, *El Pulso de España. Confesiones Políticas* (Madrid, 1904), 436.

[2] The newly appointed Minister of War, General Azcárraga, claimed later that a total of 214,333 soldiers were dispatched to the colonies over a two-year period from a standing army that totalled only 82,000 in 1895 (only 8,000 of which were in Cuba when the insurrection

Years War and the most prestigious general of the Spanish army, Arsenio Martínez Campos, was appointed as Captain-General of Cuba in the confident hope that he could repeat his previously successful strategy of conciliation in the midst of war.

Nevertheless, the Spanish army in Cuba, however augmented by troops from the metropolis, was hardly in the best condition for a new colonial war. It had little training for the specific conditions of an anti-guerrilla campaign. Army administration, like the civil administration, was corrupt and chronically deficient at all levels. The new troops were not acclimatized to an environment plagued with malaria and yellow fever. The strategic tracks and ditches built across the island during the previous campaign had been left to grow over.[3] The standing army in Spain was poorly equipped and top-heavy; there were only 5.5 soldiers for every officer and the annual army budget was barely sufficient to cover its costs. However much they took umbrage at the suggestion, regular officers were indeed reluctant to volunteer for service in Cuba, even though they won automatic promotion if they did so. The result was that some 80 per cent of lieutenants and captains serving on the island were reservists. Such was the dearth of regular officers that by 1897, teenage cadets were being offered commissions after less than a year's study at military academy if they accepted service in Cuba.[4]

Moreover, the Spanish army faced a far more formidable opponent than in the earlier wars of independence. In contrast to the Spanish military chiefs, the leaders of the Cuban independence movement had learnt valuable lessons from the Ten Years War. Their renovated military strategy relied to a great extent on economic warfare. By carrying the torch to the canefields of collaborationist planters, the Cuban insurrectionists destroyed much of the crop on which the Cuban economy rested and on which Spanish colonial rule depended. As the insurrection spread through the island, sugar production plummeted. Cuba had produced

began): *El Liberal*, 28 Sept. 1898 quoted in Helene Tzitsikas, *El pensamiento español, 1898–1899* (Mexico, 1967), 58.

[3] Shortly after the uprising began, the well-known journalist Gonzalo de Reparaz launched a bitter attack on the unpreparedness of the Spanish military in the popular illustrated weekly *La Ilustración Española y Americana*, 8 Mar. 1895. Martínez Campos's son wrote that soldiers were sometimes not paid for up to eleven weeks (or eleven consecutive payments) and when they were paid, the banknotes they were given were often worth less than their face value: Carlos Martínez de Campos y Serrano, Duque de la Torre, *La Reina Cristina y el Desastre* (Madrid, 1959). Even the Spanish secret service appeared to have been paid irregularly (Melchor Fernández Almagro, *Historia política de la España contemporánea, 1886–1896* (Madrid, 1956), vol. 2, 204 n.

[4] Stanley G. Payne, *Politics and the Military in Modern Spain* (Stanford, 1967), 72 and 76.

over a million tons of sugar in 1894, more than 32 per cent of that year's total world production of cane sugar. In 1896 it was down to 286,229 tons, accounting for only 10 per cent of world production.[5]

The burning of the plantations deprived their labourers of work but by the same token filled the ranks of the insurrectionists. For the new war of independence attracted a far broader layer of supporters than the Ten Years War had. It mobilized not just the Creole planters and the middle classes of Oriente, the easternmost province of the island, but far greater numbers of peasants, workers, and labourers in the same area and in the central provinces of Cuba. Amongst them were many ex-slaves who returned to their old plantations to set them alight. The widespread support in much of the countryside gave the insurrectionists an enormous advantage over the Spanish army; they were able more easily to live off the land and benefited from an invaluable source of military intelligence.

The greater popular support enjoyed by the leaders of the independence movement derived from their long-sustained efforts to organize support on the island. The Manifesto of Montecristi, the movement's revolutionary programme published and distributed shortly after the uprising, was designed to appeal to broad sections of the population in Cuba. It specifically addressed blacks, promising an end to racism and the adoption of equal opportunity in a free Cuba. It pledged to respect the private property of all who did not obstruct the independence movement. And to all Cubans it undertook to regenerate the economic life of the island. In short, it was a progressive nationalist programme that sought the support of both the Cuban plantation owner, the peasant, and the ex-slave.[6]

Landing covertly on the eastern coast towards the beginning of April 1895, a few days before Martínez Campos's arrival in Havana, the leaders of the insurrection quickly gathered together an army of volunteers from the Oriente province. Despite the cruel setback of the death of the supreme leader of the movement, José Martí in his first military engagement, the insurrectionists soon drove beyond the geographical limits to which they had been confined during the Ten Years War. By the beginning of 1896, their roving columns had penetrated as far as the westernmost tip of the island and to the edge of the province of Havana itself, leaving in their wake a trail of burnt plantations, dynamited bridges and twisted railway tracks.

[5] Manuel Moreno Fraginals, *El Ingenio. Complejo económico social cubano del azúcar* (Havana, 1978), vol. 3, 34.

[6] Hortensia Pichardo, *Documentos para la historia de Cuba* (La Habana, 1977), vol. 1, 483–91.

Martínez Campos's strategy of combining military operations with acts of generosity towards the rural population and offers of peace negotiations with revolutionary leaders failed to bear fruit. The insurrectionists fought a mobile guerrilla war, striking at strategic targets almost at will and obliging the Spanish forces in vain to chase their small groups of swift cavalry across the countryside whose population provided them with shelter and information. In a letter to Cánovas in July, Martínez Campos wrote despairingly:

The few Spaniards on the Island only dare proclaim themselves such in the towns; the rest of the inhabitants hate Spain . . . When one passes by the huts in the countryside, one does not see men, and the women, when asked for their husbands and sons, reply with a terrifying naturalness: 'In the mountain, with so-and-so'.[7]

As for the General's attempts to negotiate a settlement with individual rebel leaders, they were doomed by the narrow margin of concession allowed by both the Spanish government and colonial community in Cuba.

As part of his military strategy, Martínez Campos brought back into use the great defensive ditch built during the previous wars which divided the island from north to south at its centre. Some two hundred yards wide, filled with barbed wire, dynamite, and obstacles of different kinds and guarded by a string of manned blockhouses linked by railway, it was meant to confine the bulk of the insurgent forces to the eastern part of the island. From the beginning, however, small bands of rebels were able to slip through or past the defence without much problem. Martínez Campos's attempt to block supplies from Florida reaching the insurgents by controlling the shipping lanes around the island met with no greater success. The filibustering expeditions from Florida, supported by numerous American sympathizers, were too many to control by sea patrol and the numberless coves and inlets along the great length of the island provided ideal conditions for landing small consignments of arms and ammunition. These were then carried inland by local inhabitants supporting the revolutionary cause.[8]

Unable to suppress or even contain the insurrection and unwilling to

---

[7] The letter is quoted in full in Valeriano Weyler y Nicolau, *Mi mando en Cuba (10 Febrero 1896 a 31 Octubre 1897). Historia militar y política de la última guerra separatista durante dicho mando* (Madrid, 1910–11), vol. 1, 28–32.

[8] Ibid., vol. 2, 55–6. Even the British Vice-Consul (an American citizen) of Fernandrina in Florida was allegedly involved in filibustering and duly forced to resign: letter from the British Ambassador to the United States, Sir Julian Pauncefote, to Lord Gough, FO5 2265, 19 March 1895.

resort to a more repressive strategy out of moral principle, Martínez Campos resigned his command in January 1896, barely ten months after his arrival on the island. He left a demoralized army in Cuba and was greeted on his return to Spain by hostile crowds.[9] His replacement by General Valeriano Weyler, a tough professional soldier with fewer scruples, signalled a change in government policy towards a strategy of 'total war' in Cuba. Cánovas now declared that no concessions could be made to Cuban aspirations for greater autonomy until the insurrection was crushed. Indeed, the Spanish Premier had always been a firm defender of assimilation, that is, the eventual integration of Cuba into Spain with the same rights as the peninsular provinces. Such an uncompromising stance merely polarized opinion in Cuba between advocates of a Spanish Cuba and separatists, cutting the ground from under the feet of those political forces in Cuba, such as the Autonomist Party, which sought an intermediate solution.

Yet it was clear that in Spain and amongst the Spanish community in Cuba, Cánovas enjoyed widespread backing for his war policy. Amongst the families whose menfolk were called up for military service there can have been little rejoicing, but their opinions were not sought or reflected publicly. Bullfights, vaudeville, and the press all adopted a fervent nationalist tone. The bands played patriotic hymns and the soldiers marched to the ships accompanied by cheering crowds in festive spirit waving the national flag. In addition, those economic interests tied up with colonial trade—ports, colonial banking, shipping, textiles, and other consumer exports—formed a powerful lobby in favour of a purely military solution.[10] Indeed, support for Cánovas's policy appeared to be widespread amongst all sections of the well-off in Spain, to judge from their enthusiastic response when his government floated a national loan to raise money for the war effort after it had failed to obtain a loan on the international market. However, this may have had much to do with the extremely favourable terms offered to investors by the government.[11] There were other vested interests that also opposed any relaxation of Spanish sovereignty in the colonies. The colonial bureaucracy stood to lose jobs, the Church its missionary goal as well as the extensive lands and the secular

[9] Fernández Almagro (*Historia Política*), vol. 2, 263.

[10] See, for example, the position of the Catalan employers in Juan Sallarés y Pla, 'El problema colonial', *El Trabajo Nacional*, 15 Jan. 1897 reproduced in Serrano (*Final*), 162–6.

[11] Carlos Serrano, *Le tour du peuple. Crise nationale, mouvements populaires et populisme en Espagne (1890–1910)* (Madrid, 1987), 4–12. For the 1896 loan, see also Elena Hernández Sandoica and María Fernanda Mancebo, 'El Empréstito de 1896 y la política financiera en la guerra de Cuba', *Cuadernos de Historia Moderna y Contemporánea*, no. 1, 1980, 141–69.

power it enjoyed in remote parts of the colonies, and the military its identity as defender of the unity of the Spanish Empire. Finally, there were political interests in both Cuba and Spain whose power derived from their control of clientelist networks and who therefore felt threatened by any fundamental political reform in the colony.[12]

The established press and orthodox political opinion were unanimously pro-war, from the Republican parties on the Left to the Carlists on the Right. Amongst the former, only Pi y Margall's Federalists opposed the military solution, suggesting instead that the colonies should be awarded an autonomy statute similar to that of the British Dominions. Pi despaired as ordinary Spaniards succumbed to the growing war fervour.[13] The other Republican parties moved rapidly away from his principled stand to launch a belligerently nationalist campaign in defence of Spanish sovereignty. The Restoration system was attacked not because it clung on to a redundant empire but on the contrary because it was insufficiently aggressive in the defence of this empire. The ex-President of the First Republic, Emilio Castelar, while criticizing the regime for creating the colonial revolt through its failure to grant reform, was also a fervent advocate of Spain's continued sovereignty over her colonies. 'Spain made America', he wrote, 'as God made the world . . . America will be Spanish forever.'[14] As the threat of American intervention drew closer, many Republicans took to the streets to protest at the pusillanimity of the Spanish government. The Valencian Republicans, led by the novelist Blasco Ibañez, staged a violent pro-war demonstration in March 1896, storming the bullfighting stadium and wounding a Civil Guard in the process.[15]

Of the extra-parliamentary parties, the anarchists struggled to determine their attitude towards the Cuban struggle for independence. Their hesitations rested largely on the ambiguity of anarchist positions over the relationship between the national question and their ultimate goal of social revolution. This was exacerbated by nationalist divisions between Cuban and Spanish rank-and-file anarchists. Though they came to support Cuban self-determination, the anarchists tended to evade the thorny issue of

---

[12] For further discussion, see José Varela Ortega, *Los amigos políticos. Partidos, elecciones y caciquismo en la Restauración (1875–1900)* (Madrid, 1977); Inés Roldán de Montaud, 'La Unión constitucional y la política colonial de España en Cuba (1868–1898)', Tesis Doctoral, Universidad Complutense de Madrid, 1991; Francis J. D. Lambert, 'The Cuban Question in Spanish Restoration Politics, 1878–1898', Ph.D. Thesis, Oxford University, 1969.

[13] *El Nuevo Régimen*, 22 Apr., 7, 14, and 25 May 1895.

[14] *La Ilustración Española y Americana*, 8 May 1898, 270; Emilio Castelar, *Crónica Internacional* (Madrid, 1982), 140 and 449; Serrano (*Le Tour*), 193–220.

[15] Luis Morote, 'Los sucesos en Valencia', *El Liberal*, 9 Mar. 1896.

nationalism by concentrating on the harmful effects of war on Spanish workers.[16] Even more than the anarchists, the Socialists were reluctant to recognize that the Cuban struggle for independence had any connection with the needs and aspirations of Cuban workers. Clearly ignorant that there was considerable support among the latter for the insurrection, they failed to perceive the social implications of the nationalist struggle, merely reiterating at first the abstract slogans of internationalist pacifism.[17] Eventually, the Socialists recognized the validity of the independence struggle, but chose to focus their agitation, like the anarchists, on the social injustice of the system of military service in Spain.[18]

On his appointment, Weyler claimed he could bring the war to a satisfactory conclusion in two years. He replied to the insurgents' 'economic' warfare by seeking to deny them their most crucial advantage, the support they enjoyed among the people in the countryside. Upon his arrival, Weyler issued the notorious 'reconcentration' decree whereby all inhabitants of rural areas were ordered to move into urban areas under Spanish control. By emptying the countryside of its people, he hoped to deprive the insurgents of recruits, shelter, food supplies, and military intelligence. The order was carried out systematically and the Cuban countryside became barren. An American government official travelling eastwards by train from the capital described it thus: 'The country was wrapped in the stillness of death and the silence of desolation.'[19] Indeed, as one historian has remarked, the Cuban wars of independence were the first of the 'dirty' colonial wars of the twentieth century, more reminiscent of Algeria in the 1950s or Vietnam in the 1960s than the set-pieces of nineteenth-century campaigns in which professional colonial armies confronted the massed forces of declining indigenous empires.[20]

Herded into the fortified towns and cities under the reconcentration order, the rural inhabitants suffered terrible privations. Weyler had accompanied the decree with a number of measures designed to provide for

[16] Serrano (*Le tour*), 123–53. See also 'Revista internacional', *La Idea Libre* (Madrid) no. 45, 9 Mar. 1895.

[17] Weyler was the first to acknowledge the extent of Cuban working-class support for the struggle. In his account, he describes how tobacco workers in Havana were read books and articles supporting independence while they worked (tobacco workers in particular had adopted the practice of having a workmate read aloud during work-time). He was aware also of the collections made for the insurrection in the factories on pay day on Saturday; Weyler (*Mi mando*), vol. 1, 407.

[18] Serrano (*Le tour*), 64–89.

[19] William J. Calhoun, in Philip S. Foner, *The Spanish–Cuban–American War and the Birth of American Imperialism, 1895–1902* (New York, 1972), vol. 1, 117.

[20] Payne (*Politics*), 67.

the influx of people into the urban areas. However, they were totally inadequate and made worse by the chronic maladministration and corruption of the military and civil authorities. The temporary housing provided for the thousands of displaced people was insufficient; at best the country people were crowded into barely converted warehouses and at worst many had to sleep in the open. Food was in scant supply and many people starved to death or died of the effects of malnutrition. The appalling sanitary conditions of the concentration camps also gave rise to epidemics in which many lost their lives. On a visit to the Mariel concentration camp, a left-wing Spanish journalist compared it to Dante's *Inferno*.[21] Though no records were kept, many accounts suggest that at least 200,000 people died as a result of 'reconcentration'. Weyler himself attempted later to justify the policy on the grounds that it was copied shortly afterwards by the Americans in the Philippines and by the British in Transvaal; indeed, an American Commission in 1902 recognized it to have been a legitimate war measure.[22] In terms of military strategy, 'reconcentration' may have been quite effective but it destroyed the possibility of any reconciliation between Cubans and Spaniards on the lines of the Zanjón Pact.

As part of his military strategy, Weyler strengthened the defensive ditch that cut across the centre of the island and built a new one across a narrow stretch between Havana province and the westernmost province of Pinar del Río where the insurgent black general Antonio Maceo was operating. The garrisons were augmented and the ditches were illuminated with electricity at night. Like Martínez Campos, Weyler's aim was to compress the rebel forces into three areas, hunt them down separately in the west and in the centre, allowing him, once they had been destroyed, to concentrate the bulk of his forces for a final assault on the rebel stronghold in the easternmost province of Oriente.[23]

Though vastly outnumbering the insurgents, however, the Spanish troops were unable to pin them down. The Cubans were able to make repeated attacks on garrisons and towns controlled by the Spanish army. But as Weyler threw more troops in, their room for manœuvre decreased. After a bold and successful attempt to get round the great ditch in the west

---

[21] Manuel Ciges Aparicio, *El libro de la vida trágica. Del cautiverio* (Alicante, 1985). The author was jailed for publishing an article in a French newspaper criticizing conditions in the camp. Foner in *The Spanish–Cuban–American War*, 110–18 describes the effects of 'reconcentration'.

[22] Chadwick (*The Relations*), vol. 1, 493. For Weyler's self-justification see *Mi mando*, vol. 5, 329–30.

[23] Weyler (*Mi mando*), vol. 1, 277 *passim*.

in early December 1896, Maceo was surprised by a Spanish patrol and killed. His death gave rise to exaggerated hopes in Spain that the war was now won and crowds took to the streets in celebration. Though it was a setback for the Cuban forces, their guerrilla bands continued to escape encirclement and to wreak havoc in many parts of the island. Both sides claimed that they were winning the war. It is more true to say that the war was at a stalemate. If the Spanish army controlled most of the urban areas, the war in the countryside was inconclusive.[24]

Nevertheless, the physical and financial cost of the war was far greater for Spain than for the Cuban independence movement. The Spanish High Command had to put a huge army into the field to combat the small guerrilla forces of the Cubans. By 1897 just under 200,000 Spanish troops had been sent to Cuba to quell the insurrection. But because of disease the effective strength of the army was soon reduced to around 150,000.[25] By all accounts, the conditions in which the troops had to fight were atrocious.[26] Unacclimatized to the environment, the poorly nourished Spanish soldiers fell victim to yellow fever, dysentery, malaria, and anaemia. Food rations were inadequate, especially for the conditions in which they had to operate, constantly on the move through tropical heat and rain, searching out the elusive insurgents or digging trenches and building forts. A staunchly patriotic officer was shocked to see the condition of the troops on his arrival in Cuba. He remembered seeing a counter-guerrilla patrol of pro-Spanish Cubans riding past:

I seem to be witnessing a procession of dying men. All the faces [are] exaggeratedly emaciated, a greenish hue insufficient to hide the bronzed colour of skin blackened by the sun . . . The majority are dejected and indifferent. The trousers of most of them are rolled up and are the uniform colour of mud which forms a crust on bare legs marked, in most cases, with ulcers or scratches.[27]

[24] For Cuban claims, see Foner (*The Spanish*), vol. 1, 119–23, and for Spanish, Weyler (*Mi mando*), vol. 1, 19. On the basis of the diary of a Spanish soldier, Eloy Recio Ferreras argues that, contrary to Foner's view, the Cubans were constantly on the retreat and that military engagements were few: 'Diario inédito escrito por un soldado español en la Guerra de Cuba, 1896–1899', *Revista de Historia de América*, no. 112, July–Dec. 1991, 21–42.

[25] *La Época*, 6 May 1897.

[26] Amongst eye-witness accounts of the condition of the troops, the following stand out: Manuel Corral, *¡El Desastre! Memorias de un voluntario en la campaña de Cuba* (Barcelona, 1899); Ricardo Burguete, *¡La Guerra! Cuba (Diario de un testigo)*, (Barcelona, 1902). Among other contemporary accounts, see Damián Isern, *Del Desastre nacional y sus causas* (Madrid 1899), 253–68. For a recent analysis: Elena Hernández Sandoica and María Fernanda Mancebo, 'Higiene y sociedad en la guerra de Cuba (1895–1898). Notas sobre soldados y proletarios', *Estudios de Historia Social* no. 5–6, Apr.–Sept. 1978, 361–84.

[27] Burguete (*¡La Guerra! Cuba*), 69.

According to official statistics, only just over 4 per cent of the deaths registered in July 1897 were the result of battle; the rest were due to illness, of which almost 49 per cent were caused by yellow fever.[28] One contemporary account claims that during the whole of the war, 58,939 soldiers died of illness, hunger, or fatigue, that is, some 27 per cent of the army, while only 4,128 died in battle.[29] Conditions were exacerbated by maladministration and corruption. Wages were frequently held back or were not fully paid out. Food rations were inadequate and often went rotten through poor planning. But many other rations were sold illegally for profit and wine was diluted with water for the benefit of corrupt officers and sergeants. Conditions in the field hospitals were so bad that sick soldiers often preferred to stay with their platoons out on campaign rather than be sent for treatment.[30] Many officers, quartermasters, and civilian administrators working for the army were reckoned to have made tidy fortunes selling such things as supplies and passes during the course of the war.[31]

The physical and financial cost of the war was complemented by a high political cost. Doubts about the government's strategy began to surface in parliament and in the press. Antonio Maura, foreseeing a disaster, rose in parliament to challenge the military solution. From within Conservative ranks, Francisco Silvela called for radical reform in Cuba as the only way out of the war. Half way through 1897, the Liberals finally withdrew their support for the government's policy and insisted that only the offer of autonomy could end the war, thus bringing to a close a brief period of bi-partisanship.[32]

[28] According to figures published the *Gaceta de Madrid*, quoted in *El Imparcial*, 13 Aug. 1898.

[29] Corral (*¡El Desastre!*), 124. For more recent calculations see Payne (*Politics*), 76 and 477–8 nn. 28 and 29, and José Barón Fernández, *La Guerra Hispano-norteamericana de 1898* (La Coruña, 1992), 251.

[30] Recio (*Diario*), 36–7; Corral (*¡El Desastre!*), 124–31. That these conditions were typical of Spanish military organization in the late nineteenth century is suggested by Santiago Ramón y Cajal's account of his experience as a doctor during the Ten Years War in *Mi infancia y juventud* (Madrid, 1955, 1st edn. 1939), 212–15.

[31] Corrupt practices were particularly well documented in the case of the Spanish army in the Philippines. The Madrid daily paper *El Nacional* ran a campaign after the wars between March and April 1899 detailing these practices (27 Mar. to 20 Apr. 1899); as a result, two of their journalists were tried and imprisoned by the military tribunal in August 1899. The articles were published in book form in the same year: El Capitán Verdades (Juan Urquía), *Historia negra. Relato de los escándalos ocurridos en nuestras ex-colonia durante las últimas guerras* (Barcelona, 1899).

[32] For Maura, Javier Tusell, *Antonio Maura. Una biografía política* (Madrid, 1994), 40–3; for Silvela, *El Imparcial*, 6 Dec. 1896; for the Liberals, *El Imparcial*, 20 July, 1897.

More menacingly for the Spanish government, the United States became increasingly insistent on the need for a rapid and peaceful solution. At an early stage of the Spanish–Cuban War, both Houses of the American Congress had voted to give the insurgents belligerency status. Rejecting the proposal and acting more cautiously, President Cleveland, through a note sent to the Spanish government in April 1896 by his secretary of state, Richard Olney, had urged on Spain the swift concession of self-government to Cuba, offering to mediate between the two sides. The Olney Note insisted that the US government was acting on Christian principles and because it was worried about American–Cuban trade and the destruction of US property in Cuba. The note clearly suggested that should peace not come soon, the United States would intervene.[33]

Hopeful that Weyler's military strategy would soon bring the insurrection to an end, the Spanish government had rejected the Note's proposals on 22 May 1896. Weyler himself was conscious that his operations were a race against time before the US intervened.[34] As the war dragged on without a clear outcome in sight, the pressure on the American government to intervene had increased. The publicity given in the United States to conditions in the concentration camps in Cuba was arousing widespread anger. In December 1896 President Cleveland had once again urged the Spanish government to end the war, accompanying his message this time with a warning that American patience was limited.

To add to the pressures on Spain, the Philippine independence movement under the leadership of the secret society, the Katipunan, had launched their second rebellion in two years in August 1896. Supported in particular by the slum-dwellers of Manila, the insurrectionists forced the Spanish government to commit troops to a second war front; by the beginning of 1897, some 30,000 were deployed in a war similar in its conditions to that in Cuba. Like Weyler, General Camilo Polavieja had replaced the Captain-General in the Philippines in order to carry out a war of attrition against the rebels. And like the Cuban guerrillas, the enemy in the Philippines proved to be agile and elusive.[35]

Unable to make headway on the military front, Cánovas announced that the limited form of autonomy agreed by parliament in 1895 would be

---

[33] The Note is reproduced in Chadwick (*The Relations*), 452–8.
[34] Weyler (*Mi mando*), vol. 4, 315.
[35] Ricardo Burguete, *¡La Guerra! Filipinas (Memorias de un herido)* (Barcelona, 1902), 90. A right-wing officer, Burguete calls the Manila slum-dwellers 'the select reserve army of assault, impelled not by the Katipunan but by four centuries of misery and hunger which the copious pages of dominant catechism have not been able to sweeten' (73).

applied in those areas of Cuba pacified by the army. He also requested Weyler to moderate his reconcentration policy. These measures satisfied neither the American government (under the new and accommodating Republican administration of William McKinley) nor the Conservatives in Spain nor least of all Weyler.[36] It could be argued that by 1897, neither a political solution nor a military solution was possible any longer. The Cuban insurrectionists commanded too much support amongst the population for any proposals for autonomy, however radical, to be the basis for a settlement. On the other hand, had the government's strategy been, from the start, to combine the offer of radical reforms with the kind of decisive military campaign carried out by Weyler, the outcome might have been different.[37]

In any case, Cánovas's assassination in August 1897 brought to an end the strategy of total war. The Premier was shot dead by an anarchist, for reasons largely unconnected with the Cuban war, as he was on holiday in a quiet Basque spa. His replacement as Premier in October by the Liberal leader, the ageing Mateo Sagasta, was a tacit admission by the regime that his policy had failed. The new government recalled Weyler and issued a decree of autonomy for Cuba and Puerto Rico which went further than any previous proposal in devolving political power to the colonies, though it still reserved ultimate authority for the Spanish government through its representatives, the Governor-Generals.[38]

The Cuban issue now turned on whether the US government was prepared to accept the new decree. If it did, the danger of American intervention would recede and the US government might be persuaded to take sterner measures against the boatloads of aid that reached the Cuban rebels from the American coast and from other Caribbean islands or even call on the rebels to lay down their arms.[39] However, even before the decree was made public, McKinley's envoy in Spain, General Stewart L. Woodford, was convinced that autonomy under continued Spanish rule was not a possible solution. Referring to the endemic corruption of Spanish colonial administration, he wrote, in a dispatch to the President on 17 October,

[36] Weyler was disgusted by Cánovas's order but remained loyal: *Mi mando*, vol. 4, 402–5.
[37] Lambert ('The Cuban Question'), 247.
[38] Fernández Almagro (*Historia política*), vol. 3, 32–4; Foner (*Spanish*), vol. 1, 133–4.
[39] Though the American Ambassador in Spain claimed to his British counterpart that the war was costing the US 3 million dollars a month in thwarting filibustering expeditions: letter from Barclay to Salisbury, 4 Mar. 1898, PRO FO 72/2062.

Rebellion is the only possible protest against the Spanish methods of administration. The cause must be removed before the disease can be cured.

He also referred to the

utter inability of the Spanish official mind to comprehend autonomy as Americans and Englishmen understand it . . . the most liberal Spaniards seem to understand autonomy simply as a boon to be conferred and to be exercised under Spanish supervision and mainly through Spanish agents.[40]

Yet McKinley seemed to look favourably on the autonomy decree, judging from his Annual Message to Congress in December.[41] To add to official Spanish hopes, the war in the Philippines appeared to have ended when the rebels signed the peace agreement of Biyak-na-Bató in the same month. A succession of events in January and February, however, dashed these hopes and hastened the decline in relations between Spain and the United States. In one of those fateful military interventions that so mark the history of modern Spain, a group of ultra-loyalist officers and civilians smashed up the offices of a Havana newspaper which had been campaigning for autonomy and against the concentration camps. Their action prompted McKinley to send a powerful battleship, the USS *Maine*, to Havana harbour on a 'goodwill' mission that could only be interpreted as a form of pressure on the Spanish government.[42]

A second, and for the Spanish government, unfortunate event was the publication by the *New York Journal* of a private letter from the Spanish Minister in Washington, Enrique Dupuy de Lôme, to the Liberal politician, José Canalejas, which had been stolen by a Cuban agent from the latter's rooms during a visit to Havana. Dupuy de Lôme had been sending a series of bland reports to Spain encouraging his government to view relations with the US in an optimistic light.[43] In his letter to Canalejas, the Spanish Minister had made disparaging remarks about McKinley. Not particularly significant in themselves, the comments caused a furore when they appeared on the front page of the sensationalist paper under the

[40] Julián Companys Monclus, *España en 1898: entre la diplomacia y la guerra* (Madrid, 1992), 325. The dispatch is quoted in full, 323–6.

[41] Chadwick (*Relations*), 525–7.

[42] The British Ambassador in Washington clearly disapproved of the move, writing to the Prime Minister, Lord Salisbury, on 26 January that 'The Maine's presence in Havana might so easily be made the occasion of an unfriendly demonstration which would seriously complicate the situation. Nothing would suit the interests of the Separatists better than an occurrence of this kind.' Barclay to Salisbury, PRO, FO 72/2062.

[43] Thus his telegram of 24 Jan. 1898 regarding the Maine, in *Documentos presentados a las Cortes en la legislatura de 1898 por el Ministro de Estado* (Madrid, 1898), 104.

headline, 'The Worst Insult to the United States in Its History'.[44] Besides confirming the suspicion of Spanish duplicity amongst many American politicians, the publication of the letter also strengthened the tide of anti-Spanish jingoism sweeping the country which the government would find increasingly difficult to resist.

An even more dramatic event was the explosion of the USS *Maine* in Havana harbour on 15 February in which 266 American sailors lost their lives out of a crew of 354. The tragedy brought war fever to a pitch amongst wide sections of the American press and public. McKinley was able to stave off immediate action by setting up a board of inquiry. This did not prevent the *New York Journal* from publishing on 18 February eight pages of data 'proving' Spanish responsibility, leading the captain of the *Maine*, who had been ashore when the explosion occurred, to wonder if the paper had secret contacts with the alleged saboteurs.[45] The three-man commission of inquiry decided after five weeks of investigation that the explosion had been the result of an external underwater device, the clear implication being that it was planted by Spaniards. A more likely cause was that internal combustion created by heat on the engine-rooms set off deteriorating explosives within the cruiser. Numerous such accidents were to happen in battleships over the coming years.[46] If this was so, and the balance of evidence seemed to indicate it, it was a tragic accident that could not have occurred at a worse moment for the Spanish regime.

The explosion of the Maine, however, was an incidental not a causal factor leading to the Spanish–American War which followed shortly after. At the root of the impending conflict between the two countries lay the failure of the Spanish government to find either a military or political

---

[44] Joseph Smith, *The Spanish–American War. Conflict in the Caribbean and the Pacific, 1895–1902* (Harlow, 1994), 40.

[45] Edmund Morris, *The Rise of Theodore Roosevelt* (New York, 1979), 601.

[46] Indalecio Nuñez, 'Remember the Maine!', *Arbor*, número extraordinario, Dec. 1948, 369–78. A technical study by the Spanish Artillery carried out shortly after the event also argued this case: Severo Gómez Nuñez, 'La catástrofe del *Maine*', *Memorial de Artillería*, Serie IV, Tomo IX (Jan.–June 1898), 281–91. The causes of the Maine explosion have been endlessly debated since then and several new theories have been put forward; a recent one is that the explosion was touched off a hydrostatic mine, invented by a Peruvian engineer and planted by Cuban anarchists: Guillermo G. Calleja Leal, 'La voladura del Maine. Nuevas luces sobre un enigma histórico que terminó con el Imperio español', *historia*, n. 176, Dec. 1990, 12–32. An American investigation in the early 1970s conducted by Admiral Rickover concluded, like the Spanish ones above, that the balance of probability indicated an internal cause (Hyman G. Rickover, *How The Battleship 'Maine' Was Destroyed* (Washington DC, 1976). For an overview of the debate, see Louis A. Pérez, 'The Meaning of the *Maine*: Causation and the Historiography of the Spanish–American War', *Pacific Historical Review*, 58 (1989), 293–322.

solution to the Cuban insurrection. In the notes transmitted to the Spanish government by the American Minister in Spain, the continuation of the war in Cuba and the failure of the autonomy measures were cited as the cause of the US government's increasing concern about the Cuban situation. By the end of March, McKinley and his cabinet had openly stated that only Spanish abandonment of Cuba could bring the war to an end. Should Spain refuse to give up the island, the United States would be forced to intervene militarily. The US congress had already given a clear signal of American intentions by voting a military appropriations bill of 50 million dollars. This message was now conveyed firmly but sympathetically to the Queen Regent and to the Overseas Minister by the American envoy, General Woodford.[47]

The Spanish regime faced an excruciating dilemma. Both the Queen Regent and leading politicians were convinced that any voluntary abandonment of the island on their part would bring about the collapse of the Restoration system and the downfall of the monarchy. To understand why they thought so, we need to remember the fragility of that system, which had been created only twenty-three years previously and rested on an uneasy alliance of barely representative and fragmented political forces. It is easy in retrospect to conclude that their fears were unfounded. But the background to those twenty-three years of relative stability had been half a century of civil wars, uprisings, military coups, and a short-lived Republic. Even after the Restoration of 1875, there was repeated political unrest—small, localized Carlist insurrections, military mutinies, Republican uprisings, anarchist rebellions, assassination attempts, plots, and conspiracies, all of which both the government and the media took very seriously.[48] The Bourbon monarchy, contested by the defeated but restless Carlist Pretender, was represented by an Austrian Queen Regent and Crown Prince still too young to ascend the throne.

Moreover, as the conflict with the United States loomed, the overwhelming weight of public opinion appeared to be in favour of war. The press saw no other option and the less sober amongst them gave way increasingly to jingoist enthusiasms. The Church multiplied its fund-raising and morale-boosting activities in favour of war, and the mood in the streets, to judge from the frequent and boisterous demonstrations

---

[47] Companys (*España*), 211–21.

[48] Worry about the future of the monarchy was shared by the British Ambassador. In a private and confidential report to Lord Salisbury, he referred to the 'very hostile currents which may overwhelm the dynasty and perhaps the monarchical institutions, in the event of any grave reverse'. Drummond-Wolff to Salisbury, 10 June 1898, FO72/2064.

against American embassies, was belligerently pro-war. Indeed, when the government declared an armistice in the war with the Cuban rebels in a last desperate attempt to placate American demands, there were protest riots in Madrid during which trams were smashed and the Civil Guard had to make repeated cavalry charges to disperse the demonstrators.[49] It would not be surprising if the regime concluded that any gratuitous surrender of Cuba would be greeted by a much more violent and widespread revolt.

Refusing to abandon Cuba meant going to war with the United States. On the basis of existing sources, it is impossible to judge accurately how far the regime, as opposed to the jingoist press, believed Spain stood any chance of winning such a war at this stage. In the prevailing mood of belligerency in Spain, it was difficult for the Queen Regent or for ministers to express doubts about Spain's military capacity. However, there are many indications that amongst informed opinion it was taken for granted, before hostilities broke out, that Spain would lose any war with the United States. In a dispatch to McKinley on 7 March, Woodford gave an account of a long conversation he had had with a Spanish businessman whom he believed to be speaking with the full knowledge of the Premier and Overseas Minister. During that conversation, Woodford reported,

I also understood him to say that he knew that Spain would be beaten in any struggle with the United States, that he feared such struggle to be inevitable, but notwithstanding this, that he and all good Spaniards would accept the issue of war without hesitation.[50]

There is further anecdotal evidence to suggest that in the higher echelons of the regime, defeat was accepted as the only possible outcome of a war with the United States. The Overseas Minister, Segismundo Moret, confided to a friend that war with the United States would be madness because of Spain's military weakness. When urged to express this view publicly, Moret declared that the throne would fall if he did so. He had no answer when his friend, in reply, asked him, 'Do you not believe that the nation (*la patria*) should come before the throne?'[51] The Liberal politician, Count Romanones, wrote later about a meeting held in the Royal Palace between the Queen Regent and leading politicians after she had received a confidential message from the US President government offering a

---

[49] *El Imparcial*, 9 and 11 Apr. 1898.

[50] Companys (*España*), 337. In the same letter, Woodford describes another conversation in which it is suggested that similar convictions about the hopelessness of the war are widespread: 339.

[51] E. Gutiérrez-Gamero, *Mis primeros ochenta años (memorias)* (Barcelona, 1934), 34–5.

choice of war or the sale of Cuba to the United States. The unanimous feeling amongst all gathered at that meeting and in subsequent unofficial meetings held by the Queen Regent with opposition politicians was that selling Cuba was not an option that Spain could adopt and that war was necessary in order to maintain peace at home; that is, war 'was the only honourable means whereby Spain could lose what little was left of her immense colonial empire'.[52] It can be surmised, therefore, that the regime went to war with the United States knowing Spain would be defeated but believing war and defeat to be the lesser evil.

This is not to say that the regime failed to take measures to avoid war. As early as 1896 the government had sought to persuade the European Powers to block American intervention in Cuba in the hope that they opposed any alteration of the international balance of power. The Queen Regent, María Cristina, attempted to make use of her dynastic connections, appealing to her uncle, the Emperor Franz-Josef of Austria and her aunt, Queen Victoria, both of whom expressed sympathy for the Spanish cause but were unable to act decisively in its favour.[53] Only Germany had responded positively, impelled by its own long-standing interest in acquiring Spanish colonies in the Pacific and concerned therefore that the US might get there first.[54] It was only on the eve of the war, however, that the European Powers were stirred to take minimal action, presenting an anodyne collective note to the American President on 6 April urging peace and moderation.[55]

[52] Figueroa y Torres, Alvaro de (Conde de Romanones), *Las responsabilidades políticas del antiguo régimen de 1875 a 1923* (Madrid, 1925), 33; also Gabriel Maura Gamazo, *Historia crítica del reinado de don Alfonso XIII bajo le regencia de Doña María Cristina de Austria* (Barcelona, 1919), vol. 1, 359–60.

[53] For the correspondence between María-Cristina, Queen Victoria and Lord Salisbury regarding the War, see George Earle Buckle (ed.), *The Letters of Queen Victoria* (London, 1932), vol. 3, 44–5, 236–7, 239, 244, 280.

[54] María Dolores Elizalde Pérez-Grueso, *España en el Pacífico: la colonia de las Islas Carolina, 1885–1899. Un modelo colonial en el contexto internacional del imperialismo* (Madrid, 1992).

[55] For a detailed account of negotiations over European intervention see Orestes Ferrara, *The Last Spanish War. Revelations in 'Diplomacy'* (New York, 1937) and for diplomatic contacts between Spain and the European Powers see *Documentos presentados a las Cortes en la legislatura de 1898 por el Ministro de Estado. Negociaciones Generales con los Estados Unidos desde 10 de abril de 1898 hasta la declaración de guerra* (Madrid, 1898). On an issue of minor importance, Madrid was also hoping that European banks might exert pressure on European governments to intervene because of capital tied up in Spanish bonds issued to fund the suppression of the Cuban revolt. See Francisco Morales Padrón, *Historia de unas relaciones difíciles (EEUU–América española)* (Seville, 1987), 127; for a further discussion of the bonds issue, see Paul S. Holbo, 'The Convergence of Moods and the Cuban Bond "Conspiracy of 1898"', *Journal of American History* no. 55 (June 1968), 54–72.

In a last desperate attempt to avert war, María Cristina also used her pious connections with the Vatican. Pope Leo XIII was godfather to her son Alfonso and the Pope's secretary, Cardinal Rampolla, was an old confidant of hers. The Vatican had backed the Spanish cause against the Cuban revolutionaries from the beginning. The Papal Nuncio in Spain had blessed troops leaving for the colonial wars and the Pope himself had sent his blessing to a contingent departing for the Philippines in November 1896.[56] Leo XIII became the centre of last-minute efforts to avert war with the United States. Unwilling to take the initiative themselves, the European Powers had agreed that he should make representations to the American government through the Catholic bishops in the United States. At the same time, the Spanish government, fearing a backlash from the military, decreed a unilateral armistice in Cuba as if it was giving way to insistent demands from the Pope and the European ambassadors to suspend hostilities.[57]

To understand why all the European Powers, some the traditional allies of Spain, stood back and allowed the dismemberment of the residue of the Spanish Empire, we need to consider the transformation that had taken place in the international context in the previous twenty years or so. Since the 1870s, there had been an unprecedented expansion of territory colonized or controlled by the Great Powers. So rapid had been that expansion that by the 1890s most uncolonized areas in the world had been drawn into the sphere of influence of one or other of the Powers and tensions were breaking out over the demarcation of these spheres and the relative rights of trade and navigation. The partition of Africa had largely been determined in the Berlin West Africa Conference of 1885 which had also agreed on new mechanisms whereby disputes of this nature could be resolved. The new expansionism did not respect historical rights over territories or dynastic connections and indeed was justified in terms of a crude new philosophy of Social Darwinism in which the notion of the survival of the fittest was extended to peoples and nations. Older and weaker empires, obtained in an earlier period of mercantilist expansion, found stronger and acquisitive Powers chafing on their borders.[58]

As the different Powers jostled for hegemony in the 1890s, they distributed or redistributed colonies and spheres of influence amongst them-

[56] Cristóbal Robles Muñoz, '1898: la batalla por la paz. La mediación de Leon XIII entre España y Estados Unidos', *Revista de Indias*, vol. XLVI, no. 177 (1986), 251–2.

[57] Ibid. 271.

[58] Paul Kennedy, *The Rise and Fall of the Great Powers. Economic Change and Military Conflict From 1500 to 2000* (London, 1988), 249–330.

selves.[59] Compared to the great restructuring of colonies at the end of the First World War, this was a relatively modest affair, yet it established or confirmed the new contours of world power. In Southern Africa, Portugal was forced by Britain and Germany in 1890 to renounce any ambitions to extend its African colonies and its client status within the British sphere of influence was later formally confirmed. In South America, Britain had to give way to the United States over the Venezuela–British Guyana dispute in 1895, Washington insisting on its hegemonic right to resolve matters in the Western Hemisphere. French troops, pushing down the Nile Valley in 1898, were forced into a humiliating retreat by the British at Fashoda and France thereafter was obliged to confine its colonial interests in Africa mainly to the north-west.

Of all the areas in dispute, that most contested in the 1890s was the Far East. There, Russia, Britain, Japan, the United States, and to a lesser extent France, vied for ascendancy over the succulent Chinese market. Unlike Africa, the Great Powers were unable to impose any clear redistribution of territory and spheres of influence. Britain and America were determined to keep the door of this market open, while both Russia and Japan were keen to gain territory at the expense of the crumbling Chinese empire. Japanese ambitions to expand into the Chinese mainland after their stunning victory over the Chinese in 1895 had been curtailed by the Great Powers with commercial interests and colonial outposts in China.[60]

The ability to trade in this area in particular depended on naval power, especially for those Powers, such as Germany, Britain, and the US, situated at some distance away. And naval power, in turn, rested not only on expensive programmes of ship construction but also on the acquisition and creation of naval bases, coaling stations, and submarine cables across the globe. The possession of ports on the Chinese mainland and islands in the Pacific thus became an important asset for any Power with pretensions to compete in the Far Eastern market. It was inevitable, therefore, that the Spanish colony of the Philippines, in particular, but also Spain's island possessions in the mid-Pacific, should attract the interest of the great trading Powers. Its strategic potential was not being developed nor indeed was that of most of the islands actually occupied by Spain. Germany, above all, had cast acquisitive eyes at these possessions and briefly con-

[59] Pabón ('El 98'); Jover Zamora ('1898').
[60] For British diplomatic correspondence over China, see G. P. Gooch and Harold Temperley, *British Documents on the Origins of the War, 1898–1914. Volume I. The End of British Isolation* (London, 1927), 3–41.

tested the ownership of the island of Yap in the Carolines archipelago in 1885.[61] European interest in this area also had economic motives. While Cuba was specialized around the production of sugar and was losing Spain money, the Philippine economy had become highly diversified and extremely profitable. Spain's protectionist tariff barriers around the islands' trade aroused the irritation of European merchants and politicians alike.

As for the role of the Caribbean in this international context, the strategic value of Cuba to the United States was twofold. It lay ninety miles from Florida and athwart the entrance to the Gulf of Mexico, controlling the shipping passage to the Mississippi and the soft underbelly of the United States. American hegemony in the Caribbean, moreover, was vital in order to ensure the security of the sea-route to and from the proposed Isthmian Canal; in 1901, Washington would obtain sole rights to build the Canal and two years later, control of Panama itself. American possession of Cuba, as the influential naval strategist, A. T. Mahan kept reminding informed opinion, was an essential part of this strategy.[62]

The annexation of the island, in any case, had long been an aspiration of American politicians and businessmen.[63] As early as October 1897, it was being discussed as a possible solution to the Spanish–Cuban War. Though it was framed as a political imperative, based on the racist notion that the Cubans were not ready for self-government, it coincided with the wider economic and strategic interests of the United States.[64] Later, as we have seen, McKinley was secretly offering to purchase Cuba from Spain without the least reference to the Cuban independence movement. Outwardly, American diplomats were assuring their European counterparts that Washington had no covert designs on Cuba. Woodford protested to a British diplomat that annexing Cuba 'would be like assuming control of a madhouse' but the latter was not convinced and indeed reported to London that Washington was encouraging the rebels to hold out and wanted 'much more than the mere pacification of the island'.[65]

[61] Elizalde (*España*).
[62] For example, Alfred Thayer Mahan, *The Influence of Sea Power upon History, 1660–1783* (London and Cambridge Mass., 1890).
[63] Foner (*Spanish*) p. XXVIII; Fernández Almagro (*Historia política*), vol. 2, 288–9, Ramiro Guerra, *La expansión territorial de los Estados Unidos* (La Habana, 1975).
[64] Woodford was worried that even annexation might prove difficult. In a dispatch to McKinley on 17 October 1897, he wrote, 'I hope that annexation may not come until Cubans shall have learned how to rule themselves, or until enough Americans shall have gone there to make a reliable back-bone of intelligent citizenship' (Companys (*España*), 325). See also May (*Imperial*), 125 and Foner (*Spanish–Cuban–American*), 208–27.
[65] Barclay to Salisbury, 4 Mar. and 17 Apr. 1898, PRO FO72/2062.

Accordingly, any attempt by European Powers to intervene diplomatically on behalf of Spain ran the risk of upsetting the United States. None wished to incur Washington's displeasure, least of all those like Britain and Germany who were America's most important trading partners. Britain was not averse to the consolidation of United States power in the Far East, since both were committed to the 'Open Door' policy with respect to China, and Britain, which found itself diplomatically isolated at the end of the century, had more to fear in that area from its European rivals than from an increasingly kindred Washington. Moreover, with the appointment in 1895 of Joseph Chamberlain and Arthur Balfour as Colonial Minister and First Lord of the Treasury respectively, an important shift was taking place within the British political establishment towards an Anglo-American alliance.[66] Germany, as we have seen, hoped to make territorial gains from the break-up of the Spanish empire. The delicate balance of power in the Far East might be threatened should a European power gain special advantage from Spain's losses. Dynastic sympathies and diplomatic traditions were no match for *Realpolitik*.

In any case, like London, Washington was poised on the brink of a radical shift in its foreign policy. Hitherto, it had remained aloof from military entanglements abroad, moved by the belief that conquest was a violation of the basic principles of the American Constitution. A new élite of politicians, businessmen, and newspaper proprietors now challenged that assumption. According to them, America's power as an industrial and trading nation had to be backed by military and above all sea power. The acquisition of overseas territory was a vital part of this strategy; Cuba, the Philippines and the Spanish islands in the Pacific were highly suitable objects of this expansion because of their strategic position. As part of a New World version of the Social Darwinism rampant throughout Europe, it was also believed that it was America's 'Manifest Destiny', to extend its creed across the globe.[67] These views coincided with a public mood of assertive nationalism arising from the domestic frustrations caused by the Depression of the 1890s. And they were gaining enormous popularity through the press of both Joseph Pulitzer and William Randolph Hearst,

---

[66] For British foreign policy, see J. A. S. Grenville, *Lord Salisbury and Foreign Policy. The Close of the Nineteenth Century*, (London, 1970, 2nd. edn.) and R. G. Neale, *Great Britain and United States Expansion: 1898–1900* (Michigan, 1966).

[67] The bibliography of the debate in American society over expansionism is enormous. For a particularly vivid account, see Barbara Tuchman, *The Proud Tower, A Portrait of the World Before the War, 1890–1914* (London, 1966), 130–54.

FIG. 1 The US preparing for war with Spain, as seen by the Spanish jingoist press. Cartoon from the Catalan Republican periodical, *La Campana de Gracia*

who was selling 5 million copies a day of his *New York Journal* on the eve of the war with Spain.[68]

Among the most fervent advocates of expansionism in McKinley's cabinet was the energetic assistant secretary of the navy, Theodore Roosevelt. The Spanish–Cuban War brought this contradiction in the cabinet between isolationism and expansionism to the surface. It was resolved in favour of the latter, not without misgivings on the part of both McKinley and his Secretary of Navy, John D. Long and the fervent opposition outside the government of the anti-imperialists.[69] Thus American policy was shaped not simply by changing circumstances and the pressure of public opinion, as has often been asserted, but also according to already existing options outlined by naval and colonialist circles.[70] The Assistant Secretary of State, William Day's cryptic remark to Woodford in a March 1898 dispatch that 'There are many things, my dear General, which can not be written . . .' suggests that its Cuban policy was part of a wider strategy which could not be articulated in public or even in confidential dispatches because it contradicted official statements about American motivation.[71]

Indeed, McKinley's 'war' message to the US Congress on 11 April made no mention of Cuban independence. In the debate that followed several insistent voices were raised in support of the Cuban liberation movement. In the Congress resolution that ended the debate, the President was able to resist any reference to the future status of Cuba, but was forced to concede the Teller amendment whereby the United States disclaimed any intention of annexing the island. A week later, the Congress passed a joint resolution demanding Spanish withdrawal from Cuba to which Madrid replied by breaking off diplomatic relations. War was formally declared on 25 April. Neither side had wanted war but both had been impelled towards it for opposite reasons: Madrid because it considered war the only way of losing the Empire without losing the regime and Washington because, in the circumstances, war was the only way it could begin to build its own empire (Fig. 1).

The first military encounter took place in Manila on 1 May between the American Asiatic squadron under Commodore Dewey and the Spanish Pacific squadron under Admiral Montojo y Pasarón.[72] Dewey's ships had

---

[68] Holbo ('The Convergence'), 54–72.

[69] David F. Trask, *The War with Spain* (New York, 1981), 455.

[70] Elizalde (*España*), 243–4 n. 32.

[71] The quote from Day in Companys (*España*), 355.

[72] This account of the war is based mainly on the following sources: issues of *El Imparcial* and *La Epoca* between 2 May to 13 August; Chadwick (*The Relations: The Spanish–American War*), vols. 1 and 2; Pascual Cervera y Topete, *Guerra Hispano-Americana. Colección de*

gathered in Hong Kong to await instructions from Washington. When war was declared, he was ordered to sail to the Philippines as part of a strategy of striking simultaneously at different Spanish targets. Montojo, convinced that his flotilla would be destroyed in an open sea battle, had retreated to Manila Bay to seek the protection of its shore batteries and underwater mines. To avoid the bombardment of the city, however, he chose to position his squadron further downstream at Subig Bay where he discovered, to his disgust, that the shore batteries there were not ready for action. Finally anchoring by the Cavite naval station, whose batteries were in position, the Spanish ships awaited the arrival of the American squadron.

In the early hours of 1 May, under cover of darkness, Dewey's squadron steamed into the wide mouth of Manila Bay past the first Spanish defences. At about 5 a.m., the naval battle began. For two hours, the two squadrons exchanged fire, the Americans' powerful 8-inch guns causing heavy damage to the Spanish ships, whose guns were largely out of range and unable to reach their targets. The American flotilla retired briefly to reload and have breakfast and then returned to continue the battle. By mid-morning, the Spanish squadron was so badly damaged that Montojo ordered the ships still afloat to be scuttled; in contrast, the American squadron suffered only minor damage (Fig. 2). When word of Dewey's capture of the Cavite naval station reached Washington, preparations to send an expeditionary force to conquer the Philippines themselves were set in motion.[73]

Meanwhile, the Spanish Atlantic squadron under Admiral Cervera y Topete had been ordered on 29 April to set sail for Puerto Rico from the Cape Verde Islands, where it had been awaiting in vain to be reinforced by ships under repair in the Cadiz dockyards. Cervera was convinced of the folly of sailing to the Caribbean and he repeatedly conveyed his view to the Spanish Minister of the Navy that his squadron faced certain destruction by the superior American fleet which, under the command of Admiral Sampson, had been blockading Cuba from the start of the hostilities. A second American squadron under the command of Commodore Schley

documentos referentes a la Escuadra de Operaciones de la Antillas (El Ferrol, 1899); Victor M. Concas y Palau, *La Escuadra del Almirante Cervera* (Madrid, 1900, 2nd edn.); C. P., *Ante la opinión y ante la historia. El Almirante Montojo* (Madrid, 1900); Isern (*Del Desastre*); Fernández Almagro (*Historia política*), vol. 3; Smith (*The Spanish–American*); Trask (*The War*); A. B. Feuer, *The Santiago Campaign of 1898. A Soldier's View of the Spanish-American War* (Westport, Connecticut, 1993).

[73] The most detailed description of the battle is in Chadwick (*Relations: The Spanish–American War*), vol. 2, 154–213.

FIG. 2 A patriotic view of the Disaster. The Spanish fleet at Cavite, 'The Final Cry, "Long Live Spain!"' From *La Campana de Gracia*

had remained behind at Hampton Roads in view of exaggerated public fears that the Spanish fleet might attack the east coast of the United States. Surmising correctly that Cervera was heading for Puerto Rico, Sampson sailed there and not finding the Spanish squadron, bombarded the capital San Juan before returning to Florida.

Cervera's flotilla was indeed making its way to Puerto Rico but the poor condition of some of his ships caused the voyage to be painfully slow, upsetting the American commander's calculations about its approximate location and enabling it thus to evade the enemy squadron. Cervera's original intention had been to dock in Puerto Rico but in the knowledge that American ships were in that vicinity and that Havana was completely blockaded, the Spanish commander decided to make for Santiago harbour where he hoped to obtain coal and supplies. Unknown to him, a cable had been sent by the Spanish government during his voyage, giving him authority to return to Spain in view of the build-up of American ships in the Caribbean. This order was then rescinded when the Commander-in-Chief in Cuba, General Blanco, protested that the absence of the squadron in Caribbean waters would demoralize the troops in Cuba. Arriving in Santiago on 19 May, the squadron refuelled from the low level of stocks available there and contemplated making its way to Puerto Rico. By a majority decision among the commanders, however, it was decided to remain in Santiago harbour rather than risk an encounter with American ships reportedly in the vicinity. By 25 May, the Spanish squadron found itself blockaded in the harbour by the combined fleets of Sampson and Schley.

In the meantime, a huge American expeditionary force of 17,000 men had been assembled in Tampa, Florida, under the command of the rotund General Shafter. Organized into the Fifth Army Corps, it consisted of regular units as well as volunteers, of whom the most notable were Theodore Roosevelt's flamboyant Rough Riders. Largely because of the presence of the Spanish ships in Santiago, the expeditionary force set sail for eastern Cuba on 7 June and on the 11th, a detachment of marines from the American squadrons anchored nearby landed at Guantánamo, some forty miles from Santiago and seized its harbour to provide a coaling station for the American ships. The Cuban insurgents under Calixto García agreed to carry out sustained attacks on Spanish forces in the area where the landings were planned. Finally on 22 June, after a naval bombardment, American forces disembarked at Daiquirí and Siboney, meeting little Spanish resistance.

The Spanish commander in Santiago, General Linares, had created

three lines of defence around and beyond the city. The outer ring consisted of small detachments defending the coast east of Santiago. A
stronger line of defence was formed by blockhouses at a distance of a few
miles from the city. The city itself was defended by an outer perimeter
formed by a defensive ditch and numerous fortifications. As the American
troops advanced through jungle along the track leading towards Santiago,
Spanish troops in the first line of defence fell back to more fortified
positions and there the first battles took place. In these engagements, the
American troops suffered numerous casualties in the face of skilled and
determined Spanish soldiers equipped with highly effective Mauser rifles.
But the Spanish were heavily outnumbered and lacked sufficient ammunition. The fort of El Caney, for example, was defended by only 467 men
and 47 advance snipers and held only 960,000 rounds of ammunition.[74] By
2 July, the Americans had burst through the second line of defence and
now lay siege to Santiago itself.

While US troops were advancing on Santiago, Cervera's squadron had
remained in the harbour, oblivious to the urgings of Madrid and the
Captain-General in Havana that it should attempt to run the blockade to
avoid a humiliating capture by the Americans. With the enemy now
poised to seize Santiago, Cervera was ordered by General Blanco from
Havana to leave the harbour. On 3 July, the Spanish squadron sailed out
of Santiago Bay, taking the American fleet briefly by surprise. Gathering
up speed, the eleven American battleships ran down the Spanish ships
and one by one, as they were hit by superior fire, Cervera's squadron was
forced to run aground on the shore. The first to do so was Cervera's
flagship, the *María Teresa*, and the admiral, the last on board to abandon
ship, had to swim ashore with other survivors, arriving with hardly any
clothes left on him. During the engagement, the American fleet had
hardly been touched; while the Spanish had suffered 323 killed and 151
wounded, the Americans lost only one sailor and two were wounded.

American troops were now ordered to seize Santiago or force its surrender. Surrounded on all sides by the enemy, weakened by illness and lack
of food, sleep and shelter, the Spanish defenders saw surrender as inevitable. After several days of negotiations and a short bombardment of the
city by the American fleet which left the city untouched because the range
was too high, the Spanish army in eastern Cuba capitulated on 15 July
with the agreement of Madrid. The fall of Santiago, the siege of Manila
and the loss of most of the Spanish fleet left the Spanish government with

[74] A. B. Feuer, *The Santiago Campaign of 1898. A Soldier's View of the Spanish-American War* (Westport, Connecticut, 1993), 76–7.

little option but to capitulate. Moreover, it proved unable to send Spain's reserve squadron of newly repaired ships to the scene of battle. The ships had set out, under the command of Admiral de la Cámara, on the long voyage through the Suez Canal towards the Philippines with the impossible mission of asserting Spanish sovereignty in the Far East without engaging the enemy.[75] Unable to refuel before the journey through the Canal because of international laws of belligerency, however, it was forced to return to Spain in mid-July. With no further hope of resistance, the Spanish government accordingly instructed the French ambassador in Washington to explore on its behalf the American terms for a cessation of hostilities.

While these secret talks got under way, Spain's other island in the Caribbean, Puerto Rico, was also invaded by an American expeditionary force. Led by General Miles, the Puerto Rican campaign was considerably more sophisticated than General Shafter's in Cuba. Taking the Spanish command by surprise, his force landed on 24 July at Guánica on the west coast at the other end of the island to the capital San Juan. The capture of the nearby port of Ponce allowed more troops to be landed and Miles then divided his force into four columns which drove separately towards the capital, engaging in a number of skirmishes with Spanish troops as they advanced. As in Cuba, the Spanish command had spread some of its forces in garrisons throughout the island but the bulk of the army was concentrated in San Juan and along the road across the mountains to Ponce. Any further military engagement, however, was forestalled on 14 August by the news that a peace protocol had been signed two days earlier between the United States and Spain.

In the Philippines, Admiral Dewey had proceeded to occupy the naval station of Cavite, where Montojo's squadron had been destroyed, and instituted a blockade of Manila. The capital of the Philippines had already been all but surrounded by the Filipino insurgents. The Katipunan insurrectionists, who had risen in August 1896, had been forced by Spanish military to accept peace terms in December of 1897 and under the Pact of Biyak-na-Bató, its leaders had gone into exile. A new insurrection had broken out in March 1898 and by the time of the naval battle in Manila Bay, the Filipinos had captured many of the small Spanish garrisons scattered about the islands and were threatening Manila itself.

On 25 May an American expeditionary force had set sail from San Francisco bound for the Philippines. En route, it annexed the independent republic of Hawaii and seized the undefended Spanish island of Guam

[75] Aunón to Cámara, 27 May, in Chadwick (*Relations*), vol. 2, 383–8.

where it ran up the American flag. Arriving in the Philippines between the end of June and mid-July, the American troops joined in the siege of Manila. Some 13,000 beleaguered Spanish soldiers entrenched in defensive positions in and around the city, now faced 8,500 American soldiers and 10,000 Filipino insurgents. The final assault began on 13 August. After a bombardment on the city by American ships, the invading troops advanced, forcing the Spanish soldiers to fall back from one defensive position to another until the acting Commander-in-Chief of the Spanish forces, General Jaudenes, signalled his intention to capitulate. Unknown to both sides, however, the Spanish and American governments had agreed a peace protocol in Washington the day before.

The outcome of the Spanish–American War suggested that the conflict had been a totally one-sided affair; a mighty nation had inflicted a humiliating defeat on a third-rate power. And indeed, in the mythology surrounding the war that arose on both sides, it was a case, on one hand, of Spanish heroism against overwhelming odds and on the other, of American moral and military superiority against a decadent foe. In terms of potential power, however, there was no such mismatch. The Spanish army vastly outnumbered the American. It had up to 200,000 troops in Cuba, 30,000 in the Philippines, and 8,000 in Puerto Rico, while when the war began the American standing army had been a mere 28,000 men.[76] The two crushing naval defeats inflicted by America on Spain whereby the war was largely determined obscured the fact that on paper at least the Spanish navy was of similar strength to the American and that neither matched the British or the German navies, nor indeed that of a second-class naval power.[77]

The reasons why the Spanish war effort failed so dismally to match that of the American are several. The Spanish army was widely dispersed in each of the arenas of war. In Cuba and Puerto Rico, it was spread out in numerous garrisons across each island with its main force gathered in and around Havana; of the 30,000 troops in Oriente province in Cuba, for example, only 8,000 were concentrated in Santiago when the siege began.[78] In the Philippines, it was scattered about several of the islands of the archipelago. The American High Command, in contrast, was able to direct large numbers of troops at very specific points, chosen for their

[76] Smith (*The Spanish–American*), 48–9.

[77] Chadwick (*Relations*), vol. 1, 28–39. Admiral Tirpitz, on the basis of information from the German fleet, believed the Spanish squadron would defeat the American. The Kaiser was reported to be 'stupified' on learning about the outcome of the battle in Manila Bay: Jover Zamora ('1898'), 40.

[78] Fernández Almagro (*Historia Política*), vol. 3, 118.

strategic value from information supplied by the local insurgents. In Cuba in particular, the Americans depended greatly on the rebel army, which had virtually won the war in the east and kept Spanish garrisons there pinned down while the American forces advanced towards Santiago. The epic 200-mile journey of the Spanish relief column led by Colonel Federico Escario from Manzanillo to Santiago, through repeated ambushes, is testimony to the control the Cubans enjoyed in the area and the problem for the Spanish of redeployment.

For the same reason, food supplies, medicine, and ammunition were difficult to transport across the island and, once the naval blockade of Santiago began in April, were unobtainable by sea. Little food could be gathered from local sources because the land in the east of the island had been devastated by war. Santiago fell so easily because the army could neither feed its population nor hold off an American assault for lack of men and munitions. During a brief moment of euphoria before the naval battle off the coast of Cuba, Spanish troops in Santiago had paraded a cart through the streets bearing the allegorical figure of McKinley amongst others to shouts of 'Down with bacon!'. Bacon was one of the terms used by Spanish jingoists to insult Americans (because it derived from pigs); the irony was that it was also the only nutritious food left in the besieged city and it would run out shortly after the incident.[79] Moreover, the size of the Spanish army in Cuba was no indication of its strength because so many soldiers were sick. That this problem affected the American invasion force is clear from a report by a US regimental surgeon that they could not have continued the siege of Santiago much longer because yellow fever had ravaged their ranks. Indeed, Theodore Roosevelt claimed that by the time the troops were due to leave the island in August, not 10 per cent were fit for duty.[80]

The only edge the Spanish troops enjoyed over the American soldiers was their knowledge of the terrain and their experience of counter-guerrilla warfare gained over three years of war against the Cuban insurgents. An incident just before the first engagement in Cuba between Spanish and American soldiers gives some idea of the deadly effect of this experience. As Theodore Roosevelt's Rough Riders advanced north from their landing-place in Siboney through dense jungle, they kept hearing what they thought was the cooing of wood-doves and the call of a 'tropical' cuckoo, although they never saw any birds. Shortly afterwards, a hail of Mauser bullets tore through their ranks. The bird song had been the signal given by Spanish look-outs tracking the advance of the American soldiers towards the prepared ambush.[81]

It was also true, however, that many of the Spanish troops had arrived only recently and were young and inexperienced. Dressed in straw hats, white cotton uniforms, and espadrilles, many were mown down by the American Gatling guns and artillery fire. An American private in the Rough Riders described the pitiful scene in the Spanish defensive positions after the battle for the San Juan Hill:

When we arrived at the Spanish trenches, on the north slope of San Juan Hill, we saw the work of the Gatling guns. Most of the Spaniards had been shot through the head—some two or three times. So help me God, they looked like kids about twelve years old. Hundreds of them were lying there dead. It was a pitiful sight. All of us boys felt ashamed of ourselves.[82]

Moreover, amongst many of the Spanish troops, there appeared to be no strong motivation to continue fighting what was clearly a lost cause and for a population that mostly supported the independence movement. Even the General commanding Santiago, in a telegram to the Minister of War, recognized that

the ideal is lacking; for they are defending the property of those who abandoned it in their very presence and who have allied themselves with the American forces.[83]

Like the army, the Spanish navy suffered from many disadvantages in comparison to its American counterpart. In an age when the rapid advance of military technology made long-term naval planning hazardous, Madrid and Washington had chosen diametrically opposed strategies. Following the French *Jeune École* school, Spain had elected to build a swift and mobile navy of armoured and protected cruisers backed by the potentially lethal fleet of torpedo gunboats. The United States, on the contrary, had followed the British model, constructing heavily armoured battleships equipped with long-range fire-power.[84] Part of the problem for Spain was that its programme of naval construction and renovation was far from complete as the war began. To some extent, this was a reflection of Spain's

[81] Morris (*The Rise*), 642–4.

[82] Feuer (*The Santiago Campaign*), 54.

[83] Telegram of 12 July 1898 from General Linares, cited in Chadwick (*The Relations: the Spanish America War*), vol. 2, 227.

[84] Agustín R. Rodríguez González, 'Balances navales, estrategias y decisiones políticas en la guerra de 1898', in *Estudios Históricos. Homenaje a los Profesores José María Jover Zamora y Vicente Palacio Atard* (Madrid, 1990), vol. 1, 634–6.

relative industrial backwardness; many of its warships were in foreign dockyards awaiting completion or in the process of being repaired and the crews operating new or refurbished ships were unfamiliar with the recently installed technology. Also, those that were operating off the coast of Cuba had suffered considerable wear and tear during the Spanish–Cuban War.

The Spanish fleet that finally arrived in Santiago was far smaller and less well equipped and manned than that originally intended.[85] Thus Spain had only one first-class battleship compared to four American while each had one second-class battleship of similar tonnage. Spain had three armoured cruisers to two heavier American ones. Of protected cruisers, Spain had three heavy ones to eleven American and twelve unprotected cruisers to twenty. The US had six monitors while Spain had none. As for gun-fire, the US navy enjoyed a superiority of three to one in heavy armament.[86]

In contrast to the American fleet in the Caribbean, moreover, the Spanish ships in the area suffered from the immense disadvantage of operating several thousands of miles from home. The most urgent problem this posed was one of refuelling. The coal ships accompanying the Atlantic squadron were either seized by American ships or were left behind in ports on the way. Unknown to Admiral Cervera, furthermore, Santiago suffered from an acute shortage of coal. Coal was also very difficult to obtain from neutral ports. As we have seen, when Madrid attempted to send a third squadron to the Philippines via the Suez Canal under the command of Admiral Manuel de la Cámara, it was unable to proceed through the Canal for lack of fuel and had to return home. This was the result of British pressure on the Egyptian authorities not to supply coal to the Spanish fleet on the strength of international laws over belligerency. Yet the American squadron in the Pacific, in contrast, was able to obtain coal and refitting facilities from the British without undue problems.[87] Lack of coal, therefore, severely diminished the only potential advantage which the Spanish squadrons enjoyed over their rivals—speed and mobility. Holed up in a harbour or attempting to run a blockade with insufficient coal, their ships were easy prey to the more powerful American squadrons.

[85] Ibid. 649–50; Concas (*La Escuadra*), 21–2.

[86] Chadwick (*The Relations: the Spanish American War*), vol. 1, 28–39; see also Soldevilla (*El año, 1900*), 118–19.

[87] Rosario de la Torre del Río, *Inglaterra y España en 1898* (Madrid, 1988), 141–53 and 178–88; for the official British position on the Suez Canal episode, see Gooch and Temperley (*Documents*), Document 379, 28 June 1898, 319.

Spain's naval strategy had originally envisaged a different kind of war at sea, one in which Spanish ships would remain mobile, striking at targets on the East coast of the United States and then withdrawing, with a squadron stationed off the coast to defend the peninsula. The government's decision to send Cervera's squadron to the Caribbean appeared to be influenced by different strategic considerations—to raise the morale of the troops there and above all to ensure a defensive presence in the area to impede the Americans from landing troops, bombarding coastal towns and cutting communications with Madrid. Cervera and his commanders saw the situation differently. The Admiral had written a succession of letters to the Navy Minister between February and March 1898, outlining the disparity of forces between Spain and the US and the disastrous consequences of such a war, asking his views to be conveyed to the Queen Regent and to the Council of Ministers and indeed, suggesting that they probably were as aware as he was of the true situation.[88]

While his squadron had waited in Cape Verde Islands for further orders from the government, Cervera's views were conveyed to a special meeting of the Naval High Command on 23 April. The minutes of that meeting reveal wide differences of opinion amongst the assembled naval commanders as to what the squadron should do next.[89] When asked by the Navy Minister to declare their preferred option, sixteen out of eighteen had decided finally that the squadron should sail immediately for the Caribbean and the other two that it should wait until the ships under repair were ready. One Vice-Admiral, having originally argued that the squadron should return to Spain to defend its coasts, agreed that it should set sail for the Caribbean if this were necessary 'in the supreme interests of the Fatherland' but made clear his belief that this would result in certain disaster. The senior Admiral at the meeting summed up their dilemma; the squadron could not return to Spain nor remain where it was. Public opinion had overestimated the strength of the Spanish fleet and demanded the satisfaction of a military encounter. The squadron had therefore to set sail for the Caribbean with the risk that it would be defeated there.

Nevertheless, it is clear that most of the naval High Command, whilst aware that the Spanish and American navies were not equal in fighting power, did not share Cervera's conviction that the only possible outcome of the dispatch of his squadron was its destruction. Indeed, like much informed opinion in Spain, they seem also to have considerably underes-

[88] Cervera (*Guerra*), 29–72.   [89] The minutes are reproduced in Ibid. 72–82.

timated the capacity of the American navy, just as the government and the army had of the US army.[90] If Cervera and his commanders set sail for the Caribbean convinced they were being sacrificed in order to make the loss of the colonies more palatable for the Spanish public, the balance of evidence suggests that the strategy of the government and the naval High Command was not guided by such ulterior motives.

Cervera may have had more grounds for his belief subsequently. While there may have been valid strategic reasons for sending his squadron to Cuba, the decision to order it to run the blockade of Santiago Bay appears to have been taken, by the Commander in Chief of the Spanish forces in Cuba, General Blanco, largely on political grounds. Had the squadron remained in the harbour, it was likely to have fallen into American hands without a struggle. This outcome would have been unacceptable both to military pride and to the public mood in Spain. So Cervera's ships had set sail out of the harbour to face almost certain destruction. The drama of the situation, as the Spanish ships steamed out of the harbour, was later described vividly by the captain of Cervera's flagship.

The bugle gave the signal for battle to begin, an order repeated by all the batteries and followed by a murmur of approbation amongst all those poor sailors and marines anxious to fight . . . My bugle sounded the last echo of those that history tells sounded in the conquest of Granada; it was the signal that the history of four centuries of greatness was coming to an end and that Spain was passing into the ranks of a fourth-class nation. Poor Spain!, I said to my esteemed and noble Admiral and he assented meaningfully, as if to say that he had done everything possible to avoid it [the battle] and his conscience was clear.[91]

That this had been the perception also amongst the officers in the Pacific fleet is suggested by a letter from one of them shortly before the Disaster in Manila Bay. Writing to his brother, Luis Cadarso, the captain of the Spanish cruiser Reina Cristina, who was killed in the battle, had stated bitterly, 'we will have to accept so unequal a battle for the sake of national decorum'. At his trial after the War, Admiral Montojo, exclaimed, 'It has always been said: woe betide the defeated!; but now it

---

[90] Rodríguez González ('Balances'), 644–6. Underestimation of the fighting capacity of the American troops may have been influenced by Spanish Intelligence reports. A spy in Florida reported that 'Troops in Tampa are badly fed, badly clothed, and are all weak, poorly trained but were ordered to be ready for service at once. They are not well armed . . . Discipline is poor and everybody drinks heavily': AGA/AE 8061, letter dated 7 June 1898.

[91] For his account of the battle, see Concas (*La Escuadra*), 153–5.

should be added: woe betide those who are sent to be defeated!'[92] Yet it had been Montojo's choice to remain within Manila Bay behind a protective wall of shore batteries and underwater mines. The fact that not all these were yet in place or were too dispersed had been due to military unpreparedness and lack of resources. Montojo had repeatedly warned about the overwhelming strength of Dewey's flotilla and the deficiencies of the Spanish defences but the Navy Ministry had replied each time that it was unable to send further reinforcements and munitions.[93] In the event, the American ships had been able to penetrate into the Bay without problem and Montojo's squadron was picked off from a distance by the more heavily armed American battleships, largely out of the range of the Spanish gunners on ship and on shore. And the squadron had been sunk, not so much because of the destruction caused by American fire but by Montojo's order for the ships to be scuttled to avoid their capture by the enemy.

That is to say, there appears to have been no tacit conspiracy by the Spanish regime or the High Command to sacrifice the navy or to set the scene for a spectacular defeat with minimal cost in human lives in order to persuade opinion at home that the colonies had to be abandoned. Instead, Spanish naval strategy was made on the hoof and was guided by a number of conflicting considerations: the need to defend the peninsula coast and the colonies at the same time; the problem of coaling; the hope that ships in repair might be ready shortly to join the depleted squadrons; the demands of the overseas armies for naval protection and the transport of supplies and so on.[94] What made it extraordinarily difficult was the immense distance over which the navy had to operate and the endemic defects of military planning and administration. It is likely therefore, as we have already argued, that informed opinion within the Spanish regime expected Spain to lose the war but not to suffer such a catastrophe as the two naval defeats and the ignominious surrender of Santiago.

No sooner had the news of the disaster at Manila Bay reached Spain than the business of seeking blame for the defeat began. In the months that followed, few institutions and political leaders escaped blame. The

---

[92] Concas (*La Escuadra*), 5. For Cadarso's letter, Rodríguez Martínez (*Los desastres*), 126; for Cervera's commanders: Concas (*La Escuadra*), 26.

[93] C. P. (*Ante la opinión*), 78–9, 88.

[94] This is Rodríguez González' conclusion (*Balances*); see also Sylvia L. Hilton, 'Democracy Goes Imperial: Spanish Views of American Policy in 1898', in David K. Adams and Cornelis A. van Minnen (eds.), *Reflections on American Exceptionalism* (Keele, 1994), 97–128.

more serious analyses rightly pointed out the lack of direction and continuity in military and naval planning and the absence of an effective
foreign policy in an age of imperial expansion. What appeared to be least
understood at the time was that, in the new world order at the turn of the
century, Spain's overseas colonies were an anachronism. It is true that a
crucial reason for Spain's débâcle was the tenacity of the struggle for
national liberation in Cuba. But the colonies were also lost, not through
any special failing on the part of either the Spanish government or
the armed forces, but because they were remnants of an old empire
entangled in areas which had become strategically important in the new
drive for imperial expansion of the late nineteenth century. This more
global view of the cause of the Spanish defeat was encapsulated by Lord
Salisbury's famous speech in May 1898, in which he referred to 'dying
nations', which were having to give way to more vigorous, expanding
powers.[95]

The international dimension of the Spanish–American conflict can
clearly be seen in the form in which the Spanish colonies were redistributed after the war. In principle, the negotiations leading to a peace settlement involved only the two parties to the dispute. Initial peace talks were
held in Washington between the American government and the French
Ambassador in the United States, Jules Cambon, acting on behalf of the
Spanish government. A peace protocol was agreed on 12 August 1898 and
formal negotiations between the Spanish and the American commissions
towards a treaty began on 1 October in Paris. The Spanish commission
was made up entirely of representatives of the Liberal government because no other party wished to be identified with the signing away of the
Empire. The American commission, for its part, was made up of a majority of expansionists.[96] Having been comprehensively defeated in war, the
Spanish commission had no choice but to accept the harsh terms imposed
by the victors. By the Treaty of Paris, signed on 10 December, Spain
ceded Cuba, Puerto Rico, the Philippines, and the island of Guam in the
Pacific to the United States; in return for the Philippines, Spain was paid
20 million dollars.

Outside the official negotiations, however, some of the Great Powers
were staking claims on Spanish possessions. In order to reinforce its

---

[95] It was significant that these words should come from a patrician statesman such as Lord
Salisbury, whose instinctive sympathy for the Spanish monarchy had to give way to wider
British interests. For a study of the impact of his speech in Spain, see Torre del Río
(*Inglaterra*), 194–7.
[96] Smith (*The Spanish*), 195.

FIG. 3 The European Powers 'Waiting for the weather to calm down to see if they can catch something'; the 'weather' being the Spanish-American war. From *La Campana de Gracia*

ambitions to acquire part of the Philippines, Germany had stationed a squadron just beyond Manila Bay during the naval battle between Spain and America; its presence had so incensed Admiral Dewey that he had ordered one of the German ships to be boarded.[97] Once it became clear that the United States intended to annex all of the Philippines, Germany sought British support to achieve its secondary goal of acquiring the Spanish Pacific islands. Britain, anxious that America should retain the Philippines to prevent it falling into the hands of another European Power, was also keen that Berlin should be compensated for its disappointment over the Philippines.[98] As a result of these diplomatic manœuvres, Berlin, with British and American consent, secretly negotiated with Madrid the sale of all the islands except Guam for the price of 25 million pesetas, acquiring thus a string of strategic islands, useful for coaling stations and communications, stretching to its concessions in China.

[97] Gooch and Temperley (*Documents*), 14 July, 1898, Document 126, 105.
[98] María Dolores Elizalde, 'La venta de las Islas Carolinas, un nuevo hito en el 98 español', in *Estudios Históricos. Homenaje a los Profesores José María Jover Zamora y Vicente Palacio Atard* (Madrid, 1990), vol. 1, 361–80; Neale (*Great Britain*), 37–8.

The impending break-up of the Spanish colonies had sent ripples of interest and anxiety through the European Powers, who feared that the precarious balance of power in the Mediterranean might be altered as a result (Fig. 3). Russia was reported to be interested in acquiring the Spanish African enclave of Ceuta on the Mediterranean. The Italian ambassador to Spain had divulged to his British counterpart his fear that France might gain some territorial advantage from Spain.[99] There had also been considerable tension between Spain and Britain when Madrid, fearing an American attack, had ordered fortifications to be built opposite Gibraltar, thereby appearing to threaten British security interests in that vital part of the sea route leading to the Suez Canal and India. The dispute had channelled Spanish resentment against the British government whom they suspected, with justification, of favouring the United States in the War. Madrid had attempted unsuccessfully to use the issue of the fortifications to persuade the British to lobby Washington over the Philippines.[100]

While Spain's position in the Mediterranean and Morocco remained unresolved, the redistribution of her overseas colonies was thus achieved by consent and secret negotiation without upsetting the balance between the European Powers. Washington had asserted its hegemony in the Caribbean and its power in the Pacific. It was now embarked on a new career of global expansion. Indeed, there is a striking symmetry between the fortunes of America and Spain at this juncture of their histories. The United States had resolved its internal conflicts in the Civil War and then in the Battle of Wounded Knee in 1890. Having reached the limits of expansion in its own territory, America moved outwards to claim an overseas empire.[101] For Spain, on the contrary, the Disaster of 1898 signified the end of her Empire and the beginning of her internal fragmentation.

[99] Letter from Drummond-Wolff to Salisbury regarding Russia on 11 May 1898 in PRO FO 72/2063; and conversation with the Italian ambassador in letter to same on 2 Aug. 1898 in PRO FO 72/2065.

[100] Torre del Río (*Inglaterra*), 249–77; secret telegram from Salisbury to Drummond-Wolff, 11 Aug. 1898 in Buckle (*The Letters*), 264; letters from Mr Balfour to Queen Victoria, 26 and 31 Aug. 1898, 266–7 and 269–70 and from Queen Victoria to the Queen Regent of Spain, Sept. 1898, 280–1.

[101] The significance of the War for expansionist Americans was exuberantly expressed by Theodore Roosevelt in a letter to his friend Henry Cabot Lodge. As he gathered together the Rough Riders regiment in preparation for the assault on Cuba, he confided, 'I fail to get the relations of this regiment and the universe straight', Morris (*The Rise*), 121.

2

The Aftermath of Disaster

THE end of the War was greeted in Spain with a gamut of different emotions. Probably the most widespread of these were also the most private—amongst those families with young men who survived the war, a deep sense of relief at their safe return; amongst those who lost relatives, sorrow and perhaps anger at their fruitless sacrifice. Such private feelings were not made public except in the memoirs that began to appear much later on. Those whose voices were always heard, the press and parliament, sounded a common note of gloom and outrage. The profound shock that appeared to grip journalists and politicians following the end of the Empire suggested that many informed people, knowing the hopelessness of any war with the United States, had suspended their disbelief and allowed themselves to be carried away by the prevailing mood of jingoism.[1]

The Disaster exposed as a terrible delusion the belief that Spain was at least a middle-ranking world power, a belief that was a central component of the national culture. The loss of the last remnants of the Empire provoked a severe post-imperial crisis among sections of Spanish society, one that had been delayed since the early nineteenth century. Spain's political system, its national character, and Spanish nationhood itself now began to be widely questioned. This crisis was all the more acute because it occurred at the highest point in the age of empire, when the possession of colonies was seen as the bench-mark of a nation's fitness to survive. Lord Salisbury's speech on 4 May 1898 in which Spain was implicitly referred to as a 'dying nation' reverberated throughout the Spanish press.[2]

Yet the regime which had presided over such a national catastrophe remained in place and survived for the next twenty-five years. Elsewhere,

---

[1] This was one of the accusations in a long and passionate speech in parliament by the Liberal democrat, José Canalejas, *DSC*, Sept. 1898, n. 57, 1719–30. Intellectuals were also deeply affected by the Disaster; the historian Menéndez y Pelayo stopped writing letters for a while and the neurologist Ramón y Cajal's research rate dropped considerably.

[2] Rosario de la Torre del Río, 'La prensa madrileña y el discurso de Lord Salisbury sobre "las naciones moribundas" (Londres, Albert Hall, 4 mayo 1898)', *Cuadernos de Historia Moderna y Contemporánea*, no. 6, 1985, 163–80.

disasters of a similar magnitude caused profound political changes. The historical model that most haunted the Spanish establishment was the rout of Napoleon III's army by the Germans at Sedan in 1870. The consequent loss of Alsace-Lorraine had led to the fall of the Empire of Napoleon III and the proclamation of the Third Republic. In the aftermath of the Disaster, the name of Sedan also rang through political speeches and articles in Spain with doom-laden significance.[3] Such was the government's apprehension of the political dangers resulting from defeat that the day after the disaster in Manila Bay, the Minister of the Interior sent a cable to all provincial governors ordering them to prepare the Civil Guard to quell unrest.[4] As the weeks went by peacefully, politicians and journalists continued to vie with each other in the depiction of the coming disintegration. Unless something was done soon, many voices urged, the end of the nation itself was nigh. A few months after the Disaster, a popular weekly magazine wrote urgently,

today the question for us, not the main but the only and exclusive question, is one of life or death; one of whether we continue to exist as a nation or not.[5]

Yet in the immediate aftermath of the Disaster, no general rose up in revolt and the opposition of neither left nor right made any impression on a seemingly immovable regime. The Liberal government that had officiated over the ignominious defeat was duly replaced by a Conservative government in February 1899 but such changes occurred so frequently there was nothing remarkable about it. Two years later, the Liberal leader, Mateo Sagasta, to whom was attributed the major responsibility for the Disaster, was back in power with a team of ministers closely associated with the war period.

In view of the frailty of the Restoration regime, such stability needs some explanation. The simplest hypothesis is that it derived from the sheer comprehensiveness of the defeat. The mistakes, the incompetences and the corruptions of the government and the military were of little consequence next to the overwhelming display of force by the United States. It is true that great efforts were made to exorcise the Disaster by identifying scapegoats. In the Senate, the Conde de las Almenas, echoing

---

[3] For example, 'Sedan', *La Campana de Gracia*, 23 Sept. 1898.
[4] 2 May 1898, AHN, Legajo 44A, no. 19.
[5] 'Sed fuertes', *La Ilustración Española y Americana*, 8 Feb. 1899. Even the British Ambassador shared the prevailing apprehension that the regime was about to fall. In a dispatch to Lord Salisbury on 30 July, he warned that '[Spain] is exposed to great internal dangers . . . Things do not look well for Spain . . .' (Drummond-Wolf to Salisbury in PRO, FO72.2065).

a common feeling throughout the country, launched a bitter attack on the generals, demanding that 'medals should be torn from chests and sashes raised from waists to necks'.[6] During the months that followed the end of the war, several prominent military and naval commanders were put on trial, including Admirals Cervera and Montojo, but those few that were found guilty were simply struck off the active list and received the full corresponding salary entitlements.

For his part, the Archbishop of Seville attributed the Disaster to the nefarious activities of Masonic lodges throughout the world.[7] The press was blamed, and in some cases blamed itself, for creating illusions about Spain's war capacity and for stirring up jingoism. Loose accusations were thrown at the Queen Regent, at the Americans for greed, at the British for connivance with the US.[8] While the Sagasta government was to blame in particular, it seemed everyone was to blame in general. The right-wing paper *El Nacional* sprang to the defence of the armed forces against the Conde de las Almenas and his supporters, arguing that any army was only as good as the society from which it sprang; cunningly adapting the Socialists' wartime slogan against the evasion of conscription by the better-off families, 'Everybody or nobody', the editor declared all of Spain was responsible for the Disaster.[9]

A more important reason for the immobility of the political system was the absence of any alternative. The traditional arbiters of political change, the military, were divided, unpopular and indecisive about their role in a post-imperial Spain.[10] Only General Polavieja contemplated taking power for a brief while to ensure a period of stability before handing the government back to the established parties. But he was dissuaded by the firm stance of the Queen Regent, who, unlike her son twenty-five years later, understood the danger to the monarchy of any wilful disregard for the Constitution.[11] The Carlists, who had fought bitter civil wars with the

[6] *El Imparcial*, 8 Sept. 1898; according to *El Cardo* ('Al Conde de las Almenas'), 19 Sept. 1898, anti-military sentiments were widespread after the Disaster. Among other newspapers that attacked the military and the navy included *La Época* (e.g. 11 May 1899) and *El Heraldo* ('Los verdaderos culpables', 11 Aug. 1899).

[7] *El Imparcial*, 7 Aug. 1898.

[8] For the press, *El Diario de Barcelona*, 9 July, 1898, 7745; *El Imparcial*, 8 Feb. 1899. For the Queen Regent, the Americans and the British, see for example *El Diario de Barcelona*, 7 July, 1898, 7664 and 7673–4.

[9] 'Ejército y Pueblo', 8 Sept. and 'Todos o ninguno', 13 Sept. 1898. For a lengthy discussion of the contemporary search for responsibility for the Disaster, see Rafael Núñez Florencio, *Militarismo y antimilitarismo en España* (Madrid, 1990), 269–329.

[10] For more on the military reaction see Chap. 6.

[11] Joaquín Romero-Maura, *'La rosa de fuego'. El obrerismo barcelonés de 1899 a 1909* (Madrid, 1989), 17–18.

armies of Spain's regimes throughout the nineteenth century, were no longer the menace depicted by the Liberal press, for whom, however, they remained the bogeyman of Spain. Too confined geographically to mount anything but local revolts, they had also been crippled by internal divisions during the last quarter of the century. Hoping to take advantage of the post-Disaster crisis, nevertheless, the irredentist Carlists built up caches of arms and launched a small uprising in October 1900 which was easily put down.[12]

Nor were the Republicans able to mount an effective attack on the Restoration system. In the last quarter of the nineteenth century, they had been weakened by a deep split between those who had opposed the Restoration system and those led by an ex-President of the First Republic, Emilio Castelar, who had believed that more could be achieved by participating in that system. In the aftermath of the Disaster, hoping vainly for a popular revolt or a military uprising, the more belligerent Republican press thundered against the regime for having lost the colonies. A wishful cartoon on the cover of the Catalan Republican paper, *La Campana de Gracia*, shows a worker poised over a castle of cards adorned with a King and his ministers; freely translated, the caption reads, 'Suppose I blow . . . !'.[13]

However, the Republicans had an uncertain base among workers, who, if they were not absorbed in problems of jobs, wages, and prices, were more likely to support social revolution than political conspiracy. Secret but inconclusive talks took place between Valencian Republicans and Liberal General Weyler but the Republicans' hope of reconstructing the sporadic nineteenth-century alliance between the army and the urban middle classes came to nothing. The attempt by a small group to launch an uprising on their own in 1899 ended in fiasco.[14] Moreover, the Republicans' cultural subordination to the dominant model of nationalism, outside Catalonia at least, made it difficult for them to project an alternative, either during the course of the war or in its aftermath.[15]

---

[12] The authorities were clearly well informed about Carlist intentions. A telegram to Madrid from the Spanish Embassy in Washington on 8 Dec. 1899 gives details about a shipment of arms from New York destined for Carlists in Valencia: AGA (AE), 8062. For more on the Carlists, see Miguel Artola, *Partidos y programas políticos, 1808–1936*, vol. 1, 535–44.

[13] 'Ay, si bufo' . . . 'Un castell de cartas', 8 July 1899.

[14] Reig (Obrers), 282–5. See also '¡A las armas! La Patria en peligro', *El Progreso*, 6 July, 1898; 'La Revolució', *La Campana de Gracia*, 5 Aug. 1899.

[15] José Alvarez Junco, 'La cultura Republicana', in Nigel Townson, *El Republicanismo en España (1830–1977)* (Madrid, 1994), 285–90. For Catalan Republicanism, see Angel Duarte, *El Republicanisme català a la fi del segle XIX* (Vic, 1987).

The weakness of the anti-dynastic opposition was as much to do with the stagnation of Spanish society as with their own failings as organizations. Along with other 'Latin' countries in Europe, Spain had remained a relatively backward society throughout the nineteenth century. Apart from pockets of industry and urban development on her periphery, especially in Catalonia and the Basque Country, Spain's social and economic structures had changed very little over the century. At the beginning of the new millennium, two-thirds of the active population were still engaged in agriculture, many of whom worked purely for subsistence. Life in the central tableland of Spain was marked by high mortality and low birth rates. If as much as 50 per cent of the total adult population was still illiterate, the proportion must have been considerably higher in the more backward areas. The agrarian crisis of the late nineteenth century, provoked by the influx into Europe of cheap grain from America and Russia, had stimulated a hitherto negligible flow of migration towards urban areas; nevertheless, only 9 per cent of the population could be described as urban by the beginning of the century and of the cities, only two had more than half a million inhabitants compared to twenty-five in the rest of Europe.[16]

The consequence was that the Restoration system rested on a largely demobilized society controlled by the patronage dispensed by political bosses, known as caciques, through a hierarchy of clientelism from Madrid down to the smallest provincial town. Until the war of 1895–8, probably a majority of Spaniards had gone about their lives with little knowledge or interest in what happened in parliament or indeed in the nation as a whole. 'Public opinion' had been formed by the oligarchy and the city élites, who controlled political life, ran the army, owned land and businesses, or published newspapers. The dynastic political parties were not mass organizations but represented, albeit imperfectly, the interests of this narrow range of élites. The base of opposition parties or extra-parliamentary parties, on the other hand, was too limited both geographically and numerically to offer a serious challenge to the regime.

Yet another reason for the regime's stability in the post-war period was the absence of any severe economic strains. Contrary to the prognostications of the ruin that would follow the loss of the colonies, the Spanish economy did not plunge into an immediate crisis.[17] Indeed, the macroeconomic statistics for the first few years of the new millennium

---

[16] Tortella (*El desarrollo*), 28–38.

[17] The *Diario Mercantil* ('Como ayer', Aug. 1898), for example, envisaged 'veritable ruin' and *El Norte de Castilla* ('Por Castilla', 5 Aug. 1898) foresaw 'hunger, misery, desperation'.

reveal lower inflation, reduced public debt, and a higher level of capital investment.[18] While there was a fall in the level of exports, this was not as much as the loss of the protected colonial market would suggest. Many industries depended on trade with Europe rather than with the colonies and when the value of the peseta crashed in the wake of the war with the United States, they experienced an unprecedented boom in exports. Thus while exports to the colonies decreased by 263 million pesetas between 1897 and 1899, this loss was more than compensated by the increase in exports to other countries.[19]

Even for those products most reliant on colonial trade, such as cotton textiles, flour, footwear, paper, wine, and preserved foodstuffs, the effect of the loss of the colonies was uneven. For one thing, there was no immediate drop in trade; on the contrary, it picked up after the war and remained stable for at least another year as outstanding orders were cleared. Thereafter there was a considerable fall in sales of those Spanish goods which had to compete in the old colonial markets on equal terms with US products, now that the protective tariff barriers had been dismantled. Other goods, such as shoes and boots, olive oil, and garlic, however, continued to find favour amongst Cuban and Puerto Rican customers because they were more to their taste than rival American products.[20]

The effects of the loss of the protected colonial market were also cushioned by a number of conjunctural factors: the aforementioned post-war fall in the value of the peseta; the fortuitously good harvests of 1898 and 1899 which raised domestic consumption; the return to Spain of the troops who had fought in the wars overseas, with their wage arrears in their pockets and needing new clothes to replace their tattered uniforms. The economic effects of the end of the Empire were attenuated, above all, by a spectacular influx of capital from Spaniards living in Spanish America. It has been estimated that over 1,600 million pesetas (gold standard) were repatriated in the aftermath of the War.[21] Much of this was

[18] Francisco Comín, 'Estado y crecimiento económico en España: lecciones de la historia', *Papeles de Economía Española*, no. 57 (1993), 55.

[19] At its highest point, colonial trade had represented 34% of Spain's total exports; by 1901, it received only 9.5%: 'Estadísticas de Comercio Exterior de España', in Borja de Riquer, *Lliga Regionalista: la burgesia catalana i el nacionalisme (1898–1904)* (Barcelona, 1976), 60. Iron-ore production in 1899, for example, rose approximately 30% over the previous year. Bilbao, where much modern industry was located, saw a brisk revival of business and as many as 39 new large-sized companies were registered there in 1899: *Parliamentary Papers*, Commercial Reports, vol. XCVI (1900), no. 2445, 2 and 25.

[20] Ibid., no. 2460, 35 and vol. CII (1899), no. 2216, 28.

[21] J. Sardà, *La política monetaria y las fluctuaciones de la economía española del XIX* (Madrid, 1948), 294. For the cushioning of the expected crisis, see the views of the Catalan

stimulated by the fall in the value of the peseta in the wake of the war. But amongst the repatriated capital was also that of Spanish colonial settlers returning to the peninsula from Cuba and Puerto Rico and bringing with them both entrepreneurial know-how and large fortunes. Indeed, the influx of this capital boosted investment in several parts of Spain. In Galicia for example, from where many of these settlers had first departed for the colonies, the capital was invested in a range of businesses such as sugar mills, shipping, and tourism.[22] The loss of the sugar trade encouraged the production in Spain of beet sugar, especially in the Ebro Valley where soil conditions were propitious. In turn, the growth of sugar-processing plants stimulated the production of alcohol and the development of hydro-electric plants.[23]

In the short term, however, the loss of the colonial market caused a severe structural crisis in those sectors most dependent on it, such as the flour industry, the Atlantic ports and Catalan textiles.[24] In the aftermath of the Disaster, both wheat farmers and textile producers became the most vociferous supporters of the regeneration of Spain's economic and political system. Their political lobbies set to work to demand from the government the continued protection of their own industries through state subsidies which would allow them to dump their post-colonial surpluses on to new markets.[25]

The Catalan textile industry, in particular, had relied heavily on exports to the colonies. For many years, it had enjoyed both protection from foreign competition and a guaranteed overseas market. During the decade of the 1890s, the colonial market had absorbed an annual average of 50.5 million pesetas' worth of textile goods; between 1900 and 1905, these sales plunged to an annual average of under 21 million.[26] The immediate drop in exports led to bankruptcy among firms overly dependent on the colo-

employers' organization, Foment de Treball Nacional in their post-war programme, 'A los representantes de la nación', *El Trabajo Nacional*, 15 Sept. 1899.

[22] J. A. Durán, *Agrarismo y movilización campesina en el país gallego (1875–1912)* (Mexico, 1977), 137.

[23] Caja de Ahorros de la Inmaculada, *Aragón en su historia* (Zaragoza, 1990), 456.

[24] Flour production in Spain had already been in steep decline since the 1880s owing to the influx of cheap grain into Europe and a Spanish–US agreement giving preference to Cuban sugar exports to the US. In addition, Castilian wheat farmers had been severely hit by competition from Catalan producers. The combined effect of the agrarian crisis of the 1880s and the loss of colonial trade meant that by the end of the century, flour exports had fallen some 30% from their peak in the 1870s (Javier Moreno Lázaro, 'Crisis y transformación de la harinera en Castilla y León (1882–1905)', *Cuadernos de Economía de Castilla y León*, no. 1, 1992, 161–229).

[25] See for example, *La Industria Harinera*, Nov., 1898, and 'De interés nacional', *El Norte de Castilla*, 28 Nov., 1898.

[26] Riquer (*Lliga*), 60.

nial market. As early as September 1900, according to a contemporary report, more than thirty companies had collapsed in Catalonia leaving some 60,000 workers without jobs.[27]

Yet while some firms suffered the loss badly, most of the industry coped with the new circumstances with surprising agility. After the war, exports to the ex-colonies of cotton goods, overwhelmingly the dominant export of the Catalan textile industry, fell from a five-yearly average of 7,000 tons to one of just over 2,500 tons. In the same period, however, exports to Latin America and to the rest of the world almost tripled, reaching a five-yearly average of over 2,250 tons in each area. The result of this diversification of export markets was that total exports of cotton goods from Spain fell between 1895 and 1909 by an average of only 751 tons.[28] Indeed, the drastic fall in exports to the colonial markets forced the Catalan textile magnates to restructure and re-equip their factories, whose economies of scale had been based on a limited domestic market and a largely protected export market. The recovery of the industry was due in great part to their ability not only to find new markets for their goods but more importantly, to maintain competitive prices through technological innovation.[29]

Nevertheless, the shock of losing the colonial market exploded the cosy relationship between the Catalan bourgeoisie and their patrons in Madrid. Catalan industrialists mobilized to force change on the political establishment. In the immediate term, they sought to persuade the government to carry out a range of measures to subsidize the industry and to establish new markets. In the longer term, however, it was evident that domestic demand had to be raised and this required an urgent programme of modernization of the kind that no previous Restoration governments had offered, dominated as they had been by the interests of the landed oligarchy.[30]

Hopes among the Catalan bourgeoisie that their urgent needs might be recognized were raised when Polavieja, having rejected the idea of a

[27] Soldevilla (*El año, 1900*), 34. For further discussion of the loss of the colonial market on Catalan industry, see R. J. Harrison, 'Catalan Business and the Loss of Cuba, 1898–1914', *Economic History Review*, vol. 27 (1974), 435.

[28] Author's calculations from Jordi Nadal, 'La industria cotonera' in *Història econòmica de la Catalunya contemporània* (Barcelona, 1991), vol. III, 64. The buoyancy of the Catalan cotton industry is also confirmed by figures showing that its average consumption of raw materials continued to rise steadily during the last decade of the nineteenth century and the first of the new century: 59.

[29] Jordi Nadal and Carles Sudrià, 'La controversia en torno al atraso español en la segunda mitad del siglo XIX (1860–1913)', *Revista de Historia Industrial*, 3 (1993), 199–227.

[30] 'La Crisis', *El Trabajo Nacional*, 20 Sept. 1900; Riquer (*Lliga*), 69–70.

military coup, considered attempting to form a government outside the two Restoration parties. As a leading advocate of protectionism, the devout, conservative general had close links with Catalan employers. In recognition of his role in suppressing the 1896 Filipino uprising, he had received a hero's welcome in Barcelona in 1897 and an arch had been dedicated to his military triumph. Secret talks between him and leading representatives of the Catalan bourgeoisie in August and September 1898 led to an agreement whereby they would back Polavieja's bid to form a government in return for his support for their minimum demands for fiscal and electoral devolution. Accordingly, Polavieja's manifesto of September 1898, amidst calls for a nation-wide regeneration, also promised an administrative decentralization that would allow the productive regions to generate greater wealth for themselves.[31]

However, lacking a party or any kind of social base besides the support of the Catalan bourgeoisie, Polavieja was in no position to challenge the political establishment. Both the Queen Regent and the leader of the Conservatives, Francisco Silvela, who had succeeded Cánovas on the latter's assassination, sought to persuade the General to join a Conservative government rather than insist on forming his own. A pious, austere lawyer, Silvela had briefly broken away from the Conservatives in 1897 to form his own party on a regenerationist programme. In the aftermath of the Disaster, he had distinguished himself by a series of speeches in parliament and a much-commented-upon article entitled 'Sin pulso'. Echoing Lord Salisbury's speech, he had argued that the nation lacked a pulse and if governments did not radically change direction, there was a risk of 'the total rupture of national bonds' and the end of Spain's 'destiny as a European people . . .'[32] Unable to form his own government and unwilling to stage a coup, Polavieja bowed to the inevitable and agreed to become Minister of War in a new government headed by Silvela.[33]

For a while, Silvela's regenerationist government breathed fresh life into the regime. Taking office in March 1899, the new Premier raised the

---

[31] The text can be found in María Carmen García-Nieto, Javier M. Donázar and Luis López Puerta, *Bases documentales de la España contemporánea* (Madrid, 1972), vol. 5, 41–9. The manifesto was drawn up in collaboration with the Liberal politician José Canalejas, amongst others, and had the blessing of the Queen Regent. Canalejas admitted his involvement in a speech in November (*El Imparcial*, 7 Nov. 1898). For the Queen Regent's part see Romero-Maura (*La rosa*), 18 n. 29; for the correspondence between Polavieja and representatives of the Catalan bourgeoisie, see 12–23.

[32] *El Tiempo*, 16 Aug. 1898, quoted in full in Francisco Silvela, *Artículos, Discursos, Conferencias y Cartas* (Madrid, 1922–3), vol. 2, 493–8.

[33] Ibid., vol. 2, 515–18; Romero-Maura (*La rosa*), 23–8.

hopes of those élites who wished to restore the legitimacy of the Restoration system and those, like the Catalan bourgeoisie, who hoped to gain access to the centre of the decision-making process. Silvela had promised to reform public administration at all levels, to renew the armed forces, and to stimulate the economy. But he stressed that he was seeking above all to restore morality into Spain's political life.[34] Impelled by an almost missionary zeal, the new Premier set a distinctly unusual tone in cabinet meetings. He and his ministers began their term of office by hearing Mass in the government chapel, leading the anti-clerical Republican deputy, the novelist Vicente Blasco Ibañez, to propose that deputies should recite the rosary to greet the new ministers as they took their seats in Congress.[35] Silvela's emphasis on ethics in politics had its origin in the conservative idealism of the Cánovas tradition. But at another level, it was perhaps a recognition of the difficulty for any Restoration government of modernizing Spain while continuing to represent the interests of the oligarchy; a plea for moral transformation rather than structural reform may have been a wishful means of overcoming this fundamental contradiction.

Nevertheless, the new Premier's cabinet embraced a wider range of interests than was usual in Restoration politics; the Minister of Justice, for example, was a well-known Catalan jurist, Manuel Durán i Bas. After taking office, Silvela made further appointments meant to win over lobbies outside the oligarchy, above all that of the Catalan bourgeoisie. This effort was all the more significant because Silvela himself was deeply hostile to any political expression of regionalism.[36] The new government, however, had to contend with virtually irreconcilable interests arising from the aftermath of the war. The most pressing task was to reduce the crushing deficit of 300 million pesetas largely made up of debt on loans raised to finance the wars.[37] Silvela's Minister of Finance, Raimundo Fernández Villaverde, drew up plans for a budget which would balance accounts at a stroke, above all by cutting public expenditure and raising taxes; deftly, the Minister also imposed an extraordinary tax of 20 per cent on interest from the War Debt.[38]

---

[34] Silvela (*Artículos*), vol. 2, 513.

[35] Fernández Almagro (*Historia política*), vol. 2, 336 n. 2.

[36] 'El Catalanismo y sus alivios', *La Lectura*, Jan. 1902, in *Artículos*, vol. 3, 123–38.

[37] Contemporary estimates of the total cost of the war ranged from the 4,000 million pesetas calculated by the Aragonese intellectual, Joaquín Costa ('Mensaje y programa de la Cámara agrícola del Alto-Aragón' in *Reconstitución y europeización de España* (Huesca, 1924) and 1,874 million pesetas claimed by official sources: Soldevilla (*El año, 1898*), 345–6.

[38] For further details, see Francisco Comín Comín, *Hacienda y economía en la España contemporánea (1800–1936)* (Madrid, 1988), vol. II, 604–45.

Yet the cuts in public expenditure that Villaverde wished to introduce were not compatible with Polavieja's plans for military reform. The financial crisis and Silvela's natural inclination towards austerity got the better of other political considerations. Faced by the Premier's insistence on cuts in military expenditure, Polavieja resigned. In any case, the regenerationist General's usefulness was fast diminishing. His alliance with the Catalans had been frowned on by the military, who vehemently disapproved of any expression of regionalism which was not simply folklore, while his plans to restructure the army were not popular amongst officers. Moreover, his presence in the cabinet had not prevented the rise of Catalanist sentiment and he had lost the support of the Catalan bourgeoisie for his failure to ensure that the government carried out his promise of fiscal devolution.[39]

The resolution of the public deficit was a unique achievement. Thanks to Villaverde's budget, prices were stabilized, the international value of the peseta rose and for the next ten years the state enjoyed what had been impossible before and what would be almost unthinkable afterwards, an annual surplus in its balance of accounts. Nevertheless, simply by raising taxes, Villaverde's budget of June 1899 destroyed any hope that the government would win the support of businessmen and large sections of the middle classes. The tax rises generated widespread protests which spiralled into mob violence, generalized shop closures and the withholding of tax payments in many parts of Spain. The arrest of defaulters in Barcelona led to the resignation of the Mayor and then of Silvela's Catalan Minister of Justice until the Premier's carefully contrived plan to woo opinion outside the establishment lay in tatters.

Moreover, Silvela's efforts to clean up the political system of the Restoration merely served to erode it. Reforming public administration meant dismantling the machinery whereby the Conservatives and the Liberals maintained their stranglehold on Spanish political life through the exercise of nepotism and patronage. Abstaining from electoral falsification would also have allowed parties largely excluded from this system to make inroads into the dynastic parties' majorities, so Silvela continued with the time-honoured practice of fixing elections. He had learnt to his cost the dangers of relaxing central control of the electoral machinery ten years previously when, as Minister of the Interior in a cabinet headed by Cánovas, he had attempted to reform the electoral system and had merely enabled the Republicans to increase their share of parliamentary seats. His

[39] See 'Oficio por el que la Junta de adhesiones al programa del general Polavieja rompe con éste, el 18 octubre 1899', in Romera-Maura (*La Rosa*), 555–6.

Liberal opponent, Segismundo Moret, had summed up the dilemma succinctly: 'Silvela sought to do the impossible: change the electoral procedures . . . without changing the workings of the regime.'[40] Even so, the government's freedom to fix elections was diminishing, at least in some of the large cities, as Republicans and regionalists began to organize more effective electoral support.

Silvela's central dilemma—how to reform the system from within without undermining it—was exacerbated by divisions within his own unreconstructed party. Moreover, his attempt to open up the cabinet by appointing as ministers representatives of wider interests, such as Durán i Bas and later the liberal newspaper owner, Rafael Gasset, and the Basque engineer, Pablo Alzola, merely heightened the tensions within the government. During his first spell of nineteen months as Premier, Silvela appointed three different cabinets and survived seven ministerial crises. It was not surprising that he should scorn the suggestion that, in view of the political crisis, a national government should be formed. 'A government made up of elements extracted from here and there', he declared, 'would be equivalent to an exhibition of the country's produce.'[41]

However, the failure of the Silvela government was symptomatic of a deeper failure. Following the loss of Empire, the regime lost the exclusive right to be the arbiter and expression of the national interest. Its inability to retain the colonies and the manner in which they were lost loosened the tenuous bonds that held the frail political system together. These bonds had been economic to the extent that the regime had safeguarded the fruits of colonial exploitation, and ideological in so far as it had been able to project its own values as those of the nation. Both forms of hegemony had been weak in the first place. The colonial pact had rested on a grossly distorted economic relationship which was almost impossible to maintain in a rapidly changing international context. And the ideological ties had depended largely on a mirage—the belief that Spain under the Restoration system remained a world power of sorts and that this political regime had ensured the stability of an increasingly prosperous nation.

The legitimacy of the oligarchy which had created the 1875 Restoration system had rested on its ability to maintain a consensus among subordinate élites around a number of common interests: the benefits of the Empire for commerce, the military, the bureaucracy and the Church; the protection of Spanish industry from foreign competition; the grudging

---

[40] Varela (*Los amigos*), 303; Romero Maura (*La Rosa*), 75–8 (n. 41).
[41] Fernández Almagro (*Historia política*), vol. 3, 267.

agreement of the military not to intervene in political life; the need to prevent a resurgence of Carlist and Republican unrest; and the fear of revolt from below. The almost twenty-five years of relative stability which had followed the Restoration Settlement of 1875, after the turbulence of the earlier part of the century, appeared to have consolidated the regime to which the Settlement had given rise.

The loss of the Empire emptied this consensus of much of its purpose. It robbed sections of the bourgeoisie of a crucial market for their goods, it swept away the colonial bureaucracy, sapped the confidence of the military in the political system, and deprived the Church of its influence over the colonies, though not over the regime itself. The Disaster exposed the hollowness of the Restoration Settlement, leading the military, the Catalans, and sections of the middle classes, among others, to question their allegiance to it. The outward stability of the regime belied the rapid decline of its hegemony. Most of its leaders were well aware of this problem. Silvela himself declared:

The failure of the governing classes has been tremendous and a consequence of it is all that so-called regionalism, which is merely the weakness of the cerebral centre, . . . and the collapse of the respect of the people towards their governing classes.[42]

Silvela's comment identified two important components of this crisis of legitimacy. On the one hand, it was a crisis of nationalism and national identity as represented by the establishment. In comparison to France, for example, the liberal state in Spain had made comparatively little effort during the latter part of the nineteenth century to consolidate a sense of nationhood. The war with the United States had given rise to a sudden and late convulsion of national fervour. The icons of this nationalism had been paraded about in their full colours in the months leading to the Disaster. Their most typical figure was the lion, symbol of valour and nobility, as opposed to the pig, representing American uncouthness and commercialism (Fig. 4). National values were identified as patrician, anti-commercial, rural, Catholic and Castilian. The Restoration regime had also projected itself as liberal and progressive, based as it was on a marriage between the traditional aristocracy and a new landholding élite. These contradictory images had only recently been fully propagated through political speeches, vaudeville spectacles, bullfighting ceremonies, Church sermons, and the popular press.

[42] Quoted by Joaquín Costa in, 'Más sobre el regionalismo', *Revista Nacional*, 15 Jan. 1900, n. 20, 413.

Fig. 4 The Spanish lion facing the American pig: 'Grunt as much as you like, I'm not budging from here'. From *La Campana de Gracia*

The Disaster profoundly undermined the power of these late representations of national identity and enabled a range of different models to gain strength, from 'Europeanization' to nostalgic reconstructions of a mythic Spain. Of these models, that which most troubled the traditional forces in Spain was the Catalan bourgeois project which identified the supposed Catalan values of modernity, industry, and thrift as the basis for the regeneration of Spain. Indeed, in contrast to its nineteenth-century version, Spanish nationalism increasingly became the preserve of conservative reaction against the new social and political movements of early twentieth-century Spain, such as the regional nationalists and the labour movement, neither of which identified with the state or even the nation.[43]

The other component of the crisis identified by Silvela was the breakdown of the regime's authority amongst the masses. He was certainly

---

[43] José Alvarez Junco, 'Spanish Nationalism in the Nineteenth Century', in Clare Mar-Molinero and Angel Smith (eds.), *Nationalism and National Identity in the Iberian Peninsula* (London, 1996).

wrong in attributing this solely to the Disaster. The increase in popular protest was also the result of the accelerating process of modernization in parts of Spain from the 1890s onwards. The combination of this process and the effects of the wars on the poorer classes in both town and country-side was beginning to break down traditional values and allegiances, cre-ating a new potential base for opposition parties. This base was beginning to be mobilized against the regime by Republicans, anarchists, and Social-ists, above all in the industrial centres of Spain: Barcelona, Zaragoza, Valencia, Gijón, and Oviedo amongst others.

Thus, while the nation-state had become consolidated in many other European countries, that in Spain was increasingly weakened by centrifu-gal forces. This was only partly the result of the Disaster; more impor-tantly it was the consequence of the unevenness of modernization. While parts of Spain were undergoing a rapid process of social and economic transformation, vast areas of the country remained unmodernized. The widening economic gap between the two generated increasing political and cultural contradictions which made any resolution of the crisis of the political system even more difficult to achieve.

The next four chapters will examine the growth of some of these centrifugal impulses within the period of 1898 to 1909; Chapter 3, the revolt of the middle classes; Chapter 4, the rise of mass social protest; Chapter 5, the Catalan movement; and Chapter 6, the growth of military discontent. These separate challenges embodied diametrically opposed interests with the result that they failed to coalesce into a political alterna-tive to the regime. Nevertheless, they profoundly undermined the Resto-ration system and established a pattern of conflict and crisis which, to a different degree, led to the military coup of 1923 that brings this narrative to a close.

3

Regenerationism: The Revolt of the Middle Classes

COUNTESS EMILIA PARDO BAZÁN, in one of her light-hearted allegories about post-Disaster Spain, describes a duke choosing to wear his grandfather's suit of armour for a fancy-dress ball in Madrid. Since it is the wrong size he gets it welded on but during the ball it becomes uncomfortable; try as he might, however, he cannot get out of it. A friend of his remarks: 'Spain is like you . . . caught in the mould of the past and dying, because she doesn't fit in it nor can she get it loose.'[1] The story condenses self-images of the defeated Spain typical of the times: the quixotic foolishness of going to war with the United States, the technological backwardness of the military, the dead weight of tradition, the claustrophobia of an unchanging society. It also suggests a contradiction between state and society; Spain has outgrown its institutions and official ideology like the duke his family suit of armour.

Such metaphors proliferated in the vexed atmosphere of *fin de siècle* Spain. The Disaster stimulated anguished enquiries into the history and the soul of the nation. On all sides of the political spectrum, writers, journalists and politicians and, no doubt, amateur philosophers in cafes and casinos, delved into the reasons for Spain's decline and the nature of its identity. The resulting search for the essence of nationhood was informed by a determination on the part of many to avoid the rhetoric of the past. Accordingly, the philosophical enquiry was accompanied by eminently practical proposals for Spain's redemption. This widespread movement of opinion came to be known as Regenerationism. Such was its popularity, even less than two months after the Disaster, that a popular conservative illustrated magazine testily referred to

that swarm of regenerators and saviours of the country who . . . like poisonous microbes, have crawled out of drawing-rooms, literary gatherings, cafés, tabernacles and centenary celebrations of our homeland to explain to us why all these evils

---

[1] 'La Armadura', *Cuentos de la Patria* in *Obras Completas* (Madrid, 1973), vol. 1, 1520–2.

have befallen us, how they might not have occurred, who is to blame for them and what is the sole and sure means of remedying them. This is this summer's epidemic . . .[2]

The theme of national decadence was a favourite topic amongst the reading public in many parts of late nineteenth-century Europe. In France it was a fashionable malaise brought on by the decline of confidence in Progress and by France's own disaster in the Franco-Prussian War of 1870–1 in which she lost Alsace-Lorraine.[3] In Spain, the sense of national decadence was part of an old tradition stretching back to the vogue in the early seventeenth century for blueprints to restore the ailing Spanish economy. Drawn up by the so-called *arbitristas* or *proyectistas*— lawyers, state employees, amateur politicians, and others—some offered serious proposals, like a 1600 scheme for agrarian reform; others proposed more exotic ideas, such as the suggestion that a toll should be charged for ships using the Straits of Gibraltar, or that cocoa beans should be used as the means of exchange.[4] In the mid-eighteenth century, ideas of regeneration were inspired by the French Enlightenment. Despite the fierce, underlying antagonism between the two countries, intensified by the Napoleonic invasion of 1808, France almost always remained a reference point for intellectuals seeking a model of progress. Although Britain (and Germany towards the end of the century) provided a superior example of material progress, intellectuals inclined towards France for reasons of language, culture, and sentiment.

Later, the abortive experiment of the First Republic in Spain, with its chaos of cantonalist revolts and Carlist uprisings, undermined the faith of progressive intellectuals in purely political change. In the calm backwaters of the early Restoration period, they turned to educational and moral reform as the basis for a gradual transformation of society. The most influential, if controversial, voice was that of the Free Institute of Education, founded in 1876 after the expulsion of progressive teachers from the universities. Led by some of those astonishing polymaths typical of late nineteenth-century Europe, the Institute shaped the ideas of a new generation of intellectuals and professionals that would emerge in the 1890s,

---

[2] *La Ilustración Española y Americana*, 22 July 1898, 47.
[3] For a discussion of *fin de siècle* decadence in France see Eugen Weber, *France. Fin de siècle* (Cambridge, Mass, 1986), 9–26.
[4] González de Cellorigo, *Memorial de la política necesaria y útil restauración a la república de España y Estados de ella, y del desempeño universal de estos Reinos* (Valladolid, 1600). See also Carmen López and Antonio Elorza, *El Hierro y el Oro. Pensamiento político en España, siglos XVII–XVIII* (Madrid, 1989), chap. V.

many of whom would forsake their mentors' resigned acceptance of the *status quo*.[5]

As a vague movement of opinion, regenerationism pre-dated the Spanish–American War; several of the best-known works criticizing Restoration society and proposing its reform were written before May 1898.[6] The Disaster crystallized and diffused the deep unease about the state of Spanish society felt previously by a handful of intellectuals and politicians. What was new was the sense of finality. The loss of Spain's last colonies in the New World seemed to provide incontrovertible evidence of her terminal decline. From an excessive illusion of imperial status, public opinion plunged to an equally exaggerated sense of national prostration in the aftermath of defeat. Two years after the Disaster, stirring the depths of pathos, the Madrid daily newspaper, *El Correo*, exclaimed:

Everything is broken in this unhappy country; there is no government, no electorate, no political parties; no army, no navy; all is fiction, all decadence, all ruins . . .'[7]

For those who felt they had been shouting in the wilderness about Spain's true state, it was a moment of self-vindication tinged with deep sorrow, 'an instant of profound beauty . . .' as one wrote.

For a moment we could see everything clearly. The lightning from that storm suddenly illuminated all the landscape of three centuries of history . . . and in the light of that flash the true path appeared . . .'[8]

Many of those who sought to diagnose the causes of Spain's decadence resorted to a sort of pathology of the nation. The crudest diagnoses tended to confuse biological states with historical and social processes; hence the temptation for instant remedies and quack treatments. Much influenced

---

[5] For an analysis of the early stages of the Institute, see Vicente Cacho Viu, *La Institución Libre de Enseñanza* (Madrid, 1962), vol. 1.

[6] Joaquín Costa's *Colectivismo agrario en España* was published in 1898; in the same year, Angel Ganivet committed suicide after completing *Idearium español* and shortly before the Cavite Disaster; Unamuno's *En torno al casticismo* was published as five articles in 1895; Macías Picavea began his *El problema nacional. Hechos, causas, remedios* in 1891; Mallada's *Los males de la patria y la futura revolución española* appeared in 1890; other critical writers active before 1898 include Gumersindo de Azcárate (*El régimen parlamentario en la práctica*, published in 1892), Joaquín Sánchez de Toca (*La crisis agraria europea y sus remedios en España*, 1887), Rafael Salillas (whose influential study of the sociology of the criminal underworld, *Hampa*, came out in 1898); Valentín Almirall (*L'Espagne telle qu'elle est*, 1886) Pompeyo Gener (*Heregías*, 1887) and Leopold Alas (Clarín).

[7] 7 Feb. 1901, quoted in Joaquín Costa, *Oligarquía y caciquismo como la forma actual de gobierno de España* (Madrid, 1902), 13 n. 2.

[8] Miquel S. Oliver (writing in 1907), *La literatura del Desastre* (Barcelona, 1974), 113–16.

by the prevailing fashion of positivism, writers and politicians mobilized the language of medicine to describe the symptoms and remedies: germs, disease, and degeneration on one hand and therapeutic treatments on the other. Visiting Spain on behalf of an Argentinian newspaper, the Nicaraguan poet Rubén Darío smelt decay in the air: 'there is in the atmosphere an exhalation of a decomposing organism.'[9] Silvela's notorious metaphor of Spain's dead pulse was matched by Macías Picavea's description of Spanish history since the sixteenth century as 'a general infection of the whole organism' which had led to a 'chronic illness', while Joaquín Costa's last-ditch solution for Spain's regeneration was for an 'iron surgeon' who would operate on the sick body of the nation.[10]

Encouraged by this public thirst for national introspection, a host of would-be regenerators reached out to an audience avid for solutions to the nation's problems. The almost exclusive attention paid subsequently in literary and historical accounts to the so-called literary Generation of 1898 has obscured the more modest contributions made by a range of writers to the debate about wherefore and whither Spain.[11] They included journalists, lawyers, parliamentary deputies, academics, military officers, and professionals from a variety of ideological backgrounds from Carlism to Republicanism. The more reactionary accounts reiterated the familiar themes of Spanish conservatism: the prevailing decadence was due to the failure to uphold the ideals which had led to the creation of the Empire—unity, Catholicism, hierarchy. The source of the modern crisis was the erosion of traditional values such as the family and religion, and the rise of materialism and utilitarianism; the new industrial bourgeoisie were compared unfavourably with the landowning oligarchy, a case of grasping egoism versus benevolent paternalism.[12] Other more progressive accounts nevertheless found fault with apparently innate characteristics of the Spanish race. In keeping with the drama of the occasion, these were painted in lurid terms: the Spaniards were verbose, apathetic, lazy,

---

[9] 'Madrid' in *España Contemporánea* (Barcelona, 1987), 43.

[10] Ricardo Macías Picavea, *El problema nacional. Hechos, causas, remedios* (Madrid, 1899), 368–9; Joaquín Costa, *Política Quirúgica* (vol. VIII of *Biblioteca económica*, Madrid, 1914) *passim*, and *Oligarquía y caciquismo como la fórmula actual de gobierno en España: urgencia y modo de cambiarla* (Madrid, 1902), 79. The use of pathological imagery to describe the state of society was common among later regenerators as well; see for example Ortega y Gasset's speech in 1914 quoted in *Ensayos sobre la Generación del 98 y otros escritores españoles contemporáneos* (Madrid, 1981).

[11] Juan López-Morillas calls them 'the other generation of 98': *Hacia el 98. Literatura, sociedad, ideología* (Barcelona, 1972), 246.

[12] Damián Isern, *Del Desastre nacional y sus causas* (Madrid, 1899).

arrogant; in them, passion overrode reason, individualism was stronger than civic spirit, and self-delusion or *fantasía* dominated perception.[13]

The anger of the regenerators was directed above all against the political system. A strong sense of betrayal underlay their criticism. The Restoration Settlement of 1876 had seemed to usher in a long and fruitful period of calm after the storms of the mid-nineteenth century. The Carlists were no longer a serious threat, the Republicans were discredited by the experience of the First Republic, and moderate forces on the right and left of the political spectrum had been absorbed into the political system, enabling periods of government in which essential reforms, such as the introduction of universal male suffrage, could be carried out in peace. The price that the middle classes had to pay was their subordination to the established order. Though their social importance was growing as modernization made inroads into the social structures of the *ancien régime*, their access to power and privilege was still largely denied by the prevailing system of patronage. Now, however, the Restoration Settlement was seen to be a mirage. Its politicians had led Spain into a humiliating defeat, betraying the trust placed in them by the people. Their rhetoric of defiance against the United States had been hot air; they were like conjurors who had lost both wand and rabbit. *El Imparcial*, jumping on the regenerationist bandwagon, wrote:

The sad truth is that these great statesmen who do the great honour of governing us would be capable of converting the Empire of Germany into the Republic of Andorra.[14]

For these middle strata of society, the Disaster was a crisis of both identity and legitimacy: identity because their own self-esteem was bound up with that of the nation; legitimacy because those to whom they had, willingly or unwillingly, entrusted the interests of the nation had signally failed to defend these interests. It was the turn of the middle classes—the thinking people, the 'live forces' of Spain as opposed to 'official Spain'—to take up the reins of government. One regenerator wrote:

Today, confronting each other face to face are the old, corrupt, depraved, indolent Spain and the 'new Spain' pushing forward and fighting to survive.[15]

---

[13] Macías Picavea (El problema), 212–14; Lucas Mallada, *Los males de la patria y la futura revolución española* (Madrid, 1969; 1st edn. 1890), 84–5. Some of these sentiments were echoed in the press: *El Nacional* 12 Oct. 98; *La Epoca* 'Robinson', 6 Aug. 1898. See also Alzola (*Problemas*), 114 and 184–5.

[14] 'Para que conste', 13 Oct. 1898.

[15] César Silió y Cortés, *Problemas de día* (Madrid, 1900), 75.

Fig. 5 A caustic depiction of the regenerators pulling Spain in different directions until she is choked. Silvela is on the far left and Sagasta is on the far right. From *La Campana de Gracia*

For the most radical, it was no longer simply a question of replacing the discredited politicians but of changing the political system itself. '[O]ur form of government', Joaquín Costa argued in a famous lecture in 1902, 'is not a *parliamentary regime, adulterated* by corrupt practices and abuses . . . but on the contrary, a *regime of the oligarchy, served*, not mediated by apparently parliamentary institutions.'[16] Nor was educational reform as proposed by the older generation of Krausist intellectuals sufficient; the life of the nation hung on a thread and severe and immediate measures were needed to ensure its survival.

The reforms proposed by the regenerators were ones with which most of the middle classes and the bourgeoisie (and indeed some of the oligarchy like the Silvelists) were in agreement. They were debated endlessly—in the pages of the press, in parliament, in cafes and clubs (Fig. 5). Spain

[16] Joaquín Costa (*Oligarquía*), 25.

needed a comprehensive programme of public works to create the infrastructure of a modern economy. The most urgent task was the realization
of irrigation schemes to boost agricultural productivity. Amongst other
measures, the setting up of agrarian credit schemes, the extension of
communication and distribution networks (more canals and railway lines),
the decentralization of government, investment in training and basic education, the reform of the judiciary and the introduction of social security
benefits were proposed. All this had to be accompanied by electoral reform to eliminate fraud and dismantle the cacique system. The state
needed to intervene in the economy and its investment would be paid for
by a reduction in the state budget on other accounts, notably by cutting
expenditure on the military and the bureaucracy.[17] Together, the proposals amounted to nothing less than a comprehensive programme for the
modernization of Spain, taking as its models the developed countries to
the north of the continent, France, Britain, and Germany; hence the
various programmes came to be described as the Europeanization of
Spain.

In the immediate aftermath of the Disaster, such proposals found a
wide audience, in particular amongst those who were most affected economically by the consequences of the loss of Empire. Organized opposition to the political establishment coalesced around two movements for
the regeneration of Spain. The first was the Catalan movement, which
brought together industrialists and nationalist sections of the middle
classes.[18] The second began amongst the farmers and businessmen of
Castile and Aragon and spread to embrace the grievances of the middle
classes and sections of the bourgeoisie throughout Spain. The businessmen had been emboldened by the vaccuum of political authority in the
months after the Disaster to organize and agitate outside their usual
lobbies of politicians. Their most urgent grievance was the new burden of
taxation imposed by the post-war government to pay for war debts.
Heated meetings of industrial circles and Chambers of Commerce were
held throughout October 1898 and in November a mass assembly of
delegates from all over Spain met in Zaragoza where oppositional agitation was most organized.[19]

It was a triumphant meeting, attracting not just small traders and
shopkeepers but representatives of big business as well. The speeches

---

[17] See for example, Macías Picavea (El problema); Cámara Agrícola de Alto Aragón,
Mensaje y Programa in J. Moneva y Puyol, *La Asamblea Nacional de Productores (Zaragoza 1899)* (Zaragoza, 1899), 8–29.

[18] See Chap. 5.

[19] *El Imparcial*, 7 and 26 Oct.

were filled with the outrage and the new sense of confidence of a petty bourgeoisie hitherto deprived of a political voice. It was significant of the pervading anti-establishment atmosphere that a delegate who tried to defend the navy was listened to in silence while other speakers who attacked the government were greeted with deafening applause. Santiago Alba, a rising young politician from Valladolid and a protégé of the Castilian wheat baron and Liberal cacique Germán Gamazo, proclaimed that the Zaragoza meeting was the Covadonga of Spain's regeneration, in reference to the place in Asturias where, according to tradition, the Reconquest of Spain had begun. It was somewhat incongruous, therefore, that the Assembly concluded merely by sending a message containing the programme it had voted in to the Queen Regent.[20]

The contradiction between the rhetoric of the Assembly and its political timidity was noted by Joaquín Costa, who was busy organizing his own nation-wide movement of small farmers. Speaking to the Press Association of Madrid, he criticized the Zaragoza Assembly for failing to create an organization; it was an indication, he stated, that Spaniards still lived 'in a superstitious state of formulae and incantations'.[21] Costa was one of those extraordinary self-made intellectuals of the nineteenth century who collected disciplines as others collected fossils or flora. Born to a family of poor Aragonese farmers in 1846, he worked as a servant and then as a building worker, only beginning his secondary education as a nineteen-year-old studying in the evenings. A trip to the Paris World Exhibition in 1867 funded by a scholarship opened the eyes of the young Costa to newly revealed marvels of science and technology. It also exposed to him the relative backwardness of Spain. Inspired by what he saw, Costa sent to his home in Huesca sketches of a new-fangled invention on display in the exhibition and fellow enthusiasts back home constructed the infernal machine according to his diagram; it was Huesca's (and perhaps Spain's) first bicycle.[22]

After graduating in Law, Philosophy, and Literature and gaining a Doctorate, Costa plunged into the life of the Free Institute of Education where he imbibed the deeply ethical principles of the older generation of intellectuals who had founded it. But by the 1880s, he had moved away from their Utopian faith in education as a panacea for Spain's regeneration. The country needed more immediate measures to stimulate eco-

---

[20] For comprehensive coverage of the Assembly, see *El Imparcial*, *La Epoca*, and *El Liberal*, 22–28 November. The Assembly's message is printed in full in *El Imparcial*, 1 Dec.

[21] Moneva y Puyol (*La Asamblea*), 30–1.

[22] Marcelino Gambón Plana, *Biografía y bibliografía de D. Joaquín Costa* (Graus/Huesca, 1911), 8.

nomic growth. As a native of mountainous Aragon, he knew well its immense reserves of water and the aridity of much of the land in Spain. By harnessing the waters of the second most mountainous country in Europe and spreading them through a vast network of irrigation channels, the soil could be brought to life. New markets were required for the Spanish produce thus yielded and where better than North Africa, that other half of Spain's geography and culture, according to Costa, which, 'for each Spaniard begins in the soles of their feet and ends in the tips of their hair'.[23] A new developmental and neo-colonial role in North Africa would also help to restore Spain's declining international status. Inspired by European exploration and expansion in Africa, Costa also fostered initiatives to probe into unknown regions of the continent.[24]

Of Costa's early enthusiasms, only this rather naïve belief in a mutually beneficial colonialism was to be abandoned. In his cussed, courageous manner, he spoke out against the war in Cuba in 1895, joining that other lone voice of opposition, the Federalist Pi y Margall, in demanding Cuba's autonomy. Costa's first foray into politics on an anti-war and regenerationist ticket in the 1896 elections ended in defeat by the local cacique; he thus experienced first-hand the corruption of the electoral system which he and others were attacking with ever-greater vehemence. A political programme was not enough; organization was needed.

Since the early 1890s, with his customary energy and legal expertise, Costa had been organizing the small farmers and merchants of Upper Aragon who had been badly hit by the agrarian crisis of the previous decade. Shortly after the Disaster, his Agrarian Chamber of Upper Aragon published a stirring manifesto to the nation calling for a national assembly of farmers or 'producers'. It is a strange document, at once radical and conservative. While calling for a new national party that would carry out a policy of regeneration on behalf of workers and peasants (*para la blusa y el calzón corto*), it also claimed to be inspired by tradition.[25] This contradiction lay at the heart of Costa's philosophy. Surrounded by an agrarian sector in decline, hit doubly by the surplus of wheat on the world market and the loss of the colonial market, Costa sought to preserve the world of the small farmer against the encroachments of both capitalism

[23] 'Los intereses de España y Marruecos son armónicos', speech of 30 Mar. 1884, reproduced in *España en África* (suplemento) 15 Jan. 1906; see also his *El comercio español y la cuestión de África* (Madrid, 1882).
[24] He founded the Society of Africanists, organized a Congress of 'colonial geography', and edited the *Revista de Geografía Comercial*.
[25] Cámara Agrícola de Alto Aragón, *Mensaje Programa*, quoted in full in Moneva y Puyol (*La Asamblea*), 8–29.

and latifundia. His vision was of a pre-capitalist Utopia of small farmers and artisans rooted in the old collectivist traditions of the Spanish countryside.[26]

Three months after the publication of the manifesto, a nation-wide meeting of the agrarian chambers was held in Zaragoza, on the heels of the industrialists' meeting of November. As they arrived, the delegates were given credentials on which a magnificent coloured illustration was printed symbolizing the organizers' vision of Spain. In it could be discerned a matronly figure (a traditional representation of Spain) caught up in brambles, her bosom covered in blood and a broken sword in her hand. At her feet lay a history of Spain and other documents covered in blood; on the right a sheaf of wheat and an exhausted peasant boy standing on scattered farm implements and branches, wiping his brow; in the distance, by way of contrast, could be seen a windmill and a labourer ploughing the fields near a village, the scene lit by a rising sun. '[T]he past and the present, as felt by Mr Costa,' thought one unsympathetic delegate.[27] It was significant that the illustration appealed to a deeply traditional image of the countryside, void of emblems of industry or modern agricultural technology.

The Producers' Assembly was infused by the same sense of crisis and redemption as that of the Chambers of Commerce, though Costa injected a greater sense of drama into the proceedings of his own meeting. His two speeches were filled with apocalyptic metaphors and on several occasions Costa broke down and wept, to the rapture of many in the audience. His oratory was couched in the style of the times in which the ability to rouse the audience with fine imagery was almost as important as the ideas it contained. Costa employed a wide range of rhetorical devices, all calculated to appeal to his agrarian audience. His most common references were evangelical; a feature of political oratory of the day, these drew on the shared Catholic background of the audience and also on the Christian roots of Costa's own thinking through the school of Krause and the Free Institute of Education. In his apparently improvised opening speech, Costa referred to the 'desolate virgin' [Spain], abandoned by the powers 'after her son [the Spanish people] had been crucified in the Calvary of

---

[26] Joaquín Costa Martínez, *Colectivismo agrario en España. Partes I y II. Doctrinas y hechos* (Madrid, 1898). 'The tragedy of Costa', wrote Manuel Azaña, 'is that of a man who would like to cease being a conservative and cannot. A very Spanish case' ('¡Todavía el 98!' in *Plumas y palabras* (Barcelona, 1976), 180. For a penetrating study of Costa's populism, see Jacques Maurice and Carlos Serrano, *J. Costa: Crisis de la Restauración y populismo (1875–1911)* (Madrid, 1977).

[27] Moneva y Puyol (*La Asamblea*), 64–5.

Cuba and the Philippines'. The same image of virgin and son is repeated
twice more—this time the guilty party is the politicians. In this use of
religious metaphor, Costa was drawing on a common stock of images
employed among others by the Republicans.[28]

Another repeated reference, tailored to his audience of farmers, was to
nature; for example, politicians were like almond-trees, giving forth much
blossom but little fruit, promising a false spring in the midst of winter and
harming the vines by casting their shadow over them. Costa also mobilized the stereotypical images of Spanish nationalism—the 1808 uprising
against the Napoleonic invasion, Spanish honour dishonoured; Spain's
very identity was threatened with extinction. Everything in Spain, he
cried, had to be regenerated, or else it would disappear as a nation. 'Spain
is dead!' he exclaimed at the end of his speech, 'Long live Spain!'[29]

Costa's magnificent rhetoric did not persuade all the delegates. In fact,
the Assembly was riven by contradictions. Some of the delegates represented agrarian sectors close to the oligarchy who were content to stir up
pressure on the government to protect agrarian interests but were determined to limit the damage the Assembly might do to dynastic party
interests. The focus of conflict was the identity of the new movement.
Costa and his allies argued passionately for the creation of a new party.
The majority of the Assembly, on the other hand, voted for establishing a
League on the lines of that led in the 1880s by the wheat-growing oligarchy of Castile. Outside the Assembly, the national newspapers devoted
many columns to the proceedings but even those most sympathetic to its
aims were hostile to the proposal for a new party.[30] More conservative
papers, careful not to sound anti-regenerationist, concentrated their criticism on the figure of 'the sociologist Costa' and his plan for the creation of
a 'hydraulic party'.[31]

Inside the Assembly, some delegates poured scorn on intellectuals and
do-gooders. '[D]own with intellectuals' cried one; 'none of this "living
forces of the country"; there will never be unity between them because it's
impossible to unite what is incompatible.' The Assembly, wrote a con-

[28] See, for example, José Alvarez Junco, *El Emperador del Paralelo. Lerroux y la demagogia
populista* (Madrid, 1990), 408–12.
[29] Ibid. 59 and 64; *El Imparcial*, 16 Feb. 1899; Manuel Tuñón de Lara, *Costa y Unamuno
en la crisis de fin de siglo* (Madrid, 1974), 249–53.
[30] The ambiguities of the more reformist sectors of the oligarchy were reflected in the
editorials of *El Imparcial*, a Liberal paper close to Castilian wheat interests. See 'Ligas, sí;
partidos nunca', and 'Quien mucho abarca . . .', 17 and 19 Feb. 1899 respectively. Its editor,
Rafael Gasset, was shortly to become a minister in a new Silvela cabinet.
[31] *La Ilustración Española y Americana* 22 Feb. 1899, 102.

servative delegate later, was a 'small conspiracy by *intellectuals* to seize the soul of the productive masses and . . . get on to the higher echelons of the State'.[32] Costa bore the brunt of the attacks of those unwilling to turn the Assembly into more than a new lobby. There were mutterings about his manipulative demagoguery, high-handedness as chairman, and Messianic ambitions. By the fourth day, over a third of the delegates had left. Upset by all the intrigue, Costa at first refused to be President of the new League. A passionate speech by Santiago Alba (there representing the Chambers of Commerce) persuaded him to drop his objections and after an emotional scene full of embracing and weeping, the day's proceedings ended with Costa being carried away in a state of speechless nervous exhaustion.[33]

The Assembly of Producers, like that of the Chambers of Commerce, was followed with great interest throughout Spain and perhaps with some anxiety on the part of the dynastic politicians. But for the more perspicacious amongst them, it must have been clear that the Assembly represented no real threat to their interests. The new National League of Producers was more of a lobby than a political movement. Moreover, it had failed to unite the farmers. Its programme, drawn up by Costa and published in mid-April, contained admirable proposals for reform but failed to state the means whereby they could be achieved. Far from seeking to mobilize other social classes, the League seemed to exclude the participation of workers and peasants; the programme referred solely to 'the productive intellectual classes' as the instrument of change; regeneration, therefore, had to come from above. In a revealing sentence, Costa warned the better-off classes of the cataclysm which might follow if these reforms were not carried out: 'Revolutions carried out from the centre of power . . . are . . . the lightning rod which will ward off revolutions on the streets and in the countryside.'[34] The choice offered was either Costa's movement or chaos.

The discontent of industrialists and the lesser bourgeoisie was given fresh impetus, shortly after the League's foundation, when Silvela's new cabinet announced its budget. The tax reforms of the Finance Minister, Villaverde, appeared to impose even greater burdens on industry and property, while raising the *consumos*, the much-hated indirect tax on food, fuel, and drink. In an unprecedented break with legality, the new Cham-

---

[32] Moneva (*La Asamblea*), 80–1 and 255.

[33] *El Imparcial* and *La Epoca*, 20 Feb. 1899.

[34] Moneva (*La Asamblea*), 173 (who publishes the text in full). The programme is summarized and quoted at length in *El Imparcial*, 13 Apr. 1899.

bers of Commerce movement called on its members to withhold tax payments in protest and on 26 June shopkeepers in many parts of Spain responded to the call by drawing down their shutters. Their action set off a wave of popular agitation in their favour and against the Villaverde budget. Riots broke out in numerous cities. Workers went on strike in support of the shopkeepers, stores which had remained open were forced to close by roving mobs, tax offices were burnt down, trams overturned, shots fired, civil and religious establishments stoned. The action spiralled out of control into a generalized protest against the authorities lasting until early July; martial law was declared in many areas and the troops were called out to restore order.

Had the Chambers of Commerce movement harnessed this popular agitation to their cause, it might have been able to exert powerful pressure on the government. However, both its leader, the glass manufacturer Basilio Paraíso, and his allies were as hostile to the rough protest of the working classes as the ruling élites and in attempting to disassociate themselves from popular discontent, they merely exposed their own weakness. The Valencia Chamber of Commerce complained that the 'tumultuous and wild demonstrations carried out by elements alien to the mercantile classes' were 'altering the fundamental nature of the action and diminishing its importance . . .'. In parliament, Silvela seized on the occasion to reprove the middle-class protesters for 'awakening passions which have nothing to do with the injured interests of the tax-payers'.[35]

The Chambers of Commerce campaign was further undermined by lack of co-ordination. While Costa criticized the action for being too precipitate, the Barcelona shopkeepers' guilds decided to carry out their own campaign of withholding tax payments in July, shortly after the first nation-wide protest had fizzled out. Seventeen years earlier they had carried out a similar action against increases in taxes on commerce without success. This time again, with only the formal backing of Paraíso's movement, the Barcelona shopkeepers lacked the power to confront the government on their own.[36] But like their counterparts elsewhere, they were encouraged by the reigning atmosphere of crisis as well as the sympathy of the press into believing that the government

[35] *Las Provincias*, 27 June 1899; Silvela quote from *Diario de Barcelona*, 28 June 1899 (a.m.).

[36] Paraíso and Santiago Alba both spoke at a meeting in support of the action on 17 Aug. For the 1882 tax protest, see Pedro Voltes Bou, 'Las dos huelgas de contribuyentes en la Barcelona de fin de siglo', *Cuadernos de Historia Econoómica de Cataluña*, vol. V. (1971), 43–66. For more on the Barcelona employers' stance, see Chap. 5.

would give way. That their action was more than a simple protest against higher taxation was suggested by the wry statement of one of their leaders shortly afterwards:

We believed naïvely that we could do without large armies, expensive armaments and unnecessary fleets, since without colonies to defend or protect, they were of little or no use to us. We believed also that useless expenditure would be eliminated and that more funds would be spent on productive activity and that public administration would be purged of immorality, bringing an end once and for all to favouritism and making bribery and corruption impossible.[37]

By late summer, the authorities were beginning to turn the screw on the tax rebels in Barcelona. When, under duress, the Mayor signed bailiffs' orders against the first line of shopkeepers and promptly resigned in protest, the city's shops closed down and violence broke out in the streets once again. By the end of October, a State of War was declared in Barcelona and the withholding of taxes was declared seditious. The first shopkeepers—amongst them a haberdasher, a cobbler, a saddler, and a silversmith—were arrested and imprisoned. As more were detained, crowds started to gather outside the gaol and the detainees were showered with gifts, including wine and cakes.[38]

However, the Barcelona shopkeepers' action was weakened by their failure to secure the active support of either Paraíso's movement or the Catalan employers' organizations, who were attempting to negotiate a separate deal with the Silvela government. The guilds were hamstrung by their dependence on the powerful Barcelona Chamber of Commerce which had expressed its outright disapproval of shop closures; Paraíso declined their invitation to speak at a public meeting because of the hostility of the industrialists in the Chamber.[39] Moreover, their action met initially with a lukewarm response from the Catalan movement because their demands ignored the question of autonomy. By November, the so-called *tancament de caixes* or closure of tills had collapsed, despite the wave of local support. While it boosted the Catalan rebellion against the state, its failure in the most prosperous region of Spain (Catalonia provided nearly a quarter of all contributions to the state budget) emasculated the protest of the nation-wide Chambers of Commerce.

[37] José María Pirretas quoted in Joaquim de Camps i Arboix, *El tancament de caixes* (Barcelona, 1961), 12.

[38] Ibid. 46–7.

[39] *La Vanguardia*, 20 Aug. 1899. The Barcelona Chamber of Commerce attacked the tactic of shop closures because they served as a 'pretext for the enemies of society and order to carry out demonstrations and riots . . .': Ibid., 9 July 1899. See Chap. 5 for their changing positions and for further details of the Catalan movement.

The lack of synchronization between the two movements concealed a deeper division. While the loss of the Empire had encouraged regionalist sentiments, it had created an insecurity about national unity among many other Spaniards. As the Catalan movement gained strength, the under-current of misgiving towards regionalism grew among members of Paraíso's movement. This was the expression not just of a traditional centralist mentality but also of a justifiable fear that devolutionary deals between the government and the rich regions of Catalonia and the Basque Country would fatally weaken the movement. The division surfaced at the Chambers' second Assembly in Valladolid in January 1900. Despite pro-testations by Catalan delegates that 'Catalonia is as Spanish as the most Spanish of the other sister regions', others voiced fears that Catalans were going their own way by pointedly repeating the need for a united Spain. Paraíso set the tone in his opening speech:

I don't want . . . anyone to talk in the name of either class or regional interests but with and in that of Spain, which wants the union of all Spaniards'.

Yet while the Assembly was debating this issue, the Catalan industrialists' organization, the *Foment*, was holding a parallel meeting in which the call for autonomy resounded.[40] Assembly delegates close to the *Foment* had been given instructions to assert regionalism, push for decentralization and evade any vote on further action over taxes. When the Assembly placed the question of regional economic deals low on its list of priorities, Catalan support, lukewarm at its best, turned cold.[41]

Other disagreements within the Chambers' movement ripened into divisions. The question of its political identity once again became the centre of bitter argument. The moderate sections were unhappy at its increasing politicization. The Murcia Chamber of Commerce declined to join in further action because 'the mission of the Chambers is to defend the interests of production and commerce and not to get mixed up in politics'.[42] Representatives of Basque big business led by the engineer Pablo de Alzola rejected any idea that the movement should become a party, insisting instead that it give its support to the party that was prepared to accept its programme. When the Assembly decided to turn the movement into an ill-defined political organization, the National Un-ion, the Basques withdrew their support; shortly after, Alzola joined a

[40] Though the meeting sent a message of greeting to the Valladolid Assembly: *El Imparcial* 18 and 15 Jan. 1900.

[41] See letters from Albert Rusiñol in Borja de Riquer, *Lliga Regionalista: La burguesia catalana i el nacionalisme (1898–1904)* (Barcelona, 1977) appendices 11 and 12.

[42] *El Imparcial*, 17 May 1900.

reshuffled Silvela cabinet, judging that the latter's 'revolution from above' held more promise than the regenerationist movement.[43] Thus its two most powerful groups, the Catalan and Basque industrialists, abandoned the Chambers' organization, the first to create their own movement for regeneration and the second to defend their interests from within the government.

The incorporation of Costa's League into the new National Union did not stem the haemorrhage of support, once given so enthusiastically by all sectors of the bourgeoisie in the heady days of autumn 1898. Costa's own movement had suffered numerous defections, in particular those of the Andalusian agrarian chambers whose material interests were closely tied to those of the oligarchy. Fearful of encouraging further unrest in the volatile countryside of the South, Andalusian farmers were concerned not to 'provide arguments to the unconscious masses, in whose bosom dissident ideas are germinating', according to the Cadiz agrarian chamber; 'our resolutions', it went on, 'should be directed at maintaining the principle of authority'.[44]

The misgivings that many previously sympathetic groups felt towards the new National Union concerned not just the question of what political identity but what action it should adopt. Paraíso himself revealed a deep reluctance to upset the political apple-cart which accorded ill with Costa's radical impatience; thus Paraíso's press statement, issued shortly before the Valladolid meeting, referring to his attempts to change the government's mind:

for the sake of our children's fatherland we limited our demands and pleaded and begged to an incredible degree. We were asking for something, very little; the most insignificant action that might reveal an intention on the part of the government to apply taxes more usefully and productively; but everything was useless, everything in vain.[45]

Compare this sort of language with that of Costa in a speech a year and a half later denouncing politicians and their supporters as

the Gothic figures of parliament . . . the toffs of the Calatrava [a Madrid district] pavements, everything that's useless, everything that's in the way, the immense

---

[43] Carlos Serrano, *Le tour du peuple. Crise nationale, mouvements populaires et populisme en Espagne (1810–1910)* (Madrid, 1987), 260 and n. 73.

[44] Ibid. 262 n. 76. The powerful Liberal wheat baron Gamazo also withdrew his support after Santiago Alba and 11 *gamacista* councillors joined the National Union. For Gamazo's relations with the regenerators, see Maximiano García Venero, *Santiago Alba. Monárquico de razón* (Madrid, 1963), 39–50.

[45] *El Imparcial*, 30 Nov. 1899.

phalanx of spiritual TB sufferers, the parasitic scum of top-coat and frock-coat, the social mud that invaded the bullring, drunk on wine and savagery on the day of the defeat at Santiago de Cuba . . .[46]

Indeed, between Costa and Paraíso there could not have been a greater contrast: the cautious, upright Castilian businessman and the impatient, flamboyant intellectual from Aragon.

When their two organizations were merged into the National Union, there was almost instant disagreement about long-term strategy. Paraíso continued to see the use of tax 'strikes' and shop closures as a means of forcing the government to change its policies; in the meantime, he maintained regular contact with politicians of both parties. Costa, on the other hand, argued that tax revolts were only effective if there was an alternative party ready to take up the reins of government.

The purpose of the planned resistance is to provoke the fall of the Government in order to put or get another put in its place. Revolutions have no other objective. Thus passive resistance is a revolution from below . . . Today the National Union does not hold the key to either active or passive revolution, and if it tries one it will get not just its fingers but its whole body caught.[47]

Still reluctant to break from the movement, although increasingly disenchanted with it, Costa acquiesced in the plan to organize further actions.

The National Union was a shoestring organization, run by a Directory made up of Costa, Paraíso, and Santiago Alba. All three met many of the costs out of their own pockets and worked full-time without pay. Costa was based in Madrid and took responsibility for correspondence while Alba and Paraíso travelled to and fro between the capital and their hometowns and support bases of Valladolid and Zaragoza respectively.[48] Despite this flimsy organization and a government attempt to take them to court, the National Union's call for a one-day protest was widely supported. Once again it appeared that the action was backed as much by the mobs as by shopkeepers. The closure of stores was accompanied by demonstrations, riots, and stoning. The most serious incidents took place in Barcelona, where barricades were constructed in the broad avenue of Ronda San Antoni and shots were fired at the police from balconies and street corners. Paraíso claimed exultantly that 360,000 shops had joined

[46] Joaquín Costa Martínez, *Crisis Política de España. Discurso leído en los Juegos Florales de Salamanca, 15 de septiembre de 1901* (Madrid, 1901), 7–8.

[47] Paraíso even kept in touch with the discredited Conservative Romero Robledo: Serrano (*Le Tour*) 255; Costa quoted, 252 n. 62.

[48] García Venero (*Santiago Alba*), 48.

the action and predicted that the government was about to fall.[49] By mid-June, however, it was clear that the tactic of shop closures was not only having no effect but also rapidly losing support among National Union members and the Directory was forced to abandon any further action. A month later, Paraíso resigned as President.

Whilst both he and Costa continued to propose activities, neither saw any future in the continued existence of the organization. The middle-class revolt had failed; 'Now the Government knows, because the Barcelona people and the Chambers have shown them', wrote Costa, 'that the shotgun is made of cane and the loud voice is that of a jack-in-the-box; the neutral classes have no weapon left . . .'[50] Moreover, by taking action, the National Union had lost the support of reformist sections of the oligarchy and aroused the hostility of conservative elements such as the army.[51] As an opinion-making body, the Chambers movement was immensely influential. It was discussed in the cabinet; the Queen Regent received a delegation (against the wishes of the Prime Minister); Sagasta spoke of it positively on forming his new government in 1901 and then, during the cabinet crisis of November 1902, consulted Alba, substituting for a sick Paraíso, over the National Union's view of the political situation.[52] But as a political lobby, let alone organization, it was too riven by contradictions to challenge the ruling parties.

Moreover, in their concern to court respectability, the regenerators avoided any concourse with anti-dynastic forces. Though there was much sympathy expressed between the Chambers' leaders and the Republicans, the resolutely apolitical stance of most of the delegates ensured that contacts between the two movements remained informal.[53] No relations were established with the Socialists either; in this case, feelings of antipathy were mutual. In keeping with their dogmatic refusal to have truck with non-proletarian forces, the Socialists condemned the Chambers movement as bourgeois and worthless.[54] For its part, the regenerationist

---

[49] Romero Maura (*La rosa*), 94. For details of the action, see *El Imparcial*, 11 and 13 May 1900.

[50] 'Por qué fracasó la Unión Nacional', quoted in Fernández Almagro (*Historia Política*), vol. 2, 668–9 n. 13.

[51] *El Imparcial*, 21 June 1900, reported 'profound irritation' in the armed forces; for the change in this paper's attitude see editorials on 23 June ('they [the National Union] failed out of pretentiousness (por cursis); for having had aspirations absurdly greater than the means at their disposal') and 24 June 1900.

[52] Ibid., 20 June 1900 and 14 Nov. 1902.

[53] For details see Serrano (*Le tour*), 255–7.

[54] This was Pablo Iglesias's reaction to the first Zaragoza Assembly: *El Imparcial*, 13 Mar. 1899.

movement shunned any association with the working classes. Pathetic images of the poor and the suffering people abounded in their rhetoric; yet when workers, housewives, and unemployed youth took to the streets in their support they recoiled with horror. Thus isolated from most of the 'live forces' of the country which they claimed to represent, the regenerationist movement failed to gather together the different protests in *fin de siècle* Spain.

In the immediate aftermath of the Disaster, when the Restoration system appeared to have lost all credibility, the movement had brought together a broad section of reformist middle-class and bourgeois opinion that felt excluded from power. Its purpose had been to unite the 'productive classes' in an alliance that would transcend divisions of region and class and sweep aside what was seen as the parasitical oligarchy controlling the state. But the regenerators had overestimated their own strength just as they underestimated the resilience of the political system. Once the regime had recovered its balance and the dynastic parties renewed their sources of patronage, the supporters of the Chambers movement began to defect. The movement was progressively whittled down to its core in the heartlands of Castile and Aragon, to one of the areas, that is, most affected by the loss of colonial trade and the long-term decline of the traditional agrarian sector. From a global challenge against the political order, the programme of the regenerationist movement was reduced to a list of local grievances.

The regime's survival was more the consequence of the immobility of Spanish society than its own capacity to adapt, as we have seen. The crisis of legitimacy following the loss of the Empire was not accompanied by a severe social or economic crisis. In a largely unmodernized society with poor communications and a high rate of illiteracy, the traditional networks of social and ideological control continued to function in most of the countryside and the provincial towns. Indeed, Costa and his allies failed to understand the nature of the Restoration regime; this may not have been a serious failure because, whatever policies they adopted, their access to levers of political mobilization was limited. But it was important in that the lessons they derived from their failure had a deep influence on the discourse of Spanish politics on both right and left of the political spectrum.

For Costa and many other regenerators, the problem with Spain was its political class, who were defined as a tumour or unnatural excrescence on the body of the nation. This 'alien faction' held power by virtue of a system of patronage and corruption defined as caciquismo, the rule of political brokers or party bosses. The true forces of progress, the national interest, lay trapped beneath the surface; it was enough to extirpate the 'alien faction' in order to release their suppressed energies. The natural agents of this transformation were the intellectual and economic élites, who would take over the levers of the state to carry out the country's modernization and oversee, in Costa's words, 'a reintegration of Spain into the history of humanity'.[55]

The main shortcoming of this analysis is that it ignored the nature of the state. Rather than an instrument that could be turned to any use, the Spanish state was the historical expression of the rule of the landed oligarchy. Caciquismo was the consequence, not the cause, of Spain's social structure. It was significant that Costa's programme did not envisage the expropriation of latifundia but the redistribution of old communal lands. What he was proposing, in other words, was a political and not a social revolution. Without fundamental agrarian reform, however, neither the power of the cacique nor the oligarchy could be challenged.[56] For all the political invective of the regenerators, a residue of petty bourgeois ideological deference towards the establishment persisted in their strategy, expressed by constant appeals to reason and morality.

Costa's ideas were forcefully conveyed in two lectures he gave in the Madrid Ateneo in March 1901, after it had become clear that the regenerationist movement was fading. In many ways, this was an extraordinary event. Costa was by now a well-known figure in political and intellectual circles and his views were held in much respect, though, like much of the political rhetoric of the time, they seemed to have little effect on policy. The lectures had a familiar structure; one dealt with the causes of the Spanish 'problem' and the other with the remedies. What was new in Costa's prescriptions was his call for an 'iron surgeon' to carry out the regeneration of Spain from above. Costa's definition of this figure was couched in romantic terms:

an iron surgeon, who knows intimately the anatomy of the Spanish people and feels for them an infinite compassion . . . , who has good sense and the courage of a hero . . . who feels a desperate, passionate yearning to have a fatherland and as an artist of peoples throws himself into its improvisation . . .[57]

Prompting this new formula was not just Costa's impatience ('we are old,' he exclaimed, 'and want to feel some positive result of our work . . .')[58] but

[55] *Oligarquía*, 30 and 41.
[56] Jacques Maurice and Carlos Serrano, *J. Costa: crisis de la Restauración y populismo (1875–1911)* (Madrid, 1977), 157–8.
[57] *Oligarquía*, 86–7. [58] Ibid. 85.

also a pessimism about the potential for a collective challenge to the regime born out of the failure of the regenerationist movement.

His 'iron surgeon' proposal has given rise to much polemic, mainly because it was used later to justify authoritarian tendencies. But Costa was adamant that he was not proposing the substitution of parliament nor the reorganization of the state. On the contrary, he saw the 'iron surgeon' as a temporary expedient equipped only with the sort of powers held by the US President (indeed, some of Costa's historical references are to Benjamin Franklin and Abraham Lincoln).[59] Despite the ambiguities of Costa's formulation, the figure of the 'iron surgeon' had more to do with nineteenth-century pretorian liberalism than twentieth-century totalitarian dictatorship, more Rousseau than Mussolini.[60]

Another remarkable feature of Costa's Ateneo lectures was that leading politicians and intellectuals, from Antonio Maura to the neurologist Ramón y Cajal, agreed to give their responses to his ideas. The written replies amount to a collective X-ray of moderate and conservative opinion (of the organized Left only the Socialist leader Pablo Iglesias was consulted but sent no reply). There is no better illustration of the reigning confusion over the Spanish 'problem' and the wide disparity of views among the middle classes than the contradictory proposals for Spain's regeneration which they put forward, from federalism, absolute monarchy, the reform of local government to the long-term raising of the culture of Spaniards.[61] It was also evident that the debate was being conducted in a vacuum; despite widespread interest, neither the Ateneo nor indeed any other lecture hall was the forum where political decisions were made.

Indeed, the immensely discouraging fact for the regenerators was that, for all the oratory and the ideas, nothing seemed to change. In the fullness of time, the Regency of María Cristina gave way to the monarchy of the young king Alfonso XIII in 1902; in the previous year, Sagasta, the

[59] Ibid. 86–88 and 106.

[60] The notion of enlightened dictatorship was a common topic among regenerators. Pompeyo Gener in 1887 had favoured a 'scientific dictatorship exercised by a Darwinist Cromwell grafted on to a Louis XIV who would be implacable and splendid at the same time . . .' (*Heregías. Estudios de crítica inductiva sobre asuntos españoles* (Barcelona, 1888, 2nd. edn.), 255. Macías Picavea, seconded by the *Círculo Industrial de Madrid*, called for a 10-year suspension of parliament as a precondition of regeneration (*Oligarquía*, 435–44 and 511–15). For the polemic over the 'iron surgeon' see Enrique Tierno Galván, *Costa y el regeneracionismo* (Barcelona, 1961); Joaquín Romero Maura, 'Note sulle ripercussioni ideologiche di Disastro Coloniale', *Rivista Storica Italiana*, LXXXIV (1972), 32–52; Elías Díaz, *La filosofía social del krausismo* (Madrid, 1973), 189–212; Rafael Pérez de la Dehesa, *El pensamiento de Costa y su influencia en el 98* (Madrid, 1966), 69–79.

[61] *Oligarquía*, 424 ff.

politician most tainted by the Disaster, formed a new government. The concept of regenerationism had been expropriated by the establishment and was emptied of meaning; as a political slogan it was on everyone's lips and could be applied to anything. In a novel published in 1903, Pío Baroja described a shoe repairer's shop sign which had the words 'shoes regenerated' written on it. He writes:

The historian of the future will surely find in this sign proof of how extensive a particular idea of national regeneration was at certain times, and he will not be surprised that that idea, which began seeking to reform and regenerate the Constitution and the Spanish race, ended up on the sign of a corner shop in the slums where the only thing reformed and regenerated was shoes.[62]

For progressive intellectuals, the contrast between their impact on the course of history and that of their counterparts in France could not be more bitter. While French intellectuals successfully mobilized public opinion over the Dreyfus Affair and paved the way for the emergence of a democratic state, the social influence of intellectuals in Spain was very limited. Emilia Pardo Bazán wrote wistfully of how she envied French intellectuals their *cause célèbre*.[63] But Spanish writers lacked the same social base for their modernizing projects because of the small cultural market and the relative weakness of public opinion in Spain. While in France by the turn of the century the most popular newspaper sold over a million copies a day, the highest print-run of the most widely read daily newspaper in Spain, *El Imparcial*, was under 117,000.[64] With characteristic sarcasm, Unamuno suggested that the Spanish writers' real complaint was not that they were ignored but that they did not sell enough books.[65]

The lesson which Spanish intellectuals derived from the failure of the regenerationist movement was, like Costa's, a deeply pessimistic one. Unable to identify with any of the political ideologies on offer, they set off, in different directions, on their own ideological journeys.[66] Costa himself

---

[62] Pío Baroja, *La Busca* (Barcelona, 1966), 63.

[63] E. Inman Fox, 'El año de 1898 y el origen de los "intelectuales"', in J. L. Abellán, *La crisis de fin de siglo: ideología y literatura. Estudios en memoria de R. Pérez de la Dehesa* (Barcelona, 1975), 27.

[64] Eugen Weber, *France, Fin de Siècle* (Cambridge, Mass., 1986), 27. *El Imparcial*'s figure is for 11 Oct. 1898.

[65] 'Los Escritores y el Pueblo' (1908), *Obras Completas* (Madrid, 1958), vol. 4, 434.

[66] Azorín, once considered too radical for the *Imparcial*, became a correspondent of the conservative *ABC*; Maeztu, Baroja and Unamuno moved to the Right, Valle-Inclán and Antonio Machado to the Left; several, like Adolfo Posada and Ortega y Gasset helped to found the Reformist Party. Unamuno and Maeztu had collaborated with anarchist and

turned unconvincedly to the Republicans and became a parliamentary deputy in 1903 but soon retired because of ill-health. Shortly before his death in 1911, the young philosopher Ortega y Gasset visited him to exchange views about the state of Spain. As Ortega was leaving, Costa attempted to get up but fell back in his chair because of his infirmity. '[I]t seemed', wrote Ortega, 'that we had before us a symbol of our people, that man half of whose body strove to stand up while the other half lay paralysed'.[67] For Ortega and other intellectuals, Spain's paralysis derived from the inertia of both the established order and the people; only the mind, the moral and intellectual élite, strove to bring about change. But its voice was not heard.

For the most striking aspect of the intellectuals' disillusionment was their loss of faith in the masses. Visions of 'the people' changed radically during the ten years straddling the two centuries. Their idealization had been a literary and pictorial genre in late nineteenth-century Spain when a new wave of *costumbrismo* depicting the customs of the poor became fashionable. Some of these images of the lower classes were simply banal, such as the drawings in the *Ilustración Española y Americana* (the equivalent of the *London Illustrated News*), exemplifying the piety or picturesque poverty of country folk; others were informed by a genuine interest in the traditional life in the countryside. Towards the end of the century, the 'people' ceased to be a mere aesthetic object for many writers and became a subject of history, an agent of change. The regenerators saw them as potential allies in the struggle to transform Spanish society. However, they were considered passive partners in the enterprise, for they too needed regenerating, like Baroja's shoes.[68] When, on the contrary, working people took to organizing or protesting, their actions and de-

Socialist papers but abandoned their early revolutionary affiliation. The contact with the dogmatic Socialist Party had been a particularly uncomfortable experience. Maeztu wrote in 1904: 'Experience has shown that intellectuals are dangerous for socialism . . . better double-lock them up in the sacred ark of the tabernacle and drive out the flies': quoted in Serrano (*Le Tour*), 313.

[67] *Ensayos sobre la Generación del 98 y otros escritores españoles contemporáneos* (Madrid, 1981), 23.

[68] For example, Paraíso's statement to *El Español*, 'Not only should the habits of the government be regenerated but also those of the people': quoted in *La Vanguardia*, 13 Aug. 1899. Opening the academic year in Oviedo University in 1898, Rafael Altamira said, 'The people cannot create the impetus for regeneration, since they are the first that need to regenerate themselves through culture': quoted in Tuñón de Lara (*Costa*), 43. In 1896, Unamuno had referred to the liberal middle-classes' 'solidarity of interest with manual workers' (quoted in Serrano (*Le Tour*), 311 n. 36).

mands hardly conformed to the spirit of moral self-improvement or dedication to national productivity wished for by the petty bourgeois regenerators.[69]

Even Miguel de Unamuno, the most ardent defender of the people against the paternalism of regenerators, began to show a subtle change of emphasis in his definition of who the people actually were. In his earliest works of regeneration, they were men and women of flesh and blood, the working people of the countryside, for whom the Disaster meant little but renewed sacrifices. This 'people' or *pueblo*, contrasted with the nation (a purely superstructural entity) is seen as the vital source from which Spain would be renewed. By 1908, however, it had become more of a concept than a reality; the people are contrasted with the masses (*la plebe*) or the crowd, who have not yet achieved the status of the people; by going down to their level, intellectuals merely get in the way of 'the holy work of the conversion of the masses into the people, work currently in progress'.[70]

The city mobs, the workers' strikes, the growing violence in the Andalusian countryside, indeed the sudden increase in organized labour, awoke fears that lay deep in the intellectuals' sense of class identity. In a counterpoint of opposite images, the people were seen as noble, innocent and deserving on one hand, and vicious, violent and irrational on the other. For Costa in 1902, they were

imperfect, without muscle and without soul, outwardly deformed, impoverished like the soil, without red cells in their blood, with only crepuscular flashes in the brain and with only the free will allowed them by the parasites of caciques and oligarchs.

In Baroja's baroque vision of an industrial future, they are 'a multitude of lecherous, drunk, egotistical men full of dirt and misery'. Blasco Ibañez uses the image of a bonfire at night, keeping out the poor like wild animals, as a metaphor of the coming social war,

[69] For a discussion of the relationship between intellectuals and workers, see ibid. 308–17 and Sebastian Balfour, 'The Solitary Peak and the Dense Valley: Intellectuals and Masses in *Fin de Siècle* Spain', *Tesserae* no. 1 (Winter 1994), 1–19.

[70] For his earlier position, see his two articles 'La vida es sueño. Reflexiones sobre la regeneración de España' (Nov. 1898) and '¡Adentro!' (1900) in *Obras Completas* (Madrid, 1958), vol. 4, 407–17 and 418–27. The quotation is from 'Los escritores y el pueblo', ibid. 437. For a discussion of Unamuno's concepts of people and nation see Tuñón de Lara (*Costa y Unamuno*).

the great struggle, the fight in the shadows, the overwhelming crush of the crowd, the assault of the monsters of darkness to seize the riches of happy people . . .[71]

This growing apprehensiveness about the lower depths of society was a common topic among the 'respectable classes' throughout Europe. It was fuelled by the growth of slums and by the desperate acts of anarchists such as Ravachol in Paris and Santiago Salvador in Barcelona who threw a bomb into the bourgeois audience of the Liceo opera-house in 1895 killing twenty-one people. It was part of a wider sense of insecurity, a decline in the nineteenth-century faith in rational progress caused partly by the negative effects of industrialization and the Great Depression of the 1870s. The ideological and aesthetic crisis of *fin de siècle* Europe was encouraged by new perceptions about the complexity of the natural world and human nature that challenged the certainties of positivism; parallel to Freuds's exploration of the unconscious, Bergson was championing the role of intuition and Max Planck and Einstein were overturning ingrained concepts of time and space. The 'objective' world of the Realists and Naturalists gave way to the cult of subjectivity and metaphysical idealism; *Symbolistes* and impressionists charted new, more intuitive areas of human experience and expression.

In Spain, the parochial crisis of identity felt by intellectuals flowed into this wider crisis of ideology. Their preoccupations were not only to do with the national question and the 'social problem' but also the upheaval of aesthetic forms. But their feelings of pessimism ran deeper than elsewhere because of the seemingly insurmountable contradictions of Spanish society—between traditional and modern, inertia and mobility, rural and urban, peasant and worker, religious and anti-clerical, aristocratic and bourgeois culture, and so on. Pessimism sometimes ran to despair because of the intellectuals' sense of their own impotence.[72] The contrast between the buoyant response of Catalan writers and artists to the perceived challenges of the new century and the growing pessimism of their Spanish counterparts is revealing. In Catalonia, a burgeoning nationalism was combining with a newly assertive industrial bourgeoisie to challenge the established order. While Catalan creative artists and intellectuals celebrated modern, cosmopolitan currents in reaction to the medievalism of the Catalan Renaixença, many of their counterparts elsewhere in Spain turned to the past in an attempt to overcome the contradictions of the new

[71] Costa (*Oligarquía*), 67–8; Pío Baroja, 'Nihil' in *Cuentos* (Madrid, 1983 12th edn.), 85; Vicente Blasco Ibañez, *La Horda* (Barcelona, 1948), 89.
[72] The combination of *fin de siècle* and post-regenerationist despair can be found in particular in Azorín's novel, *La Voluntad* (Madrid, 1902).

age. Their nostalgic meditations about medieval Castile, their Utopian visions of a past society in which social harmony reigned, were a compulsive flight from the dilemmas of modernization.

The regenerationist movement had been an effort to reconcile traditional and modern sectors of the economy. Its failure reinforced the sense of precariousness of the petty bourgeoisie, abandoned by the industrial bourgeoisie and threatened by industrialization and the rise of popular agitation, just as their tax revolt had been almost engulfed by the mobs. The feeling of insecurity was compounded by the decline of lower-class deference; an echo of the new, rough, more assertive voice of the city mobs, directed sometimes against 'respectable' citizens, can be heard in newspaper accounts of riots.[73]

Threatened by a changing world and unable to influence the course of history, many petty bourgeois intellectuals sought for a model of identity in an unchanging emotional landscape—a rural arcadia as in the illustration of Costa's League or Unamuno's concept of *intrahistoria*, a traditional culture abiding under the turbulent surface of events.[74] Castile and Quixote re-emerged as powerful icons of Spanish identity, whereas they had become by implication somewhat discredited in the political discourse of the aftermath of the Disaster. The progressive intellectuals' distaste for the brash rhetoric of the war period, in which the spirit of the Reconquest was evoked to encourage nationalist fervour, had been summed up by Costa's demand that El Cid's tomb should be locked and bolted. Now Castile, especially the Castile of the Middle Ages, re-appeared as a source of inspiration for a renewed Spain. The image of Castile, like the image of the people, was ambivalent; present-day Castile was gloomy, bigoted, decaying, but in its old churches and ruined castles could be found the authentic identity of Spain. Likewise, Quixote, having absurdly charged the lethal windmills of the American ironclads, was ready to set out again on his third mission, this time to bring Spanish spirituality to a materialistic world.[75]

[73] Doubtlessly voicing a common feeling among the middle classes, *El Imparcial* ('Factores de Disciplina' 2 June 1901) complained about the decline of respect towards the established order among workers: 'The Spanish state has failed to be loved and ceased to be feared.'

[74] For a discussion of this tendency in literature, see Lily Litvak, *Transformación industrial y literatura en España (1895–1905)* (Madrid, 1980).

[75] For example: Costa's speech in 1901 (*Crisis Política*), 20; Azorín (*La Voluntad*) and *La Ruta de Don Quijote* (Madrid, 1905); Miguel de Unamuno, *La vida de Don Quijote y Sancho* (1905) in *Obras Completas*, vol. 4, 377. For a discussion of the use of myths by the 1898 Generation, see José Luis Abellán, *Sociología del 98* (Barcelona, 1973).

Thus turning away from the brief illusions of the post-Disaster period, many writers and intellectuals resorted to traditional myths that gave them a sense of permanence in a changing society. Many of these images they shared with traditional Spanish conservatism. Indeed, there is a strong vein of Carlism in Costa and Unamuno; for example, the evocation of rural life in early twentieth-century Spanish writing is dominated by a typically Carlist theme, nostalgia for a way of life threatened by industrialization.[76] For the most part, country life is seen in mythical terms, a rural Utopia without caciques, starvation or violence, like Costa's vision of the past. In contrast, city and industry are portrayed as dehumanizing. The bleakest picture of industrialization is painted by Baroja; he describes a plain covered with factory chimneys belching smoke: 'The landscape is black, desolate and sterile; a landscape of feverish nightmares . . .'[77]

Through these myths, disillusioned intellectuals helped to give legitimacy to anti-democratic tendencies in Spain. Though they may have been distorted subsequently, their images seeped into the discourse of Spanish nationalism. Their attacks on parliament fed a growing anti-parliamentary tendency. Costa's iron surgeon was evoked by Primo de Rivera to justify his dictatorship in 1923. Similarly, the evocation of a legendary Castile sanctioned the construction of a myth of nationhood that denied the plurality of identities in contemporary Spain.[78] Creative writers and intellectuals thus helped to articulate the insecurity of social groups whose identities appeared to be threatened by the process of modernization.

In the ferment that followed the Disaster, no concrete alternative to the political system emerged from among the disaffected sectors of the middle classes. Divided by distinct economic and regional interests and disdaining any alliance with anti-dynastic organizations, the regenerationist movement failed to capitalize on the crisis of legitimacy of the established order. But regenerationism profoundly altered the way many Spaniards saw their country. Writing many years later, Azorín conceded that the spirit of the movement, 'that vast and mordant spirit of social criticism . . . is now embodied solidly, strongly and profoundly in the

---

[76] Unamuno explicitly recognized their shared debt to Carlism; see his speech 'Sobre la tumba de Costa' in *Obras Completas*, vol. 3, 1127–45.

[77] 'Nihil' in *Cuentos*, 80–7.

[78] Unamuno, on the other hand, fought against this monolithic view of Spanish identity; for example, his 1906 article of 'Más sobre la crisis del patriotismo' in *Obras Completas*, 1010–26.

masses'. It injected a powerful dose of realism into political discourse and prepared the ground for new assaults on an unchanging order.[79]

After the failure of the National Union's tax protest in June 1900, the reformist-inclined Liberal newspaper, *El Imparcial*, dedicated an editorial to Joaquín Costa, berating him for the overambitiousness of his political agenda:

The men of the middle classes . . . can no longer speak seriously about revolution; at the most, of revolts and riots to seize power from each other. The true revolution has passed on to other hands; to those of the workers who show without doubt a much better appreciation of the objectives and of power.[80]

Now that the middle classes had failed, was it not, Costa himself asked in 1903, the turn of the people?[81]

[79] Azorín, *Clásicos y modernos* (vol. XII of *Obras Completas*) (Madrid, 1919), 248. For a discussion of the influence of regenerationism on the Republicans, see Romero Maura (*La rosa*), 96–8.

[80] 'Para Joaquín Costa', 24 June 1900.

[81] Quoted in Serrano (*Le Tour*), 317 n. 43.

4

Dancing with Corpses: Popular Responses
to War and Disaster

POPULAR reaction to the Disaster was notoriously muted. Apart from a
few angry demonstrations led by students, most Spaniards appeared to
greet the news with indifference. This at least was the conclusion drawn
by many commentators at the time. Unamuno, contemplating field labourers threshing corn, felt that the national catastrophe had hardly
touched their lives.[1] Journalists were scandalized by the fact that on the
very day the news of the Cavite defeat reached Spain, the Madrid public
turned up to watch a bullfight as if nothing had happened; this one event
became for many observers thereafter a token not just of the fickleness of
public opinion but of the backwardness of the Spanish people.[2]

The seemingly unconcerned response of people to the Disaster was all
the more shocking to these commentators because it was in direct contrast
to the wave of patriotic fervour which had gripped the country on the
outbreak of the war with the United States. Since the beginning of the
Cuban insurrection some three years previously, the affairs of war had
spread to the remotest corners of Spain. The growing demand for troops
and the increasing financial sacrifices occasioned by the war led to a
mobilization of Spanish society which was both physical and ideological.
By 1898 over 200,000 conscripts were on duty in Cuba and the Philippines; by the end of the war, some 13 per cent of the Spanish population
had been enlisted at one time or another.

However, because military service could be avoided by buying an ex-

---

[1] 'On the very day of the disaster of Cervera's fleet, I was in an area of meadowland,
having cut myself off for several days to avoid newspapers, in which the labourers were
peaceably threshing corn, unaware of anything to do with the war and I'm sure that there
were throughout Spain many more people working in silence, concerned only with their
daily bread, than others worried by the public events': from a letter to Ganivet quoted in
Fernández Almagro (*Historia Política*), vol. 2, 621.

[2] According to the Marques de Alta Villa, for example, it showed 'decadence . . . criminal
indifference' (¡A los toros!, *El Cardo*, 6 May 1898); see also José Francos Rodríguez, *El año
de la derrota 1898. De las memorias de un gacetillero* (Madrid, 1936), 233–6.

emption from the state for 2,000 pesetas or simply paying for a substitute at a cost of anything between 500 and 1,200 pesetas depending on the stage of the war, the burden of conscription fell on the poorer social classes who could not raise that kind of money. Indeed, the colonial armies were made up not of volunteers but of the poorest peasant and working-class men.

That military service was widely evaded by the better-off is suggested by the surge in state receipts from the purchase of exemptions, rising from between 9 to 12 million pesetas before the 1895 insurrection to an average of almost 40 million during the war, dropping once again after the Disaster to around 12 million pesetas.[3] Other less legal means of evasion, such as paying bribes or using contacts to have a son declared unfit for duty, were also solely available to the better-off.[4] The only means of dodging the draft open to poorer people was to emigrate illegally but this was feasible only in those regions close to the frontier or bordering on the sea from where emigration traditionally sprang, so that while overall figures for desertion remained relatively low across Spain, the proportion rose to up to 13 per cent of the call-up in these regions.[5]

Evidence of evasion of or flight from conscription, however, should not lead to the conclusion that the war was unpopular. Any assessment of popular responses towards the conflict as it unfolded is bound to reveal contradictory impulses. Military service had always been unpopular and had provoked frequent riots throughout the nineteenth century; not only did it forcibly separate relatives but it also led to hardship amongst poorer families because they were deprived of a breadwinner and the wages paid to the recruits were totally inadequate to cover this loss.[6] However, at times of heightened patriotism such as the period from 1896 to 1898, such resentments were more difficult to express or indeed were forgotten in the atmosphere of nationalist fervour generated by the press and the political and social élites.

[3] Nuñez Florencio (*Militarismo*), 225.

[4] Some idea of the scale of these forms of exemptions can be gathered in 'La quinta de 1896', *El Imparcial*, 2 Oct. 1896.

[5] Serrano (*Le Tour*), 12–40. *El Imparcial* ('Emigración de Quintos', 3 Aug. 1896) quoted a *Voz de Galicia* report that half of the draftees in some areas of Galicia had fled the country before being called up. The military's concern about desertion was perhaps reflected in the peremptory tone of the standard letter to all Mayors announcing the drafting of individual recruits in which 'without excuse or pretext of any kind' the draftee had to report to the relevant barracks, while 'he who does not present himself on the appointed day will be punished as a deserter': Montblanc municipal archive, *Correspondencia militar*, 1. 11, Caixa 58 and 59.

[6] Sales ('Servei militar').

Throughout most of the nineteenth century, popular nationalism had been confined to urban centres and to the middling and working classes—students, shopkeepers, artisans, market-stall holders, and the like—who formed the backbone of the resistance against absolutism. Its most potent symbol was the Second of May uprising by the Madrid populace against the French invader in 1808. After the Peninsula War, however, the appeal of nationalism was limited by the absence of any external threat. Neither the monarchy nor the liberal state seriously attempted to project any symbols or rituals of national identity which might compete with religious and local definitions of self so predominant outside urban areas.

In the last quarter of the century, however, the process of modernization laid the potential basis for a more widespread sense of national identity, as the urban population grew many times over and parts of the countryside began to be drawn into the urban nexus. In contrast to a revitalized traditionalism, propagated by the Church, the Carlists and conservative élites, which drew on the myths of the Reconquest and the conquest of the New World and emphasized the civilizing Christian mission of Spain, this popular nationalism was modernizing, Republican and increasingly imperial in tendency. In the first decade of the new century, its two most characteristic exponents were Alejandro Lerroux and the Valencian novelist and politician Vicente Blasco Ibañez.

This emergent nationalism was nourished by the growing international tensions over colonial partition. A military campaign against rebellious tribesmen in Morocco in 1859–60 led by the popular Liberal generals O'Donnell and Prim had aroused the first widespread enthusiasm for overseas ventures. It had adopted an imperial character when, in 1885, Germany had briefly threatened to occupy a remote island in the Pacific that Spain claimed as its own. In a foretaste of the anti-Yankee demonstrations of 1898, crowds had taken to the streets to rip down the Kaiser's coat of arms and burn the German flag.[7] Enthused by these events, a young navy lieutenant called Isaac Peral had donated his blueprint for a submarine to the state and in 1889, the new invention was launched with the blessing of the Queen Regent. Amidst salvoes from nearby warships and great public excitement, the machine took to the water with an ecstatic Peral waving kisses to the cheering crowd from the turret. In a world buzzing with the magic of new technology, the submarine appeared to the popular imagination to give Spain an invincibility when combined with

[7] María Dolores Elizalde Pérez-Grueso, *España en el Pacífico. La colonia de las Islas Carolinas, 1885–1899* (Madrid, 1992), 54.

the fabled valour of its soldiers and sailors.[8] In 1893 Morocco once again became the focus of public attention after a detachment of Spanish troops led by General Margallo was massacred by the Rif rebels and General Martínez Campos was sent to pacify the tribesmen amid renewed enthusiasm for military exploits in North Africa.

The outbreak of the Cuban insurrection of 1895, in contrast, aroused little popular emotion; it was the third such insurrection in twenty-five years or so and Martínez Campos was once again the man to put it down. As it grew into a full-scale war, however, most Spaniards began to be drawn into its sufferings and excitements. The intensity of popular reaction varied according to the different stages of the war. General Weyler's replacement of Martínez Campos, which led to a new strategy of total war, stirred the first widespread enthusiasm for the campaign against the Cuban insurrectionists. The death in 1896 of the black Cuban General, Antonio Maceo, aroused intense patriotic excitement. In his memoirs, the Catalan journalist Gaziel remembers the feeling of triumph that seized him and his fellow schoolboys at the news of the death of that legendary figure whose image adorned chocolate boxes and cartoons. Public jubilation overflowed into riots in Zaragoza and Valencia. Such general rejoicing, however, might have arisen from the mistaken belief that Maceo's death signalled the end of the war.[9]

There was little sign, on the other hand, of any popular opposition to the war, at least on a collective level. The anti-war left-wing groups—Socialists, anarchists, and Federalists—faced growing hostility from an increasingly bellicose public and their attempts to organize collective protest aroused little support.[10] Much has been made of the so-called 'Mothers' demonstration' in Zaragoza on 1 August 1896 to suggest diffuse popular opposition to the war. On that day, a small group made up mainly of women and teenagers gathered in front of the Civil Government in

---

[8] Fernández Almagro (*Historia política*) vol. 2, pp. 113–16. Peral's subsequent fate and that of his submarine became one of many symbols of Spain's fall from illusion in the aftermath of the Disaster. The submarine was rejected on technical grounds; Peral died shortly after, a broken man, and his assistant went mad. In his Memoirs, Pío Baroja quotes a popular song poking fun at the illusions raised by the invention: *Memorias*, vol. III, 25. See also 'Un recuerdo a Peral', *Nuevo Mundo* 27 Apr. 1898. A later version of this public illusion in new inventions in military technology was the Daza torpedo of 1897–8: 'Lo del torpedo Daza', *El Cardo*, 17 June 1898.

[9] Gaziel, *Tots el camins duen a Roma. Història d'un destí, 1893–1914* (Barcelona, 1958), 99. 'With Maceo dead, the insurrection is dead also', wrote the *Diario de Zaragoza* on 10 Dec. 1896 ('La muerte de Maceo'). For the demonstrations in the two towns see *El Liberal* and *Diario de Zaragoza*, 10 and 11 Dec. 1896.

[10] A notable exception was the anti-war meeting organized by the Federalists in Zaragoza in Jan. 1898 which attracted some 2,000 people: *El Imparcial* 17 Jan. 1898.

Zaragoza carrying a banner inscribed with slogans which presaged the Socialists' campaign of 1897 against the inequalities of the war effort: 'Long live Spain! No more troops to Cuba! Let rich and poor go!'. The demonstrators marched to several workshops—a small espadrille factory, a leather store, a corset factory—bringing out their largely female workforces. Shortly afterwards they were dispersed by the local Civil Guard and six people were arrested, including a boy and a girl each aged 13 and a man who had disturbed the peace by threatening the demonstrators; indeed, the press reported great hostility towards the demonstrators on the part of the mainly male onlookers.[11] The protest revealed the growing strain of military recruitment on the working classes but cannot be used on its own to suggest any widespread opposition to the war.

It is clear from numerous sources that the war was not uniformly popular, contrary to the image given by most of the press. Writing after the Disaster, the writer Macías Picavea, for example, claimed that the war had been 'unpopular, decidedly unpopular from beginning to end' and that during his numerous journeys throughout rural Spain, the dominant note of his conversations with a wide cross-section of people was 'that the Cuban war was a stupid mistake'.[12] The degree to which the war was unpopular, however, cannot easily be assessed and more research into this question, for example amongst any extant private correspondence between soldiers and their families, needs to be undertaken. It can be argued, nevertheless, that the war was least popular amongst the urban and rural working classes, those, that is, who suffered most from the deprivations occasioned by the war, and that, in the absence of collective channels of protest, this private dissension took the form of passive resignation and a deepening resentment towards the government.

At the same time there can be no doubt that the war met with approval amongst wide sections of Spanish society. It was above all the increasing intervention of the United States in the conflict that roused the nationalist fervour of much public opinion in Spain, however mixed the feelings of many Spaniards were about the personal sacrifices they were increasingly having to make. Indeed, as the mobilization of recruits intensified, na-

[11] *El Imparcial*, 2 and 3 Aug.; *Diario de Zaragoza*, 2 Aug.; *Heraldo de Aragón*, 1 Aug. (p.m.) and 3 Aug.

[12] *El problema* p. 276. Gaziel remembers workers protesting against the embarkation of troops in the Passeig de Colom near the port (*Tots el camins*, 100). For further evidence, see Elena Hernández Sandoica and María Fernanda Mancebo, 'Higiene y sociedad en la guerra de Cuba (1895–1898). Notas sobre soldados y proletarios', *Estudios de Historia Social*, nn. 5–6 (1978), 361–84.

tional concerns penetrated into the most undeveloped parts of Spain, challenging old definitions of self with new perceptions of national identity. The call-up was accompanied by ceremonies in which patriotic marches such as the *Marcha de Cadiz* were played. Food, wine, and gifts were offered to the departing soldiers and local dignitaries—mayors, Civil Governors, landed gentry, bishops—gave speeches about duty to the Fatherland and the Empire to raw recruits, some of whom probably had little idea of what these concepts meant.[13]

In his article 'La obsesión', Joan Maragall conveyed the feverish atmosphere that gripped the country in the days before the war with the United States:

War, war! . . . War with the United States! There's no way of talking about anything else. Talking! . . . not even thinking or dreaming about anything is possible without war in the background. Our affairs, our hobbies, our possessions, our interests, even those most private, most intimate, most remote from public life, are now subordinated to the idea of war, are impregnated with it . . .[14]

That this 'obsession' was shared by all classes is suggested by Claudi Ametlla's recollection of groups of illiterate people gathered every day in bars in Catalonia to hear someone read aloud the latest news about the war in the newspapers.[15] A pharmaceutical firm seized the opportunity of heightened jingoism to try to undercut the sales of a competing product, the American-produced Scott Emulsion, claiming that 'those who directly or indirectly help the New York merchants are unworthy of calling themselves Spaniards'.[16] And Gaziel recalls a popular game amongst youngsters consisting of a postcard-sized picture of the USS *Maine* costing 10 céntimos which contained a small explosive charge at the end of a tape that could be set alight; he claims to have blown up a whole fleet for one peseta though he and many of his schoolmates ended up with holes in their shirts and trousers.[17]

It was clear also from the innumerable money-raising activities in support of the war effort that it enjoyed widespread backing. The national subscription, launched by the Queen Regent in April 1898, was administered in each town by a committee made up of the local élite, including the mayor, the priest, the judge, the teacher, and a master craftsman.

[13] A description of a typical ceremony of this sort can be found in *Heraldo de Aragón* ('El embarque de las tropas'), 29 Sept. 1896 (p.m.).

[14] *Artículos (1893–1903)* (Barcelona, 1904), 8.

[15] Claudi Ametlla, *Memòries Polítiques (1890–1917)* (Barcelona, 1963), 47.

[16] *Nuevo Mundo*, 13 Apr. 1898.

[17] (*Tots*), 104–5.

These committees raised donations from a wide cross-section of the population—from the clergy, Chambers of Commerce, white-collar workers, primary school children, sports clubs (such as the Madrid Cyclists Association), bullfighters and the bullfighting public, and so on.[18] Newspaper accounts of pro-war demonstrations in cities in the days leading up to the war with the United States also suggest support from workers, though the bulk of the demonstrators evidently were students.[19]

The Church played an important role in stirring up jingoist sentiments. Its enormous moral authority in a largely devout society was mobilized in ways that far exceeded its supposed spiritual mission. The product themselves of a narrow and bigoted intellectual training, clergymen saw in the Americans a double enemy, as Protestants and as opponents of the Spanish Empire. In a typical sermon in the Cathedral of Madrid on 2 May 1898, a clergyman exclaimed:

These barbarians come from the West, mounted on great steam machines armed with electricity; they come disguised as Europeans. As all barbarian tribes, they have no ideal other than greed, nor any other code but their unbridled will.[20]

Many popular spectacles in this period were also impregnated with jingoism and nationalist enthusiasm. In particular, the so-called national spectacle, the bullfight, played an important role, not just in raising money and morale but in reinforcing traditional and comforting myths about Spanish identity.[21] Breeders and bullfighters gave their services free and costumes, ribbons, decorations, women's fans and even the sand of the arena were all displayed in the national colours. Spectators and readers of the bullfighting press were encouraged to see the *corrida* as a metaphor for war and the bullfighter as an emblem of Spanish military virtues. In a long article in a Zaragoza newspaper shortly after Maceo's death, the war in Cuba is described entirely in bullfighting metaphors and a journalist, writing in a Madrid bullfighting magazine on the eve of the Disaster at Cavite, dismisses any thought of defeat with the words:

How can the country of bullfights fear the pigs? Impossible! . . . I'd like to see what General Miles himself would do with his 50,000 men . . . if we let loose on them 50 of Miura's bulls![22]

    [18] *La Publicidad*, 23 Apr. 1898; *El Imparcial* in April and May 1898 gives details every day of the money raised for the subscription.
    [19] For example, the participation of Madrid railway workers in a demonstration on 23 Apr.: *La Publicidad*, 24 Apr. 1898.
    [20] Fernando Soldevilla, *El año político 1898* (Madrid, 1899), 197.
    [21] A bullfighting journalist called the *corrida*, 'The eternal and indissoluble marriage of our manly bullfights with the national sentiment', *Madrid Taurino*, 12 May 1898.
    [22] 'Notas Taurinas', *Diario de Zaragoza* 12 Dec. 1896; 'Pesimismos estúpidos', *Madrid Taurino* 1 May 1898.

The popular verses or *coplas* often used by bullfighting correspondents to give a lyrical and mythical dimension to the exploits of both bulls and bullfighters became a natural vehicle for the expression of nationalist sentiments. Songs and poems about the war abounded in the press and in popular shows in singing cafés, zarzuelas and the so-called *género chico* genre of short dramatic plays accompanied by music which had become fashionable in the last quarter of the century.[23] While many of these simply repeated the jingoistic clichés of the times, others reflected more accurately the people's experience of the war.[24] One of the most popular zarzuelas of the time, Miguel Echegaray's *Gigantes y Cabezudos*, is filled with references to contemporary problems affecting working people. A riot by women market vendors against a rise in taxation takes place on stage, one of the women singing a spirited song against the authorities; in another song, a woman sings the contents of a letter from the boy-friend of one of her companions, who is illiterate, about his sufferings as a soldier in Cuba. On a barricade which they have built in preparation for an attack by the forces of law and order, the women sing:

> If women ruled
> instead of men
> it'd be oil on troubled waters
> of nations and people.[25]

It is true, however, that *Gigantes y Cabezudos* was performed after the Disaster in November 1898 and therefore expressed the more critical views proliferating in all the media in the post-war period. In the popular press, in particular, there was a dramatic change of images in the wake of the defeat. During the Spanish–Cuban War, the Cuban insurrectionists were often portrayed as 'golliwog' figures in newspaper cartoons (of both Republican and Conservative papers), black, barefooted, primitive and therefore no match for the Spanish soldier.[26] As the war with the United States loomed, racist stereotypes of the Americans invaded the media and popular culture. The commonest image of the American was the pig, a

---

[23] José Deleito y Piñuela, *Origen y apogeo del 'Género Chico'* (Madrid, 1949); Antonio Valencia, *El género chico. (Antología de textos completos)* (Madrid, 1962).

[24] Carlos García Barrón in *Cancionero del 98* (Madrid, 1974) has made an exhaustive study of poems and songs as they appeared in the press but his conclusion that they reflected popular opinion is questionable because the established press was uniformly pro-war.

[25] This is a very free translation of: 'Si las mujeres mandasen / serían balsas de aceite / los pueblos y las naciones', Miguel Echegaray, *Gigantes y Cabezudos. Reseña y explicación de la Zarazuela cómica en un acto y tres cuadros* (San Sebastián, 1899). There is a description of the first performance on 29 Nov. 1898 in E. Gutiérrez-Gamero's *Mis primeros ochenta años (Memorias)* (Barcelona, 1934), vol. 6, 75 7.

[26] A typical example is a cartoon entitled 'De Manifiesto' in *El Cardo*, 11 Mar. 1898.

metaphor denoting voraciousness, greasiness, uncouthness, and dirtiness but also vulnerability as the most slaughtered animal in the Spanish diet. The Republican daily, *La Publicidad*, merrily forecast that

> If the war lasts a long time
> the price of ham will fall
> because of the many Yankees
> that the Spaniard will kill.[27]

Immediately after the Cavite defeat, the illustrated weekly, *La Ilustración Española y Americana* referred to 'the healthy and greasy pig trampling on the dying lion'.[28] Other racist images of Americans depicted them as a cowardly, thieving, and money-grabbing race made up of the scum of the earth. The Americans' supposedly commercial spirit was held up to ridicule as denoting an absence of honour and spirituality.[29]

These representations of the 'other' were juxtaposed with stereotypes of Spanishness. The commonest image of the Spaniard was the lion, whose nobility and bravery contrasted with the alleged vices of the pig. Another icon representing Spain that appeared frequently in cartoons and illustrations was a young woman, a sort of virgin queen, who was often accompanied by a lion. This mixture of monarchy and religion, Isabel the Catholic, and the Virgin Mary, condensed the traditionalist view of Spain as the defender and propagator of the true faith and contrasted with the Republicanism and protestantism of the Americans (Fig. 6). The Republican press also used images of a young woman representing Republican Spain. She was often portrayed in an intimate and touching light, dismayed, puzzled, wiping her brow.[30] Halos, and saints like St George, patron saint of Catalonia, were also deployed visually in support of nationalist propaganda, even by the most anti-clerical of newspapers: in the Republican *La Campana de Gracia*, for example, St George is depicted bayoneting a pig which is spurting blood from the wound and vomiting money from its snout (Fig. 7).[31]

The popular press also showed a concern to suggest that support for the war encompassed all classes in Spanish society. Sentimental stories about poor widowed mothers and their sons or the patriotism of the working man were meant not only to induce pathos but also to reassure the reader

---

[27] 'Cantares', 24 Apr. 1898.
[28] 'Crónica General', 8 May 1898.
[29] For example in a poem by Carlos Luis de Cuenca in ibid., 30 Apr. 1898.
[30] The cartoonists of the Republican *La Campana de Gracia* in particular excelled at these images.
[31] Número extraordinario, 23 Apr. 1898.

Fig. 6 'Saint Spain, ex-virgin and martyr'. From *La Campana de Gracia*

that the working classes were on the right side. In the illustrated magazine *Blanco y Negro*, part of a short story describes a bricklayer giving up his daily wage of 2 pesetas to the national subscription while around him rich men are making fat donations; yet it is the worker from whom 'majesty shined'.[32]

[32] 'Por la patria' in *Blanco y Negro*, 21 May 1898.

FIG. 7 St George, patron saint of Catalonia bayoneting the American Pig. From *La Campana de Gracia*

In the weeks leading up to the war with the United States and for a short time after, much of the press was full of reassuring images of Spain's military capabilities. Photos and huge illustrations of Spanish warships and cannons adorned the front covers of illustrated magazines and soldiers and sailors were depicted in heroic poses.[33] Not all papers, however, expressed such optimism, however self-enforced. The perception amongst much informed opinion that the Spanish fleet was no match for the American was clearly shared by a much wider public. A bullfighting paper declared on the eve of the Cavite Disaster that 'All we have really are the rowing boats on the pond in the Retiro [Madrid's park].'[34] And in the characteristic tone of fatalism of the bullfight ritual, an imaginary

[33] For example in ibid. and in *La Ilustración Española y Americana*.
[34] Carlos Crouselles, 'Pesimismo estúpido', *Madrid Taurino*, 1 May 1898.

bullfighter who has volunteered to fight in Cuba sees not victory ahead but defeat and death.

> Perhaps in the first encounter we'll suffer defeat . . .
> Let us fight without respite, so that at our tomb
> The nations can contemplate examples to emulate.[35]

After the capitulation at Santiago, there was a brusque change of tone in the popular press. Hyperbole and jingoism were replaced by pathos and censure. The scale of the defeat was conveyed by images of the damaged or sunken ships of the Spanish fleet and maudlin pictures of mourning mothers. Spanish soldiers and sailors are now portrayed as heroic in defeat, with the implication that they are the sacrificial victims of bad policies. The harrowing scenes of the repatriation of wounded and diseased veterans are vividly described in tones combining sentimentality with anger at their treatment by the government.

By August 1898, however, the popular magazines were returning to traditional themes and illustrations as if to forget that anything had happened. Images of war were replaced by familiar drawings of picturesque regional costumes and habits. Single female readers of a middle-class magazine were encouraged to lay aside their sorrows by the popular lyricist José Jackson Veyán because thousands of single officers, 'burning with love', were returning from combat: 'A sea of husbands crossing the sea!'[36] For their part, the bullfighting correspondents abandoned their bellicose images; it was no good crying over spilt milk, one wrote, 'since we've got the corrida / Let's enjoy ourselves'. From a vicarious form of war, the bullfight became a form of escapism from the consequences of defeat.[37]

The new tone of criticism in the popular press was directed not just at the government and politicians but at the people. There was widespread condemnation of their apparently passive reaction to the Disaster.[38] In a characteristically belligerent article for which he was briefly jailed, the Republican leader Alejandro Lerroux railed not just at the political establishment (whom he recommended should be shot or hanged) but also at

---

[35] Antonio Soler, 'Un Voluntario', ibid. 25 Apr. 1898.

[36] 'Actualidades', *Blanco y Negro*, 20 Aug. 1898. The above condensation of press reactions is drawn from the following: *Blanco y Negro, La Ilustración Española y Americana, Madrid Cómico, Nuevo Mundo, Instantáneas, El Enano*, and *El Cardo*.

[37] *El Enano*, 'Plaza de toros de Madrid', 2 May 1898; see also the account of the bullfights in San Sebastián on 20 Aug. 1898.

[38] For example, Franciso Capella, 'Justo Castigo', *Instantáneas*, 10 Dec. 1898; 'Después de la derrota', *Don Quijote* 20 Jan. 1899, quoted in García Barrón (*Cancionero*), 246.

the people, 'a docile, exaggeratedly docile people'. Yet the Republican leaders' disappointment with the masses was at odds with their own sanctification of them as the source of all Spanish virtues, especially those of virility and pride in contrast to the supposed effeminacy of the regime.[39] While it was recognized that elections were largely fraudulent exercises, the widespread abstentionism of the people was also a source of frustration for those wishing to see reform in the aftermath of the Disaster. A cartoon in a reformist conservative paper shows a policeman standing in front of an empty polling booth and a dog urinating on the wall. 'Thank God *someone* has turned up!', says the policeman (Fig. 8).[40]

Were the Spanish people generally 'docile'? Did they really react to the war and the Disaster with total passivity? There is a consensus amongst most historians who have written about the period that Spain was a largely immobile country; until at least the 1920s, communications were very poor and villages and provincial towns were trapped in an inner-looking world oblivious to national issues. According to this view, social relations in the countryside were dominated by semi-feudal attitudes; the caciques and their allies exercised effective control through either patronage or occasional repression. The spasmodic outbursts of popular anger were merely the expression of an archaic tradition; only in a few cities on the periphery could there be found an incipient organized agitation.[41] Such a view is amply supported by statistical evidence showing that Spain remained a largely unmodernized society until the second half of the twentieth century, characterized by stagnant economic and social structures and traditional political behaviour.[42]

It could be argued, however, that these macro-economic data hide important shifts in political attitudes amongst many layers of the population. Indeed, the picture of a largely dormant society is difficult to reconcile with the extraordinary rise of popular agitation that spread across Spain during the war with the United States and especially in its aftermath. Although there are few data on social disturbances, it is clear from

[39] For typical Republican championing of the people see 'Ministerio femenil', *El Progreso*, 8 July 1898 and Lerroux's article, 'Hierro contra hierro' in *El Progreso*, 4 July 1898. A cartoon in the same paper on 10 Dec. 1898 entitled 'The attitude of the people' shows a typical Spaniard taking a siesta against a wall; a second image shows him in the same position at night with nightwear on; the caption reads 'Before the peace signature and after the peace signature. The same but with fewer clothes on!!' Alvarez Junco notes that this pessimism about the people was not a good starting-point for a strategy based on their mobilization (*El Emperador*), 212.

[40] 'Las elecciones', *El Cardo*, 19 Sept. 1898.

[41] For example, Tortella (*El desarrollo*) and Varela Ortega (*Los amigos*).

[42] See Chap. 2.

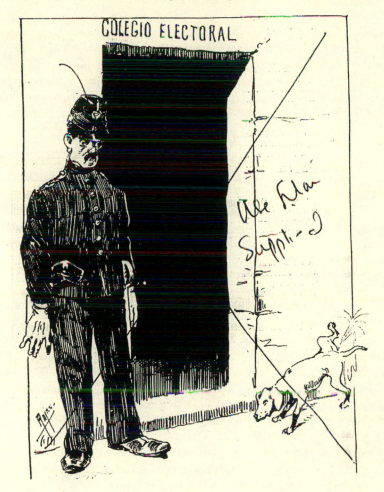

FIG. 8 A satirical view of elections in Spain at the turn of the century, from *El Cardo*. The caption reads, 'Thank God someone's turned up!'

existing sources that their number multiplied from May 1898 onwards. The first wave of protest originated from the sudden rise in the price of bread and flour early in that year as a result of the wartime fall in the value of the peseta. This came on top of increasing demand for Spanish flour from the French market because of a poor harvest in the autumn of the previous year, the consequent diversion of flour from the domestic market and the practice by flour merchants of stockpiling to evade tax and artificially to force prices up.[43] The protest about bread was combined with a grievance over the rise in the enormously unpopular tax on articles of primary necessity, the so-called *consumo* tax on food, fuel and drink which was collected by semi-official tax offices situated in markets and at the entrance to towns.

The first riot broke out in the port of Gijón in Asturias at 9 a.m. on 2 May, the day after the disaster at Cavite, when women fishmongers gathered in the town square to protest against the tax rise. Their action sparked off two days of general strike, violent clashes with the police, the destruction of tax offices, and the looting of shops and factories.[44] On 3 May, a bread riot began in Cáceres and in the following week riots spread to most parts of Spain. By 11 May martial law had been declared in all provinces in Spain except Alava. The protest was led largely by women, as indeed had been the tradition in cases of bread riots throughout the nineteenth century. As homemakers, women had a particular concern with the consumption needs of their families and were immediately affected by any rise in the price of basic foodstuffs.[45] But in their role as vendors of food in the markets (in particular, the vegetable vendors, the *verduleras*, who were the origin of many riots), they were also directly affected by rises in the *consumo* tax. In the more industrial centres where many garment and processing plants used cheap unskilled female labour, women played an important role in halting the city's production over issues relating to consumption rather than to the labour process.

Indeed, the major protagonist of the 1898 riots appeared to be women and they were reported in many towns to be armed with knives, axes, fire, stones, and clubs. One account describes women rioters in Logroño

[43] Federico Marqués, 'La cuestión del Trigo', *El Imparcial* 8 Apr. 1898; *La Epoca*, 4 and 6 May 1898.

[44] *El Noroeste*, 3 May 1898; *El Diario de Barcelona*, 5 May, reproduced in Serrano (*Final*), 196–8.

[45] Louise A. Tilly, 'Collective Action and Feminism in France, 1870–1914' in Louise A. Tilly and Charles Tilly (eds.), *Class conflict and collective action* (London and Beverly Hills, 1981), 207–31.

armed with sticks and axes carrying small children in their other arm and telling their men to keep away, presumably because they were more likely to be arrested.[46] The target of the rioters' protest was usually warehouses and trains in which wheat was stockpiled and transported, as well as bakers' shops, the *consumo* tax offices, the Town Hall, the Civil Governor's building, and the Civil Guard or troops defending them. The national and regional press reported deaths, numerous injuries, and large-scale destruction of property, including religious establishments. Male workers, notably miners, came out on strike in support of the protest in many parts of Spain and the riots in these areas sprang from their demonstrations.[47] By mid-May the agitation had died down, partly through exhaustion, partly as a result of the dispatch of troops but also because the local authorities acquired supplies of flour to meet the demand or subsidized the purchase of bread.[48]

The riots of May 1898 have been considered merely an expression of the traditional social agitation of nineteenth-century Spain, that is, an archaic form of protest in an archaic society.[49] It is true that riots had been a recurrent feature of urban and rural life throughout the century. They had taken different forms—protests against conscription, anti-clerical violence, riots over problems of subsistence in general, even riots in protest against the transfer of an Archbishop's see[50]—although the line dividing these was not always clear and one kind of riot could lead to another. The bread riots, in particular, had been imbued with a sense of legitimacy in the use of violence in order to ensure a generally accepted view of what was a fair price for a loaf. In this sense, they corresponded to those typical of the 'moral economy' described by E. P. Thompson in the case of the eighteenth-century English riot; far from challenging the social order, they had often ended up cheering the local cacique or one of the political parties in power or indeed, demonstrating support for the war. In

---

[46] *La Epoca*, 11 May.

[47] There were miners' strikes in La Unión (Cartagena), Langreo, Mieres, Oviedo: *La Publicidad* 5 May 1898.

[48] This brief description of the May 1898 riots is condensed from newspaper reports in *El Imparcial*, *La Epoca*, *La Publicidad*, *El Noroeste*, *El Diario de Barcelona*, and *El Progreso*.

[49] Serrano (*Le Tour*), 40–54; María Luz Arriero, 'Los motines de subsistencias en España, 1895–1905', *Estudios de Historia Social*, XXX (July–Sept. 1984), 193–250; Demetrio Castro Alfín, 'Protesta popular y orden público: los motines de consumo', in José Luis García Delgado (ed.), *España entre dos siglos (1875–1931): continuidad y cambio* (Madrid 1991), 109–23.

[50] Antonio Pirala for example, in *España y la Regencia. Anales de diez y seis años (1885–1902)* (Madrid/Havana, 1904), mentions riots in Calahorra against the transfer of its See to Logroño: vol. 3, 156.

the absence of channels of negotiation over grievances, they were, in Eric Hobsbawm's phrase, a form of 'collective bargaining by riot'.[51]

Before the 1890s, these spasmodic outbursts of popular anger arose from perennial animosities and were directed against traditional targets—not so much the local gentry or the local bourgeoisie with whom there existed a certain degree of solidarity built on patronage or shared interests, as with the representatives of government and state, those distantly perceived agencies for exacting taxes and imposing order.[52] By the early 1890s, however, their number had multiplied to such an extent that the government became concerned about the preservation of law and order across the nation. A circular from the Minister of the Interior in 1892 warned provincial governors that the riots were acquiring 'extraordinary publicity and resonance' and that the authorities were in danger of being overwhelmed unless they suppressed them energetically.[53]

Moreover, towards the end of the century the subsistence or tax riots in some parts of Spain began to attract the support of newly organized workers and of peasants' associations imbued with new perceptions about social class.[54] The May 1898 riots were an explosion of popular anger which combined traditional protest with a relatively recent form of agitation, the strike. They revealed a mixture of different cultures of protest—a still powerful residue of moral claims about the food supply rooted in an old system of paternalist market regulation, and new forms of agitation

[51] For anti-conscription riots see Nuria Sales, *Sobre esclavos, reclutas y mercaderes de quintos* (Barcelona, 1974), 207–77. E. P. Thompson, 'The Moral Economy of the English Crowd in the Eighteenth Century', *Past and Present* 50 (1971), 76–136; see also Thompson's later discussion of this question in *Customs in Common* (London, 1991). Eric Hobsbawm, *Labouring Men* (London, 1964), 7. Commenting on the May 1898 riots, an editorial in an Asturian daily wrote, 'many towns, knowing instinctively that they will achieve nothing by quiet and reasonable demands, resorted to violence as the most effective means of getting their grievances heard': 'Aplazamiento', *El Noroeste*, 8 May.

[52] The most important riots had occurred in 1856 in Castile and the eastern provinces and in 1892 and 1897. For the latter two see AHN, legajo 44 A, no. 18. For the 1856 riots, see Nicolas Sánchez-Albornoz, *Las crisis de substencias de España en el siglo XIX* (Rosario, 1963), 92–8. For the ties binding together social classes in the same locality, see for example Gabriele Ranzato, *La aventura de una ciudad industrial. Sabadell entre el antiguo régimen y la modernidad* (Barcelona, 1987), 108–19.

[53] 'Motines por consumos', AHN (Interior) Serie A, File 44 n. 18. Indeed, the 1892 disturbances were in many respects an antecedent of the 1898 riots. Their location was similar and so was the combination of traditional anti-fiscal protest with a newly emergent labour agitation: Rafael Vallejo, 'Pervivencia de las formas tradicionales de protesta: los motines de 1892', *Historia Social*, n. 8 (Autumn 1990), 3–27.

[54] For the Galician case, see J. A. Durán, *Agrarismo y movilización campesina en el país gallega (1975–1912)* (Mexico, 1977).

borrowed from collective action in the workplace.[55] What was new also was the scale of the protest and the degree of violence that went with it. The rioters' slogans reported by the press also hinted at more radical social attitudes; among those quoted were 'Death to the rich', 'Death to the guilty', and 'Down with the *consumos*', 'Death to the government!', 'Death to the bourgeoisie!' and 'Long live the workers' party!'[56] Though some of the slogans were clearly anarchist-inspired, betraying the growing influence of left-wing organizations in some areas, they also suggested that traditional attitudes of deference towards local élites and party representatives were giving way to more class-based positions.

While the May 1898 riots retained strong traditional characteristics, the same cannot be said so easily about the new wave of riots between June and July of 1899. They were ignited by the protest of shopkeepers and small businesses against an increase in taxes proclaimed by the post-war government. The latters' tax 'strike' unleashed a wave of popular protest against the related rise in the *consumo* tax. The renewed riots, if we can rely on a comparison of press reports on the protests of 1898 and 1899, were concentrated in the larger towns and the agitation affected above all Andalusia, the Levante, Catalonia, parts of the Basque region, and the mining areas of the peninsula.[57] But the forms they took were similar—attacks on the *consumo* offices, religious establishments, and military and civil authorities. They were accompanied by strikes, the overturning of trams, cavalry charges by the Civil Guard, and for the first time since the mid-nineteenth century, clashes between rioters and troops. Crowds roamed the streets of towns seeking out shops that had not joined the small businessmen's action and forcing them to close. In the more industrial centres, flying pickets went round the factories bringing out their workers. The rioters were a motley working-class crowd, according to newspaper accounts, including women market-sellers, unemployed youths (responsible in the judgement of many journalists for most of the violence), and industrial workers.

The riots in Zaragoza, in particular, revealed an awareness of national

[55] For further discussion of the roots of popular agitation, see Louise A. Tilly and Charles Tilly (eds.) (*Class conflict*) and George Rudé, *Ideology and Popular Protest* (London, 1980).

[56] *El Imparcial* and *La Publicidad*, 6 May.

[57] Press reports on the riots focus on Zaragoza, Valencia, Madrid, Seville, Barcelona, Murcia, Granada, La Coruña, Burgos, Gijón, Reus, Alicante, and Puerto de Santa María but there are numerous references to actions in smaller towns. The newspapers on which the following analysis of the 1899 agitation is based are: *El Heraldo de Aragón*, *El Norte de Castilla*, *El Imparcial*, *La Epoca*, *El Diario de Barcelona*, *La Vanguardia*, *Las Provincias*, *El Diario de Zaragoza*, *La Campana de Gracia*, *El Noroeste*, *El Globo*, and *El Liberal*.

issues among the rioters, for all the violence they used, that accords ill with the archaic label usually attached to disturbances in this period. Among other actions, the demonstrators marched to the local Chamber of Commerce and called for its representatives to appear on the balcony to receive their applause and then to lead their demonstration. They also demanded that a telegram should be sent to Chamber's leader, Basilio Paraíso, to offer him their support for the nation-wide protest against the budget. The same crowd sacked the Civil Government headquarters, to cries of 'Death to the government', throwing out and burning its furniture and decorations, including a portrait of the Queen Regent. The windows of rich citizens were smashed by stones and a local Jesuit College was attacked, its main gate petrol-bombed and its façade damaged by stones. A section of the crowd attempted to seize the sword that General Polavieja, now Minister of War, had presented to the Zaragoza cathedral in commemoration of a distant victory in Cavite against the Cuban insurrectionists.[58] Not all of these targets of popular ire were new; when combined, nevertheless, they amounted to a formidable assault on the ruling class as a whole: the local representatives of the government, the police, the army, and the Church.

The press reported occasional cries of '¡Viva España!' during the riots of 1899. If this slogan can be interpreted at all, however, it represented a very different view of Spain to the one propagated by most of the press and the regime during the war. It was perhaps one imbued with the traditional values of nineteenth-century Spanish Republicanism—the Jacobinist notion, for example, of an alliance of the people and the army against the *ancien régime*; of a secular, democratic bourgeois state. But it was not remotely like that of the regenerators, either. A cartoon by Cecilio Pla in the illustrated weekly *Blanco y Negro*, was probably an accurate reflection of popular opinion about the intellectuals who articulated the regenerationist programme. Entitled 'Scenes from Madrid. A regenerator of the country', the full-page drawing depicted a top-hatted orator on a platform with a banner inscribed with the words, 'I save the country with my elixir'; a man is seen walking away from the small, mainly working-

---

[58] Details from *Diario de Zaragoza* and *El Heraldo de Aragón*, 27–29 June 1899. The extent to which the rioters enjoyed popular support can be gauged by the money raised by a Republican paper, *El Clamor Zaragozano*, through a subscription for the families of the hundred or so rioters jailed by the authorities; donations came not just from factories and workshops but also from middle-class people, including a 100-peseta donation from the main local Casino or Republican club (21 and 28 Sept. and 22 Oct. 1899).

class audience, yawning with boredom and with a bandage around his head as if he had a headache.[59]

The fact that these new riots were largely urban-based does not mean that rural grievances were absent nor that there was a clear dividing line between new and traditional kinds of protest, as we have already suggested.[60] In fact, both modern and traditional sectors of the economy were involved in the riots. In towns with some industry, protest over problems of subsistence converged with strikes over wages and conditions. What bound the two together were declining living standards affecting both the agricultural and industrial workers' families.[61] In any case, there was not always that well-marked division between rural and urban life that characterized more developed and urbanized economies. Villages and small provincial towns in Spain at the turn of the century were relatively more populous than some sixty years later. At the same time, most towns retained close links with the countryside and their influence irradiated throughout the surrounding areas. Sheep were driven through their streets to the markets, pigs and chickens rooted about in the sewers, and crowds of peasants moved in every day to sell their produce. Even the capital retained a marked rural character, as in Blasco Ibañez' vivid description in *La Horda* of low life in Madrid at the turn of the century.[62] It was often at the point of entry into the town, at the *fielato*, the customs post responsible for the collection of the *consumo* tax which was a privatised public service, where riots began.

Indeed, the transition from the traditional 'legitimizing' riot to more modern forms of collective protest such as strikes or political demonstra-

[59] 15 Oct. 1898. Two weeks later, *Blanco y Negro* took to task intellectuals, the chattering classes, and the would-be educational reformers epitomized by *El Liberal* and *El Globo* ('A ocho días vista', 5 Nov. 1898). Emilia Pardo Bazán suggested that most people were too plunged in bullfighting, scandal, and crime to worry about national problems: *La Vida Contemporánea*, 63.

[60] The two brief accounts of the riots of 1899 conclude, wrongly I believe, that they were merely traditional forms of protest, like those of May 1898 (Arriero ('Los motines') and Castro Alfín ('Protesta') while, surprisingly, Serrano (*Le Tour*) makes no reference to them at all. The 1899 riots were followed by similar disturbances in 1900 in support of the shop closures. The geographical spread of these riots—not just to the industrial cities but also to towns in the agrarian heartlands such as Segovia—suggests that popular anger against the *consumo* tax was universal. For details, see Soldevilla (*El año, 1900*), 151–6.

[61] For details, see Manuel Tuñón de Lara, *El movimiento obrero en la historia de España* (Madrid 1972).

[62] See also Brigitte Magnien, 'Culture Urbaine' in C. Serrano and S. Salaun (eds.), *1900 en Espagne (essai d'histoire culturelle)* (Bordeaux 1988), 85–103. For a similar picture of French towns see Eugen Weber, *Peasants into Frenchmen. The modernization of rural France 1870–1914* (London, 1979), 232–40.

tions was not linear. While there was a virtual general strike in Zaragoza
in support of the protest against the rise in taxation in June 1899, the
demonstrators in the small town of La Constantina in Andalusia ended
their march cheering the local Liberal cacique outside the party headquarters.[63] Politics in the countryside and in the small provincial towns continued to be rooted in personalities and personal loyalties rather than in the
abstractions by which social conflicts were beginning to be expressed in
the cities.

Similarly, it is difficult to demarcate economic from political protest.
This is particularly true of anti-clerical agitation. At the turn of the
century there was a marked increase in the number of anti-clerical riots in
the larger towns up and down the country. Although strongly influenced
by anarchists and Republicans, the actions were too widespread to be
imputed solely to political organizations of the Left. They involved
a broad section of the population, from students to workers to unemployed youth and they were often accompanied by attacks on the *fielatos*.[64]
Indeed, the social spread of riots of all kinds is as striking as their
geographical extension. Press reports attempt to characterize the rioters as
rent-a-mobs, unemployed layabouts, or children with nothing better to
do.[65] But it is clear from the same reports that the rioters were drawn
from a wide range of ages and occupations: housewives, market-sellers,
unemployed teenagers, cobblers, women shirt-makers and milliners,
factory-workers and artisans and the like. Amongst these, also, were
veterans of the Cuban wars.[66] In this assorted crowd, the Socialists,
Republicans, and anarchists found a new and wider constituency for
political protest.

The broad context for this rise in popular agitation was the quickening
of the pace of modernization in the last quarter of the century. The growth
of industry and urbanization, the crisis in the countryside, affecting wine-
and wheat-producing areas in particular, and the rapid extension of the
railway network all helped to accelerate changes in a society that had
hitherto been evolving comparatively slowly. The new urban dwellers
were rural migrants hit by the agrarian crisis and many must have brought

[63] *El Imparcial*, 3 July 1899.
[64] For example see the detailed reports in the February, March and April 1901 issues of
El Imparcial.
[65] Typical epithets were *trinxaires, grandullones, granujos*, which could be translated as
hooligans, overgrown imps, and urchins.
[66] For references to the rioters as social outcasts see for example *Diario de Barcelona* and
La Vanguardia in July 1899. For details of the occupations and background of individual
rioters, see *El Imparcial*, 26–28 June 1899.

with them old traditions of collective protest. Like all migrants, they also absorbed new values as they became integrated into city life. As industry grew, the size of the workforce increased and the first large-scale strikes began in the early 1890s and burgeoned at the beginning of the new century. The transformation of industrial structures, in particular the decline of the factory colony in the interior of Catalonia, led to an erosion of the paternalist authority of employers.

In the post-Disaster period, industrial protest was fuelled by a fall in the living standards of workers, and by the offensive against textile workers by Catalan employers intent on raising the low levels of productivity to compensate for the loss of the colonial market. Villaverde's budget, moreover, threatened to close many factories affected by the rise in tax on sugar, alcohol, salt, and other commodities.[67] The graph of strikes rose steeply from the turn of the century onwards; the first mass general strikes took place from 1901 onwards. There was a spectacular rise in the membership of the UGT from around 6,000 in 1896 to 29,000 in 1900, 40,000 in 1902, and almost 57,000 in 1904.[68] No less striking was the increase in the influence of the anarchists though this is not easily quantifiable; by 1900, nevertheless, they were confident enough to organize a new national anarcho-syndicalist federation. In 1901 Silvela warned his fellow Conservatives that social agitation was spreading to the countryside and a leading liberal daily alerted its readers to the quiet, relentless expansion of anarchism throughout rural Andalusia. The Republicans made a sustained effort to build up support in the area, sending several leading orators, such as Alejandro Lerroux and Blasco Ibañez, on speaking tours. Indeed, between 1902 and 1903, a rash of violent strikes broke out in the province of Córdoba.[69]

The more specific context of popular agitation was the war years of 1895 to 1898 and their aftermath. The wars had dislocated the lives of innumerable working-class and peasant families, casting sons, brothers, or fathers into a distant and brutal campaign or forcing them to flee abroad to avoid conscription. The hardship caused by the temporary or permanent loss of a breadwinner had been exacerbated towards the end of the

[67] J. M. Alonso de Beraza, 'Las Clases Obreras', *El Liberal*, 11 July 1899. For the effect of the loss of the colonies on Catalan textile workers, see Jordi Nadal and Carlos Sudrià, *Historia de la Caixa de Pensions* (Barcelona, 1981), 17–24.

[68] Tuñón de Lara (*El movimiento*), 305–32.

[69] For Silvela's speech, *El Imparcial*, 9 June 1901; the article is 'La Clave del Problema' in *El Globo* 5 July, 1902; for the Republican campaign and the strikes in Andalusia, see Juan Díaz del Moral, *Historia del las agitaciones campesinas andaluzas—Córdoba. (Antecedentes para una reforma agraria)* (Madrid, 1967—1st edn. 1929), 186–207.

war by the bread crisis. The rise in indirect taxation announced in the Villaverde budget came as an additional blow. Yet all their sacrifices had culminated in a sudden and ignoble defeat. The poor did not need to be able to read the papers to know that it had all been in vain and probably unnecessary.

The inarticulated moral shock of the defeat can only have been deepened by the conditions in which the veterans of the wars were repatriated. The contrast between the manner of their departure and that of their return caused widespread anger. As early as 1897, the Socialists had campaigned against the lack of proper medical care and sanitation on board the ships transporting sick and wounded soldiers back home. Their paper gave a particularly harrowing account of the voyage of a ship called the *Isla de Panay* which left Havana on 30 August 1897 with a cargo of some 900 sick soldiers many of whom were seriously ill. The inadequacy of conditions on board—according to the paper, for example, there was only one doctor—led the civilian passengers to protest to the authorities before the ship set sail. During the voyage, over sixty soldiers died and another fifty-five had to be unloaded en route at Puerto Rico. On their arrival in La Coruña, 359 soldiers had to be hospitalized.[70]

An exclusive contract for the transport of troops to and from the colonies had been awarded to Compañía Transatlántica whose director, the Marquis of Comillas, was a close friend and associate of the Minister of War, General Azcárraga. The company was paid 32 pesetas per soldier by the government for the voyage, more, according to a contemporary calculation, than the fare paid by ordinary passengers.[71] At the end of the war, with over 150,000 troops due to be repatriated, many if not most of them sick, the same company was awarded a new contract by the US government which had taken on the responsibility of repatriating the Spanish troops, according to the terms of the capitulation.[72] The appalling conditions in which the troops were transported back to Spain resulted in many deaths at sea. There were riots by relatives in the ports of disembarkation in protest at the bureaucratic delays and negligent treatment given to the returning soldiers (Fig. 9).[73]

---

[70] See, for example, '¡Asesinos!' *El Socialista*, 24 Sept. 1897.

[71] *El Nuevo Régimen*, 7 Jan. 1897, in Hernández Sandoica and Fernanda Mancebo ('Higiene'), 365.

[72] Tomás Alvarez Angulo, *Memorias de un hombre sin importancia (1878–1961)* (Madrid, 1962), 236. In this book, Alvarez Angulo gives a harrowing account of his own repatriation from Cuba.

[73] For the riots in Vigo, see *El Imparcial*, 16, 20, and 22 Sept. 1898; also, Tuñón de Lara (*Costa*), 33–4.

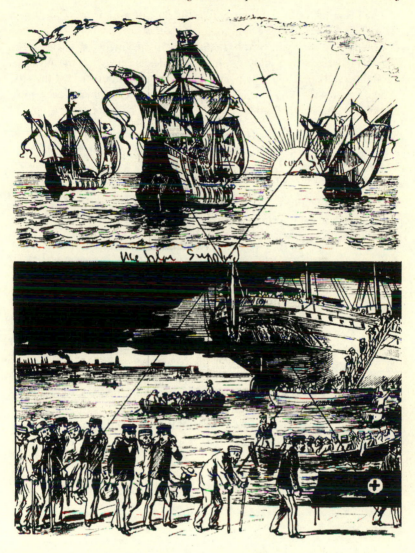

FIG. 9 A Republican view of the Disaster. The caption reads: 'The discovery of America, "How it began, how it ended"'. From *La Campana de Gracia*

The veterans' ordeal did not end at the port of disembarkation. They were then transported by rail to inland cities from where they were expected to make their way back to their home towns or villages. So distressing was the appearance of many that it was rumoured the authorities deliberately unloaded the troops at night or in the outskirts of the city to avoid protests.[74] The journalist Joaquim Nadal remembered the shock he experienced as a child on seeing the returning soldiers.

How much suffering, pain, anguish, misery in those emaciated faces, yellow as parchment—the colour of wax, the colour of bile—and in those skeletal bodies, so thin, so insubstantial that it seemed . . . they were going to vanish into thin air from one moment to the next . . .[75]

The citizens of Madrid were reportedly dismayed at the sight of groups of ragged veterans wandering about the streets of the capital, begging for money. According to *El Imparcial*:

There were many unfortunate [soldiers] who, exhausted by dysentery, malaria or tuberculosis, could not walk and dragged themselves along the streets, sowing grief and pity everywhere they went.[76]

Harrowing stories were told of their return home; of the soldier who arrived home at night too feeble to wake up his parents and was found dead on the doorstep by them the next morning; of the rural labourers, father and mother, who were unable to recognize their son on his return, he was so emaciated.[77]

The intense press coverage given to the shocking condition of the veterans was part of the widespread attack on the government by newspapers and the political opposition in the immediate aftermath of the Disaster. But while there were numerous charitable acts to help the veterans from eminent people such as the Queen Regent, bishops and noblemen, little interest was shown in their long-term welfare. They were given 20 pesetas each on their return in advance of back wages which the govern-

[74] 'Los soldados que regresan' *El Imparcial*, 2 Sept. 1898; *La Campana de Gracia*, 17 Sept. 1898 and 25 Feb. 1899.
[75] *Cromos de la vida vuitcentista* (Barcelona, 1946), 275–6.
[76] 'El regreso de los soldados', 1 Sept. 1898.
[77] The first anecdote is recounted by Ruben Darío in *España Contemporánea* (Barcelona, 1987), 43 and formed the basis of a sentimental story, 'El repatriado', in *Blanco y Negro* 21 Jan. 1899; the second is from 'La repatriación. Soldados en Zaragoza', *El Mercantil de Zaragoza*, 1 Sept. 1898. For contemporary writers' accounts of repatriation, see for example Joan Maragall's poem, 'Cant del retorn' in 'Poesies', *Obres Completes* (Barcelona, 1929), vol. 1, 103–4 and Emilia Pardo Bazán's short story '¡Poema humilde!' in *El Socialista*, 18 Oct. 1897.

ment owed them and a pension of around 7.50 pesetas a month. The daily wage of an unskilled labourer at the turn of the century was around 2.50 pesetas while it cost about 3.60 pesetas a day to feed a family of four on a basic diet.[78] Charitable funds to supplement the meagre payments given to the veterans soon dried up and some were forced to resort to begging.[79] As late as 1903, many had still not been paid their wages, as the Ministry of War issued a statement that it now had sufficient funds to pay all claims.[80]

As with all popular attitudes of the time, few records exist of the views of the veterans and their families on their return and of the relatives of those who died. The grief and the hardship remained private and went unrecorded. But some anecdotal evidence of the sense of injustice that was no doubt felt by many of them can be found in the reports of the riots that accompanied the disembarkations and of demonstrations by groups of veterans protesting against the government's failure to pay them their full wages.[81] We know from press reports that there were Cuban veterans among the ringleaders of the 1899 riots. During the riot in Zaragoza, for example, the Civil Guard shot dead a young cobbler called Gregorio López who had served five years in Cuba and had taken part in the battle of Peralejo in which the Spanish General Santocildes had fallen dead at his feet. The dead veteran's father, a local miller, lifted his body up for the rioters to see, crying, 'He came from Cuba! He was a sergeant! He hasn't been paid his wages! He tried to protest against the Government!'; his words, according to a newspaper, 'raised the crowd's feelings to the highest pitch'.[82]

The connection between the effects of the wars and the waves of riots that followed the Disaster were noted by contemporary commentators. Countering Silvela's claim that the nation lacked pulse, the Republican *El Nuevo País* claimed that the riots in the ports showed that the nation was

[78] Antoni Jutglar, *Ideologías y clases en la España contemporánea* (Madrid, 1969), vol. 2, 59–63. Details about veterans' pay are from Rafael Pérez Delgado, *1898. El año del Desastre* (Madrid, 1976), 394 and Santiago Galindo Herrero, *El 98 de los que fueron a la guerra* (Madrid, 1952), 104.

[79] Zaragoza Municipal Archives (Gobernación, 1898–9, Armario 78 Legajo 12, file 126; Legajo 14 file 81 and 336.) Of twelve unemployed people listed as a charitable gesture by *El Clamor Zaragozano* (23 July 1899) to help them find jobs, seven were veterans of the Cuban war. *El Imparcial* ('¡Pobre soldado!', 11 Apr. 1899) recounts the plight of one soldier who raised money by selling his credit with the government to a money-lender at 50% interest.

[80] *La Conca de Barbará*, 11 Oct. 1903.

[81] For the latter, see for example 'Incidente lamentable' *El Nuevo País*, 12 Dec. 1898, and *El Imparcial*, 23 Mar. 1899.

[82] *El Heraldo* and *El Heraldo de Aragón*, 28 June 1899.

indeed alive, adding somewhat primly that the only problem was that 'it cannot manifest its feelings except through the fisherwomen of La Coruña, the poorest families of Santander and the Vigo mob'.[83] An editorial in the leading daily, *El Imparcial*, argued that the cause of the riots was the inequality of the sacrifices being demanded by the government for restoring the health of the Spanish economy and it noted that the protest was taking the shape of a social war.[84] The small businessmen's leader, Basilio Paraíso, while vehemently rejecting the form which the popular protest was taking, suggested that

the movement responds to a generalised state of discontent. Women are taking part because they cannot forget the sufferings they went through in giving their sons to the war.[85]

An echo of this widespread unrest can be found in the increasing references in the press and in parliamentary debate to the so-called social question. The phrase became almost as significant as that other incantatory word 'Regeneration'. Debates were held in the Madrid Atheneum and the Crown Prince himself organized a competition to find solutions for the agrarian problem in the South.[86] A number of reforms were passed from 1900 onwards in an attempt to contain these pressures from below.[87] Outlining the programme of his first post-Disaster government in 1901, the Liberal leader Sagasta stated that the two most vital issues facing him were the religious and the social questions.[88] Indeed, these two problems increasingly became interwoven from the beginning of the century. The traditional link between subsistence riots and anti-clerical riots has already been noted but some explanation is required for the popular rancour against the clergy in many parts of Spain.

The roots of anti-clericalism in Spain lay in the protracted civil wars in the nineteenth century, first between liberals and absolutists and then between liberals and Carlists. The Church hierarchy's support for the absolute monarchy and the Carlists' deliberate identification of their cause

---

[83] 'Hay pulso', *El Nuevo País*, 17 Sept. 1899; Canalejas' paper, *El Heraldo de Madrid*, also noted 'the spirit of protest which is throbbing throughout Spain': 'Curar y no enconar', *El Heraldo de Madrid*, 3 July 1899. See also the editorial in *El Liberal*, 4 July 1899.

[84] 'La mejor defensa', 4 July 1899.

[85] 'Temores', *El Imparcial*, 1 July 1899.

[86] Díaz del Moral (*Historia*), 226.

[87] These included the Workers' Compensation Act; a law regulating the work of women and children; a third prohibiting work on Sundays; and yet another creating the Instituto de Reformas Sociales to collect data about working and living conditions among working-class families.

[88] *El Imparcial*, 15 Mar. 1901.

with Catholicism ensured that the clergy became the target of hatred of those who supported the democratic and progressive cause, whether liberal or Republican, urban or rural. The campaign of terror conducted by Carlist guerrillas in the countryside of Catalonia and the Basque Country in particular was answered by atrocities against the clergy.[89] To the bitter legacy of those old conflicts was added popular resentment against the privileged status of the Church, which received massive subsidies from the state. Using official figures, a Republican paper calculated that the Church cost the State 43 million pesetas annually.[90] Moreover, the Church was fully identified with the establishment. The parish priest was a familiar figure of authority in each village, forming part of the local élite rather than defending the poor. He was not renowned, either, for his intellectual abilities or cultural level.[91]

Anti-clerical feelings were directed above all against the religious orders, amongst which the Jesuits were a special target of hatred. This was partly connected with their special status in Spain which set them above the laws governing the lives of Spaniards, allowing them to be answerable only to Rome. The influx of Jesuits from France following the anti-clerical reforms of the Third Republic in the early 1880s only served to fuel popular anger. But anti-clericalism derived its force also from the economic advantages enjoyed by all the religious orders. They produced much merchandise for sale which was not subject to tax, such as embroidered and printed goods, shoes, market-garden produce, chocolate and sweets; they also provided services such as laundry and sewing. The fact that their labour force was made up of inmates of the various Catholic welfare institutions also severely undercut the local labour market.[92] As the main source of charity, they were able to wield considerable economic and ideological power; for example, it cost 25 pesetas to marry in a church, in contrast to the 1 peseta charged by the Town Hall but couples not married in a religious ceremony were barred from the social benefits administered by the Church.[93]

After the Disaster, moreover, the loss of the Philippines was attributed in many popular circles to the nefarious activities of the clergy, who were largely responsible for administering the islands. A cartoon in a Republi-

[89] Josep Benet, *Maragall i la setmana tràgica* (Barcelona, 1968, 4th edn.), 182–5.
[90] 'Una bancarrota', *La Campana de Gracia*, 13 Aug. 1898.
[91] Julio Caro Baroja, *Introducción a la historia contemporánea del anticlericalismo español* (Madrid, 1980), 215–16.
[92] Joan Connelly Ullman, *The Tragic Week. A study of anticlericalism in Spain, 1875–1912* (Cambridge, Mass., 1968), 326–8.
[93] Gerard Noel, *Ena: Spain's English Queen* (London, 1984), 117–21.

can weekly shortly after the Disaster shows fat, ugly friars leaving the Philippines in rowing-boats carrying with them huge sacks of money.[94] And indeed, it was the Republicans who led the campaign against the clergy at the beginning of the century. They were able to appeal to a new social base amongst the burgeoning population of the urban centres. To the traditional anti-clerical circles—students, urban-based artisans, skilled workers, and shopkeepers amongst others—were added new layers of unskilled or unemployed workers who had migrated to the cities and were absorbing new urban values which ran counter to the religiosity of parts of the Spanish countryside.[95]

Perhaps because of this diversity of classes, the Republicans' anti-clerical campaign drew on traditional popular animosities against the clergy rather than on modern secularism, thus concealing their own internal contradictions. The rituals and icons of Catholicism were held up for ridicule as being no better than the 'grotesque' fetishes of Congo villages.[96] At the same time, Republican leaders appealed to misogyny and repressed sexuality by encouraging popular beliefs about strange goings-on behind convent walls. In a notorious article in 1906, the Republican leader in Barcelona, Alejandro Lerroux, invited his readers to sack the convents and 'raise the veils of nuns to convert them into the category of mothers'.[97]

The Republicans' ability to mobilize urban masses on the clerical issue forced the Liberals, concerned at the possible haemorrhage of their support towards the Left, to put it at the centre of their political agenda.[98] The political consensus from the Centre to the Left on the clerical question paved the way for a new wave of agitation against the clergy at the beginning of the century. It was sparked off by the staging of Benito Galdós' new anti-clerical play, *Electra*, at the beginning of 1901. This

[94] *La Campana de Gracia*, 4 June 1898; see also Carlos Ría-Baja, *El Desastre filipino. Memorias de un prisionero* (Barcelona, 1899), 35–7.

[95] The Cardinal Archbishop of Toledo ordered a survey of religious observance in Madrid in 1909 which found that only 4% of its population complied with the Easter duties of confession and communion: Pike (*Hispanismo*), 101.

[96] Vicente Blasco Ibañez, 'El corazón de Jesús', *El Clamor Zaragozano*, 29 Oct. 1899.

[97] '¡Rebeldes, rebeldes!', *El Progreso*, 1 Sept. 1906, reprinted in Alejandro Lerroux, *De la lucha. Páginas de Alejandro Lerroux* (Barcelona, 1909), 119–20. For a discussion of popular culture and Republican anti-clericalism, see José Alvarez Junco, 'Cultura popular y protesta política' in Maurice (*Peuple*), 157–68 and in his own *Emperador*, 401–14. A typical display of anti-clerical prejudice can be found in a series of articles run by the Republican daily *El País* (briefly renamed *El Nuevo País* to escape censorship) in Nov. 1898, in which the Jesuits were described as an effeminate, strange, and baroque cult.

[98] Manuel Suárez Cortina, *El reformismo en España. Republicanos y reformistas bajo la Monarquía de Alfonso XIII* (Madrid, 1986), 1–2.

coincided with two other events: a much-publicized lawsuit in which a mother won the final appeal in her case against the Church for persuading her daughter to enter a convent, apparently against her will; and the brief visit to Madrid of the Count of Caserta, who had led the Carlist troops in the last Carlist war, for the wedding of his son to the Princess of Asturias. The confluence of the three events generated violent anti-clerical demonstrations in Madrid which spread to Valencia, Barcelona, Granada, Zaragoza, and other cities, forcing the authorities to declare martial law therein.[99]

Popular anti-clerical feelings were also expressed in feasts such as the Mardi Gras Carnival. In a fairly repressive society such as early twentieth-century Spain, feasts and popular rituals were a safety-valve for the expression of collective grievances as well as for the release of individual inhibitions. It was an old tradition to satirize figures of authority, such as the clergyman, the doctor, the local cacique, or indeed the government itself, in masked pageants such as the Carnival. It was also common practice during these rituals for men to dress up as women and vice versa even though this cross-dressing was condemned by the Church as a sin against the Sixth Commandment.[100] In the first decade of the century, the Carnival became once again a focus of disapproval, not only of the Church but of the military and conservative opinion in general, because it expressed new and sharper social criticism. A parody of the Maundy Thursday religious procession during the Carnival in the Catalan town of Montblanch in 1908 caused great indignation amongst Catholics. In the same town shortly after the Disaster, the military had also been mocked by Carnival revellers for losing the war.[101] In an article in *La Vanguardia* in 1904, the Catalan magnate, Güell i Ferrer, lamented the transformation of the Carnival into a socially divisive feast, full of 'rude masks' and 'venomous insults'.[102]

What they were complaining about, in fact, was the emergence of a working-class culture which had cast off the traditional social deference of previous generations and was beginning to assert itself politically. This

[99] *El Heraldo de Madrid*, 31 Jan., 5–13 Feb. 1901; *El Imparcial*, 8–14 Feb. 1901; *El Almanaque de las Provincias*, 1902. Francisco Pi y Margall and Francisco Pi y Arsuaga, *Historia de España en el siglo XIX* (Barcelona, 1902), vol. VII (1921–2).

[100] Julio Caro Baroja, *El Carnaval (análisis histórico-cultural)*, (Madrid, 1965), 85–90. For a discussion of such forms of popular protest in eighteenth-century Europe, see Charles Tilly's introduction to Louise A. Tilly and Charles Tilly (eds.) (*Class Conflict*), 13–25.

[101] Arxiu Històric Comarcal de Montblanc (Fons A. Rosselló Rg. 25, Llig. 4); 'Militares y paisanos', *La Correspondencia Militar*, 15 Feb. 1899.

[102] 9 Feb. 1904. The provincial paper *La Conca de Barbará* also complained in the same year about the 'decadence' of the Carnival, its lowering standards of morality: 21 and 28 Feb.

change in social relations was most marked in the cities, as we have seen. Modernization was transforming urban physiognomy and culture. The industrial centres were filled by a new layer of unskilled workers from the countryside who found work on the building sites, in the foundries and, in the case of women, as domestic servants. The rise of the working-class population was accompanied by the spread of suburban slums and the growth of unionism. Because there was not work for everybody, an 'underclass' of unemployed or semi-employed people grew, seen by respectable society as petty criminals, young 'hooligans' and so on. Traditional forms of social control such as patronage and paternalism were eroded by the growth of anarchist and Socialist organizations and new, populist movements such as those mobilized by Lerroux in Barcelona and Blasco Ibañez in Valencia. The people's voice was becoming increasingly assertive and insolent.[103]

The growing social agitation to which we have referred throughout this chapter was the result, therefore, of two converging processes: on one hand, a structural transformation common to other European countries (though far less acute in the Spanish case) and marked in Spain by agrarian decline in central and southern provinces, urbanization on the periphery, and a rise in labour organization; and on the other, a crisis of legitimacy as a result of the war and the Disaster which reached down into many layers of the working and labouring classes. The two processes cannot easily be separated nor is it possible to calculate their relative impact. It can be argued, nevertheless, that the wars of 1895–8 and their aftermath helped to undermine a social consensus that was already fragile. In many parts of Spain, there was a new climate of popular disenchantment with the established order and its local representatives, combined with a new combativeness over issues of land and work. An editorial in the Gijón Republican paper *El Noroeste*, referring to the 1899 riots, commented shrewdly,

We are not dealing here with a movement with a concrete or fixed aim . . . the popular elements are not moved by any well-defined or single aspiration./ Why this ambiguity?, this vagueness? In our modest opinion, the recent action by the people does not signify condemnation of the government project nor of an aspect of its policies but a protest against the whole regime, whose rule coincides with the deepest and most acute crisis faced by Spain. . . .[104]

---

[103] Magnien ('Culture urbaine'); Alvarez Junco ('Cultura popular y protesta política' and *El Emperador*); Romero Maura (*La Rosa*). For Blasco Ibañez' movement, see Ramir Reig Armero, *Obrers i ciutadans. Blasquisme i movement obrer. València, 1898–1906* (Valencia, 1982).   [104] 'La España que revive', 5 July 1899.

Two years later, commenting on the violence of the general strike in La Coruña, *El Imparcial* noted the changing political mood among workers: 'The Spanish state has failed to be loved and has ceased to be feared.'[105]

The dual crisis of legitimacy and modernization weakened the ability of the Spanish state either to draw upon traditional values to re-establish its authority or to create a popular base for a new nationalism based on military and commercial penetration into Africa. This was in marked contrast to the surge of interest in imperialism in many other parts of Europe in the same period.[106] The Disaster exposed the hollowness of the patriotic rhetoric orchestrated by the local and national élites and cut short any incipient growth of popular imperial sentiments.

The events of the Tragic Week of July 1909 embody, in many respects, the foregoing analysis of popular attitudes in the post-Disaster period. They were precipitated by the military campaign against the Rif tribesmen in Morocco authorized by the Premier, Antonio Maura. A decree on 11 July ordered the mobilization of reservists from lists drawn up as early as 1903. Many on the list had since started a family and as the ex-Minister of War, General Fernando Primo de Rivera, acknowledged, had thought themselves free of any further obligation to do military service.[107] The decree provoked virulent protests which in Barcelona in particular, partly because it was the port of embarkation, turned into a violent and prolonged confrontation with the authorities.

The circumstances in which the reservists were mobilized could not fail to evoke bitter memories of the war of 1895–8. The company responsible for the shipment of the troops was the same, the policy of selling call-up exemptions was still in force, the same or similar notables were sending off the recruits with patriotic speeches to the accompaniment of bands playing popular marches, and as in many send-offs during the colonial war, devout middle-class ladies were distributing religious medals and free cigarettes to the soldiers.[108] While there had been a degree of patriotic enthusiasm amongst the troops in the war against the United States, the conflict in Morocco was widely perceived to be solely for the benefit of Spanish investors whose financial interests were threatened by the Rif tribesmen. As the band played the Royal March in the port at Barcelona,

---

[105] 'Factores de disciplina', 2 June 1901.

[106] See for example Winfried Baumgart, *Imperialism. The Idea and Reality of British and French colonial Expansion, 1880–1914* (Oxford, 1982).

[107] In a statement to *Le Journal* quoted in José Brissa, *La Revolución de Julio en Barcelona* (Barcelona, 1910), 8; Soldevilla (*El año, 1909*), 241–2.

[108] Connelly Ullman (*The Tragic Week*), 135.

the crowds whistled in derision and the conscripts threw the medals overboard.[109]

The week of violence in Barcelona and in the industrial towns surrounding the city began on Monday 26 July with a spontaneous strike against the Moroccan War by metalworkers in Barcelona, who had staged the first general strike in Spain in 1902.[110] Their protest was taken up by workers throughout the city, after flying pickets had done the rounds of the main factories, until Barcelona was at a standstill; simultaneously, strike action paralysed the nearby textile town of Sabadell and then spread to other towns in the province. Groups of youths and women, many wearing the white bow that became an emblem of the anti-war protest, went round closing down shops and cafes, meeting little resistance and some sympathy; when shopkeepers showed resistance, their windows were smashed following the tradition of popular actions exemplified in the riots of 1899.

The first clashes with the police (the Civil Guard and the Security Guards) took place when demonstrators attempted successfully to stop the trams, which were run by scab labour. The growing violence prompted the government to declare martial law but when the troops were called out, they, and indeed some of their officers, showed a reluctance to fire on the strikers. There were many instances of fraternizing between soldiers and workers; a Socialist worker remembered seeing, as a 7-year-old, troops marching through the working-class district of Gracia surrounded by the Civil Guard to ensure there was not contact with the local population.[111] The result was that the police continued to be used to repress the agitation. Further clashes took place when rioters, some armed with pistols and carbines, attempted to assault police stations where arrested strikers were being held.

On the night of 26 July the first act of burning Church property took place in the working-class district of Poble Nou. It was followed during the next two days and nights by a wave of incendiarism directed against convents, monasteries, and religious schools and institutes throughout Barcelona. At the same time, news reached the rest of Spain, Barcelona's

[109] 'Lo que haya de caer, caerá', *El Progreso*, 19 July 1909.

[110] The following brief synthesis of events in Barcelona is based on a number of accounts: AMA archives (Legajo 151), Connelly Ullman (*The Tragic Week*); Angel Ossorio y Gallardo, *Barcelona. Julio de 1909 (Declaración de un testigo)* (Madrid, 1910); Brissa (*La Revolución*); Antonio Fabra Rivas, *La Semana Trágica. El caso Maura* (Madrid, 1975) and other sources mentioned below.

[111] Alberto Pérez Baró in Antonio Fabra Rivas, *La Semana Trágica. El caso Maura* (Madrid, 1975), 11.

communications by rail and telegraph having been cut off by the strikers, that Spanish forces in Morocco had suffered a disastrous defeat at the Barranco del Lobo (the Ravine of the Wolf). By Thursday 29 July just under half of the city's religious establishments had been damaged, some burnt to the ground. That morning, Barcelona was wreathed in plumes of smoke. Armed clashes continued between the police and demonstrators firing from behind barricades built by the men, women and children of the working-class neighbourhoods. As the troops and police gradually took control of the streets, they were repeatedly shot at by snipers. By Saturday, the last pockets of resistance were overwhelmed and order was restored. During the week some 104 civilians had been killed, many more had been injured and hundreds had been arrested.

In the meantime, the nearby town of Sabadell had been taken over by strikers. After a mass meeting on Wednesday declared for a Republic, the town was run briefly by a revolutionary committee. The first troops sent to restore order were greeted with applause and there was some fraternization between soldiers and demonstrators but the arrival of further troops on Saturday and the news that Barcelona had been pacified led to the collapse of the rebellion.[112] In Granollers similarly, a revolutionary committee was set up and decisions were made by acclamation in mass meetings in the town square. A hostile conservative account describes one such decision concerning the problem of whether the tobacconists should remain open or not since only shops selling articles of primary necessity were allowed to trade. While the women argued that they should close and the men should 'smoke their own fingers', the latter argued that smoking was a vital need; a compromise was agreed whereby tobacconists would remain open for two hours a day.[113]

In other industrial towns of the province, such as Manresa, Mataró, and Terrassa, strikers also seized brief control after clashing with the local *Somatén*, the vigilante volunteer police force. During the disturbances, tax offices and religious establishments were burnt down, as had been the tradition in popular disturbances throughout the previous century. Outside Catalonia, however, protest against the war failed to develop beyond isolated demonstrations, such as the dramatic scenes in the Madrid station from where recruits were being transported to Barcelona.[114] An attempt

---

[112] José Comaposada, *La revolución en Cataluña. Segunda parte de la revolución en Barcelona* (Barcelona, 1910), 10–14; n.a., *La Semana Sangrienta. Sucesos de Barcelona: Historia, descripciones, documentos, retratos, vistas etc.* (Barcelona, n.d.), 185–6.

[113] Ibid. 189–91.

[114] For a graphic account, see *El Globo*, 22 July 1909 (p.m.).

by the Socialists to call a nation-wide General Strike was pre-empted by the government's action in arresting their leaders and closing down their printing presses.

The most striking characteristic of the Tragic Week was that it combined both modern and traditional forms of social agitation—the General Strike and the riot. The co-existence of both forms was perfectly logical in the context. What had begun as a protest against the call-up of reservists developed into a challenge against the regime itself. By bringing the city's commercial and industrial activity to a halt, the General Strike posed the question of state power. Judging by numerous eye-witness accounts, many of the rioters had some picture in their minds of an alternative form of state, whether it was a vaguely perceived workers' state or, as most accounts suggest, a secular bourgeois republic based on an alliance of the army and the people. Rioting, similarly, was a necessary corollary of this challenge for power; the trams had to be stopped to prevent the movement of scabs and troops, and the streets had to be taken over.

What is more difficult to explain is that the target of subsequent rioting was almost exclusively the religious establishments. Many hypotheses have been put forward in an attempt to explain this aspect and it will continue to remain a debatable issue since the data are too patchy to allow any definitive conclusion. A number of these explanations, however, can be discarded. The burnings were not the work of Maura's opponents, intent on forcing his resignation to prevent the passage of his local reform law.[115] Nor were they simply the actions of a fanatical minority or the degeneration of the anti-war protest into irrational mob violence, as the more conservative press claimed.[116] An even less convincing argument is that they were the result of the Radical Republican leaders' efforts to encourage anti-clerical violence as a means of defusing revolutionary tensions.[117] While many of them were organized by local officials of the Radical party and extremist members of its youth organization, they were joined or backed by much wider sections of the population than those who were active supporters of Lerroux.

There is no evidence to suggest, either, that different social groups were involved in each kind of action. The vast majority of those arrested were workers while 60 per cent were Catalan-born, implying that there

---

[115] According to an unsigned report submitted to Maura ('Antecedentes para determinar la naturaleza del movimiento revolucionario de Barcelona', n.d., AM, Legajo 151, no. 18.)

[116] For example, Ramón Rucabado, 'L'Apoteosis', *La Veu de Catalunya*, 26 Aug. 1909 (a.m.).

[117] This is suggested in Connelly Ullman (*Tragic Week*), 324–5 and 332.

were no differential factors of either occupation or geographical origin amongst the demonstrators which could explain their behaviour. The fact also that officers and their troops showed a certain degree of passivity towards the mob and that middle-class people reportedly came out on to their balconies to witness the burnings suggest at least that there was no vehement opposition to the actions and that antagonism towards the Church was widespread.

It is clear also that the anti-clerical rioting was directed not so much against the personnel of the Church but the expressions of its power; despite the violence of the rioting, only three monks were killed during the Tragic Week, one by asphyxiation as he hid in a cellar. Eye-witness accounts suggest, moreover, that looting was not widespread. The rioters seem to have been more concerned with destroying the Church's symbols than carrying off its belongings. Their special venom was directed against statues; one shocked eye-witness account described how a group of children spent some time spitting and hitting at a statue they had dragged out of a chapel before throwing it on a bonfire. At another church, the rioters were especially keen to tear down the church bells, going to great lengths and some physical risk to bring them down.[118] In a further case, chickens belonging to the nuns of a convent were thrown on to the fire, where furniture and clerical robes were burning, because the rioters wanted to make it clear they were not thieves, that is, that their actions were politically motivated.

The almost exclusive attention paid to assaulting clerical property and the form in which this was carried out suggest that the Church was considered by the rioters to be an important prop of the ruling ideological order. It was also an institution and an ideology which reached into or interfered in the lives of all of them, through education, welfare, and economic competition.[119] The Church, moreover, was the most visible and accessible target for anti-establishment protest, with convents, schools, and welfare institutions dotted about the city. The fact that popular anger was not directed against bourgeois property indicates the small influence of socialism and anarchism amongst the mob and, conversely, the thrall of Republican ideas, which played down class divisions and focused its rhetoric against the residue of the *ancien régime*.

---

[118] *La Semana Sangrienta*, 128 and 159.

[119] Connelly Ullman, 326–8. However, Romero-Maura (*La Rosa*), 521–2, rightly points out that in Barcelona at least the convents were not important sources of economic competition. See also Gustau Barbat and Jordi Estivill, 'L'anticlericalisme en la revolta popular del 1909', *L'Avenç*, no. 2 (May 1977), 28–37.

This is not to say that the rioters were driven by purely rational motives.[120] Behind their actions lay the residue of popular myths, prejudices,
and superstitions about the clergy. For example, it appears from numerous anecdotes that the rioters expected to find evidence of all sorts of
malpractice within the convents. Many nuns were popularly believed to
be there against their will while the rest were thought to be the victims of
false consciousness. A young rioter was asked by nuns what he wanted of
them. 'I have come', he replied, 'to liberate you and to burn down the
convent.'[121] Large amounts of money were mistakenly thought to be
stashed away by the clergy and arms for the Carlist cause were also
searched for in vain. The lurid propaganda of the Radicals had excited
long-held popular fantasies of torture and sexual deviance within the
convent walls. The crowds had expected to find foetuses. In one convent
a room fitted out with chains and strange installations was discovered and
rumours abounded that it was a torture chamber. A play entitled *The
Mysteries of a Convent or the Nun Buried Alive* had been running to packed
houses in Barcelona; it was based on a supposedly true story of a man who
had witnessed a procession of nuns and the burial of a live nun as he was
stealing oranges on the wall of a Hieronymite convent. When that same
convent was ransacked during the Tragic Week, the rioters tore open the
tombs and found the corpses of nuns with their hands and feet tied
together. The crowd did not know that the practice of burying bodies in
this way had been a common practice for centuries in Catalonia and they
proceeded to parade the corpses through the streets as evidence of clerical
barbarism.[122]

Yet there was also a festive spirit amongst the rioters as they ransacked
the convents and churches which suggested that the violence was also a
kind of Dionysian rite of liberation from the repressive morality represented by the Church. Some of the scenes described by eye-witnesses
remind one of the traditional Carnival festivities mentioned earlier. In one
building, rioters dressed up in the priests' robes which they had found
inside and performed a satire of a religious ceremony, while others seized
some musical instruments and played them in the patio.[123] In an incident
which became notorious, a man picked up one of the nuns' corpses that

---

[120] As Joan B. Culla i Clará argues in *El Republicanisme lerrouxista a Catalunya (1901–
1923)* (Barcelona, 1986), 212. This is also refuted by Alvarez Junco (*El Emperador*), 386–7.
For an incisive analysis of the cultural roots of anti-clericalism see the latter, 397–414.
[121] Ibid. 94–5.
[122] Ibid. 173–6; for the play: Comaposada (*La Semana Trágica en Barcelona*), 23 and 34.
[123] *La Semana Sangrienta*, 148.

were so exciting the curiosity of the crowds and danced with it in the street.

The Tragic Week was therefore a largely spontaneous explosion of popular protest which brought into play traditional and modern forms of agitation, mixing socio-economic and cultural grievances with vestigial myths and rituals. At its heart lay what Joan Maragall called 'social impotence', that is, the sense of alienation of ordinary people from the regime and its ideology. Shortly after the Tragic Week Maragall wrote:

we have here a great conglomeration of individual energies that has not been able to create a social organism proportionate to its mass, still badly integrated in the totality of the State.[124]

Whatever its causes, the preponderance of anti-clerical violence during the week dissipated the protest against the regime. The religious buildings were not centres of power but at the most, symbols of the prevailing ideology. The failure of the General Strike to prevent the war or to change the regime, though Maura was forced to resign shortly after, was due both to its isolation within Spain and to the spate of church burnings which undermined its political impact.

The violence of the Tragic Week profoundly altered political perspectives. It strengthened the belief among some intellectuals that ordinary people were not ready for participation in a modern polity. It discouraged conservative Catalanists from opposing the regime and contributed to a rightward shift among military officers. For sections of the left such as the Socialists, the Tragic Week was a disaster, the waste of a unique opportunity to organize the labour movement into a political force against the regime.[125] The terrible repression that followed had also an important impact on the left. Under the newly appointed Governor of Barcelona province, Crespo Azorín, martial law was extended, all organizations of the left of centre continued to be banned and over 150 lay schools and progressive institutions in the province of Barcelona alone were closed down. The new anarcho-syndicalist federation in Catalonia, Solidaridad Obrera, suffered the arrest of its leaders and the closure of its centres.[126] If the Radicals celebrated the events as the 'Glorious Week', the repression that was unleashed hit their own followers hardest. Their numerous

[124] Josep Benet, *Maragall i la setmana Tràgica* (Barcelona, 1968; 1st edn. 1963), 118–19.
[125] Fabra Rivas (*La Semana Trágica*), 56.
[126] Throughout the country there were 990 arrests, according to *La Veu de Catalunya* (28 Aug. 1909), of which some 60% were in Catalonia; Connelly Ullman (*Tragic Week*, 284) adds that this figure represented a mere third of the total number detained. Figures for the closure of schools are from the latter, 283.

centres and clubs were closed down and many of their officials arrested. Because they were the main target of government repression, however, the Radicals' reputation as being the main opponents of the regime was sustained and their continuing hold on the popular vote in Barcelona was confirmed in the May 1910 elections.

The regime wreaked both real and symbolic revenge on the social forces that had taken part in the Tragic Week. Of the numerous trials that followed, those in the military courts were largely concerned with the crime of treason or 'armed rebellion'. The five people who were sentenced to death, however, could hardly be described as guilty on that charge. None were accused of homicide or manslaughter and none had been involved in any important incidents; it is difficult not to reach the conclusion that they were singled out for exemplary punishment because of what they symbolized rather than what they did.[127] The most notorious trial was that of Francisco Ferrer, the anarchist and founder of the Escuela Moderna, a network of libertarian schools whose centre was in Barcelona. Absurdly, he was accused of being the 'author and chief of the rebellion' when in fact he had been very much on its margins, although he was a fervent advocate of violent revolution.[128] To the thousands of demonstrators in many countries who rallied in vain to demand that the Maura government should pardon him, it was clear he was being executed for his ideas. Ferrer died true to these beliefs, according to a sympathetic report based on an eye-witness account; standing up before the firing-squad, having been granted a last request not to kneel, he shouted 'I am innocent! Long live the Escuela Moderna!'[129]

Another execution with strong symbolic overtones was that of the man who had danced with the mummified corpse of a nun. Although he was in fact charged with participating in an armed rebellion because he had helped build a barricade, it was clear that he had been singled out for profaning religion; as he himself said as he was taken out to be executed, 'there were many people who were more guilty than he was . . . and they were free!'.[130] Ramón Clemente García, or 'the charcoal lad' as he became known during his trial, was a poor and, according to reports, slightly mentally retarded 22-year-old who had done military service at the age of

---

[127] Ibid. 288–9.

[128] For detailed evidence, see Connelly Ullman (*The Tragic*), 298–304; for differing views of Ferrer, see Romera Maura (*La Rosa*) and Alvarez Junco (*El Emperador*). Ferrer's radicalism can be gauged from leaflets and programmes seized from his room by police and reproduced in AM, Legajo 151, no. 10.

[129] Brissa (*La Revolución*), 290–3.

[130] Ibid. 209.

15 and was employed in a charcoal workshop in Barcelona. During the events of the Tragic Week, it was reported, he had been 'delighted to find he could be of use as a revolutionary' and had considered dancing with the corpse 'an amusement'.[131] In contrast to Ferrer, Clemente's last moments were filled with pathos; kneeling before the firing-squad in his shabby clothes, he sobbed as they fired into his body.[132] In executing the anarchist teacher and the charcoal-burner, the regime was perhaps, unconsciously or not, trying to exorcise both the new threat of revolutionary ideas and the old spectre of popular revolt.

[131] Comaposada (*La revolución de Barcelona*), 247.
[132] Brissa (*La revolución*), 207–10.

5

Between the Mobs and the Troops: The Catalan Challenge

SHORTLY after the fall of Cuba, the Acting British Vice-Consul in Barcelona sent a report to the Prime Minister, Lord Salisbury, warning him of the growing peril of Catalan separatism. This, he wrote,

was at first confined to the younger members of the upper and middle classes but it has gradually spread through all classes of the community in Catalonia and men—both young and old—may now be constantly heard, in the cafés and clubs of this city, advocating in loud terms the policy of 'decentralization' and in milder tones the policy of separation of Catalonia from the rest of Spain . . . [I]t might in the event of political troubles in other parts of Spain . . . develop suddenly into a mighty movement fraught with great danger for the integrity of the kingdom.[1]

The Vice-Consul undoubtedly overestimated the strength of separatist feeling in Catalonia. Few Catalans seriously considered the possibility of an independent Catalan state. In fact, 'separatism' was a loose term wielded by Spanish nationalist opinion of all hues to deride regional movements for autonomy. The word acquired a special resonance after the loss of the colonies since they, like Catalonia, had been seen as an integral part of Spain. But most Catalan nationalists sought autonomy not independence and many were staunch Spanish patriots. The Vice-Consul was right, however, in seeing Catalanism as a potential threat to the state. In the wake of the Disaster, bourgeois disaffection and a revived Catalan nationalism converged in a movement that swept aside the established parties in Catalonia and appeared briefly to challenge the Restoration system itself.

Catalan national identity was not simply an expression of an ethnolinguistic difference but had deep historical roots. As the regions of northern Spain united in the Middle Ages around a common endeavour to oust Islam and then to colonize America, Catalonia, like several others, had

---

[1] Letter from Witty to Barclay, 26 July 1898, PRO FO 72.2064.

retained a certain degree of political autonomy, first within the Crown of Aragon and then under the Castilian monarchy. Until the Bourbon reforms of the eighteenth century, the Spanish Crown had maintained a sort of contractual relationship with the historic regions of Spain, allowing them to retain a variety of constitutional arrangements based on ancient rights dating back to the medieval kingdoms. Indeed, at the end of the nineteenth century, Navarra and the Basque country still enjoyed special tax rights which Catalan nationalists, with increasing stridency, were claiming for themselves. After twice revolting against the monarchy in 1640 and in 1701, Catalonia had lost the last remnant of its limited autonomy, the Catalan parliament or Corts. Under the more efficient administration of the Bourbons, however, the élites of the different Spanish regions began to enjoy the fruits of a captive colonial market. As a result, the sense of a separate regional identity was subsumed by a common interest in maintaining the empire. Local challenges to the central rule became confined to popular revolts against food shortages or against the repressive policies of the absolutist monarchy.

The loss of the continental Empire in the early nineteenth century only partially undermined this common imperial relationship. More important in generating friction between the regions and the state were the Liberals' determined but largely abortive attempts throughout the century to create a modern centralized state. Despite their efforts, the Spanish state remained too weak to impose a uniform culture and administration on the country. Local or regional impulses developed two diametrically opposed forms. On one hand, urban-based federal Republicans attempted to create a democratic federal state based on a pact between autonomous regions.[2] The failure of the First Republic in 1873 indicated the weak social base for such a project. Nevertheless, Catalanist federalism—the notion that Spain could be regenerated through strengthening the regions—remained a powerful tradition amongst the Catalan middle classes and sections of workers and artisans.[3] The other centrifugal tendency in nineteenth-century Spain was the Carlist movement, a reaction by traditional rural society against the secular, centralist, and modernizing efforts of liberal and Republican regimes. In rural Catalonia in particular, it was closely associated with the Church, which became a

---

[2] F. Pi Margall, *Las nacionalidades* (1876) (Madrid, 1972).

[3] Thus Almirall's statement in 1886, 'the regional spirit is the only element of regeneration that we have left'. Valentí Almirall, *Lo Catalanisme* (Barcelona, 1886), 328. For the popular base of Catalan federalism in the late nineteenth century, see Josep Termes Ardévol, *Federalismo, anarcosindicalismo y catalanismo* (Barcelona, 1976).

powerful defender of the Catalan language and culture, seeing them as the source of traditional values.[4]

The failure of the Liberals and Republicans to create a modern nation-state was compounded by the slow pace of modernization in all but the periphery of Spain. Most of the country remained in the thrall of an agrarian, largely subsistence economy dominated by an oligarchy made up of the old aristocracy and a new class of landowners and bankers who had acquired wealth and prestige through the disentailment of Church lands. After the collapse of the First Republic, this oligarchy created the Restoration state in its own image, building a system of political patronage which articulated with local power networks. Parts of the periphery, on the other hand, had been undergoing a process of modernization which increasingly widened the social and economic gap between them and the relatively stagnant centre and south.

Yet the bourgeoisie of the industrialized periphery depended on the state for the protection of their economic interests. The state provided the legal and administrative framework in which Catalan and Basque industry could exploit the limited domestic market. It was responsible for the defence of the colonial markets, so vital to Catalan manufacturers, and protected Spanish industry, to varying degrees, from foreign competition. The subordination of regionalist demands was therefore necessary for the greater needs of the Empire and the profits derived therefrom.[5] Moreover, while the peripheral bourgeoisie had little direct representation in the state, they were closely linked to the ruling élites through a shared national interest and a common culture. In turn, the ruling oligarchy was responsive to the economic needs of the industrialists. Thus the Catalan and Basque lobbies of Madrid had been powerful instruments of regional representation, not the embryo of revolutionary bourgeois nationalism.[6]

On the other hand, the widening cultural gap between Catalonia and the rest of Spain had encouraged a latent sense of a separate national identity among sections of the new Catalan middle classes. Influenced by

---

[4] Josep Torras i Bages, *La tradició catalana* (1892) in *Obres Completes* (Monserrat, 1984), vol. 1, 225–716.

[5] 'Memorial de Greuges' (1885), in J. A. González Casanova, *Federalisme i autonomía a Catalunya (1868–1938). Documents* (Barcelona, 1974), 501.

[6] A view partially expressed or implied in *El Regionalismo*, Barcelona 1887, by the influential conservative Catalan Joan Mañé Flaquer. See also: Elena Hernández Sandoica, 'Pensamiento burgués y problemas coloniales en la España de la Restauración', Ph.D. Thesis, Universidad Complutense de Madrid, 1982, 2 vols.; Jordi Solé-Tura, *Catalanisme i revolució burguesa* (Barcelona, 1967), and Antoni Jutglar, *Els burgesos catalans* (Barcelona, 1966).

the wave of romantic historiography in the early nineteenth century, Catalan intellectuals had set out to construct a new and somewhat glorified picture of Catalonia's past and to renew the Catalan language and its old culture in the literary movement known as the *Renaixença*. In contrast to the Carlists, they saw Catalan traditions as the harbinger of a modern progressive society. While the textile bourgeoisie practised a sort of economic regionalism, Catalan intellectuals promoted a new cultural nationalism. Catalan national identity was seen as a result of historical destiny. It was defined largely in terms of the 'other', the Castilian 'character' as opposed to the Catalan 'character'. The latter displayed common sense (*seny*) and hard work while the former was inclined to idleness and an excess of imagination.[7]

A parallel process of cultural differentiation had been taking place in the Basque Country. But in contrast to Catalanism, Basque nationalism, as formulated by its founder Sabino de Arana, was a reaction against modernity and modernization. Arana constructed a myth of Basque nationhood that was based on racial exclusivity and the exaltation of the traditional rural values of the region; it was no coincidence that Arana came from a fervent Carlist background. In his own brand of fundamentalism, both the immigrant working class and the industrial bourgeoisie of the region were defined as anti-Basque.[8]

It was not surprising, therefore, that the links between Basque and Catalan nationalism remained tenuous. Moreover, in contrast to its Basque counterpart, the Catalanist movement had established a significant social base by the end of the century. It was a loose federation of associations grouped together into the Catalanist Union, the Unió Catalanista. The Union's programme, the Bases de Manresa of 1892, called for the restoration of the historic autonomous government and its legal codes, a special tax regime for Catalonia, the continued protection of Catalan industry, and the institution of Catalan as an official language. The social composition of the Union can be gauged from the delegates to the Manresa meeting of 1892. Just under half were from the professional middle-class—lawyers, doctors, chemists, writers, clergymen, and so on—while almost 33 per cent were mainly rural proprietors and 10 per cent were bankers and manufacturers. Of the rest there was only one manual worker, a carpenter.[9]

---

[7] *La Renaixensa*, 'Secció Política', 6 July 1898. For a brief discussion of Catalanist traditions, see Josep M. Colomer, *Espanyolisme i catalanisme. La idea de la nació en el pensament polític català (1939–1979)* (Barcelona, 1984), 12–23.

[8] Marian Heiberg, *The Making of the Basque Nation* (Cambridge, 1989), 49–57.

[9] Jordi Llorens i Vila, *La Unió Catalanista (1891–1904)* (Barcelona 1991), 28–9.

Whilst the Union shared a common political aspiration, however, its components sprang from widely different impulses. At one extreme, it was a provincial, conservative movement closely linked to the Carlists and to the local Church, clinging to traditional forms of social and legal organization. At the other extreme, Catalanism was a fiercely nationalist middle-class movement, seeking the greatest possible degree of autonomy from a central state for which it felt deep contempt.[10] Between these two poles lay a wide range of opinions and strategies for the assertion of Catalan identity, embracing federalism, regionalism, that is the defence of regional interests of an economic or political kind, and nationalism, the notion of a separate national interest based on a distinct ethnic and linguistic identity.[11] The core of Catalanist opinion, however, did not envisage the formation of a new nation or state. During the debates in the Manresa meeting delegates had repeatedly stressed that theirs was not a separatist movement. The Girona delegate, Joaquim Riera i Bertran, for example, had exclaimed,

we do not and have never tended towards such a senseless path as wishing to isolate Catalonia from the nation as a whole of which it is an integral and glorious part. We have never been nor are now nor could ever be so reckless as to seek to do away with centuries of [this] reality.[12]

Nevertheless, there was an ambiguity at the centre of the Catalanists' position on the national question which allowed a range of different views on the subject to co-exist. The more extreme nationalist position came out into the open in 1897 when a group of Catalan intellectuals issued a public statement of support for the Greek King, who had just sent an expedition to free Crete from the Turks, in which they drew explicit parallels between 'foreign domination' in Crete and Catalonia. The consequent repression unleashed by the government against the Catalanist press galvanized the nationalist movement and attracted the support of Catalan federal Republicans. On the other hand, the colonial wars were interpreted as nothing more than a struggle between autonomy and centralization; the most militantly nationalist of the Catalanist papers merely called for the concession of home rule to Cuba, as an embryonic nation with the

[10] This tendency was undoubtedly responsible for the notorious incident in 1899 when French naval officers on a visit to Barcelona were greeted with the cry of 'Long live French Catalonia!' and a rendition of the Marseillaise during a function in their honour at the Tivoli Theatre: *El Imparcial*, 22 July 1899.

[11] For a discussion of the meaning of regionalism and nationalism at the time see Lluís Durán i Ventosa, *Regionalisme i Federalisme* (Barcelona 1905).

[12] Ibid. 30.

same right as Catalonia to be an autonomous part of a Greater Spain.[13] This may not have been unconnected with the fact that the Catalan economy was heavily dependent on trade with the Cuban colony. Nevertheless, Catalan nationalists distanced themselves from the more bellicose position of the local bourgeoisie, opposing outright both the colonial war and the conflict with the United States.[14]

The Disaster immeasurably heightened the alienation felt by Catalanist opinion towards the ruling élites. The contrast between the wartime jingoism of the Spanish government and press and the pathos of the débâcle at Cavite and Santiago undermined any lingering illusions in the capacity of the Restoration system to defend the interests of Catalonia. The Disaster also reinforced the feeling among many Catalans that they had a separate national identity and a different historical destiny and that these were incompatible with those of Castille. Whereas Catalanists had tended previously to refer to Catalonia as a region, it was now increasingly conceived of as a 'nation' and Spain as the 'state'.[15] Moreover, Castille and most of Spain were regarded as backward, an encumbrance on the development of Catalonia. The architect Domènech i Montaner contrasted the 'sepulchral silence', the crumbling buildings, the weeds and the moss of a supposedly typical Castilian town with the atmosphere of Barcelona with its great smoke stacks, its streets bustling with commerce.[16]

The polemic about national characteristics tended to degenerate into the hostile exchange of stereotypes or mere racism. The discourse of Catalan regenerationism, as indeed that of its Castilian version, was filled with references to the cultural and racial superiority of the Anglo-Saxons and Germans, with whom Catalanists tended to identify.[17] References to the 'semitic blood' of Castilians and Andalusians, to their 'Muslim inheritance', and to their 'African' attitudes to work abounded in the Catalanist press. A notorious short story which appeared in the Catalanist satirical paper, *La Tralla* in 1907, dramatically entitled '¡Era castellana!' suggested that Castilian women tended to be unfaithful wives and bad mothers. In the same issue, Catalan women, on the contrary, were described as beautiful, upright, dutiful, and possessing a developed sense of social conscience.[18]

---

[13] Lluís Duran i Ventosa, *La Renaixensa*, 27 Sept. 1896.

[14] *La Renaixensa*, 7 July 1898.

[15] Joan-Lluís Marfany, *La Cultura del Catalanisme* (Barcelona, 1995), 89–97.

[16] Lluís Domènech i Montaner, *Estudis Polítics* (Barcelona 1905), 75–6.

[17] For example 'El por que de la superioridad de Alemania', *El Trabajo Nacional* 30 Apr. 1899.

[18] 15 Jan. 1907.

In a speech in March 1899, the Mayor of Barcelona, Dr Bartolomeu Robert, set out to give scientific respectability to the feelings amongst many Catalans that they were racially superior to the Castilians. Drawing on Social Darwinist theories fashionable at the time and making explicit reference to Lord Salisbury's famous 'Dying Nations' speech, he implied that the supposed degeneration of Spain was linked to the racial characteristics of Castilians as revealed in their cranial features. The speech was a big event, enjoying widespread and notorious publicity throughout Spain, and the venue, the Barcelona Ateneu, was so packed out that many spectators were turned away at the entrance for lack of space.[19]

As so often, the debate about national identity also crystallized around the bullfight. For progressive European-minded Catalans it was a barbaric sport, similar to the Roman circus, a manifestation of the backwardness of Castilian culture, 'an unworthy symbol of national identity', according to the painter Santiago Rusiñol.[20] Dr Robert himself organized a meeting against bullfights in 1901 in which a motion was passed calling on the government to ban the spectacle or at least to introduce safety measures and tax it to provide funds for more healthy sports facilities.[21]

Indeed, the Disaster exposed more sharply than ever before the gap between the two Spains—the entrepreneurial and culturally innovative periphery and the inert, backward-looking centre which, according to Catalanist opinion, had allowed the catastrophe to happen. Shortly after the battle at Cavite, the Unió Catalanista issued a passionate statement condemning the war:

Catalans have not spent a century of heroic efforts to create an advanced civilization in this corner of Spain only for it to be thrown away in a spell of drunkenness and for the sake of the unreal phantom of national honour needing the blood of battles to be satisfied.

The lesson was clear: the future of Catalonia depended on altering the balance of political power both in Catalonia and in Spain.

[I]t is of urgent and absolute necessity that Catalonia has a government representing its own internal interests and that it influences the direction of external interests in proportion to its own strength . . . (the Catalan people) will see that

[19] Dr Joan Freixas, 'La rassa catalana', *La Veu*, 16 Mar. 1899 (a.m.). In another speech in the Ateneu the following year, Robert defined the Catalan character, in direct contrast to the Castilian, as individualistic, practical, hard-working, refined, and artistic and the Catalan language as a crisp, virile language which expressed thoughts directly: *La Vida Barcelonesa*, 13.

[20] 'La cogida de Mancheguito', *Madrid Cómico*, 6 Aug. 1898.

[21] *La Vida Barcelonesa*, 16–17.

the present imbalance between our great economic strength and our political nullity within Spain threatens their prosperity.[22]

Despite its rapid growth in membership, however, the Catalanist movement was too weak on its own to influence national policy or indeed to challenge the regional bosses of the Restoration system.[23] It was the shift of opinion among sections of the Catalan bourgeoisie that created the basis of a powerful movement of opposition in Catalonia. Until the colonial wars, the wealthiest Catalan manufacturers and landowners had been content to remain politically subordinate to the oligarchy as long as they were guaranteed access to the overseas markets and protection for their industry from foreign competition. While Cánovas was in power, the Catalan bourgeoisie enjoyed the patronage of Conservatives wedded to the dogma of protectionism. Their relationship with the Liberals, however, was problematic, among other reasons because Liberal governments had been keen to lower tariff barriers. Through successive campaigns to block their free trade measures, those Catalan industrialists and landowners not tied to the Liberals' network of patronage developed an early sense of their own separate economic needs.[24]

The loss of the colonies was a potential catastrophe for Catalan business. The colonial market, especially the Philippines and Cuba, had absorbed up to one-fifth of its most important product, cotton textiles; at the same time, it had supplied goods to the Catalan market, in particular sugar and coffee, on which many merchants and shopkeepers depended for their livelihood. Many Catalans, not just businessmen, were bound to Cuba by strong sentimental ties; men of different generations had done their military service there during the colonial wars and a great number of families had relatives who had emigrated to Cuba, many of whom were forced to return to Catalonia after the war. The fortunes of most Catalan capitalist dynasties had derived from colonial trade and in particular from the lucrative slave trade of the early nineteenth century.[25] The failure of the government to hold on to the colonies was compounded by its inability, as Catalan business saw it, to negotiate favourable terms of trade with the US as part of the Paris Treaty.

[22] 'Manifest de la Unió Catalanista en favor de la pau (12 de juny de 1898)' in Riquer (*Lliga*), 323.
[23] According to Llorens i Vila (*La Unió*, 66), the conglomeration of local associations that made up the Unió embraced between 2,500 and 5,000 members.
[24] Pedro Voltes Bou, *La política de fin de siglo, a través de la prensa barcelonesa de la época*, vol. XXII, *Documentos y estudios* (Barcelona 1978).
[25] Josep M. Fradera, 'Catalunya i Cuba in el segle XIX: el comerç d'esclaus', *L'Avenç*, no. 75 (Oct. 1984), 42–7.

They were further alienated from the regime by the tax burden it imposed on them to pay for the consequences of war. Villaverde's budget was greeted with anger and incredulity. The powerful Catalan employers' federation, the Foment del Treball Nacional, sent a strongly worded exposition to the Premier in July 1899 attacking what they argued was its extremely unfair distribution of taxes and cuts in public expenditure. What Spain needed, they asserted, was investment in production and infrastructure not further military expenditure. The regenerationist message was completed by a plea for the decentralization of a 'decrepit and corrupt political regime'.[26]

Perhaps more important than any economic grievance, however, was the profound psychological shock which the Disaster caused amongst Catalan bourgeoisie. Unlike Catalan nationalists, they had been closely bound to the regime by ideological ties; some administered the regional machinery of the Restoration clientele system. Strongly patriotic, many shared the conservative values of the oligarchy and the monarchy— religion, order and hierarchy. This ideological attachment had been reinforced by economic self-interest. Most of the Catalan industrial bourgeoisie had been especially grateful to the Conservatives for their defence of Catalan industry and colonial trade against foreign competition. In 1892 Cánovas had been made honorary member of the Foment in recognition of his concession of a new tariff barrier. Indeed, lamenting the death of Cánovas, the Foment's paper claimed that 'the protectionists in Spain have become conservatives after the conservatives became protectionists'.[27]

However, the trust they had placed in the Restoration regime now gave way to deep misgiving. The Disaster exposed the weakness of its politicians and the emptiness of their jingoistic rhetoric. In a poll of business opinion in Catalonia conducted shortly after the conclusion of the Paris Treaty, the commercial newspaper *Diario Mercantil* revealed widespread irritation with the political system among Catalan manufacturers and businessmen. According to the opinions canvassed, Spanish politics were characterized by corruption, intrigue, personal ambition, and incompetence. The need for 'less politics' was repeatedly stressed. The administration had to be reformed and decentralized, the electoral system should

---

[26] Fomento del Trabajo Nacional, *Exposición elevada al Presidente del Congreso de los Diputados* (Barcelona, 1899).

[27] *El Trabajo Nacional*: J. P. S., 'Cánovas proteccionista', 30 Aug. 1897; also 'Antonio Cánovas del Castillo', 15 Aug. 1897. For relations between Catalan business and the Conservatives, see Guillermo Graell, *Historia del Fomento Nacional* (Barcelona, n.d.).

be replaced with a corporatist representation and, according to some, businessmen had to take over from professional politicians.[28]

The most urgent task for Catalan manufacturers was to seek new markets for their goods. Two such markets were Latin America, where Spain might count on cultural and linguistic advantages, and Morocco, which visionaries such as Costa had long identified as a promising area for neo-colonial expansion; the Catalan-based press and many other regenerationist newpapers elsewhere were filled with earnest pleas for commercial expansion into Morocco.[29] Another imperative was to raise domestic demand by developing a modern agrarian system. Any attempt to raise living standards in the countryside, however, threatened to undermine the interests of powerful sections of the ruling oligarchy, such as the Castilian wheat-growers and the Andalusian wine producers, whose prosperity depended on low wages. Agrarian reform, therefore, had political implications. While it lasted, Costa's and Paraíso's movement for the regeneration of Spain found widespread support among Catalan manufacturers and landowners as a kind of corollary to their own efforts to support plans for a government led by General Polavieja. An expansion of irrigation, infrastructural investment, credits, training, agrarian reform, all these were measures which the Catalan bourgeoisie backed enthusiastically because they would help to create an internal market.[30]

By 1900, however, it was clear that the two regenerationisms on offer had failed. The collapse of the Polavieja initiative drove home to businessmen that little could be achieved for the time being by the traditional lobby of the Restoration system or by the token presence of Catalans in the cabinet.[31] Costa's attempt to set up a nation-wide movement was foundering on political and regional divisions; the Catalan business leaders who had supported the Unión Nacional, shocked by its lack of support for their demands for tax devolution, withdrew their active support.[32]

---

[28] Issues of Dec. 1898 and Jan. 1899.

[29] 'We will never tire of repeating', wrote *El Diario Mercantil* in 1899, 'that now we have lost the safety valve offered us by Cuba, Puerto Rico and the Philippines, we need seriously to undertake the task of bringing Spanish products to Morocco and the South and Central American republics.' See also issues of 5 Aug. 1898 (Juan Sallarés y Plá), 25 Dec. 1898 and 7 Jan. 1899 and *El Trabajo Nacional*, 18 Jan. 1902.

[30] *El Trabajo Nacional*, 30 Sept. 1899.

[31] See, for example, the President of the *Foment*, Albert Rusiñol's letter to Emilio Orellana in Riquer (*La Lliga*), 336–8; also Guillermo Graell, the Secretary of the Foment and a fervent defender of protectionism: *La cuestión catalana* (Barcelona, 1902).

[32] See Albert Rusiñol's letter to Paraíso in Riquer (1977), 340. The Pact of Lleida in Oct. 1902 whereby Catalan business leaders and Paraíso agreed to cooperate came too late to incorporate the Catalan protest into the Unión Nacional. For the Catalan view of this Pact

Moreover, the growing crisis of Catalan industry made the search for new policies an urgent priority. Neo-colonial expansion and internal economic development required new political leadership. What Spain needed was to adopt the Catalan model of efficiency and modernity. This could only be achieved by a shift in political power, beginning in Catalonia itself. As the young textile magnate and President of the Foment, Albert Rusiñol, exclaimed in a speech to businessmen in January 1900, 'We must organize ourselves and form a small nation in order to save ourselves and save all of Spain.' The writer Joan Maragall compared Spain to Hamlet dying at the feet of the Catalan Fortinbras.[33]

The strategy which the Catalan bourgeoisie were urged to adopt was to regenerate Spain from a politically resurgent Catalonia. As articulated in 1906 by its most vigorous proponent, the young Catalan nationalist Enrich Prat de la Riba, it meant destroying the corrupt electoral system of the established parties in Catalonia and replacing it with a new political force led by the Catalan bourgeoisie. From their new power base, the Catalans could more easily take over the state and impose their model of modernization on a backward Spain. The intention was to 'save the Spanish state from total ruin, to reconstruct it and direct it', as a Catalanist paper later put it.[34] For Prat de la Riba this was only the first stage in a long-term project to restore Spain's status as a world power. His words were filled with the concepts of late nineteenth-century imperialism; Catalonia's mission was to modernize Spain, unite the Iberian peninsula, and then establish a new empire that would civilize the backward peoples of the world.[35]

Prat de la Riba's ambitions, however, were not shared by the notoriously prudent Catalan bourgeoisie. Between them and some of the nationalistic middle-class intellectuals who led the Unió Catalanista there was a wide ideological gap, exemplified by the deferential and patriotic tones of the message to the Queen Regent by the Presidents of the five leading economic corporations in Barcelona and the manifesto of the Polavieja supporters in Catalonia.[36] However, the failure of Polavieja and the Silvela

see 'El pacte de Lleyda', *La Veu* 25 Oct. 1902 (p.m. edition) and for Paraíso's reaction see his letter to Santiago Alba in Romero Maura (La Rosa), 582.

[33] Rusiñol's words from 'Meeting Catalanista' *El Imparcial* 15 Jan. 1900; Joan Maragall, 'Hamlet' in *Artículos (1893–1903)* (Barcelona, 1904), 80.

[34] 'Escandol de Congrés', *La Veu de Catalunya*, 31 Oct. 1904, quoted in Yvan Lissorgues, *Clarín Político* (Barcelona 1980), vol. 1, 297.

[35] Enrich Prat de la Riba, *La Nacionalitat Catalana* (Barcelona, 1910), esp. 140–1. The belief in Spain's imperial destiny was widespread in Catalonia: see, for example, Joan Maragall's article in *Diario de Barcelona*, 16 July 1898.

[36] The message is reproduced in *El Trabajo Nacional*, 15 Nov. 1898 and the manifesto in Borja (*Lliga*), 331–4.

government to support their interests drove leading figures of the Catalan bourgeoisie into seeking a new political alignment outside the Restoration system. Their convergence with sections of the Catalanist movement was helped by a split within the Unió Catalanista in late 1898 and by the extraordinary rise of middle-class protest against the government in the two following years.

It has already been stressed that the Catalanist movement was a broad church embracing a whole spectrum of political and ideological tendencies. Within the leadership itself, though it was narrowly based on Barcelona intellectuals, there was a growing division about strategy which masked a more fundamental ideological difference. One tendency, whose mouthpiece was the daily paper *La Renaixensa* (already twenty years in existence and still the only Catalanist daily), viewed with suspicion any dilution of the nationalist programme of 1892. Their members refused to support the Foment's campaign for a new tax regime, in which Catalonia would be able to raise its own indirect taxes after paying an annually agreed amount to the Exchequer.[37] Moreover, their experience of local elections in 1897, when a Unió Catalanista candidate had been easily defeated by the clientele machine of the Restoration system, had persuaded them against any further electoral participation.

This ideologically purist stance contrasted with the more political and pragmatic outlook of a new generation of Catalan nationalists within the Unió leadership, headed by Prat de la Riba and grouped around the weekly paper *La Veu de Catalunya*, for whom any opportunity to gain a platform for Catalanist views was worth seizing. The divisions between the two tendencies came to a head over the support given to the Polavieja initiative by the pragmatists, notably by the architect Lluís Domènech i Montaner, President of the Unió (and of the prestigious Barcelona Ateneu). In December 1898, a daily version of *La Veu de Catalunya* was launched as a rival to *La Renaixensa*, financed by a group of rich manufacturers associated with the Polavieja group; shortly afterwards, the reformist tendency abandoned the Unió.[38]

The convergence of opinion between influential industrialists and the more political wing of the Catalanist movement was hastened by the events surrounding the 'tax strike' of shopkeepers between July and November 1899. Silvela's Finance Minister, Villaverde, had sought in his first budget to reduce the massive debt arising from the war by raising considerably the burden of taxation on industry and commerce. Catalonia already paid nearly 25 per cent of the state's revenues and unlike the

---

[37] *La Renaixensa*, 1 Oct. 1898.   [38] Riquer (*LLiga*), 117–21 and 155.

shopkeepers' protests that swept across Spain a couple of months later, the Catalan action had a strong regionalist component in that the tax hike was seen as a further attack by Madrid on Catalan interests. It was symptomatic of the rise of Catalanist feelings that when the president of one of the leading economic corporations in Barcelona opened his speech in Castilian Spanish at the first protest meeting, as was the custom among the Catalan bourgeoisie, a spectator shouted to him to speak in Catalan: 'We pay too much here in Castilian, let's at least protest in Catalan', prompting the orator to switch language.[39]

The tactic of withholding tax payments in protest at their increase had been tried already unsuccessfully by factory owners and shopkeepers in 1882.[40] Although equally unsuccessful, the action of 1899 had considerably greater impact. As the government began to send the bailiffs in to seize the property of shopkeepers who had withheld their tax contributions, the action escalated into shop closures and violent demonstrations led by students, as we saw in Chapter 3. The university was closed, martial law was declared, and constitutional guarantees were suspended. Leading Catalan politicians and industrialists were forced to take sides. The elderly Catalan senator Manuel Duran i Bas, Minister of Justice in the new cabinet, and the Mayor of Barcelona, Dr Robert, a much respected figure amongst the Catalan bourgeoisie, both of whom had been appointed by Silvela in a concession to regionalist feelings, resigned from their posts, Robert after dutifully signing the first bailiffs' orders.

By the end of October, the first shopkeepers were being jailed. Amongst those who visited them in jail were leading industrialists and even the Catalanist Bishop of Barcelona, Josep Morgades, another Silvela appointment made to conciliate regionalism, made a much-publicized call. Although many sections of the Catalan bourgeoisie gave their formal support to the shopkeepers' action, they did not approve of their lawbreaking and did not contribute any funds to the campaign.[41] Nevertheless, the *tancament* was a turning-point for them; on one hand, it frayed their already tenuous links with the Silvela Conservatives and on the other, it revealed the potential support that existed among the population of Barcelona for a policy of direct opposition to Madrid.

The already tense relations between Barcelona and Madrid worsened

[39] Camps (*El tancament*), 20.

[40] Pedro Voltes Bou, 'Las dos huelgas de contribuyentes en la Barcelona de fin de siglo', *Cuadernos de Historia Económica de Cataluña*, vol. 5 (1971), 43–66.

[41] Camps (*Tancament*), 53–4. Nor did the executive committee support the action; although they paid a visit to the gaol, they declined to give formal backing because it was a purely economic protest. 'Al poble català', *La Renaixensa*, 11 Dec. 1899.

during the official visit to Catalonia in May 1900 of the Minister of the Interior, Eduardo Dato, who had been responsible for ordering the repression in Catalonia during the shopkeepers' action. His arrival was greeted by a protest shutdown of shops and he was whistled at wherever he appeared. He was even whistled at as he arrived to take his seat for a performance of *Carmen* at the Barcelona opera-house, the Liceu, prompting the Civil Guard to burst in and make arrests while sections of the public sang the Catalan national hymn, *Els Segadors*; the fact that the protest took place in such an exclusive venue indicated the extent to which some sections of the upper-middle class had lost faith in Madrid politicians.[42] The violent demonstrations that accompanied Dato's visits led once again to the imposition of martial law and the suspension of *La Veu*. Significantly, the directors of the Foment decided not to attend the official reception for Dato nor to invite him to visit their headquarters, breaking a long-held precedent of amicable relations with the government.

The collapse of the Silvela government in October 1900 eroded the hope amongst sections of big business in Catalonia that Spain's regeneration could be effected from within the Restoration system. When new general elections were announced for May of the following year, their leading representatives finally threw off their links with the Conservatives and joined with the ex-Unió members to form a new Catalan party, the Lliga Regionalista, to contest the local hegemony of the two centralist parties. The choice of the term regionalist to describe the party was significant. The Catalanist movement was now using the terms nation, nationality, and nationalism to describe itself. A leading conservative member of the new Lliga, Lluís Duran i Ventosa, justified the reference to regionalism by claiming, among other things, that the term nationalism would attract the hostility of Spaniards and in any case would run foul of the law.[43] The semantic smokescreen could not conceal the moderate tone which the industrial and agrarian bourgeoisie brought to the new party. Evading any reference to nation, the first statute of the Lliga affirmed that the party would work 'by all legal means to achieve the autonomy of the Catalan people within the Spanish State'.

---

[42] *El Imparcial*, 'El Señor Dato en Barcelona', 5 May 1900. Cambó later claimed that he had initiated the whistling campaign and that it had been supported by workers in Sabadell and Terrassa: *Memorias (1976–1936)* (Madrid, 1987), 70–1.

[43] *Regionalisme y Federalisme* (Barcelona, 1905), 10–11. It is worth noting also that after splitting with the General, the ex-Polaviejistas in Catalonia had formed the Unió Regional while the reformist wing of the Unió Catalanista had formed the Centre Nacional Català.

Regionalism, therefore, meant dual loyalty—first to the state, which would, if reformed, embrace different ethnicities and provide the political, administrative, and defence framework for the regions, and secondly to the *Volk*, or the ethnic community.[44] Moreover, this autonomy was seen by the leaders of the Catalan bourgeoisie as a lever to regenerate Spain. In his maiden speech to Parliament after the elections, the first President of the Lliga, Dr Robert, declared that the party had as its aim the regeneration of all of Spain 'because . . . we desire not only the good of Catalonia but . . . also the good of all the regions of Spain'.[45] Thus the Lliga was more of a regionalist than a nationalist movement; it sought to assert Catalan interests, not in pursuit of any essentialist vision of Catalonia as a nation but in order to modernize Spain by shifting political power to the industrial bourgeoisie of the periphery.[46]

Indeed, as the Lliga gathered strength, it gained support above all from more moderate and conservative sections of Catalonia. The progressive current within the party, made up of professional middle-class people such as intellectuals, was overshadowed by the backing of industrialists, landowners, shopkeepers, Catalan churchmen, Carlists, and some local Conservatives who brought with them the extensive clientele they had built up through the Restoration party's patronage system.[47] Many of the Lliga's outstanding leaders, such as Prat de la Riba himself and the rising young politician Francesc Cambó were deeply conservative. Cambó could well have been speaking for many of his comrades in the Lliga when he wrote years later in his memoirs

sentimentally, I was a passionate and fervent Catalanist; cerebrally, the conservative ideology of Cánovas, with his sense of authority and hierarchy, seemed to me the only form of good government.[48]

Over a period of four years, the Lliga and their rivals, the newly resuscitated Republicans, destroyed the electoral base of the Restoration system in Barcelona. The general election of 1901, in which all four Lliga candidates in Barcelona won their seats alongside two Republicans and one

[44] Ibid. 30.

[45] Dr Robert, *Legislatura de 1901. Discursos del Dr Robert* (Barcelona, 1902), 4–5. The Lliga Statute is quoted in Isidre Molas, *Lliga Catalana. Un estudi d'Estasiologia* (Barcelona, 1973) (2nd edn.), vol. 1, 47.

[46] The national question in Spain has been the object of intense debate among Spanish, Basque, and Catalan historians from Vicens Vives and Pierre Vilar to Juan Pablo Fusi, José María Jover, J. J. Linz, and Andrés de Blas Guerrero. For a recent and polemical contribution to the debate, see Marfany (*La Cultura*).

[47] Molas (*Lliga*), vol. 1, 43–5; Riquer (*LLiga*), 206–8.

[48] *Memorias*, 27–8.

monarchist, was a triumph of mobilization by Lliga activists against the fraudulent electoral practices of the local bosses of the Restoration parties backed by the Civil Governor. Political life in Barcelona was transformed. For years thereafter, elections in the city would be contested no longer by Liberals and Conservatives but by Catalanists and Republicans.[49]

The Lliga's increasingly conservative character posed a fundamental problem. If it was the party representing Catalan interests, it had to reflect a broad spectrum of opinion in Catalonia. However, the popular vote was rapidly being monopolized by a new political phenomenon, the Republican leader Alejandro Lerroux. The notoriously fragmented Republican movement had been brought together in 1901 by one of its historic leaders, Nicolás Salmerón, into a fragile electoral alliance, the Unión Republicana. The rising, volatile star of the Unión, Lerroux was also beginning to mobilize workers angry at the effects of the economic crisis in Catalonia resulting from the loss of the colonies. His main invective was directed against the Lliga, as the party of the bosses, and against Catalanism as an anti-working-class and unpatriotic movement. Lliga politicians made dark hints that Lerroux was financed by Madrid to undermine Catalanism. While the Republican leader did indeed receive secret government funds as well as the ostentatious support of the Civil Governor during elections, these hardly explain his sudden popularity amongst Barcelona workers.[50] The rise of Lerrouxism was connected both with the changing social base of Republicanism in Barcelona as a result of the accelerating process of modernization since the mid-1870s and with Lerroux's own capacity to mobilize the discontent of new social strata.

The general strike in Barcelona in February 1902, the first general strike in Spanish history, helped to define Lliga even more as a party of law and order and at the same time drove deeper the wedge between the Catalan bourgeoisie and the government. The strike was seen by the Barcelona employers purely as the work of international anarchist

[49] For the electoral figures, see Riquer (*LLiga*) and Molas (*Lliga catalana*).

[50] For secret government funds paid to Lerroux, see Alvarez Junco (*El Emperador*), 61, 217 and 336 and for the Civil Governor's support, 218–19. Another less well-known attempt to counter the spread of Catalanism to popular sectors which is likely to have enjoyed government favour was the creation in 1900 of the daily paper *La Patria* by Juan de Urquía y Redecilla (Capitán Verdades). The short-lived paper set out to curry favour among popular Catalan opinion by praising Catalan virtues, attacking caciquismo, advocating regeneration and defending workers' rights while at the same time denouncing Catalanism as an egotistical, separatist vice: 'A lo que vengo' and 'Patria: Libertad: Regeneración y trabajo' both in issue 13 Oct. 1900; also 'Paseo Histórico', 15 Oct. and 'Vida obrera', 20 Oct. 1900; see also 'El Govern contra Barcelona', *El Poble Català*, 15 July 1909.

agitators. The vast majority of workers, according to the Lliga's paper, had a 'deeply rooted sense of honour and nobility' but being innocent and having little culture, had been used by revolutionaries intent on destroying the social order. In their subversive task, the agitators had been helped by government funds and police provocateurs. Once the strike was over, the paper complained, the government was doing nothing to bring to justice those responsible for the strike, deepening the 'national debauch'.[51]

The shock of the experience led Catalan employers to develop a whole range of initiatives to try to prevent the reoccurrence of a general strike. On one hand they campaigned for greater repressive measures against political agitators, encouraging the creation of local vigilante groups, the *Somatén*, to quell disturbances and establishing a closer relationship with the local Captain-General. On the other, they carried out a series of paternalistic measures—superannuation schemes, joint consultative committees, company unions, and the like—in an attempt to preserve the loyalty of their workforce. They did not share the progressive views of the Minister of Agriculture, José Canalejas, who was advocating the reform of labour relations. On the contrary, the strike reinforced their deep-seated paternalism, impelling them to cling to old notions of corporatism—the guild structure and the 'industrial family'—that were entirely out of step with social relations and the changing mode of production.[52]

The Lliga's rightward drift, as it began to pull in Catholic and rural conservative opinion, proved especially uncomfortable for the more progressive sections within its ranks. Their restlessness came to a head during the visit to Catalonia of the 17-year-old king and the new Conservative premier, Antonio Maura, in April 1904. Maura's decision to organize the royal visit was carefully calculated. He undoubtedly weighed up the risks that were involved. There was the problem of the king's safety and that of Maura himself in a city renowned for terrorism. There was a political risk to his own credibility should the separate forces of Catalanists and Republicans empty the streets or indeed fill them with protesters. These hazards had to be set against the potential benefits of a *rapprochement* with leaders of the Catalan bourgeoisie who had, after all, been clients and collaborators of the Conservatives until recently. Maura must also have

---

[51] *La Veu de Catalunya*: 'Ensenyansas', 7 Jan.; 'La vaga general a Barcelona', 24 Feb.; 'No ha passat res', 28 Feb. 1902.

[52] See the Foment's letter to Canalejas in *Trabajo Nacional* 15 Apr. 1902 and its report to the annual general meeting in 1903 in ibid., 30 Jan. 1903. For a further analysis of the impact of the strike on the Catalan employers, see Gemma Ramos and Soledad Bengoechea, 'La Patronal Catalana y la huelga de 1902', *Historia Social* (Autumn 1989).

counted on what Joan Maragall called the 'secular roots of royal sentiment' among the community, in the hope of mobilizing a new social base for conservatism in Catalonia.[53]

In the event, his calculations proved to be correct. Although an attempt was indeed made on Maura's life, the visit was a resounding success. The king behaved impeccably, rousing the enthusiasm of the crowds wherever he went and, on one occasion at least, expressing a desire to learn Catalan in order the better to communicate with the peasants.[54] Ignoring the decision of the Lliga's executive to boycott the visit, a number of its leading conservative members arranged an audience with the king in their capacity as city councillors. Cambó, as the youngest of the councillors, was entrusted with outlining the demands of Catalan regionalists.[55] His eloquent speech was politely listened to by the king but the demands were brushed aside as a matter for the government and not the Crown. For his part, Maura (a Mallorcan himself) repeatedly stressed his admiration for Catalans during the royal visit and promised a number of devolutionary measures, including a reform of local administration which would give greater powers to the regions and municipalities.

Cambó later claimed, rather improbably, that had it not been for his speech, a new Maurista party would have emerged as a result of the royal visit. It was certainly the case that the basis for a renewed understanding between sections of the Catalan bourgeoisie and regenerationist Conservatives began to be laid during that visit.[56] The conservative instincts of the Catalan bourgeoisie were too strong to resist the overtures of Maura. However, the issue of Cambó's speech to the king finally split the Lliga leadership. The left wing left the organization, convinced that Catalanism needed a more progressive voice. Its newly founded paper, *El Poble Català*, argued that while the Catalan cause remained dominated by a socially conservative party, the masses would never be attracted to Catalanism and would fall prey to the demagogic and centralist agitation of Lerroux. The duty of Catalanists was to win them over. Such was the

[53] Joan Maragall, 'De les reials jornades' in *Obres Completes*, vol. XIII (Barcelona, 1932), 51.

[54] In one incident recounted by Maragall, a small child was hurt by the horses of the royal carriage. The king halted the procession and carried the child in his arms into a nearby tavern where he called for his own doctor to tend the child and took the address of the parents. Maragall added that he wished he had the opportunity to leave such good memories behind: ibid. 55.

[55] For the speech, see *La Vanguardia*, 8 Apr. 1904; the Lliga's manifesto 'Al poble català' calling for a boycott of the royal visit is published in Lliga Catalana, *Historia d'una política. Actuacions i documents de la Lliga Regionalista, 1901–1933* (Barcelona 1933), 30–3.

[56] Cambó (*Memorias*), 100.

polarization of political life in Barcelona that Catalanism merely attracted, in the words of the architect Domènech i Montaner, 'the repulsion of the masses'.[57]

Yet the strategy proposed by the new group was not one likely to attract the social strata that Lerroux was beginning to mobilize. *El Poble Català* called for harmony between all social classes in Catalonia on the grounds that ethnic identity was more important than class allegiance. Catalans of all classes, according to a leading article in its first issue, had to unite around 'the undefined vagueness of the sentiments of all the people'.[58] Caught between two political blocks, Republicans (or jacobins, as the Lerrouxists were described) and reactionaries, the intellectuals of liberal Catalanism could only have challenged Lerrouxism by adopting working-class demands; instead, they confined their activity to issuing moral appeals for unity and tolerance.[59]

Nevertheless, there was a huge, still untapped constituency for progressive Catalanism amongst the middle classes. The ransacking by a mob of army officers in November 1905 of the satirical Catalanist paper *¡Cucut!* and the Lliga's mouthpiece, *La Veu de Catalunya*, galvanized this potential political base. The incident was seen as an attack by an increasingly interventionist army against not only Catalan identity but also democratic rights. Popular indignation was heightened by the response of the new Liberal government which declared martial law in Barcelona and gave in to military opinion by issuing a new law, the Law of Jurisdictions, extending military jurisdiction to so-called offences against the army and the Fatherland.

In the parliamentary debate that followed the declaration of martial law in November 1905, Nicolás Salmerón, ex-President of the First Republic, rose to deliver an extraordinary speech in which he offered the alliance of the Republican movement with the Catalanists. Salmerón, nicknamed the Hollow Man by political foes because his oratorical power was allegedly not accompanied by ideological substance, was a non-Catalan Republican deputy for Barcelona and his speech was filled with references to the

[57] 'La catalanisació d'Espanya', *El Poble Català*, 29 Apr. 1905; see also 'Passem balans', 30 Sept. 1905.
[58] Joan Ventosa i Calvell, 'La crisi del Catalanisme', *El Poble Català*, 12 Nov. 1904; for a similar position, see Jaume Carner, 'Divagacions', 26 Nov. 1904, and 'Crida Patriótica', 31 Dec. 1904.
[59] Such as in J. Lluhí Rissech's article, 'L'esquerra autonomista', ibid., 6 January 1906. Cambó's partisan criticism of the group was not entirely unfounded: 'the dissidents called themselves men of the left, but they felt a real repulsion not only towards the working-class, but even towards the petty bourgeoisie.' (*Memorias*), 101.

dangers of Catalan (and Basque) separatism typical of the centralist ideology of the majority of Republican groups. It was an unusual speech in another sense; Salmerón made clear that in offering an olive branch to the Catalanist movement, his aim was to divide it. Catalanism, he explained to the assembled Spanish deputies, was made up of two tendencies, a clerical, reactionary wing and a liberal, progressive wing. Together, these two formed an 'indigestible combination'; unless separated, they would result in a powerful force united against Spain. By forging an alliance with the liberal tendency, Salmerón implied, Catalanism could be absorbed into the mainstream of Spanish politics and the separatist threat destroyed.[60]

The Republican leader's ambitions were matched by those of the Lliga leaders who wished to move out of the regional ghetto of Catalonia into the wider political arena. Moreover, it was a moot point who would gain most from the alliance, the Republicans or the Lliga. Learning of Salmerón's offer in a corridor outside the parliamentary chamber, Cambó, who was not yet a deputy, immediately gave instructions to the Lliga representatives to agree to it. 'Accept! Accept with your eyes closed, at once . . . !'[61] The result of this strange marriage between monarchist regionalists and jacobin Republicans was the formation of Solidaritat Catalana, a united front which, during its brief life, aroused the hopes of hundreds of thousands of people in Catalonia and elsewhere in a democratic transformation of political life in Spain.

The history of Solidaritat Catalana stretches from its ecstatic launch in February 1906 to its divisions of 1907 and eventual disintegration in 1909. While it lasted, it transformed what had been a range of divided nationalist and regionalist movements into a popular civic movement for the assertion of Catalan rights and the regeneration of Spain. Solidaritat Catalana brought together Republicans, Catalanists, Carlists, and Catholics on one hand, and huge sections of the middle-class and petty bourgeoisie, on the other—shopkeepers, doctors, lawyers, intellectuals, and avant-garde artists (including some of the bohemians of the now-defunct Quatre Gats café) and so on. Indeed, what stamped the new movement with an image of modernity was the backing of the professional middle classes of Barcelona.

What was conspicuously lacking in Solidaritat Catalana, however, was the support of the working classes. Catalanism was still perceived by most

[60] The speech is quoted in full in Romero Maura (*La Rosa*), 596–603.
[61] From Josep Pla, *Francesc Cambó* (Barcelona, 1928–30), quoted in Alvarez Junco (*El Emperador*), 319.

workers as a bourgeois, clerical movement. This perception was encouraged by Lerroux, who, after hesitating about what position to adopt over the officers' assault on the Catalanist press, published a sensational article in which he praised it as a patriotic gesture. Using unusually bloodthirsty and scatological language, Lerroux denounced Catalan 'separatism' and boasted that had he been an officer he 'would have gone to burn down *La Veu*, *¡Cu-cut!*, the Lliga and the Bishop's palace at least'. Lerroux's position was not as irrational as it might appear. He had much to lose from a united front of left and right Catalanism and his courting of military favour was entirely consistent with Republican traditions, which had pinned perennial hopes on gaining support amongst sections of the military. But it was a serious miscalculation, as he himself recognized later, in that it cast him out of the more orthodox milieux of political life in Barcelona and destroyed any potential support from middle-class voters.[62]

Solidaritat Catalana took shape around the campaign to combat the passage of the Law of Jurisdictions in parliament. The Lliga threw its considerable resources into the campaign, perceiving it as a golden opportunity to extend its rather narrow social base towards the left. Moreover, the new movement offered the possibility of expansion beyond Catalonia, the possibility, in the effusive words of the Lliga's paper, of saving Spain from ruin.

The immense peninsula stretches out in front of Catalonia, and one's heart almost gives way contemplating all the deserts that will have to be traversed, so many rivers, so many mountains, so many dormant towns, so many persecutions yet to come . . . But like a lover, Catalonia . . . once again is dreaming of her Spain, of the new Spain, the Spain that will owe her freedom to Catalonia.[63]

The identity of Solidaritat Catalana and the nature of its popular support can be judged by the day of action organized on 20 May 1906 to welcome the return to Barcelona of the deputies who had fought against the Law of Jurisdictions in parliament. The events, which, according to the organizers, attracted an unprecedented 100,000 people, were an assertion of the rights of both Catalonia and Barcelona against the repressive centralism of the state and of Madrid. The speeches and the icons displayed throughout the day were intended to demonstrate the ethnic and

---

[62] Alvarez Junco (*El Emperador*), 356–7; Lerroux's article 'El alma en los labios' in *La Publicidad*, 9 Dec. 1905. For a discussion of Lerroux's policies towards Catalanism, see Joan Culla i Clará, *El Republicanisme lerrouxista a Catalunya (1901–1923)* (Barcelona, 1986).

[63] Josep Pijoan, *La Veu de Catalunya* 28 Feb. 1906 (a.m.); for other typical expressions of the hopes placed in Solidaritat Catalana, see issues of 8 and 13 Feb.

civic virtues embodied by the region and the city, in tacit contrast to the vices of traditional Spanish nationalism, whose most recent expression had been the sacking of the Catalanist newspapers.

One of these virtues, stressed repeatedly by journalists sympathetic to the event, was the civilized orderliness displayed by the organizers and the demonstrators alike. Banners hung up above the crowds proclaimed:

Catalans: the best [display of] enthusiasm is order. Do not shout—stop anyone who does. When you see a white sign, move forward; when you see a red sign, stop.

And indeed, from the crowd, as one newspaper remarked approvingly, hats and handkerchiefs were waved and applause broke out but few shouts were heard and the demonstration was remarkably well organized, despite the crush.[64] No doubt the comments about the civil behaviour of the crowds was also meant, unconsciously or not, to illustrate the respectability of the overwhelmingly middle-class demonstrators in contrast to the violence displayed by the lower classes—the hooligans of the inner-city slums, the anarchists who supposedly threw bombs into crowds, the strikers who had, only a few years previously, fought pitched battles with police in the streets of the city centre.

Not all the support for Solidaritat Catalana emanated from the middle classes of the city. As the deputies' train made its way through the Catalan countryside towards Barcelona, peasants cheered and waved their caps and the deputies were greeted by crowds at each station. But the procession that filed along the San Joan Avenue in Barcelona that afternoon came fundamentally from the urban and provincial middle classes. The clubs, groups, and parties taking part embraced a broad spectrum of middle-class Catalan opinion, from Carlists to federal Republicans, from choral societies and ramblers' associations to artisans' guilds.

Indeed, the whole demonstration that day was also an effort to sustain the illusion of a community united by a common language, culture, and destiny. The sense of elation among the crowds, reported by sympathetic newspapers, perhaps came from the feeling that political differences within the Catalan political family had been overcome by the creation of Solidaritat Catalana. The deputies, who appeared on the stand to witness the march past, included the Carlist Duke of Solferino, the Republican Salmerón, the Lliga businessman Albert Rusiñol, and Emili Junoy,

---

[64] *El Diluvio* 21 May 1906, from which most of these details are drawn. The description of the events also draws on *La Vanguardia* and *Diario de Barcelona* 21 May. For Prat's own account, see 'E pur si muove', *La Veu de Catalunya*, 22 Oct. 1906.

Lerroux's right-hand man who rejected the latter's opposition to Solidaritat Catalana. All of them made a point of embracing each other and walking arm-in-arm, to the apparent delirium of the crowd. Salmerón, 'his face transfused by a prophetic fury', as one left-wing Catalanist remembered, had earlier made a speech to demonstrators assembled in the Plaza de Cataluña in which he painted a visionary picture of a united Catalan community:

A few days ago, there might have been differences amongst you; now, there is nothing but a common aspiration, the same, identical spirit . . . this union of the living forces of Catalonia.[65]

Yet the celebrations contained obvious displays of different political agendas. The British diplomat who had warned about Catalan separatism would have been surprised by the presence of Spanish flags alongside those of Catalonia while national flags belonging to the Republican Lerrouxist clubs were conspicuously wrapped up in red cloth. When Salmerón and Rusiñol spoke to the crowds earlier on, they had stressed different strategies; the first saw the task of the new movement as 'the high and noble mission of redeeming Spain', while the second claimed that its purpose was to construct 'a regional Spain alongside a great Catalonia'.

In the procession, displays of devout Catholic sentiments competed with anti-clerical Republican banners. Behind manifestations of Catalan nationalism came an elaborate float made by the federal Republicans, much appreciated by the crowd according to a paper sympathetic to the federal cause. Pulled by six horses with grooms representing each region of Spain, the float carried the shield of each of the forty-nine provinces. In the centre, surrounded by foliage, was a large bust of the recently deceased federal leader and ex-President of the First Republic, Pi y Margall, for whom the assertion of Catalan rights was part of a campaign to devolve power from an artificially centralized government to local communities throughout Spain.[66] Lerroux, dismissing Solidaritat Catalana's attempts to unite 'the most incompatible elements: clericals and rationalists, monarchists and Republicans, liberals and absolutists, workers and bosses', asked sardonically, 'What superior force obliges us to make this sacrifice? Has our nation been invaded by foreigners?'[67]

---

[65] Ibid. The description of Salmerón is from Pere Coromines, *De la Solidaritat al catorze d'abril*, vol. 2 of *Diaris i records* (Barcelona, 1974), 11.

[66] *El Diluvio*, 21 May 1906.

[67] Alejandro Lerroux (*De la lucha*), 167.

In Madrid, the government received a telegram from the Civil Governor of Barcelona reporting a striking absence of workers in the demonstrations; in one incident, it claimed that the members of a Republican club to which Salmerón paid a visit during the day's events, hissed him and there were cries of 'Long live Lerroux!' Nevertheless, the Civil Governor warned the government that the demonstration was a very grave matter because it combined a protest against institutions with a 'coldness towards Spain'.[68] The fact that it was joined by delegations from Republicans in Valencia and by regionalists and Carlists from the Basque country, Navarra and Aragón appears to have escaped his notice but the spread of the Solidaritat Catalana model raised potentially serious problems for the government. Indeed, a year and a half later, a Galician version was set up, Solidaritat Gallega, and *La Veu* reported similar moves in Valencia, the Balearic islands and Extremadura.[69]

The Civil Governor's fears appeared to be borne out in the general elections of April the following year when Solidaritat Catalana almost swept the board in Barcelona. Campaigning on a moderate programme of regional autonomy and national regeneration, its candidates won over 80 per cent of the votes in the highest electoral turn-out—58 per cent of the eligible voters—ever registered in the city and one that was not to be repeated until the Second Republic. Even Lerroux lost his seat. Meeting later in a Madrid café, Cambó and other Catalanist politicians felt they were on the verge of a national breakthrough and a campaign was planned to take the Solidaritat message to the rest of Spain. 'We must go to the provinces', Cambó exclaimed, 'and demolish that whole network [of caciques].'[70]

But Solidaritat Catalana was a problematic alliance. From the outside, its members were harassed by supporters of Lerroux. Although they still belonged to the same party, the Unión Republicana, Lerrouxists and Salmerón's followers were at loggerheads over the latter's backing of Solidaritat Catalana. From mid-1906, Lerrouxist mobs had stoned the buildings and ransacked the press of their rivals. Catalanists had responded with belligerence. The growing climate of violence in the city was exacerbated by a wave of terrorism probably linked in part to the work of *agents provocateurs* and aggrieved police informers.[71] Such was the

[68] AHN archives, Ministerio de Gobernación, Serie A 41 A no. 5.

[69] Solidaritat Gallega's manifesto is published in *La Veu de Catalunya*, 25 Sep. 1907. See also '¡¡Desperta Galicia!!' in issue of 30 Sept.

[70] Quoted in Moles (*Lliga*), vol. 1, 77–8.

[71] For details of the violence, see Soldevilla (*El año, 1907; 1908*); Alvarez Junco (*El Emperador*), 324–8, and Joaquín Romero-Maura, 'Terrorism in Barcelona and Its Impact on

polarization between the solidarios (or supporters of Solidaritat Catalana) and the anti-solidarios that it was claimed each could be recognized by their clothes. And their respective presses poured out invective against each other and against the ethnic or class stereotypes that the other allegedly stood for.[72] The hostility had culminated, just before the local elections in April 1907, in the attempted assassination of Cambó, which had left him at death's door. It had been almost certainly the work of Lerrouxist supporters and the resulting outrage had undoubtedly contributed towards the massive swing of votes to the Solidaritat Catalana slate shortly afterwards.

At a deeper level, the polarization of political life in Barcelona was the result of the twin crisis to which we have referred throughout this book, that of modernization and political legitimacy. Lerroux was organizing the discontent of both the newly militant working class of the city and the traditionally restless marginal sectors of urban society, whose numbers had grown enormously since the end of the 1880s. The Lerrouxist vote in Barcelona was first and foremost a working-class vote and only secondarily an anti-Catalan vote by immigrants. What is striking, however, is that Catalanists and Republicans shared the same criticism of the corruption and incompetence of the Restoration system and a similar programme for the regeneration of Spain through honest elections and economic renewal.[73] The problem was that the project of each was hegemonized by class. Having lost the opportunity of drawing in the middle-class Catalanist vote by the rise of Solidaritat Catalana, Lerroux made a rhetorical lurch to the left in an attempt to shore up his electoral position. On the other hand, the hegemony of the right-wing representatives of the Lliga in the leadership of Solidaritat Catalana, in addition to its large conservative following, made the new movement an uncomfortable place for progressive or left-wing Catalans of whatever hue.

The contradictions within Solidaritat Catalana had been well understood by Maura when he was called on by the king to form a new government to replace that of the Liberals at the beginning of 1907. Maura's greatest ambition was to modernize political life in Spain by dismantling the Restoration system of patronage and encouraging widespread electoral participation; out of this regeneration of local politics, he hoped, the opportunity would emerge to build a new conservative party with authen-

[72] Romero Maura (*La Rosa*), 427–30.
[73] Alvarez Junco (*El Emperador*), 351–5.

tic social roots. Despite his own origins as a Mallorcan Catalan, Maura was hostile to Catalanism or any form of regional nationalism.[74] Moreover, the existence of Solidaritat was a potential threat to his project of political regeneration because it created a united front of left and right around regional interests. He could, however, let the 'fermentation of that mixture [Solidaritat Catalana] follow its logical course . . .', as he wrote later in private correspondence; 'the irreducible heterogeneity of its components would produce a salutary diversification of right and left, revolutionary people and law and order people, moderates and extremists'.[75]

But Maura also set out to woo sections of the Catalan bourgeoisie, who were already sympathetic towards his idea of 'revolution from above'. Francesc Cambó, now the leading spokesman of the Lliga, had established a close rapport with him since his first speech in parliament and the Catalan politician saw the Lliga as precisely the kind of party Maura was hoping to establish throughout Spain.[76] Indeed, there were many aspects of Maura's regenerationism which were attractive to conservative Catalanists, not least its heterogeneous mixture of pre-liberal tradition—corporatism and paternalism—and post-liberal economic nationalism—the use of state intervention to protect and develop industry. The Catalan bourgeoisie were tied to a culture of dependency on the state for protection from both foreign competitors and their own workers. Despite his distaste for regionalism, Maura offered Catalan industrialists an irresistible combination of ideological rapport and reformist vigour. Once again, they thought they had found their man in Madrid.[77] But Maura was a catalyst in Spanish political life. His uncompromising stance sharpened existing divisions and Solidaritat Catalana, already deeply divided by political and strategic differences, did not survive his efforts to legislate change.

Three issues in particular served to bring the divisions within Solidaritat Catalana to the surface. Both left and right within the united

[74] 'There is no greater evil, nor more terrible and dangerous germ', he had said in a speech in parliament, 'than a local party like Catalanism . . . The same error as with the Cubans is being repeated here . . . and I . . . am opposed, totally opposed to all species of particular concessions to Catalonia': quoted in C. S., 'El maurisme a Barcelona' *El Poble Català*, 23 Dec. 1905. See also 'En Maura', 17 Feb. 1906.

[75] Quoted in Romero Maura (*La Rosa*), 424.

[76] See the text of two of Cambó's speeches in Oct. 1907 in *La Veu de Catalunya* 6 Oct. and 20 Oct.

[77] Cambó's support for Maura's policies is clear in his correspondence with the latter during his 'long government': AM, Legajo 19, nos. 1–3. Indeed, Maura's friend and fellow Conservative, Angel Ossorio, wrote to Maura in 1911 that the two were like twins: Legajo 80.

front sought to get parliament to abrogate the Law of Jurisdictions against which they had joined together in the first place. But while the Lliga deputies were prepared to accept Maura's vague promise of a review of the law at a later date, the progressive nationalists opposed any delay.[78] Maura's attempt to introduce a new law against terrorism giving draconian powers to the authorities also divided the two wings of Solidaritat Catalana. But it was above all the new Premier's Law of Local Administration which broke the uneasy alliance between the Lliga people and progressive Catalanists. Both had agreed to work within parliament to modify the proposed law. For the left, this meant opposing outright Maura's proposal for corporate representation in local government. For the Lliga, on the contrary, the corporative vote was an essential part of the traditions of Catalan regionalism and a dyke against the dissolvent consequences of a wider franchise.[79] In order to put pressure on parliament, Cambó warned deputies that there was a new generation in Catalonia who despised all those present and that if the law was not ratified, the leadership of the Catalan movement might be swept aside by one more radical.[80]

The split was consummated by the beginning of 1909. In the local elections of May that year, Lerroux's Republicans (now calling themselves the Radical Party having been expelled from the Unión Republicana), took control of the Barcelona city council after left and right in Solidaritat Catalana presented separate slates. For the next few years, elections were contested by three major political formations, the Radicals, with some 32,000 votes, the Catalanist Republicans, with 25,000 votes approximately, and the Lliga, with around 18,000.[81]

The Tragic Week of July 1909 destroyed any lingering hopes that Solidaritat Catalana could be reconstituted. Catalan conservatives, unable to understand the social and economic roots of violence in Spanish society, sought to explain the behaviour of the mobs in terms of the backwardness of the lower classes. All the old class bogeys were wheeled out; the masses lacked education and discipline, they were prone to pantheistic bouts of violence, they had been ideologically poisoned by anarchists and

---

[78] Francesc Cambó, *Catalunya y la Solidaritat. Conferencia donada al Teatre Principal el día 26 de Maig de 1910* (Barcelona, 1910), 61–4.

[79] Ibid. 51. For the left's position see 'La Solidaritat Catalana i el sufragi universal', *El Poble Català*, 12 Dec. 1907.

[80] DSC, 26 Oct. 1907, no. 79, 2080–1.

[81] These figures correspond to the December municipal elections: Molas (*Lliga*), 86.

Lerrouxists.[82] The shocking events, graphically depicted in the news-papers, deepened the fear that lay in the heart of 'respectable society' throughout Europe since the French Revolution that one day the mobs would destroy it too. As the Lliga's senators and deputies warned in a manifesto, 'the generation that one day burned convents and churches will tomorrow burn factories and banks, houses and shops . . .'. The mob violence strengthened the already firm conviction amongst conservatives that the people were not ready for democracy, that greater social discip-line and a clamp-down on the proliferating forces of subversion were necessary.[83]

What made any *rapprochement* with the left wing of Solidaritat Catalana difficult was the perception amongst Lliga leaders that it had been partly responsible for stirring up the mobs by trying to compete with Lerroux for the working-class vote. Prat de la Riba wrote bitterly that 'some elements' in Solidaritat 'had organized a "competition" of radicalism'. For his part, Cambó blamed the disintegration of Solidaritat Catalana on the sectarianism of the left and their jealousy of his personal ascendancy within the new movement.[84] Neither accusation was entirely off the mark. The Catalan left, or Esquerra, were well aware that there was a consider-able political constituency for progressive Catalanism which was not ad-equately represented in the leadership of Solidaritat Catalana. Amongst many sections of the Barcelona middle classes, in particular, there was a strong Republican tradition which was hostile to both the Lliga and Lerroux's populist brand of Republicanism. Moreover, while Solidaritat Catalana continued to be associated with the Conservative establishment, the working-class vote would remain with Lerroux's Radicals.[85]

[82] For typical reactions, see Ramón Rucabado, 'L'Apoteosis', 26 Aug. 1909 (a.m.) and Lluis Durân i Ventosa, 'Solidaritat social', 14 Aug. 1909 (p.m.), both in *La Veu de Catalunya*.

[83] 'Manifest dels Senadors y Diputats regionalistes', *La Veu de Catalunya*, 18 Aug. 1909. For the 'pantheism' of the masses, see Ramon Rucabado, 'L'Apoteosis', ibid., 26 Aug. 1909; for similar reactions, see Lluis Durân y Ventosa, 'Solidaritat social', 14 Aug. and for the unpreparedness of the masses for democracy: 'Per la nostra educació', 9 Sept.

[84] Enric Prat de la Riba, 'El Radicalisme', *La Veu*, 3 Sept. 1909; Francesc Cambó (*Catalunya*), 21–40.

[85] And indeed when the Esquerra went to the polls separately, they appeared to pick up some of the Radical votes, though their main support clearly emanated from Catalanist voters. Details of the votes can be found in Molas (*Lliga*), 78–88. According to the Catalanist Republican Pere Coromines, 'Catalan tradition is democratic, and even if it were not, we could not allow this Barcelona of seventy thousand Republican votes to succumb to the arbitrary domination of a provincial oligarchy': 'Al prohoms de la Lliga Regionalista. Adeu Siau!', *El Poble Català*, 5 Dec. 1909. The Esquerra's candidates, however, were

It should be remembered that the Lerrouxists were not anti-Catalan but anti-Catalanist and their leader's lurid rhetoric was directed as much against the Madrid establishment as that of Barcelona. The Esquerra's bland reformism was no match for his radical populism. Indeed, privately, Prat de la Riba regretted that the Esquerra were not more left-wing; 'if they had been,' he said in a conversation with one of their leaders, 'they would have understood that their task was to attract our popular masses with a certain social radicalism . . . rather than trying to act like government ministers'. The resulting void on the left had been filled by the Lerrouxists.[86]

For their part, the Esquerra argued that the Lliga were partly to blame for the Tragic Week; by giving Solidaritat Catalana such a 'retrograde character', they allowed Lerrouxist demagoguery to flourish. In answer to Prat de la Riba's accusation that they were trying to compete with Lerroux, they countered that the Lliga were involved in their own competition with conservative forces to see who could be most right-wing.[87] A cartoon in the popular Republican paper portrayed the Esquerra before a tribunal of the Inquisition representing the Lliga; the judges ask, 'Do you wish to form an electoral alliance with us?' to which the Esquerra reply 'No!!! . . . we've been duped once too often'.[88]

The collapse of Solidaritat Catalana brought to an end the post-1898 Catalan challenge against the Restoration system. Its political components were too heterogeneous to maintain the alliance and indeed nurtured contradictory ambitions for it. After their earlier disappointment with Silvela, the Lliga's illusions in conservative regenerationism had been reawakened by Maura, even before the formation of Solidaritat Catalana. Francesc Cambó saw Maura's 'long government' of 1907–9 as the last hope for a regeneration of political life in Spain and Solidaritat

overwhelmingly middle-class. Of their seventeen candidates in the December 1909 local elections, eight were lawyers, six were classified as industrialists or landowners, one a university professor and another a journalist, and only one was a worker: *El Poble Català*, 6 Dec. 1909.

[86] Amadeu Hurtado, *Quaranta anys d'advocat. Historia del meu temps* (Barcelona, 1964), vol. 1, 179.

[87] 'Regionalistas y reaccionarios', *El Diluvio*, 8 and 14 Sept. 1909.

[88] *La Campana de Gracia*, 20 Nov. 1909. This view was succinctly expressed by an Esquerra leader, Ildefons Sunyol: 'Twice, Catalan forces of the right and the left have joined together and on both occasions the same thing happened; almost fatefully, the right imposed their leadership on the left and the block grew more and more conservative. This provoked the creation first and then the strengthening of another, radical block which has been not only anti-Catalanist but on occasion . . . has taken on a very unCatalan character!' ('El meu parer', *El Poble Català*, 17 Nov. 1909).

Catalana as the realization of the first stage of his 'revolution from above'.[89]

Having briefly shed their subordinate partnership with other Spanish élites, the Catalan bourgeoisie now returned to the fold, persuaded that they had more to gain by collaborating with reformist Conservatives in Madrid than by rebelling against the Restoration system. Unable to identify with progressive or left-wing Catalanist projects, their ideological instincts towards the pursuit of purely regionalist politics within the established order were encouraged by the rise of Maura. After the Tragic Week, moreover, any alternative was too terrifying to contemplate. Cambó wrote:

The July events have made many sensible Catalans understand the abyss of misery and desolation that the Republic would open up before our feet. The policy of the present Government represents a rectification—not yet as thorough as we would wish—of the policy of hostility against Catalonia pursued by [previous] governments of the monarchy.[90]

The explosion of popular protest and the anti-Catalanism of an increasingly interventionist army also counselled a return to the traditional relationship with Madrid. The writer Joan Maragall beautifully distilled the new pessimism of the Catalan bourgeoisie in a letter to a friend shortly after the Tragic Week:

I believe that *we, the ruling classes*, are not up to it and if we aren't, is it strange that the lower orders aren't either? All we have here are the troops [*la tropa*] (after so many years of Catalanism) and the mobs [*la turba*] (for all our civility) and between the mobs and the troops our life goes on.[91]

As for the progressive and left wings of Solidaritat Catalana, it became clear that while they remained subordinate partners of the movement they could not tap the deep well of popular support for policies linking the defence of Catalan rights with democratic reforms. A new Solidaritat, according to one Esquerra leader, could only be based on a left-wing alliance of the Esquerra and the Socialists modelled on that formed by the French radicals and Socialists; support for this alliance, in his overly optimistic vision, would be drawn from Catalan workers who had abandoned both anarchism and Lerrouxism.[92]

---

[89] *Memorias*, 133; 'El moment polítich' *La Veu*, 5 Nov. 1909. For further discussion, see Chap. 7.

[90] 'Al Brusi', *La Veu*, 13 Sept. 1909.

[91] Quoted in Benet (*Maragall*), 73–4.

[92] Gabriel Alomar, 'Orientacions cap a una Solidaritat venidera', *La Campana de Gracia*, 18 Dec. 1909.

Perhaps a more important reason for Solidaritat Catalana's demise was that, on a popular level at least, it had been a movement of protest, not an organization representing specific economic or social interests. This was both its strength and its weakness. As a Republican Catalanist paper argued a year later, 'what was mainly a feeling of popular indignation was taken to be an expression of Catalanist sentiment. These great movements have no solid base.'[93] The failure of the campaign to get the Law of Jurisdictions repealed, added to the bitter divisions between its two wings and the trauma of the Tragic Week, brought to a halt the momentum that had been generated by the *¡Cu-cut!* affair.

Nevertheless, Solidaritat Catalana profoundly transformed political life in Catalonia. It popularized and politicized what had been a largely apolitical and intellectual movement.[94] Through it, many Catalans acquired a new sense of nationhood based on a common ethnic and linguistic identity. This tended to displace older loyalties ranging from an affection for the monarchy to an attachment to the *patria chica*, or village or local area. In an article in 1907, Maragall vividly described the awakening of nationalist feelings among ordinary people during a political meeting:

You should have seen these country people at first as they entered the meeting place, suspicious by nature, thrifty with their feelings because of their harsh struggle for a living from the soil, looking out of the corner of their eyes and with a cold, slightly mocking smile on their lips. But bit by bit, the words got through to them and their faces began to change and lose colour; the feeling of patriotism, so deep within their hearts and therefore so pure and strong, began to spread through their bodies and they trembled and their eyes lit up and . . . Oh miracle! in the end they were weeping.[95]

Yet the source of Catalana nationalism was as diverse as its expression. The peasant who wept with new-found patriotism and the textile magnate who substituted Catalan for Castilian Spanish in public were responding to different impulses. At one extreme, Catalanism was the consequence of modernization; migration, the spread of railways, the growth of towns, and so on often meant that local identities began to be subsumed by a wider sense of collectivity. The weak national projection of the Spanish

[93] Fulmen, 'La qüestió catalana', *La Campana de Gracia*, 12 Nov. 1910.
[94] Through Solidaritat, according to a leader of the Esquerra, Catalanism became a 'school of politics', moving from federalism to autonomy, merging country-bred regionalism with city-based federalism: Gabriel Alomar, 'Sobre la representació històrica de la Solidaritat', *La Campana de Gracia*, 4 Dec. 1909.
[95] 'L'alçament', *La Veu*, 13 Apr. 1907. Cambó argued that previously, 'royalty was stronger than nation'; now the immense majority of Catalans were 'a political being with a national consciousness': *Memorias*, p. 175.

state, its inability, for example, to establish a universal educational system
or offer a set of national symbols and rituals, allowed regional nationalisms
to become the most important focus of these new self-perceptions. At the
other extreme, Catalanism was the result of the crisis of legitimacy in
Spain following the loss of the Empire, a reaction, that is, against the
failure of the state to uphold the interests of Spain as they were defined by
broad sections of the Catalan population. Thus for many, Catalanism was
compatible with Spanish patriotism in that it offered an alternative model
for the regeneration of Spain. While he wrote movingly about the awakening of Catalan sentiments, Maragall could also write 'Long live
Spain . . . the true Spain!'[96]

[96] 'Visca Espanya', *Articles Polítics* (Edicions de la Magraña, 1988), 133-4.

6

The Rifle Without a Target: The Military in the Aftermath of the Disaster

OF all sections of Spanish society, the military was that most traumatized by the defeat of 1898. The loss of the remaining colonies had resulted in a considerable erosion of the army's political influence and the disappearance of an important source of financial benefits. Moreover, the Disaster burned a deep sense of injustice on the minds of professional officers. According to widespread military opinion, the navy had been needlessly humiliated by an incompetent government which had failed, as its predecessors had failed, to create a modern fleet able to do battle on an equal footing with the American warships. In its own self-perception, the army had fought bravely against overwhelming odds and had been forced by the politicians to surrender on degrading terms. Having battled to defend the honour of Spain on behalf of the Spanish people, the military were shocked to discover that many Spaniards blamed them for the defeat. While in 1897 the generals were cheered by the crowds, they were jeered at after the Disaster. Officers were jostled in the streets, humiliating jokes were made at their expense in carnivals and street festivals and half the press seemed to be out to insult them.[1]

The Disaster threw officers on the defensive and like insecure people they responded with aggression. While the military press[2] lashed out at all critics, groups of angry officers took action on their account against newspapers considered to have insulted the armed forces. This sort of violence was an old tradition amongst the military; in the aftermath of the Disaster, physical attacks on the press by officers multiplied. On 1 May 1900, for

---

[1] 'Militares y paisanos', *La Correspondencia Militar*, 15 Feb. 1899; 'Remedio radical', 13 May 1899; 'Graves colisiones', *El Imparcial*, 13 May 1899. After a riot in Vigo in Aug. 1898, *El Ejército Español* called on the government to suppress such demonstrations of anti-military feeling by the 'loutish mob' ('A ponerse en guardia', 16 Aug. 1898).

[2] Two kinds of military press could be distinguished, the so-called politico-military press, published outside the armed forces largely for a military readership, and the professional military press. Since there are no fundamental differences of opinion between the two, both will be referred to as the military press.

example, fifty officers in plain clothes destroyed the print-shop of the Valencian weekly paper belonging to the fiery Republican novelist Blasco Ibáñez, *El Progreso*, in retaliation for publishing an anti-military poem; the assailants were then besieged in the railway station by an angry crowd and only got away thanks to the intervention of the local Civil Guard. Elsewhere, newspapers that dared print unfavourable references to the army were subjected to assaults or threats of violence.[3] The anti-press violence, as we saw in Chapter 5, culminated in the assault on the Catalanist papers *¡Cu-cut!* and *La Veu de Catalunya* in 1905, and led to the Law of Jurisdictions which awarded the military extensive powers of censorship over newspapers.

The latent scorn felt by many officers towards the politicians of the Restoration regime was immeasurably deepened by the apparently inept handling of the wars by the successive governments. Dark threats were made in parliament and in the military press that the army would take over and sweep aside the old order. In the Senate, General Weyler was goaded by the Conde de las Almenas' intemperate accusations against the military into stating ominously that unless the government protected the army's reputation, 'it will have to take justice into its own hands'.[4] The military's long-held suspicion not just of the political parties but of parliamentary rule itself was strengthened by the Disaster. In an article in June 1899, the military daily *La Correspondencia Militar* declared:

Parliamentarism, which has been progressively discredited since some time ago, is now revealing itself to be incapable of anything good or useful or great for the Nation . . . The parliamentary system and government . . . has lost all confidence and prestige in the conscience of the Nation . . . there is no other remedy except temporary dictatorship.

Instead of parliament, the paper proposed a form of corporate representation on the lines of the medieval parliaments of Castile and Aragón, a model that was to become an obsession of the right.[5]

---

[3] For the assault on *El Progreso*, see *Diario de Barcelona*, 7 May 1900 and Ramir Reig, *Obrers i ciutadans. Blasquisme i moviment obrer. Valencia, 1898–1906* (Valencia, 1982), 247–8. Other incidents include an assault on staff of *El Correo de Guipúzcoa* by naval officers (*El Imparcial*, 1 Sept. 1901) and threats against the Alcoy newspaper, *La Humanidad* (Manuel Ballbé, *Orden público y militarismo en la España constitucional (1812–1983)* (Madrid, 1983), 277.

[4] DSC (Senate), 12 Sept. 1898.

[5] 'El remedio, la dictadura', 27 June 1899. For a similar view, shared by most of the military press, see the *Correo Militar* editorials, 'Cuestión previa', 13 Oct. 1898, and 'Ni honradas, ni patriotas', 3 Apr. 1900.

Amongst the current military leaders untainted by the Disaster, however, there were none prepared to stage a coup. General Polavieja had briefly contemplated seizing power to ensure stability in the aftermath of the wars but had prudently decided to seek a more legal way to further his aims. The most likely hero of the hour, General Weyler, was a staunch supporter of the Constitution, for all his ruthlessness as a military strategist. On his return from Cuba in October 1897, he had been courted in vain by Carlists and Republicans alike, who had each sent a boat to the harbour where Weyler's ship had anchored.[6] When approached by two fellow generals soon after the Disaster with the suggestion that the army should rise up, he declined to lead the coup or even to take part.[7]

In fact, for all the threats of the military press, there was little likelihood of a coup. It would not have had widespread support among civilians nor would the army have been united. Indeed, amongst the leading generals of the time there could not have been greater differences: Polavieja was an ex-sergeant, a devoutly religious and politically conservative man; Martínez Campos (who died in 1901) was a staunchly monarchist liberal whose military strategy of concession had been at the opposite pole of Weyler's; Weyler himself, a Liberal supporter until he was dismissed from his post in Cuba in 1897, was well known for his anti-clerical views; Luque, on the other hand, was suspected of harbouring Republican sympathies.[8] The ominous but vague threats of military spokesmen were more of a knee-jerk response to the public humiliation occasioned by the Disaster than part of a considered political strategy.

In any case, officers were too much on the defensive and too absorbed in the problems of demobilization to contemplate a military take-over. Much space in the military press was devoted to the acute professional

---

[6] Fernández Almagro (*Historia Política*), vol. 2, 432.

[7] Julio Romano, *Weyler. El hombre de hierro* (Madrid, 1934), 143–4, and José Ramón Alonso, *Historia política del ejército español* (Madrid, 1974), 427. Weyler also failed to respond to an invitation by Lord Ashburnham to meet the Carlist Pretender, Don Carlos, on board the English lord's yacht off Majorca (Ibid. 433–4 n. 39). Weyler later opposed the dictatorship of Primo de Rivera on the grounds it was unconstitutional, for which he was arrested, though subsequently absolved.

[8] Indeed, amongst the officers' ranks there were a number of Republicans, though most Republican supporters were non-commissioned officers or rank-and-file soldiers. For Luque see Alonso (*Historia*), 450 and 461 n. 29. Between 1878 and 1911, there were at least six Republican uprisings in Spanish garrisons. The organization responsible for the uprisings in the early 1880s was the *Unión Republicana Militar*, an offshoot of Manuel Ruiz Zorrilla's Republicans. It was formed in 1880 and had members in 22 garrisons: Gabriel Cardona, *El poder militar en la España contemporánea hasta la guerra civil* (Madrid, 1983); see also Alvarez Junco (*Emperador*), Chap. 3.

problems arising from the abrupt termination of the war. Once the badly handled business of repatriation was completed, the military and the government were faced with the conundrum of what to do with the excessive number of officers left over from the wars. The number of soldiers still in service at the end of 1898 amounted to around 80,000. Commanding this standing army were 499 generals, almost 600 colonels, and 24,000 or more officers of lower rank, that is, one general for every 160 soldiers and one officer for every three men approximately. With a standing army of 180,000, France had six times fewer officers than Spain. The disproportion in the Navy was even more striking: after the destruction of two out of Spain's three squadrons, there were 142 admirals left for two warships.[9] Moreover, the wars had resulted in a spate of promotions and decorations which had created chaos in the officer ranks and a sense of injustice among those who had not served abroad: some 17,000 citations and military crosses had been awarded to officers on duty in the colonies (as well as 341,000 to soldiers out of a total of 350,000 rank-and-file troops).

There was no disagreement about the need to effect some reductions in the number of officers. In General Polavieja's abortive budget of 1899, 12 million pesetas had been set aside for redundancy out of a total of 28 million.[10] By 1908 some 10,000 officers, a large majority from the Reserve List, would have retired or been made redundant under the generous terms offered by the government, leaving only around 14,000 officers on active service.[11] The real problem at the end of the wars concerned the distribution of such compensation (whether, for example, officers on the Reserve List were to receive as much as those on the Active List); the lack of mobility for those remaining on the Reserve; and the substantial cut in officers' pay, amounting to up to half of their salary, that took place as a result of the termination of the war, exacerbating what they claimed to be an already low income.[12] There were other difficult issues to resolve as well, such as the imbroglio of professional scales inherited from the policy of easy promotions during the wars and the need to place redundant military personnel into civilian jobs.

For at least two years after the Disaster, the military were as engrossed in these professional matters as they were with the political

[9] Figures from Alonso (*Historia política*), 439–42 and Julio Busquets, *El militar de carrera en España. Estudio de sociología militar*, (Barcelona, 1971, 2nd edn.), 25.

[10] *La Correspondencia Militar*, 4 May 1899.

[11] Alonso (*Historia política*), 449.

[12] Jorge Cachinero, 'Intervencionismo y reforma militares en España a comienzos del siglo XX', *Cuadernos de Historia Contemporánea*, no. 10 (1988), 155–84.

situation.[13] Moreover, they were acutely conscious of the weaknesses of army organization exposed by the war. Successive Ministers of War— Polavieja, Linares, Weyler, and Luque—drew up reform projects to tackle both the problem of promotions and that of internal structures embracing territorial organization, administrative overmanning, and overcentralization. Although these plans were welcomed by the military press,[14] little came of them, largely because of the vulnerability of governments to conflicting military pressure; between October 1897 and October 1909, there were fifteen different cabinets and the post of Minister of War was re-shuffled twenty times. Liberal and Conservative cabinets were also more concerned with cutting military expenditure, as part of a compulsive effort to reduce the state deficit, than reorganizing the armed forces. They failed, for example, to make military service compulsory until 1911, despite widespread support for such a measure, especially amongst officers themselves.[15]

All these questions had to be solved within the narrow limits of a state budget deeply in debt as a result of the war. The question of the budget concerned not simply the resolution of problems inherited from the wars but also the future of the armed forces. Despite a progressive reduction in numbers, and indeed partly because this restructuring was accompanied by generous compensation, the army remained an over-staffed, under-equipped, poorly trained, relatively badly paid, and inefficient fighting-force. Even worse, there was virtually no navy, at a time when naval power was the principal means whereby nations and colonies were defended or extended. According to military opinion, the future of the nation itself hinged on the state of its armed forces. Much was made of the French model; France's extraordinary recovery after the disaster at Sedan in 1870 had been due to its programme of military reconstruction.[16] Without a powerful army and navy, Spain risked the loss of her remaining posses-

[13] For examples of this preoccupation see 'Problemas militares pendientes', *El Correo Militar*, 28 Feb. 1900 and 'Hay que hacer algo', *El Progreso Militar*, 9 Oct. 1900.

[14] Looking back on the year 1901, for example, *La Correspondencia Militar* warmly approved the performance of successive Ministers of War: '1901–2', *La Correspondencia Militar*, 1 Jan. 1902.

[15] Cachinero ('Intervencionismo'). The imposition of compulsory military service would have alienated many powerful supporters of the dynastic parties who were able to buy exemption for their sons under existing legislation. General Martínez Campos had also suggested towards the end of the century that it would be dangerous to have educated recruits in the army: 'one cannot bring into the Army a revolutionary yeast of 20 to 25,000 young men educated in advanced principles because it would cause the ignorant mass to ferment and would very seriously undermine the ruling order': quoted in Pirala (*España*), 171.

[16] 'Hay que hacer patria', *La Correspondencia Militar*, 19 May 1899.

sions in Africa and indeed the possibility of a military invasion of the peninsula itself.[17]

The wars had left a deep sense of insecurity amongst the military. Spain's traditional allies had deserted her. Britain had supported the enemy, prompting fears during the war with the United States that Gibraltar might be taken over by the Americans. Moreover, increasing competition among the major European powers for control in the Mediterranean and in Africa was creating acute international tensions. If only for defensive reasons, Spain had to embark on an immediate programme of rearmament, according to the widespread view of the officer class.[18] In contrast to much business opinion, the military press showed relatively little interest in expanding Spain's role in Morocco, at least for the first few years after the Disaster.[19] With the sobriety born of defeat, *El Ejército Español* commented at the end of 1898,

Unlike those café politicians and armchair commentators (*comentaristas de tertulia*), we don't believe our future lies in Africa; at present our future lies nowhere.

Though destined eventually to rule Morocco, the writer continued, Spain needed to reorganize her forces simply to defend the territory she already controlled.[20]

What the military meant by reorganization was above all a massive programme of investment in arms and equipment.[21] While there were many well-meaning references in the military press to the need for internal restructuring to ensure the creation of an efficient modern fighting-force, their lobbies were concerned above all to ensure the highest possible slice of the budget for the military.[22] Their campaign for greater military

[17] The *Memorial de Artillería* felt in 1900 that war with Britain was 'likely': 'Voz de alarma', Jan.-June 1900, 71–6.

[18] For example, the editorial, 'Patria, ejército y marina', in *La Correspondencia Militar*, 9 Jan. 1899.

[19] During these years there were occasional articles in the military press urging action in Morocco (e.g. *El Correo Militar*, 3, 5, and 19 May 1900, *El Ejército Español*, 12 Sept. 1899, *La Correspondencia Militar*, 14 Feb. 1902) but professional matters and budgetary problems dominate its pages.

[20] F. P. y E., 'Pensemos en mañana', 10 Dec. 1898.

[21] For the military campaign for greater expenditure on arms see for example the editorial in *La Correspondencia Militar*, 'Patria, ejército y marina', 9 Jan. 1899 and 'Crónica', *El Ejército Español*, 9 Dec. 1898.

[22] See, for example, the two open letters to the Minister of War by the editor of *Memorial de Artillería* 'Crónica Interior', July–Dec. 1900, 516–19, and Jan.–June 1901, 68–71; 'Patria, Ejército y marina', *La Correspondencia Militar* (editorial), 9 Jan. 1899. For an example of the military lobby, see *El Globo*'s report in 1899 on the visit of 130 infantry officers to Polavieja on the eve of cabinet talks on the budget (25 Aug. 1899).

expenditure exasperated Antonio Maura, the politician most identified with the policy of re-building the fleet, who remarked scornfully that the military showed

a total absence of that supreme concern for converting the armed forces, within the limits of the budget, into the most efficient possible force for the defence of the territory, which is the only thing that justifies the immense sacrifice the Nation has to make to support them.[23]

However, the military were equally exasperated by the failure of governments to recognize that the first priority of defence was rearmament. Their sense of alienation towards the political system grew all the deeper as a result.[24]

Military policy on defence was part of a wider though ill-defined programme for the redemption of Spain. The central plank of this barely articulated programme was the construction of a new nationalism. 'Hay que hacer patria' ('We must construct the fatherland'), cried an editorial of *La Correspondencia Militar* on 19 May 1899. The true interests of Spain had been betrayed by the Restoration system; like a moth, caciquismo had eaten away the national fabric.[25] It was the turn of the military, the heart of Spain, to lead the nation into a new era. The only force capable of carrying through this transformation was the army because it was above narrow party interests and above the class struggle and was, besides, the only healthy institution left in the country.[26]

For all their common rhetoric, the regeneration envisaged by the military had little to do with that advocated by the Chambers of Commerce and Agriculture. Both had drawn completely different lessons from the Disaster. While officers believed passionately that the country needed a stronger army and navy, the Chambers were calling for a cut in military expenditure in order to finance investment in infrastructure. This disregard for the interests of the armed forces was foolhardy, the military believed, because without their support the regenerationist movement was unlikely to succeed. 'In their wisdom, those apostles of revolution have wounded the military classes to the quick', wrote *El Ejército Español*, 'and, driven by a suicidal instinct, have divorced themselves completely from them.' Indeed, the regenerators' proposals were seen simply as an

---

[23] Quoted in *La Correspondencia Militar*, 'Destruyendo prestigios', 20 Jan. 1902.
[24] Cachinero ('Intervencionismo'), 168.
[25] 'Algo sobre la formación del soldado' (F.P.E.), *El Ejército Español*, 9 Dec. 1898.
[26] 'Frente a frente', *La Correspondencia Militar*, 9 Feb. 1899.

'ignoble campaign against the Army', aimed at destroying the 'only healthy element in the country'.[27]

This military phobia towards the regenerators contained more than a hint of anti-capitalism. In the emerging nationalism of the army, there was little room for the economic market, for private enterprise, for the Europeanization advocated by the regenerators. Bourgeois values were seen as essentially egotistical and were therefore anti-patriotic. The diatribes of the military press against the 'grocers' of the National Union reveal the contradictory impulses within the army, a mixture of residual populism and embryonic corporatism.[28] Basilio Paraíso, one of the founders of the National Union and the archetypal small businessman, became the target of a ferocious campaign of abuse. 'He has emerged', exclaimed one military paper, 'like worms do when decomposition sets in.'[29] When the businessmen staged their tax 'strike', military impatience boiled over: 'Enough of shop closures;' cried *La Correspondencia Militar*, 'enough of Chambers of Commerce meetings; enough of daylight conspiracy against public tranquility . . . And if reason is not enough, if persuasion does not prevail, then bayonets will.'[30]

Contrary to the regenerators, the military believed that the first priority of Spain's regeneration was the reconstruction of the armed forces. In order to achieve this, civil society 'had the moral and material duty to sacrifice itself for the army . . .'[31] Industry had to be geared towards arms production, the army had to be professionalized and military service had to be compulsory. This was not simply a militaristic programme; the military version of regenerationism also laid stress on the internal reform of the country; education and training, honest and firm administration and the reform of the Church were its three fundamental demands.

That sections of the military press should support democratic reforms

[27] 'Crónica', 17 Oct. 1899 and 'Tiros al ejército' (A.C.) *El Ejército Español*, 7 Oct. 1898; A+B, *Apuntes en defensa del honor del Ejército* (Madrid, 1898), 208.

[28] *La Correspondencia Militar*, 27 June 1899, and *Correo Militar*, 'La Unión Nacional' (editorial) 25 Apr. 1900; and successive issues in June 1900. According to the *El Ejército Español*, Basilio Paraíso 'could have become the founder of the crusade of the honourable, enthusiastic and humble against the sceptics and sordid potentates of all classes' (Incognito, 'Crónica', 1 Dec. 1899).

[29] 'Crónica', *El Ejército Español*, 10 Aug. 1899.

[30] 'El único remedio', 27 June 1899. The formation of the National Union led to an almost obsessive campaign of denigration by sections of the military press, such as *El Correo Militar*, between Apr. and June 1900.

[31] 'El Ejército y el pueblo', *La Correspondencia Militar*, 15 May 1899; 'El Ejército y la política', 17 Jan. 1899.

should not come as a surprise. It is easily forgotten, considering the subsequent role of the military in Spain, that the army at the turn of the century contained a wide range of political tendencies. During the early part of the nineteenth century, the army had embraced many progressive elements. A large number of generals had been freemasons and radical liberals and many had risen from the ranks, profiting from the opportunities for promotion offered by the repeated civil wars of the nineteenth century. Most had been opposed to the *ancien régime* and many had been at odds with the oligarchy. Regimes were made and unmade by generals in a battle between liberals and absolutists and then between progressive or moderate liberals and conservatives. The army had even been tempted by Republicanism. However, the chaotic and divisive experience of the First Republic had eroded the influence of Republican ideology. Under the terms of the Restoration Settlement of 1876, the army finally withdrew from the political arena which it had dominated for so long in exchange for a tacit pledge that governments would not intervene unduly in military affairs and for considerable political and financial benefits accruing from its control of the colonies. Instead, the military became the guarantor of the establishment. Under the 1878 Law of the Constitution of the Army, one of its main functions became that of defending the nation against internal enemies.

Cánovas then strengthened constitutional rule by integrating the top layer of officers through selective promotions and the award of lucrative political appointments, while the most distinguished generals were given aristocratic titles. The army had been further wedded to the regime by the cultivation of Alfonso XII as an army man. Moreover, the continued menace of Carlism, against which the army had fought repeatedly, helped to ensure its loyalty to the restored monarchy. In the last quarter of the century, two new threats appeared to have emerged that also required a consensus between the rulers and the military: the rise of organized labour protest and the emergence of regional movements for autonomy. Both these new movements helped to consolidate the rightward drift of officers in subsequent years.[32]

[32] In a speech in the Madrid Ateneo, Cánovas declared, 'For some time now, perhaps for ever, armies will be the robust bulwark of the present social order, and invincible dyke against attempts at illegality by the proletariat who will gain nothing except vainly to shed their blood in unequal battles': quoted in Ballbé (*Orden*), 248–9. For an analysis of the military in the nineteenth century, see Stanley G. Payne, *Politics and the Military in Modern Spain* (Stanford, 1967); Caroline P. Boyd, *Praetorian Politics in Liberal Spain* (North Carolina, 1979), and Daniel R. Headrick, *Ejército y política en España (1866–1898)* (Madrid, 1981).

The price that had to be paid for neutralizing the army as a political force was the postponement of military reform.[33] It had become reconciled to the regime but neither integrated nor professionalized. Officers continued to claim they were poorly paid and educated and their social status remained low. Until the colonial wars of 1895–8, many spent tedious lives in provincial garrisons trying to make ends meet.[34] Yet the military had never ceased to intervene when it felt its interests were threatened or its sense of honour challenged. Threats or action against newspapers judged to have insulted the armed forces were frequent in the years preceding the Disaster.[35] The attempt in 1887 by the Minister of War, General Cassola, to introduce much-needed reforms was blocked by the generals and the specialized forces such as the artillery, and subsequent efforts had been directed more at reducing the number of troops than making the forces more efficient.[36] Indeed, the unpreparedness of the military for the 1898 war had been due as much to their unwillingness to contemplate reform as to government ineptitude.

While the bulk of the officer class came to identify with the established social order, they by no means approved of all its values. All sections of the military asserted the need for hierarchy, order and stability, national unity, and rearmament. Within that political frame, however, there existed a range of views opposed to elements of the dominant ideology and practice of the establishment. There was an almost unanimous opposition in the army press to caciquismo.[37] A strong vein of anti-clericalism also ran through military opinion which had its origins in the long-drawn-out struggle against Carlism during the nineteenth century. One of the leading military dailies openly attacked the Church's resistance to change in

[33] Rafael Núñez Florencio, 'El presupuesto de paz: una polémica entre civiles y militares en la España finisecular', *Hispania*, XLIX/171 (1989), 197–234.
[34] Joaquín Romero-Maura, *The Spanish Army and Catalonia. The 'Cu-cut! Incident' and the Law of Jurisdictions, 1905–1906* (Beverly Hills, 1976).
[35] For example, the arrest of the director of *El Ejército Español* in Jan. 1889; the destruction of the printing presses of *El Resumen* and *El Globo* in 1895; the assault on the Havana paper *El Reconcentrado* in 1897.
[36] For the Cassola project, see Fernando María Puell de la Villa, 'El general Cassola, reformista militar de la Restauración', *Revista de Historia Militar*, no. 45 (1978), 173–96 and by the same author, 'Las reformas del general Cassola', *Revista de Historia Militar*, no. 46 (1979), 143–74. See also Antonio Pirala, *España y la Regencia. Anales de diez y seis años (1885–1902)* (Madrid, 1904), vol. 1, 170–2.
[37] Even before the wars, General Cassola, in a letter to a friend, had referred to 'the odious tyranny of *caciquismo* . . . To dream of any beneficial reform, while such a state of affairs continues, is a vain quimera, and a revolution is necessary . . . to do away with all that gang of men and procedures, without changing the form of government, which is after all incidental', Pirala (*España*), vol. 2, 171.

an editorial in 1902, stating that 'the triumph of liberty and the victory of the democratic spirit that inspires the Army and the country makes it vital to spare no effort to bring to an end this all-absorbing clericalism'.[38] The same paper enthusiastically endorsed the new programme of anti-clerical and social reforms launched in 1902 by the radical Liberal, José Canalejas. In a cartoon in one issue, he was presented as the new Cid, mounted on a steed named Democracy.[39] It was significant that Canalejas was a firm supporter of strengthening the army.

On the question of democracy, however, the military were ambiguous. On one hand, their spokesmen praised radical reformist programmes as long as they favoured the interests of the army; on the other, they made frequent, albeit vague, references to the need for a dictatorship of the army based on the consent of the people. This was in part the residue of the authoritarian populism typical of the late nineteenth-century military. Like other movements of opinion at the time, the people were seen as downtrodden and deserving. The army perceived itself as the custodian of the rights of the poor and of the working classes in general, the 'national mother-in-law' as one paper put it.[40] The rich, on the other hand, were sometimes portrayed as selfish. In the aftermath of the Disaster, one military paper went so far as to advocate seizing part of their assets by taxing them to up to half of their income; while the poor had made terrible sacrifices during the wars, it argued, the rich had shown insufficient patriotism.[41]

Like other movements of opinion also, the army saw the education of the people as the key to Spain's regeneration. While there was a genuine current within the military that envisaged a social, educational, and moralizing mission for the army, the overwhelming consensus viewed education as more the inculcation of national values than the raising of the general level of culture.[42] *El Ejército Español* argued that the regeneration of the people should start with military service, during which conscripts

[38] *La Correspondencia Militar*, 'El clericalismo en acción', 9 May 1902.
[39] 18 June 1902. See also issues on 26 May and 5 June of the same year. *La Correspondencia Militar* placed its faith in the parliamentary action of the Moret government in 1902, in which Canalejas was Minister of Agriculture: 'El patriotismo y el parlamento', 14 Apr. 1902. It is interesting that as late as 1906, *La Correspondencia Militar* invited such staunch Republicans as José Nakens, Francos Rodríguez, and Jacinto Benavente to contribute to the front page of its special issue on 14 Mar. celebrating the Army's feast-day.
[40] 'La suegra nacional. El pueblo y el ejército', *El Correo Militar*, 7 May 1900.
[41] 'La solución', *El Ejército Español*, 7 July 1898 and 'Los pobres y los ricos', 2 Nov. 1899.
[42] Manuel Espadas Burgos, 'La Institución Libre de Enseñanza y la formación del militar español durante la Restauración', in *Temas de Historia Militar*, vol. 1 (Zaragoza, 1982). See also Joaquín Fanjul, *Misión social del Ejército* (Madrid, 1907)

should learn respect for the uniform and for the Nation.[43] Where people did not show this respect, they were branded as uncouth or worse. The angry scenes in Vigo in August 1898, when large crowds demonstrated against a general returning from the wars, prompted a military paper to call them 'loutish plebs'.[44]

As with the intellectuals, the rise of labour protest in the 1890s had begun to challenge this tradition of military paternalism. Since there was no modern police force responsible for law and order, the Civil Guard and the *Carabineros* being para-military forces, the army was increasingly used as a last resort to put down strikes and demonstrations. The military were acutely conscious of the resulting gap that was growing between workers and the army.[45] Unamuno himself noted in 1906 the increasing unpopularity of the army amongst both the rural and urban populations.

The army is not popular. In the countryside, amongst the rural population, as I have been able to observe more than once, those who served in the ranks, those who have returned from military service, conspire against its popularity. Added to this is the profound antipathy in the cities here and everywhere that workers in factories and workshops feel towards the armed forces. Above all, if these armed forces have intervened in strike disturbances.[46]

The changing attitude of the military towards the working-class movement can be traced in the course of the metal strike in Barcelona in 1902. In the early part of the dispute, an article in a military daily known for its relatively liberal views, *La Correspondencia Militar*, took the side of the metalworkers against that of the employers, the latter defined as 'the rich, with their traditional egoism and with their proven ambitions'. As a result of the employers' obstinacy, the paper asserted, the army had been forced to impose law and order and confront the workers.

[T]he powerful have turned out to be the revolutionaries, those who upset the soldier, forcing him to go out into the streets, those who set the military against the civilian when civilian and military should come together in a fraternal embrace that will solidly invigorate the country's organisms.[47]

However, as the dispute intensified, the same paper began to modify its views. In successive editorials, it stated that social conflict threatened to

---

[43] 9 Dec. 1898 and 23 Nov. 1899 ('Moral militar. Educación del pueblo').

[44] 'Populacho socz', 'A ponerse en guardia', ibid., 16 Sept. 1898.

[45] In a letter to *El Ejército Español*, for example, an infantry officer wrote lamenting this widening gulf: 'The Army and a people should be united' (12 July, 1899). An editorial in *La Correspondencia Militar* ('El estado de guerra', 7 Jan. 1902) argued against the imposition of martial law because it set army against workers and eroded the former's neutrality.

[46] 'La Patria y el Ejército', *Obras Completas* (Madrid, 1951) vol. 3, 975–91.

[47] R. Mesa de la Peña, 'Bocetos', 6 Jan. 1902.

engulf Spain; Spaniards were ungovernable because they were illiterate and uncouth; workers were ignorant and ambitious, prey to the manipulations of separatists, anarchists and Carlists; unless they were educated and unless the army was strengthened, a disaster beckoned.[48] By mid-February the editor had decided that social agitation was the most urgent problem facing Spain:

What is undermining our country is social indiscipline and we have to bring an end to this danger before a catastrophe occurs which will drag us all into the bottomless abyss of discredit and ruin.[49]

To overcome labour conflict, *La Correspondencia Militar* advocated more than simple repression; what was needed as well was legislation to prevent the exploitation of workers so that there would be no excuse for strike action.[50]

For the most part, however, the army was more obsessed by the apparent dangers posed by Catalanism than by labour agitation. Workers challenged economic and social structures whereas the regionalists threatened the integrity of the nation itself.[51] More than any other movement in Spain, it was regionalism, in particular the Catalan variety, which gave shape to the new nationalism of the military. In their violent reaction to the growth of Catalanism, there was a suffusion of wounded pride, elemental machismo, and a quite overt racism. Little distinction was made between the different wings of the Catalan movement. For the overwhelming bulk of the military, Catalanism meant separatism.

To understand their obsessive campaign against Catalan nationalists, we have to remember the extreme insecurity felt by the military after the loss of the last remnants of the Empire. The sacrifice of Cuba, in particular, had created amongst officers a psychosis of national disintegration. The colonies had been seen as an extension of Spain, as part of the fatherland. Thousands of officers had served in them before and during the wars and many, of course, had died in defence of the Empire. The demand for autonomy for Catalonia and the Basque Country was considered the thin end of the wedge, a continuation of that process of disintegration. *La Correspondencia Militar* spelt out the parallels in July 1899:

[48] 'Consecuente', 14 Jan. 'Ingobernables', 15 Jan. and 'Remedios contra el conflicto' 18 Feb. 1902.
[49] 'Síntomas', 17 Feb. 1902.
[50] 'El Ejército y las Huelgas', 6 June 1902.
[51] Payne (*Politics*), 94. 'Los sucesos de Barcelona', *La Correspondencia Militar*, 2 Jan. 1902.

In Barcelona, separatism is growing in a very similar way to the form in which it appeared in Cuba . . . There, as in Catalonia, the separatists' fig-leaf is autonomy . . . We do not want to separate from the mother country—the Cubans used to say—but we want administrative autonomy. Everyone now knows the consequences; we feel and we weep over the results today.[52]

It should also be remembered that throughout the nineteenth century the military had fought to create a united and centralized nation against the centrifugal forces of Carlism, federalism, and cantonalism. Their function was the defence of sovereignty and their identity was based on a concept of national integrity rooted in a traditional reading of history which valued unity and Empire under Castilian hegemony; this was perfectly reconcilable with support for nineteenth-century liberalism which had sought to sweep aside the remnants of the *ancien régime* and integrate the nation into a modern state. The putative loss of Catalonia, with its wealth, expertise, and tax contributions to the Exchequer, would indeed be a mortal blow to Spain. As one military newspaper put it, 'the colonial empire which we once possessed is nothing next to the dismemberment and dissolution of Spain'.[53]

On a less dramatic plane, any concession to Catalan demands would undermine the military's project to rebuild the armed forces and regenerate the nation; autonomy for the Catalan bourgeoisie meant above all controlling their own tax revenue, so depriving the central government of vital funds. The military version of regeneration, with its stress on centralization, state intervention, social discipline, and so on, was difficult to reconcile with any form of Home Rule; it was also remote from the urbane, Euro-centric values of Catalan nationalism. Furthermore, the Catalanists were known to favour the reduction of the military budget and the rationalization of the officer ranks. Behind the nationalistic rhetoric of the military, genuine as their feelings were, lay a more practical consideration of the consequences of the rise of a powerful Catalan lobby.

The military press campaign against Catalanism was sparked off by events surrounding the visit to Barcelona of a French fleet in July 1902. At a reception in their honour in the Tivoli theatre, part of the audience sang the Marseillaise and the Catalan hymn 'Els Segadors', while there were

---

[52] 25 July, 1899. For an analysis of military reaction to Catalanism, see Josep M. Solé i Sabaté and Joan Villarroya i Font, *L'Exèrcit i Catalunya (1898–1936). La premsa militar espanyola i el fet català* (Barcelona, 1990). In a burst of irrationality, one military newspaper went so far as to blame the Catalans for the loss of Cuba on the grounds that their demand for protectionist policies had weakened the nation: see the quote from *El Ejército Español* in ibid. 93.

[53] *Correo Militar*, 3 Mar. 1900.

derisive whistles when the Spanish national anthem was played. Worse, a few cries of 'Long live French Catalonia!' were heard.[54] The reaction of the military press was predictably frenzied. *El Ejército Español* declared,

Whoever attacks the sacred integrity of the Fatherland is a criminal unworthy of forgiveness. He should be carted off to prison or the madhouse; but in any case, that social leprosy must disappear.[55]

As the Catalan movement gathered force, the military reaction became more violent and irrational. Catalanism was decadent, eccentric, ridiculous; Catalans were traitors, egotists, misers, effeminates. The latent anti-semitism of many officers rose to the surface; Catalan nationalists should be expelled from the country, wrote one paper, and 'condemned to wander across the world, without a fatherland, like the cursed Jewish race'.[56] Behind Catalan calls for independence, asserted one paper, lay the shady influence of Jesuits.[57] The residual populism and anti-capitalism mentioned earlier also made an appearance in the anti-Catalan diatribes. The Catalanists mostly 'belong to the upper bourgeoisie, the boss class, who call for help from the forces of law and order as soon as their workers go on strike'. They are 'insatiable industrialists', 'plutocrats', 'monopolists of protectionism'.[58]

The Catalanophobia of the military was not without provocation. The weekly satirical magazine *¡Cu-cut!*, in particular, repeatedly needled officers with its cartoons lampooning the army and the navy. Throughout 1905 the magazine's cartoonists made fun of the military; they were portrayed as hilariously inept, uncouth, lisping (because of the dental c and z of Castilian Spanish) and overfond of uniforms and medals. The army was seen as overmanned, the navy had a tendency to sink, and frequent references were made to the failure of both in battle on land and sea. Most of its issues contained derogatory references to the defeat of 1898, implying that the military lost the war through incompetence or cowardice. A brief description of two typical cartoons may help to explain the explosion of anger among officers stationed in the Barcelona garrison in November 1905. The 8 June issue had contained an article attacking the govern-

---

[54] *El Imparcial*, 22 July 1899.

[55] 'Energía, energía, energía', 1 Aug. 1899.

[56] 'Lllamada al patriotismo', *La Correspondencia Militar*, 3 Oct. 1905, quoted in Solé and Villaroya (*L'Exèrcit*), 75. For other typical outbursts, see 56 and 64; also '¡Viva España!', and 'Signos de decadencia', *Correo Militar*, 3 and 15 Mar. 1900.

[57] *La Correspondencia Militar*, 30 Dec. 1905.

[58] 'Separatismo criminal', *La Correspondencia Militar*, 29 Nov. 1905, and 'Contra el Catalanismo justa y natural reacción', 9 July 1907, quoted in Solé and Villaroya (*L'Exèrcit*), 68 and 97–8.

ment's failure to suppress anarchist terrorism and suggesting that it was typical of the Spanish state's failure to serve the needs of Catalonia. The article was accompanied by a cartoon depicting a French cavalry charge; two bystanders are conversing, one French, one Spanish; the first remarks, 'Monsieur, they're really going fast, aren't they?' to which the other replies, 'Oh no! You should have seen how fast our lot went in Cuba, and they were on foot!'[59] The 10 August edition contained a cartoon depicting two bathers, one wearing a pair of swimming-trunks with the colours of the Spanish flag. A very free translation of their dialogue would be: 'What an odd pair of trunks you're wearing', says the first, to which the second replies, 'Yes, but the colour is really long-lasting'. 'Really?', answers the first. 'I thought that colour always loses.'[60]

Both editions were reported to the authorities by the local military for insulting the army and the nation. Under existing legislation, the press could be sanctioned for such offences by the civil authorities. In the second case, *¡Cu-cut!* was forced to withdraw the cartoon but in the following issue provocatively included a new one portraying the same bathers; this time, one of them is wearing trunks with the United States flag on them: 'So you've got a new pair of trunks?' 'Yes, sir', answers the second, 'but these don't lose'.[61] Military anger finally boiled over in November when a new issue of *¡Cu-cut!* once again made fun of the army. The offending cartoon was not perhaps the most provocative but it was the last straw. It was a small black-and-white cartoon showing a soldier and a civilian watching the crowds entering a stadium in Barcelona at a time when the Catalanists were celebrating massive gains in local elections. Significantly, the conversation is in Spanish, though the magazine appeared in Catalan. The soldier is asking: 'There's a lot of people there; what's being celebrated?' 'The Victory Banquet', replies the second. 'The Victory Banquet?' the soldier answers. 'Ah, they must be civilians then.' (Fig. 10)[62]

On the evening of 25 November, two days after the issue came out on sale, some two to three hundred officers stormed into the printing-press of *¡Cu-cut!* and smashed everything in sight, lighting a bonfire with the remains. One group moved on to the offices of the magazine and proceeded to sack them. The demonstrators then turned their attention to the

[59] 8 June, 361.
[60] 510. In the original Catalan, the words describing the colours are 'sofert' (tough, long-lasting) and 'perdis' (losing).
[61] 17 Aug., 517. Again, the Catalan word is 'perden' (lose).
[62] 23 Nov., 742.

FIG. 10 The cartoon from the satirical Catalan magazine *¡Cu-cut!* that provoked military retaliation in 1905

Catalanist paper *La Veu de Catalunya*, destroying its plant and beating up passers-by who failed to respond to their cries of 'Long live Spain!' with sufficient ardour. Forty-six people were injured, some seriously as a result of sabre wounds.[63] Their action was greeted with enthusiasm in garrisons throughout Spain; messages of support poured into Barcelona and military delegates to Barcelona were sent off and greeted at stations by large and excited crowds of officers. The authorities, unable and unwilling to impose order on the garrisons, failed to take action against the officers and instead declared martial law in Barcelona, closing down newspapers and arresting Catalan journalists. In the Liberal cabinet of Montero Ríos, Weyler, as Minister of War, refused to sack the military chiefs in com-

[63] Nuñez (*Militarismo*), 364; Alvarez Junco (*Emperador*), 317–18; Ametlla (*Memòries*), 238–9; Romero-Maura (*The Spanish Army*), 18–26; Castellví Papers (AHCB). The military press had been inciting officers to take matters into their own hands. An editorial in *El Ejército Español*, on the day the offending issue of *¡Cu-cut!* appeared, had exclaimed, 'military men, who, more than most others are obliged to feel for the Fatherland because of their career, cannot and must not tolerate that it be offended. Against the foreigner who dares to, there is war; against the unworthy Spaniard who commits the crime, the law. If the law . . . does not punish him, individual initiative' ('Bon cop de fals', 23 Nov.).

mand of the rebellious officers. The President himself, faced by a reticent king who was supposed to have supported the action privately, was forced to resign. His place was taken by a colleague, Segismundo Moret, with the brief of placating the military, while Weyler was replaced by General Luque who had distinguished himself during the action as one of its most fervent supporters.[64]

The *¡Cu-cut!* affair was a turning-point in the post-war fortunes of the military. It raised their standing amongst the numerous sections of the population in Spain who were hostile to Catalan regionalism. It encouraged the lower ranks of the officer class to organize independently of their superiors, who had greeted the initiative with hostility or reticence. In a presage of the Junta movement of 1917, these officers formed a committee to consider a wide range of grievances beyond that of Catalanist insults.[65] Moreover, as a result of the regime's capitulation to officer opinion, the Law of Jurisdictions was approved in March 1906 giving military courts wider jurisdiction over civilians than they had ever enjoyed except during periods of martial law and suspension of constitutional rights.

Before 1900 offences judged to be 'against the army' could be tried under the Code of Military Justice whether their perpetrators were soldiers or civilians. Since then, the civil courts had taken on this responsibility, affording the military ample protection against press 'abuse'. The civil courts, on the other hand, had been entirely responsible for crimes against the state and the nation.[66] Under the new law, however, the military courts were given the right to try all offences against both the armed forces and the nation. They were thus handed a powerful instrument of social control. The fiction of military neutrality in civil affairs, so carefully cultivated by Cánovas and his successors, was destroyed at a stroke.[67]

The new law polarized opinion. Most of the left, including the left-wing of the Liberal party, rejected the law outright. Both Antonio Maura and the right-wing Carlist Vázquez de Mella at first opposed the law, the former on the grounds that it undermined the civil rights of Catalan

---

[64] Romanones (*Notas*), 352–7; Cambó (*Memòries*), 111–14.

[65] Romero-Maura (*The Spanish Army*), 24–5.

[66] For a brief history of legislation as it affected the military see Nuñez (*Militarismo*), 345–55 and 369–70.

[67] Not all the military press greeted the law with enthusiasm. In an editorial on 21 Mar. 1906, *La Correspondencia Militar* expressed reservations on the grounds that the law went too far in undermining constitutional liberties; by doing so it contradicted the essentially liberal character of the army and would arouse hostility towards the military ('La verdad ante la ley').

citizens and the latter because 'Parliament cannot legislate under the threat of the sabre.'[68] The Law was almost universally opposed by the intellectuals. Unamuno delivered a scathing attack in an article in the periodical *Nuestro Tiempo*. In it, he argued that the military could not be above civil law nor had they the right to speak for the nation; it was as absurd for the military courts to try cases against the nation as for judges to go to war. Just as the Church tried to restrict religion to its own doctrine, so the military were reducing patriotism to their own narrow vision. It was the religion and the patriotism of the parish pump ('*Iglesia chica, Patria chica*').[69]

To the extent the new law related to Catalanism, however, it was applauded by conservatives and the more virulently centralist Republicans.[70] For the military, on the other hand, the Law of Jurisdictions confirmed what they had come to believe since the Disaster; that they, not the government nor any other institution, were the true custodian of the national interest. As *El Ejército Español* wrote shortly after the *¡Cu-cut!* incident, 'the army is the sublime and august incarnation of the Fatherland'.[71] Moreover, the government's surrender to military violence tipped the fragile balance of power between civil and military authorities in the army's direction. The military had always had an influential voice in Restoration governments, first through the Minister of War, who was invariably a general, and secondly, through their own effective lobbies. Henceforth, governments would find it even more difficult to legislate against their wishes.

The military also had a potent ally in the young king. Alfonso XIII, crowned when he came of age in 1902, was a military man like his father, an admirer of Prussian militarism, delighting in parades, uniforms, horses, and the camaraderie of fellow-officers.[72] He shared the belief

---

[68] Carlos Seco Serrano, *Militarismo y civilismo en la España contemporánea* (Madrid, 1984), 240.

[69] Miguel de Unamuno, 'La Patria y el Ejército', *Obras Completas*, 976.

[70] Of the newspapers, for example, the conservative *La Correspondencia de España* supported the Law (as opposed to the liberal daily papers such as *El Heraldo de Madrid* and *El Globo*). The Republican paper *La Publicidad* was also in favour, though Alejandro Lerroux, for all his anti-Catalanism, opposed the Law. Alvarez Junco (*Emperador*), 318 n. 11 and 320–2; Romero Maura (*Rosa*), 355–6; Nuñez (*Militarismo*), 370–2.

[71] 27 Nov. 1905, quoted in Cardona (*Poder*), 51.

[72] For a personal portrait of the King, see two rather anecdotal and sycophantic accounts: Julián Cortés Cavanillas, *Alfonso XIII. Vida, confesiones y muerte* (Madrid, 1956) and Sir Charles Petrie, *King Alfonso XIII and His Age* (London, 1963). In a speech to the Barcelona garrison in 1922, according to Gabriel Cardona, Alfonso praised the authoritarian, aristocratic model of the military in Wilhelmine Germany, as opposed to the more liberal model of the Allies: (*El poder*), 40–2.

common amongst them that the key to Spain's regeneration lay in a strong army and navy. In a somewhat childish entry in his diary one year before the coronation, he had written,

It is necessary to have an army and a navy, whatever it may cost and whoever has to pay for it, because without those two hands, so to speak, which are holding Spain up, it would fall like a ball to be fought over by England, Germany, France and the United States.[73]

Alfonso had astonished the first cabinet over which he presided by insisting on his constitutional prerogatives over Ministers. Only a month after the coronation, he was attempting to block or control appointments and awards proposed by the cabinet.[74] He was known to be impatient of parliamentary procedures and party factionalism. During the *¡Cu-cut!* affair, he had played a key role in persuading the military rebels to return to the barracks and await the action of parliament but in doing so he had clearly shown that his sympathies lay with them by promising action over military demands to make political Catalanism illegal and to extend the jurisdiction of military courts.[75]

The Law of Jurisdictions gave the military a new sense of self-esteem. As Ortega y Gasset pointed out, however, no army can have self-respect without the possibility of war[76] and the military were unhappy with their role as defenders of law and order for a regime against which they felt increasingly alienated. However, a fresh opportunity for military endeavour abroad arose with Spain's new involvement in Morocco. In a series of international agreements with France and Britain between 1904 and 1912, Spain was given responsibility for policing most of northern Morocco. Such a task required the renewed investment in arms and equipment for which the military had long been clamouring, and indeed, the new Conservative President in 1907, Antonio Maura, had set in train a long-cherished ambition to re-build the navy. However, the army remained woefully unprepared for war in North Africa; the demobilization after the

[73] Diary entry dated 1 Jan. 1901: J. L. Castillo-Puche, *Diario íntimo de Alfonso XIII* (Madrid, 1960), 65.

[74] Figueroa y Torres, Conde de Romanones, *Notas de una vida (1868–1901)* (Madrid, 1934), quoted in José Luis Vila-San-Juan, *Alfonso XIII: un rey, una época* (Madrid, 1993), 34–5. For his interventions in cabinet, see 'Más cavilaciones', *El Imparcial*, 29 June 1902. For further criticism of the king by this paper see the editorial, 'El Rey y los ministros', 4 Nov. 1902.

[75] Alvarez (*Emperador*), 319–20.

[76] José Ortega y Gasset, *España Invertebrada. Bosquejo de algunos pensamientos históricos* (Madrid, 1981), 56.

colonial wars meant that military conscripts had to be raised from the Reserve List, that is among men who had never expected to fight.[77]

The new alliance with the Entente Cordiale of Britain and France was not one which many sections of the military favoured because they were deeply suspicious of French expansionist intentions in Morocco; they would have preferred an alignment with France's main rival in the area, Germany, through which Spain might have acquired greater status and more territory. But to incur the displeasure of Britain and France was too great a risk. As a military newspaper ruefully commented, 'because we are weak, we have to content ourselves with the crumbs of a feast which should be ours alone'.[78]

Military interest in the Moroccan question revived with this award to Spain of an international role in Morocco. Previously, their press had seen Morocco mainly in terms of Spain's security. Warning about French ambitions in the area, they had suggested Spain should quickly move outwards from her two possessions on the northern coast, Ceuta and Melilla, to pre-empt an expansion of France's sphere of influence in the crumbling Sultanate.[79] Spain's new role in Morocco re-awakened imperialist aspirations amongst the military which had lain dormant since the Disaster. When in July 1909, the army in Morocco went into action against the rebellious Rif tribes near Melilla, their enthusiasm for war and military expansion flowed over,[80] although the campaign began with a new disaster when Spanish troops were massacred in the Barranco del Lobo ravine.

For any officer steeped in military traditions, North Africa was imbued with a mythical resonance. Popular myth had turned the messy and occasionally disastrous skirmishes with Moroccan tribes of the nineteenth century into heroic campaigns. It was common amongst many Spaniards, not least amongst army officers, to see Morocco as a natural extension of the peninsula; Spain possessed the towns of Ceuta and Melilla, control of

[77] Emilio Mola Vidal, 'El Pasado, Azaña y el Porvenir', in *Obras Completas* (Valladolid, 1940), 935–6.

[78] 'Mirando al exterior', *La Correspondencia Militar*, 16 Mar. 1906. For a pro-German stance, see also the editorial in the same paper, 'Africa en España', 12 Feb. 1906.

[79] Federico Pichereau, 'El provenir de España', *El Ejército Español*, 12 Aug. 1899; 'Francia en Marruecos. Exploraciones africanas' and 'La cuestión marroquí. España dormida', *El Correo Militar* (editorial), 19 and 21 May 1900; 'Sigamos el ejemplo', *La Correspondencia Militar*, 14 Feb. 1902.

[80] A typical article in *El Ejército Español* looked forward to 'a bright and glorious future and faith in the energies and the fortitude of our race . . . Let us feel, once more, enthusiasm, faith, hope and let us repeat, as good Spaniards do, Long Live the Army! Long live national honour!': 'Las operaciones en el Riff', 20 July 1909.

the northern littoral was seen as an essential component of the country's defence, and the influence of Spain, through commerce and immigration, was still strong in many parts of North Africa.

Army opinion was also permeated by the new spirit of imperialism which had gripped the imagination of the European powers since the middle of the nineteenth century. To the traditional perspective which had seen North Africa in terms of an unfinished religious crusade against the infidel was added a new role for the military as the trail-blazers of modern civilization against barbarism. Echoing the government line, a military newspaper wrote

[A]rms will plough the virgin soil so that agriculture, industry, mining should flourish in it, so that through it roads will open that will be the arteries of commerce.[81]

For some of the military, also, Morocco held an exotic appeal, fed by the romantic colonialism typical of *fin de siècle* Europe; much popular literature also contained stirring accounts of war in Morocco and picturesque descriptions of Moorish customs.[82] A few days before the Tragic Week, an editorial in the army newspaper, *El Ejército Español*, had let itself be carried away by these seductions, seeing in Morocco

a fatal attraction, an irresistible urge, a mysterious calling, whose voice of enchantment is heard, from time to time, leading us fatally and irremediably, shackling our will, forcing us sometimes against our own desires, towards the fields of Africa.[83]

The military, however, were evidently taken by surprise by the strength of these opposing desires among the conscripts and their families, as revealed by the riots in Barcelona and demonstrations elsewhere in July 1909. Unable to understand the nature of the popular protest against the Moroccan campaign, they fell back on conspiracy theories, accusing anarchists, Catalans and Radicals, whom they saw as the enemy within, worse even than the Moroccan foe, of whipping up the mobs for their own perverse purposes.[84] The Tragic Week and the mobilization of intellec-

---

[81] 'Política africanista; la empresa de ahora', editorial in *El Ejército Español*, 7 Aug. 1909. See also 'España en Africa' (24 July 1909) and 'Momentos de expectación' (editorial, 5 Aug. 1909).

[82] Lécuyer and Serrano (*La Guerre*), 121–225.

[83] 'España en Africa', 24 July 1909.

[84] *El Ejército Español*: '¡Ave España!', (editorial) 30 July 1909; 'Castigo necesario' (Ricardo Espí, Teniente coronel), 31 July 1909; and 'El enemigo de casa', 17 Aug. 1909. Earlier, the same newspaper made a rather feeble attempt to woo working-class opinion by claiming that the military campaign in Morocco was necessary to protect Spanish workers building the railway-line attacked by Moroccan tribesmen; it also claimed incorrectly that it was no

tuals against the war widened the gap between the army and the people, deepening the officers' sense of alienation towards the institutions of civil society. The Minister of the Interior, Juan de la Cierva, no enemy of the military himself, was profoundly disturbed by the reaction of officers to the anti-war sentiments displayed by the crowds in Barcelona. In a private letter to the Premier, Antonio Maura, he described how the Captain-General of Barcelona seized by the neck a demonstrator who had shouted 'Down with the war!' and, with the help of other officers, began to beat him up. According to La Cierva, this was 'a deplorable spectacle for a thousand reasons'. But he was even more shocked by the General's comment immediately afterwards. 'General Brandeis turned to me saying, I don't know for what reason, that he didn't have the slightest need for the civil authorities.'[85]

Indeed, according to General Kindelán, who was to make his name in the Moroccan campaign in 1913 as the first pilot to bomb from the sky, the widespread opposition to the war,

obliged the military to turn in on themselves, to isolate themselves, to live a self-effacing life, as in a closed compartment, a privatisation carried to the extreme, scornful of the civilian classes whom they suspected were infected with anti-patriotism, immorality, materialism and indifference towards the real national essence. The generic contempt [of the military] . . . focused most sharply and intensely on the press and the politicians.[86]

Faced by what they saw as a disintegrating nation riven by separatist and anti-patriotic movements and weakened by a corrupt political system, the military began to view themselves as the sole defender of Spanish nationhood. Their growing intervention in politics was in part driven by a sense of historical responsibility to uphold their conception of the national interest in the absence of any class or political force with which they could identify. Secular nationalism was weaker in Spain than in many other European countries because of the feebleness of the Spanish bourgeoisie and the relative backwardness of much of Spanish society.[87]

longer possible for the sons of the rich to avoid military service because cash redemptions were no longer possible in wartime; however, it was forced to rectify the last point a few issues later: 'Marruecos y ciertos obreros españoles', 10 July 1909.

[85] Letter of 18 July, 1909 in AM, Legajo 151, no. 10.

[86] (*Ejército*), 180–1; although informed by a desire to justify subsequent actions by the military, his description was not inaccurate. Military impatience with parliament was also reinforced by the sense of urgency surrounding the Moroccan campaign: see the editorial, 'El coco del Parlamento', in *El Ejército Español*, 7 Aug. 1909.

[87] Shubert (*Social*), 204–5.

The nationalism that the military constructed outlawed the divisions of class and region which were the product of an uneven but accelerating process of modernization and which threatened the national identity of Spain as they saw it. They sought to create a unifying vision of Spain that denied its historical complexity. In their distorted interpretation of history, traditional symbols were mobilized, such as the Celtiberian resistance to Roman invasion epitomized by the siege of Numancia, the Reconquest against the Moors, the Catholic Monarchs, the Conquest of America, the popular uprising against the French on 2 May 1808, and so on, to suggest the continuity of national traits and thereby temper the experience of division.

In the language used by the military press to assert this monolithic view of national identity there was little room for rational discourse. Apart from traditional references to the valour and honour (*hidalguía*) of the Spanish race, the glorious past and 'the tombs of millions of heroes', the nation was repeatedly personified as the Mother, abandoned or slapped by an ungrateful son (Catalanism).[88] The Fatherland, understandably perhaps, was declared intangible because it

is everything: the air we breathe, our children's cradle, the tomb of our parents. To offend the Fatherland is to offend our own mother. He who allows Spain to be insulted, would allow the woman who carried him in her womb to be insulted.[89]

As it emerged in the first decade of the twentieth century, military nationalism shared few of the characteristics of Spanish conservatism, despite their common rhetoric. The military, in general, opposed the oligarchic system of the Restoration, which they saw as responsible in part for the decline of Spain. In fact, the new military nationalism contained the kernel of a neo-conservative regenerationism that would come to fruition in the Dictatorship of Primo de Rivera in 1923 and that of Franco in 1939.[90] At the same time, the war in Morocco from 1909 forged a new generation of officers who were to lead the revolt against the Second Republic in 1936. Glossing somewhat over the divisions within the army that the war had created, Ortega y Gasset wrote in 1921,

Morocco turned the soul of our army into a closed fist, morally disposed to attack . . . [F]rom that moment, the military became a loaded rifle without a target against which to fire.[91]

[88] For example, *La Correspondencia Militar*, 14 Oct. 1899, quoted in Solé and Villaroya (*L'Exercit*), 38.
[89] Ibid. 55.
[90] Manuel Vázquez Montalbán, *Los demonios familiares de Franco* (Barcelona, 1987), 36.
[91] (*España Invertebrada* (Madrid, 1967), 15th edn.), 82.

7

The Revolution from Above

THE strategy of the so-called revolution from above, associated with Francisco Silvela and above all with his successor as leader of the Conservatives, Antonio Maura, was a coherent attempt to regenerate the regime in the troubled conditions of post-Disaster Spain. Because they had both been long-standing critics of the *status quo*, their very appointment as party leaders was a clear sign that the political establishment was conscious of the urgent need for change. Indeed, the more far-sighted amongst them believed that unless the political system was radically reformed, it would be swept aside by a revolution from below. Maura had formulated the problem succinctly a year after the Disaster. In a speech to deputies in the Congress in July 1899, he had warned,

It is a conviction of all of us that Spain has to go through a revolution; if we do not make it here, it will be made in the streets.[1]

Two years later, he had depicted this revolution from above as: 'reforms carried out by the Government *radically*, *rapidly*, *brutally*.'[2] The increasing assertiveness of social and political forces on the margin of the Restoration system, such as those examined in the previous chapters, made this revolution even more urgent as the first decade of the century progressed.

This view was also shared by the king, insofar as the revolution from above would serve to bolster the monarchy. Even before he was crowned in 1902, Alfonso had shown a youthful desire to carry out reforms in Spain; he wrote in his diary about the need to reinvigorate political life, to carry out social reforms to help the 'needy classes', and to rebuild the army and navy. A prophetic entry in his diary, written on the eve of his coronation, reads,

---

[1] *Revista Nacional*, nos. 7 and 8, 9 July 1899, 129.
[2] Juan Velarde Fuertes, 'Los planteamientos socioeconómicos del Gobierno Largo Maura (1907–1909), o bien El inicio del populismo económico en España: el Gobierno Largo Maura (1907–1909), o bien el Nacimiento del populismo económico en España: el Gobierno Largo Maura (1907–1909)', Unpublished article, Madrid, 12 Oct. 1984, 7.

I can be the King that covers himself with glory regenerating the fatherland, whose name will pass into History leaving an imperishable memory of his reign; but I can also be a King who does not govern, who lets himself be governed by his ministers and, finally, is conveyed to the frontier.[3]

Thereafter, he had shown a keen sense of the need to maintain the broadest possible political consensus for the monarchy even at the expense of any residual loyalty to his Premiers, as Maura would later find out to his own cost.

Antonio Maura took on the leadership of the Conservative Party and then the Premiership of Spain with an impeccable regenerationist pedigree. He had been a protégé (and son-in-law) of the wheat baron and Liberal minister of the 1880s and 90s, Germán Gamazo, who, long before the Disaster, had advocated a programme of economic and social reforms similar to that now accepted by many establishment politicians. As Liberal Minister for the Colonies between 1892 and 1894, Maura had made strenuous but largely unsuccessful attempts to extend the franchise in the colonies and give them some degree of administrative autonomy. In and out of government, he had campaigned consistently for the need to bridge the gap between the state and what he described as public opinion; that is, to make government responsive to those élites excluded from direct participation in political power.[4] As Minister of the Interior in Silvela's cabinet of 1902–3 (having just joined the Conservatives) and then as Premier of a short-lived government in 1903, Maura had proposed measures of decentralization to awaken local political life from the somnolence induced by patronage and chronic electoral fraud.

Finally, in January 1907, he formed his second government with a comfortable majority in parliament, confident that he could now begin to carry through a programme of reforms without internal disruption, having seen off all challenges to his leadership within the Conservative Party. Now 54, a tall, austere, and imperious figure with a trim white beard, Maura was admired or feared for his devastating oratory and his uncompromising probity. He brought a new confrontational style to a Congress used to compromise and rhetorical niceties. Whether in power or in opposition, he was a formidable figure who could rouse the emotions of jaded deputies or demolish a debating opponent with a richness of vocabulary only rivalled perhaps by the far less couth Alejandro Lerroux.

[3] Castillo-Puche (*Diario íntimo*), 109–10.
[4] Two typical examples are his speech in Congress on 11 Jan. 1892, quoted in Diego Sevilla Andrés, *Antonio Maura. La Revolución desde arriba* (Barcelona, 1954), 85; and a public speech in Apr. 1900 quoted in *El Imparcial* ('En Sevilla'), 15 Apr. 1900.

Maura's revolution from above began with an explosion of White Papers. After about sixteen months, some eighty legislative projects had been presented to the Congress for approval. The normally placid life of parliament was transformed. Bitter and lengthy debates took place over his cabinet's proposals and deputies complained of exhaustion.[5] The centrepiece of his legislative blitz was his proposal to reform the electoral system and his White Paper on Local Administration. In contemporary Spain, the town halls and the provincial councils were not the democratic expression of local life but a sort of market-place where the spoils of patronage were negotiated between representatives of central government, such as the Civil Governors, and the local caciques. By eliminating electoral fraud and giving local councils greater autonomy, Maura hoped to shatter the web of interests that constituted the system of clientelism in Spain. Through this, he intended to make the political regime more responsive to social and economic realities, widening its social base and educating Spaniards for participation in political life.[6] Local politics, he would say later, was 'an educational gym through which the people reach public life'.[7] To prevent the caciques simply packing local administration with their hand-picked men, the White Paper also proposed that half of the Councils' representatives should be drawn from corporations such as the Chambers of Commerce, agrarian leagues, and professional guilds.

The proposal was intended not so much to bring mass democracy to local government as to attract middle-class and bourgeois élites into a political system dominated until now by party notables and members of the oligarchy.[8] Maura was exasperated by the resistance to change of the political establishment. In a hard-hitting parliamentary speech defending the proposal, he pointed out that the patronage system was doomed by the 'immense, profound transformation' taking place in Spain.[9] Although his plans for local government pre-dated the revolt of the Chambers of Commerce in 1899 and the formation of the National Union, they can only have been reinforced by this expression of middle-class disaffection. The rise of the Lliga Regionalista and the formation of Solidaritat Catalana made the reform of local government even more urgent so that their more moderate sections could be coaxed back into the regime's fold. Indeed,

---

[5] Soldevilla (*El año 1907*), 329–30 and 355–6.

[6] *DSC*, 18 Oct. 1907, vol. 70, 1824; César Silió, *Maura. Vida y empresas de un gran español* (Madrid, 1934), 121.

[7] Speech to the Ateneo in Soldevilla (*El año 1917*), 572.

[8] Ramón Punset, 'Maura y el Maurismo. Perspectiva histórica de la revolución desde arriba', *Sistema* no. 233, Nov. 1979, 131–3.

[9] *DSC*, 29 Oct. 1907, vol. 81, 2124.

Maura had already established a close rapport with the Lliga leader Cambó with whom he shared similar ideological convictions and a common strategy for political change. Moreover, his efforts to attract the Lliga were being helped by the growing tensions within Solidaritat Catalana between left and right.

Maura's confidence that the new system of local government could mobilize the so-called 'live forces' in Spain may have had some basis in the more urban areas but it was difficult to imagine the politics of the agrarian heartlands changing as a result of such a superimposed structure. The patronage system there was based on the social and economic reality of a largely backward society. It was the only connecting link between government and people. As *El Imparcial* put it in 1901,

Caciquismo is the inevitable result of the grafting of a representative system on to an inert society . . . lacking habits of civic life, political culture, education, public opinion, an electorate. [None of] that could be improvised nor was it at hand; it was necessary to contract it and the contractor was the cacique.[10]

Nor were Maura's own supporters all that keen to change the system. A friend of Juan de la Cierva, Maura's Minister of the Interior, argued unashamedly for maintaining the backwardness of rural society:

I don't want roads to be built [in my province] because they don't suit me electorally. My district is mountainous and I go about it on horseback and win the elections. Nobody can compete with me contacting villages of such difficult access.[11]

Another dilemma facing Maura was that where change did take place as a result of greater electoral honesty, the dynastic parties tended to be the losers. The Conservatives, for example, had been virtually wiped out in Barcelona following the rise of the Lliga Regionalista. Indeed, every time reforming governments insisted on greater electoral transparency, the Republicans or other non-dynastic parties gained extra votes in the cities; thus during Maura's term as Minister of the Interior in the Silvela government of 1902–3, the Republicans had won control of the Madrid council in the local elections, to the king's consternation.[12] Moreover, Maura's campaign against patronage upset members of his own party. His close friend, Angel Ossorio y Gallardo, warned him in a letter in 1909 of the extreme discontent amongst Aragonese Conservatives: 'the party here exists only to curse your policies which have closed the door of favourit-

[10] 'Tema inagotable', 5 May 1901.
[11] Juan de la Cierva y Peñafiel, *Notas de mi vida* (Madrid, 1955, 2nd. edn.), 24.
[12] Tusell (*Antonio Maura*), 65–6.

ism for friends'. The result, he went on, was 'a state of disgust, indiscipline, and dispersion which threatens our next and future ventures'.[13]

Maura's ambitious plans to reshape local politics thus met resistance on all sides. It was vigorously opposed by Republican deputies (including those from Solidaritat Catalana) for its corporatism, and by conservative Catalanists for failing to recognize regions as essential elements of local government.[14] It was also criticized by some business organizations for being insufficient on its own to eliminate patronage and electoral fraud.[15] Furthermore, the passage of the proposed law through Congress was held up because of its sheer complexity—it contained over 400 articles. By the end of Maura's 'long' government of 1907–9, only part of the Paper had been approved. Through his attempts to reform the electoral system and its practice, Maura merely alienated traditional sections of his party, frustrated expectations of change, and stirred up opposition to his government.

The second plank of Maura's revolution from above was a programme of state intervention to develop national production. Its focus was the creation of a strong merchant and military navy, which would in turn stimulate the coal, steel, and shipyard industries. In this policy also, Maura had shown a remarkable degree of consistency since the beginning of his political career. As the Liberal opposition spokesman on defence in 1890 and as Overseas Minister in 1892–4, he had uttered warnings about the potentially disastrous consequences of neglecting Spain's naval power, warnings which in retrospect would appear prophetic, though many others could also claim to have been prophets of disaster in that doom-laden decade.[16] Spain's new international role after 1904 counselled a massive injection of funds into the re-building of the navy and, after the loss of the colonial market, Spanish trade needed the boost of an improved merchant marine.[17] Maura's proposed Law of Maritime Communications

---

[13] Letter of 6 Oct. 1909, in AM, Legajo 80.

[14] See Cambó's speech in *DSC*, 25 and 26 Oct. 1907, vol. 78, 2050–4, and vol. 79, 2076–82.

[15] 'Ynforme del Fomento del Trabajo Nacional sobre el Proyecto de Ley de Administración Local', *El Trabajo Nacional*, 16 Oct. 1907; 'Informe sobre'l projecte de lley d'Administració local', Federació Agrícola Catalana-Balear, July 1907, *AHCCINB*, caja 85, exped. 25.

[16] For Maura's speeches on this theme in the early 1890s, in one of which he referred to Spain's 'glorious history of disasters', see J. Ruiz-Castillo, *Antonio Maura: treinta y cinco años de vida pública. Ideas políticas recopiladas por . . .* (Madrid, 1953), 96–116.

[17] 'Our future', declared Maura after the Disaster, 'lies in the merchant marine': Soldevilla (*El año 1899*), 436.

and Naval Armaments was passed in Congress in January 1908, despite popular opposition to renewed military spending which Maura freely acknowledged.[18]

This and other associated laws introduced by Maura's government had the equally important purpose of protecting Spanish trade and industry. Further limits were placed on the participation of foreign capital in certain sectors of Spanish industry. State organizations were obliged to purchase specified amounts of products or services based in Spain. And government subsidies, grants and tax rebates were offered to private conglomerates to stimulate national production.[19] In adopting protectionist policies, Maura was following Conservative tradition. He was also in tune with the mood of economic nationalism prevalent among capitalists in Spain and elsewhere since the late nineteenth century. The *fin de siècle* economic crisis had encouraged the view that the presence of foreign capital simply perpetuated Spain's backwardness and that a policy of autarky was the best means of developing her economy. Newly created business organizations, such as the Liga Vizcaína Marítima in the Basque Country and the Liga Marítima Española, set up in 1894 and 1900 respectively, served as powerful lobbies for this strategy.[20]

Maura's policy of economic nationalism had a political objective as well. Through his measures of state intervention, he was counting on wooing back those more conservative sections of the Catalan bourgeoisie who felt unhappy at the involvement of the Lliga in such a radical movement as Solidaritat Catalana. He was hoping also to attract disaffected business sections elsewhere such as those mobilized previously by Costa and Paraíso. These were amongst the 'living forces' in Spain which could bring stability to the political system and provide a potential base both for the Conservatives and for the regime in general.[21]

Maura hoped to organize support for his programme of economic nationalism by involving business organizations in national economic planning. A decree in 1907 set up a national assembly of business which in turn created a permanent Council of Production and at a lower tier, regional councils. This new corporatist venture was designed both to

[18] Ibid. 136–7.
[19] Velarde Fuertes ('Los planteamientos'), 57–63.
[20] José Luis García Delgado, 'Nacionalismo económico e intervención estatal, 1900–1930' in Nicolas Sánchez-Albornoz (comp), *La modernización económica de España 1830–1930* (Madrid, 1985), 176–93.
[21] Letter from Guillermo Boladeres to Maura, AM, Legajo 125, no. 10.

co-ordinate and stimulate national production and to create, in the words of the decree, 'a bond between governors and governed'.[22]

The trouble with such initiatives from above was that, in a country characterized by an extremely uneven development, they had to satisfy a range of clients with widely differing needs and cultures. Protecting textiles in Catalonia, engineering in the Vizcaya, coal in Asturias and cereals in Castille (all sectors represented by powerful lobbies) entailed undermining other sectors heavily dependent on exports such as mining, wine, and fruit.[23] Moreover, Maura could not afford to ignore the traditional base of the Conservatives amongst farmers, merchants, trawler-owners, and the like in the more backward agrarian areas of Spain, many of whom were the very caciques Maura was intent on eradicating as a political force. The mouthpiece of the Catalan industrialists, *El Trabajo Nacional*, complained that, in comparison to agricultural and commercial interests, industry was poorly represented in the new Council of Production, which 'will merely reflect the age-old antithesis which exists in our country between the world of politics and the world of work'. As a result, the paper went on, the national assembly to set up the Council had been replete with well-meaning phrases but lacked concrete proposals.[24]

Maura's plans were also frustrated by the deep vein of scepticism among many businessmen about politics and politicians, a scepticism reinforced by the failure of Costa's National Union and Silvela's regenerationism. The President of the Oviedo Chamber of Commerce, for example, wrote to Maura's Minister of Industry,

permit me to doubt the eventual success of such noble and patriotic aspirations [as the Council] because experience and time, the revealers of reality, suggest yet

---

[22] AHCCNB, caja 29, expediente 26. Maura's initiatives appeared to be gaining support in many business quarters. The President of the Barcelona Chamber of Commerce, for example, wrote to all deputies and senators representing Catalonia urging them to support the Premier's White Paper on Maritime Communications; he also sent a letter to Maura himself to inform him of his campaign to gather support for the Bill from Chambers of Commerce throughout Spain and abroad: letters of 31 Mar. and 22 Apr. 1909 in AHCCNB, Caja 74, Exped. 8. For further evidence of support for Maura's economic policies, see also the following editorials in *El Trabajo Nacional*: Francisco Marragas Barret, 'El Ministerio de Hacienda', 1 June 1907 and J. Aguilera, 'La Ley de Protección al Trabajo', 16 July 1907 and 'Exposición que la Junta Directiva de esta Corporación ha elevado a la Comisión parlamentaria que entiende en el Proyecto de Ley para el fomento de las industrias y Comunicaciones marítimas nacionales', 1 Mar. 1908; also the book by the influential Catalan industrialist, Guillermo Graell, *Hacia la Nacionalización de la Economía* (Barcelona, 1908).
[23] García Delgado (*Nacionalismo*), 186–7.
[24] Francisco Moragas Barrett, 'Toque de alarma', 16 June 1907; 'La Asamblea de la Producción', *El Trabajo Nacional*, 16 May 1907.

another disillusionment, a new disappointment, so prodigiously common to the history of our public customs.[25]

Yet, while they failed to take root in the short period of his Premiership, Maura's corporatist enticements laid the basis for future programmes of economic nationalism such as that of the dictator Primo de Rivera in the 1820s.

Alongside political and economic reform, Maura's revolution from above also sought to tackle the so-called social problem. His measures were prompted by the unprecedented growth of labour protest, urban rioting and terrorism since the 1890s. Typically, Maura embarked on an energetic and audacious programme of social legislation whose purpose was to protect, moralize, and educate the masses rather than empower them. During his three-year government, a range of laws was put forward on national insurance, child labour, factory inspection, health and safety measures at work, arbitration and conciliation, strikes, land redistribution, and primary-school education, all of which attempted to extend existing legislation or create new forms of protection for workers and their families.[26] Maura's Minister of the Interior and close friend, Cierva, managed to retain the services of leading liberal reformers in the state Institute of Social Reforms, which Maura had created during his first government.[27]

Yet, Maura was not convinced that either the effects of the market or of his own laws were sufficient in themselves to solve the social problem; what was needed above all, he felt, was to foster a strong moral culture amongst the people.[28] The new legislation was therefore informed by a deeply conservative morality. As Governor of Madrid, Cierva had been notorious for his repressive measures, such as his police round-up, one summer's evening, of the city's homosexuals. Even more controversial, perhaps, had been his ban on the wearing of the fashionably large women's hats in the capital's theatres.[29] No doubt with Maura's blessing, he was now, as Minister of the Interior, legislating for a moral change in social

---

[25] In a possibly implicit reference to Costa, he went on to attack the facile rhetoric he found in the meetings being held up and down the country to launch Maura's initiative: 'the assemblies are the field of action of men of letters, and industrialists, because of the nature of their work cannot bear such an atmosphere nor are suitable material for such public competitions', Letter from A. San Román to González Besada, 24 Apr. 1907, in AHCCNB, Caja 29, exped. 26.

[26] Velarde Fuertes ('Los planteamientos'), 63–73.

[27] Such as Adolfo Posada and Adolfo Buylla: Cierva (*Notas*), 119.

[28] Cristóbal Robles, *Antonio Maura. Un político liberal* (Madrid, 1995), 117.

[29] Ibid. 57 and 53–4.

customs as part of the revolution from above, for example by forcing bars, theatres, and restaurants to close early.[30] Such measures were in accord with the revivalist spirit among religious circles whom the Conservatives counted as real or potentially important clients.[31]

Since its foundation by Cánovas in the late nineteenth century, the Conservative Party had managed to attract the more moderate sections of the Catholic right into collaborating with the State. However, the loss of the colonies and the growth of a virulent anti-clericalism in the first decade of the new century had reinvigorated a fundamentalist regenerationism among religious circles whom the Conservatives could not afford to alienate.[32] Through its control of education and its social and charitable work, the Church penetrated into the lives of millions of Spaniards. Wielding this powerful ideological influence, the bulk of the Church hierarchy campaigned relentlessly against the liberal establishment which had disentailed much of the Church's land in the first half of the nineteenth century. Even the most open and well-informed of Bishops were convinced of the existence of hidden enemies who, encouraged by Satan, were bent on destroying the Church's power. Of these enemies, the most important was the 'international Masonic conspiracy'.[33] Amongst traditionalists, indeed, participation in the Restoration system was incompatible with the faith itself. One of the Queen Regent's confessors and tutor to the future king had published an article in 1900 attacking the Liberal José Canalejas in the following terms:

Remember, Mr. Canalejas, that there are no true and legitimate politics under the sun or above it than *the politics of God*; no government other than *the government of Christ*.[34]

Maura's ability to build a mass base among Catholics was thus limited by the reactionary ideology encouraged by sections of the Church among

[30] Though the times he fixed do not appear early in contemporary terms (12.30 a.m. for theatres and bars and 1.30 a.m. for restaurants and cafés), entertainment and café life in *fin de siècle* Madrid commonly went on till dawn: Ibid. 120–3.

[31] A strongly worded pastoral by the Bishop of Salamanca in 1899, for example, had called for the 'purification of the spiritual environment, such as [public] spectacles, the different centres of leisure and above all the periodic press': quoted in Fernando García de Cortázar, 'La Iglesia en la crisis del estado español (1898–1923)' in M. Tuñón de Lara *et al*, *La crisis del estado español, 1898–1936* (Madrid, 1978), 349.

[32] Ibid. 350–2.

[33] For the relatively progressive prelate, Enrique Reig i Casanova, who would be named Archbishop of Barcelona in 1914, the colonial wars had been attributable first and foremost to the 'abominable sect' of the Masons: *Sacrilegios y traidores, o la masonería contra la Iglesia y contra España* (Palma, 1897). See also, Mauricio, *La gran traición* (Barcelona, 1899).

[34] Padre José Fernández Montaña in *El Siglo Futuro*, 24 Dec. 1900, quoted in Soldevilla (*El año 1900*), 438.

large numbers of the faithful.[35] While devoutly Catholic himself, Maura was also a liberal who believed in the separation of the Church from the State. Yet he was too much of a Restoration politician to wish to upset the delicate balance between right and left of the regime and he was careful in his second mandate as Premier not to confront anti-clerical opinion in such a way that might have endangered his government.[36]

Furthermore, Maura's more progressive social views were balanced by the instincts of a traditional Conservative. Confronted by social agitation, he resorted to repression rather than negotiation. 'Without strong social discipline', he would write in a letter in 1910, 'without deep respect towards authority and the law, neither society nor even life are possible.'[37] Indeed, it could be said that his paternalism and his strong attachment to law and order were different sides of the same coin. Yet his demonization as a despot after the Tragic Week was wide of the mark. He was a convinced constitutionalist for whom, as he had declared in a speech during the *¡Cu-cut!* crisis of 1905, 'each suspension of [constitutional] rights is a sudden halt on our path towards progress . . .'.[38] Thus an important component of Maura's revolution from above was the reform of existing legislation so that the rule of law could be maintained without recourse to martial law. Even though he was guarded about when he might repeal it, Maura was a staunch opponent of the Law of Jurisdictions.[39]

The most acute problem, however, was that of terrorism. Its epicentre was Barcelona, where Maura himself had escaped assassination by a hair's-breadth in 1903. The Liberal politician Count Romanones calculated that between 1905 and 1907, over sixty bombs had been set off in the 'city of bombs' alone.[40] Maura appointed his friend Ossorio as Civil Governor of Catalonia with a special brief to root out the terrorists. The Lliga-controlled Town Council in Barcelona also attempted to tackle the rash of bombs by hiring a Scotland Yard detective to organize a special anti-terrorist squad.[41] Neither succeeded. One year later, Ossorio tendered his

[35] Robles (*Antonio Maura*), 195–8, 200–4, 280, 329.
[36] Tusell (*Antonio Maura*), 106–7.
[37] Fernández Almagro (*Historia política*), 54–5.
[38] Speech of 28 November 1905, AHCB, Castellví papers.
[39] Tusell (*Antonio Maura*), 103. Cambó urged Maura to repeal the Law on the grounds that it gave the left in Solidaritat Catalana an opportunity to mount a campaign against Maura which would harm both the Premier's and Cambó's interests (undated letter from Cambó to Maura: AM, legajo 19, no. 3).
[40] Figueroa y Torres (*Notas*), 277.
[41] Charles Arrow, *Rogues and Others* (London, 1926), 192–209. For Maura's views, see his letter to Ossorio of 19 Mar. 1908, AM, Legajo 149, no. 2.

resignation (unsuccessfully) because, as he wrote despairingly in a letter to Maura, 'the bombs continue and will continue'.[42] Acting on Ossorio's advice, Maura drew up a White Paper which proposed enlarging the powers of the authorities to such an extent that they would be able to close down the anarchist press and their centres and expel anarchist propagandists. The draft law drew the fire of the parliamentary opposition, already disgruntled by Maura's proposals for local administration. It provided a focus for the growing disquiet of the Liberals over the scale and pace of Maura's revolution from above while enabling Republicans to portray the Premier as a tyrant.

Like Maura, the Liberals were anxious to widen the social base of their party, which had been widely discredited after the Disaster and now risked being left behind as left-wing parties began to mobilize ever-increasing numbers of people in the industrial cities.[43] They had traditionally sought to co-opt or at least to gain the support of the more moderate Republican forces to their left. Maura's White Paper gave them the opportunity to do so once again. The resulting united front against the proposed law, the Left Bloc, brought together Liberals and Republicans (minus the Lerrouxists) and even attracted the support of Socialists who had recently reversed their principle of not collaborating with bourgeois forces.

For Maura, such an alliance was a denial of the Restoration system so painstakingly put together by Cánovas in 1876. The two-party constitutional monarchy was for him the cornerstone of the Spanish nation. 'The institution of the monarchy', he had said in 1907, 'is the brooch, the bond, the personification of national unity . . . the person of the monarch . . . is the living fatherland itself.'[44] Maura was prepared to extend democratic rights to, and work with, all those political forces which accepted the framework of the Restoration Settlement. By allying themselves to those dedicated to overthrowing the monarchy, the Liberals, he believed, were breaking the consensus that held Spain together. 'Constitutional life has ended', he declared, 'because the Constitution cannot function with only one party.'[45]

The events of the Tragic Week, some fifteen months after Maura's proposed Law on Terrorism, brought the division between the two parties of the Spanish establishment to a head. They began, as we have seen, as a

[42] Letter to Maura on 18 Feb. 1908, AM, Legajo 80.

[43] Thus Segismundo Moret's speech on 18 Nov. 1908: Duque de Maura and Melchor Fernández Almagro, *Por qué cayó Alfonso XIII, Evolución y disolución de los partidos históricos durante su reinado* (Madrid, 1948, 2nd edn.), 125–6.

[44] Duque de Maura and Fernández Almagro (*¿Por qué?*), 126.

[45] Sevilla Andrés (*Antonio Maura*), 394.

protest against the call-up of reservists for military service in Morocco after the intermittent war between Rif tribesmen and Spanish troops had flared up once again in July 1909. The decision to mobilize reservists from the most restless region in Spain undoubtedly carried risks but there was no particular reason for the government to have foreseen such a violent reaction. Besides, after the extensive demobilization of the post-war period, there was little option but to draw from the official reserve lists. There was no disagreement between the two parties over the presence of the Spanish army in Morocco; indeed, the Liberals were far more enthusiastic about the advantages of Spain's involvement in Morocco than the Conservatives.[46] The Disaster had exposed as a terrible fallacy the policy of semi-isolationism and reliance on dynastic contacts followed by the regime before the Spanish–American War. In its aftermath, Spanish governments sought to re-enter the web of international alliances to defend national security. In any case, Spanish presence in Morocco was as old as its ex-colonies in America. Since the Catholic kings, the control of northern Morocco, or at least of its littoral, had been seen as a vital part of the defence of Spain. 'Our natural frontier', Cánovas had reiterated, 'is the Atlas mountains.'[47]

The willingness of Spanish governments after 1898 to intervene once again in Morocco was motivated above all by the strategic insecurity of the post-Disaster period. This sense of insecurity was heightened by the increasingly volatile international situation. In northern and western Africa, Britain, France, and Germany were competing for hegemony over trade and territory. The first two had come close to military confrontation at the Sudanese outpost of Fashoda in 1898; France had backed off and accepted British hegemony in the Nile Valley, while reserving part of Morocco as its own sphere of influence. Britain, anxious about France's ambitions in north-west Africa, had encouraged Spanish involvement in Morocco as a buffer against French expansionism.[48] She was also concerned about the security of Spanish insular possessions in the face of German competition and was therefore keen to draw Spain into an alli-

---

[46] On 17 July 1909, the Liberal spokesman accused the Conservatives of abandoning Morocco in 1904 to French expansionism: Soldevilla (*El año 1909*), 244.

[47] Fernández Almagro (*Historia Política*), vol. 2, 364. Maura declared in a speech in 1907, 'the northern part of the African continent is an essential condition of our independence and national integrity . . . And that is not a question of expansion or one of social and economic development, it is the right to life, the right to the integrity of the sovereign autonomy of Spain', J. Paulis and F. de Sorel, *Maura ante el pueblo* (Madrid, 1915), 174.

[48] Ambassador Henry Drummond-Wolff to Lord Salisbury, 2, 13, and 14 Aug. 1898, PRO/FO 72.2065 and 9 Dec. 1898 in PRO/FO 72, 2066.

ance. Indeed, Spain's weakness after her defeat by the United States favoured her new positioning in the international balance of power in the western Mediterranean and in western Africa. Discarding German attempts to woo her, Spain had aligned herself with the Franco-British Entente Cordiale in 1904 in order to ensure the security of her defensive borders and to safeguard her interests in west Africa. In a succession of talks and agreements between 1904 and 1907, therefore, she was awarded jurisdiction over a large slice of northern Morocco, amounting to some 20 per cent of Moroccan territory.

This newly enhanced role in Morocco was embraced enthusiastically by some Liberals, the army, and the neo-colonial lobby in Spain.[49] Conservatives were more wary, both of an alliance with Britain, whose pro-American role in the Spanish–American War was still deeply resented, and of a new military commitment in Morocco, where several expeditions had come to grief in the nineteenth century. The Spanish Ambassador in Tangiers confided to his British counterpart in 1904 that, 'Spain was not in a position to undertake control of any portion of the Moorish littoral: the task was beyond her strength'.[50] Yet successive Spanish Premiers recognized that there was no other option but to maintain a military and administrative presence in Morocco as part of the agreements with Britain and France.[51]

During Maura's second term of government, however, Spain's position in Morocco came increasingly under strain because of two related processes. The first was the progressive disintegration of the Moroccan empire due to its internal contradictions, exacerbated by the opening of the interior to international trade. The second was France's expansion into Morocco in response to German commercial penetration in the area, an expansion which was beginning to threaten Spain's own sphere of influence in northern Morocco. Spain's growing military intervention was intended to maintain her hegemony there. But Spanish troops were increasingly under attack by the anti-Sultan tribes of the Rif who saw themselves as fighting a war of national and religious liberation against colonialists. In 1909, miners of a Franco-Spanish iron-ore company were attacked as well as Spanish workers constructing the railway line to take the minerals to the coast. The threat of French intervention to restore

[49] For example, the Congreso Africanista, *Primer Congreso Africanista* (Barcelona, 1907), 21.

[50] Nicolson to Landsdowne, 22 Apr., PRO/FO 99.413.

[51] See for example: Silvela (*Artículos*), vol. 111, 115; and the private correspondence between Maura and Canalejas in Duque de Maura and Fernández Almagro (*¿Por qué?*), 185–96.

order forced a reluctant Maura to order troops into the interior beyond the coastal enclaves; the resulting massacre of a detachment of Spanish soldiers by Rif tribesmen in July led to the mobilization of reservists in Spain for duty in Morocco and the flare-up of protest in Barcelona.

The reaction of Maura's government to the unrest in Barcelona was not especially controversial. It was customary to suspend constitutional guarantees and impose martial law in circumstances far less violent than the events of the Tragic Week. Maura chose to ignore the advice of Ossorio in Barcelona, who, backed by Maura's own son, argued that the police could handle the situation. He elected instead to follow that of his Minister of the Interior, Cierva, who wanted to mobilize the army.[52] Maura's handling of the unrest had the support of the Liberal opposition, even when the first executions began of those judged guilty of serious criminal acts during the events. The undoing of Maura's Premiership started with the trial of the anarchist pedagogue Francisco Ferrer in the second half of August and his execution on 13 October. Ferrer had not been in Barcelona at the time the events of the Tragic Week took place and none of the evidence presented at his trial indicated as much. It was clear to many, therefore, that he was being tried for his ideas rather than his actions. Ferrer's case became an international *cause célèbre*, provoking demonstrations throughout Europe and a widely publicized campaign for the commutation of the death sentence. It helped to renew a traditional view abroad of Spain as a land of intolerance and obscurantism.

In Spain, the parliamentary opposition, which had coalesced in the Left Bloc, now found itself the spearhead of a popular movement of protest whose motto was 'Maura No!' The Liberals could not fail to respond to this opportunity to widen their appeal and oust the government; should they not do so, there was a risk that the moderate Republicans might be drawn into a left alliance independent of them.[53] In October their ageing leader, Segismundo Moret, launched a bitter attack against Maura in parliament. Cierva retorted with a speech against the opposition of such rhetorical violence that it went beyond the cut and thrust of parliamentary conventions. Maura unwisely shook Cierva's hand after the speech, giving

---

[52] Although he disapproved in principle of using military force, Maura may have been closer to Cierva in the latter's manichean view of popular agitation; while Ossorio maintained that the riots were spontaneous, Cierva appeared to see in them the guiding hand of separatists and revolutionaries: Cierva (*Notas*), 132 and 156.

[53] A. Robles Egea, 'Formación de la conjunción Republicano-Socialista de 1909', in *Revista de Estudios Políticos*, no. 29, 1982, 153.

the clear impression that he sanctioned this assault on the spirit of consensus that had informed relations between the two establishment parties.
Faced by the combination of international protest and internal political
crisis, the king chose to replace Maura by a Liberal government headed by
Moret. Alfonso justified his decision many years later when in exile:

I subscribed to the Maura No! [campaign], and I stood by it afterwards, because
I was convinced that I could not prevail against half of Spain and more than half
of Europe.[54]

The manner in which he dismissed Maura reveals something of the awe
in which he held him. Relations between the two were cordial but stiff;
Maura was the only politician to whom the king spoke in the formal
'usted' form. Although Alfonso referred to him as 'Papá Maura' when he
spoke to others, Maura was a formidable and sometimes disapproving
father-figure for the young and genial king. Immediately after the explosive debate in parliament, Alfonso had not given Maura any reason to
doubt his support. Firmly convinced that Alfonso would stand by him,
Maura went to the Palace the next day with a purely formal offer of
resignation. Fifteen minutes later, he was back at his home where, according to his son, he said,

When I entered the King's study, he came up to greet me, and embracing me with
particular affection, said to me without giving me the chance to open my mouth,
'You have come alone? I knew you would do the Fatherland and the Monarchy a
great service. What do you think of Moret as your successor?'

Maura, unable to continue his account, then fell into his son's arms and
wept for a long while, 'an irrepressible but silent weeping', wrote his son,
'that of an orphan who has just lost what he most loved in the world'.[55]

The fall of the Maura government polarized the already tense relations
between the two parties of the establishment. Maura, returning to the
opposition benches, retreated into a wounded silence, punctuated by an
occasional speech, the first of which declared 'implacable hostility' to the
Liberals.[56] His sovereign contempt for his parliamentary opponents and
erstwhile colleagues was most vividly expressed in a speech some two
years later during which he shook his frock-coat theatrically at the Liberals seated on the other side of the chamber (frock-coats were the standard

---

[54] Maura and Fernández Almagro (*¿Por qué?*), 156.

[55] Ibid. 155. Cierva also describes Maura's arrival shortly afterwards at a cabinet meeting
when his ministers were still drinking their breakfast hot chocolate; collapsing into an
armchair, he burst into tears: (*Notas*), 152.

[56] Ibid. 159; Soldevilla (*El año 1909*), 413–16.

dress of parliamentarians), exclaiming, 'The dust of your conduct has reached us; I have risen to shake it from me.'[57]

In traditional views of the October 1909 crisis, however, the Liberals' actions are seen as just one factor among several. Maura's revolution from above, according to this interpretation, was blown off-course by treacherous winds: an unpredictable attack by volatile Rif tribesmen, an equally unexpected outburst of mindless violence by the Barcelona mobs, both compounded by the Liberals' opportunism and the king's disloyalty to his Premier.[58] But Maura could also be blamed for navigational errors—his miscalculation of the opposition to Ferrer's execution and his stubborn support for Cierva. More importantly, he had steered a course wilfully using charts which were out of date. On his ship named the revolution from above, there was room only for those who accepted the ideological framework of the Restoration. He regarded the new political currents which challenged it merely as subversive. His impatience with alternative ideologies and his confrontational style drove moderate and radical opponents into each other's arms. A year after his dismissal, he wrote in a letter to a Conservative deputy,

Those Spaniards who are concerned with public life are divided into two great groupings: one, in which are assembled the supporters of riot, looting, arson and revolution and those who sympathize with or make concessions to them; and the other which includes all those of us who hold the deep-rooted conviction that without strong social discipline, without a profound respect for authority and the law no society is possible nor even life itself.[59]

Maura's government had lasted longer than any other since the Disaster and had carried out an unprecedented number of political, social, and economic reforms. If it had failed, it had done so only in terms of the ambitious goals Maura had set himself. His fundamental objective, as we have argued, had been to consolidate the liberal monarchy by extending political participation beyond the web of the traditional oligarchy. By doing so he hoped to make the regime more representative of the new social and economic élites that were emerging out of the process of modernization. But he had managed to get only a small part of his cherished reform of local administration and politics on to the statute book; he had not entirely convinced business with his programme of economic nationalism; and he had not won over the Catholic Right. Moreover, he had

---

[57] DSC, 1912, no. 77, 2061–3.
[58] For example, Maura and Fernández Almagro (*¿Por qué?*).
[59] Fernández Almagro (*Historia política*), 154–5.

signally failed to deal with the problem of law and order. Finally, in his attempts to attain a new international role for Spain, he had embroiled the army in a messy war in Morocco. Unamuno's epitaph on Maura's government some years later was cruel but pointed:

Maura is a man of words and a lawyer. Very sincere and honourable but a lawyer concerned to prove the alibi. And even when he spoke of the rapid and radical revolution from above, he was [merely] coining . . . another phrase.[60]

The man to whom the king now entrusted the solution of the political crisis was the Liberal José Canalejas, a politician much respected for his eloquence and forthrightness. Within the narrow ideological confines of the regime, this was a bold choice. Canalejas had been the *enfant terrible* of the political establishment, having flirted with the Republicans earlier in his career and formed two parties whose ostensible aim had been the democratization of the monarchy.[61] Moreover, he was known to favour freedom of worship and the separation of Church and State, policies which, while they threatened to stir up a storm amongst the powerful Catholic Right, promised to take some of the sting out of Republican anticlericalism. Canalejas's widely publicized views on the need for state intervention to reform social relations also offered an alternative means of dealing with the increasing problem of labour agitation in Spain. Indeed, within the ranks of the Liberal Party, the incoming Premier was the outstanding proponent of the new European liberalism, whose most typical figures elsewhere were Lloyd George and Giolitti. Like them, Canalejas argued for legislation to encourage the development of a reformist labour movement that would seek improvements through negotiation and controlled strikes rather than insurrection. He also favoured land reform to create a new layer of smallholders in place of an impoverished and landless agrarian proletariat prone to violence. Both policies were meant to provide the political and economic stability so conspicuously and increasingly absent in Spain.[62]

Alfonso's first choice to replace Maura had necessarily been Moret, the doyen of the Liberals, whom he had appointed without bothering with the customary protocol of consultations with leading politicians. Moret's efforts to preserve the Left Bloc had failed, however, and the tide of radicalization had led the Republicans to abandon the Liberals and to

[60] 'Maura-Venizelos', *España*, 14 May 1915.
[61] Salvador Forner Muñoz, *Canalejas y el Partido Liberal Democrático (1900–1910)* (Madrid, 1993).
[62] Ibid. 17–35 and 56–74.

form an alliance with the Socialists. To the king's alarm at the ferocity of the protest against Ferrer's execution, both in Spain and abroad, was added his concern with the growing popularity of the Republicans and the Socialists, amongst whom were some of the leading intellectuals of the day.[63] Moreover, what could happen to kings as a result of a post-imperial crisis was illustrated by the dramatic events in Portugal in February 1908 when the Portuguese king and the Crown Prince were both assassinated. The parallel with Spain was ominous. The crisis in the neighbouring country had begun when Britain and Germany had blocked her further expansion in Africa. Alfonso's growing intervention in Spanish politics was therefore motivated more by self-preservation than sympathy with any faction of the Restoration parties.

Canalejas offered the king singular advantages as Premier. While he was well known as a radical reformist, he was not as closely identified as Moret with the moribund Left Bloc. Thus his Premiership might conceivably attract the more moderate Republicans into the Restoration fold; yet he was also far more likely to win back Maura's grudging cooperation than any other Liberal leader because of his independent status within the Party. There is no evidence to support the accusation made by the Socialist leader, Pablo Iglesias, on Canalejas' nomination, that

We are being asked to swallow the bait that the monarchy is turning towards democracy . . . [I]n naming Canalejas, the monarchy is seeking only to fire the last Liberal cartridge in order to justify the return of the Conservatives.[64]

Yet for all their differences, Canalejas's strategy was in several respects a mirror-image of Maura's revolution from above. In their separate ways, both sought to modernize the Restoration state but while Maura's government had held the promise of reforms which the right might grudgingly accept, Canalejas's strategy offered the possibility of wooing the moderate left or at least of stealing the left's thunder. As Liberal Premier, he declared in a speech in parliament,

I don't believe that the agitators, the troublemakers, the professional revolutionaries will disappear but with intense and extensive work we can remove [from them] . . . the climate, the sympathy, and the attraction which they enjoy . . . [amongst] intellectual circles, whom I would like to see integrated into the forces of the monarchy.[65]

---

[63] Robles Egea (*Formación*), 154.
[64] Quoted in Diego Sevilla Andrés, *Canalejas* (Barcelona, 1956), 310.
[65] *DSC* no. 77, 2064.

Both Maura and Canalejas favoured state intervention in order to create the conditions for modernization. Both defended the monarchy because it provided the stability without which political change might lead to anarchy.[66] Both also shared the instinctive paternalism of the Spanish ruling élites towards the working classes. But while Maura found it difficult to come to terms with the rise of mass politics, Canalejas believed it could be defused by reforms. In the aftermath of the October 1909 crisis, Maura's speeches were filled with a bitter disillusion with democracy. 'Universal suffrage came and look how far it's got us,' he declared in a speech in parliament in February 1912. In reply, Canalejas reminded him that, 'neither the Conservative Party nor any other party can make the water run down another channel. Politics in Spain can't be oriented any other way than it is. It is a sign of the times, it is a phenomenon, it is a fact beyond our own will.'[67]

Unlike Maura, Canalejas led a party still divided by political clans. He was able to command a degree of consensus amongst their leaders but had to be on constant guard not to upset the balance within the party lest this should lead to the fall of his government.[68] Like Maura, on the other hand, his freedom to make policy was hampered by the recurrent war in Morocco. Abandoning the Spanish Protectorate in North Africa, according to Canalejas, would damage Spain's commercial interests and her international standing. The war obliged him to tone down reforms in order to preserve a relative degree of political consensus at home. It also prevented him from carrying out his much desired aim of rationalizing the army.[69] Moreover, the policy of rewarding officers on active duty in Morocco with promotions, which Canalejas had inherited from Maura, stirred up discontent amongst those stationed in the peninsula.[70]

The polarization of political life in Spain after the October 1909 crisis also inhibited Canalejas's ability to attract support for his policy of reforms. While the left argued his government was a manœuvre to get the Conservatives back in power, the conservative right claimed he was a prisoner of the left.[71] The increasing climate of political and labour

---

[66] Forner (*Canalejas*), 40–1.   [67] Debate of 31 Feb. 1912, *DSC* no. 77, 2064 and 2067.

[68] José Canalejas, *El Partido Liberal. Conversaciones con D. José Canalejas* (Madrid, 1912), 3. In the wake of his dismissal, Moret was described as 'embittered and very disgruntled': José Francos Rodríguez, *La vida de Canalejas* (Madrid, 1918), 499.

[69] Ibid. 6–15. For Canalejas's policy on Morocco, see also his speech on 8 Apr. 1911, *DSC*, no. 28, 645–8 and his letter to Maura on 9 Sept. 1911 in Maura and Fernández Almagro (*¿Por qué?*), 186–9.

[70] Seco Serrano (*Militarismo*), 253; Sevilla (*Canalejas*), 312.

[71] As the leading conservative daily, *La Epoca*, wrote on 8 June 1911, 'The Canalejas government is led by a Committee of Republican tutelage', Práxedes Zancada, *Canalejas. Político y Gobernante* (Madrid, 1913), 226.

agitation during his term of office in government forced him to use the army to repress agitation, damaging his democratic credentials. His biggest challenge was the national railway strike in September 1912. Following the example of the French Socialist President, Aristide Briand, he militarized the 12,000 rail-workers and sent the army in to keep the trains running.[72]

Indeed, repeatedly during his premiership, the streets of Barcelona, Valencia, Madrid, and other industrial centres were filled with anti-war protesters and strikers. The Socialist Union, the UGT, almost doubled its membership between 1908 and 1911 to just under 78,000 while the new anarchist federation, the Confederación Nacional del Trabajo, formed in 1911, had over 26,000 members on its books. The Republicans in Valencia, led by the novelist Blasco Ibañez, were, by 1913, selling 10,000 copies of their daily paper, *El Pueblo*.[73] Canalejas himself calculated that between the beginning of his Premiership in February 1910 and July 1912, some 10,581 meetings of a political nature were held, of which almost half were in Barcelona.[74]

Despite these obstacles, Canalejas's government was able to achieve some important reforms. Universal military service was introduced, bringing to an end the loophole whereby the better-off had been able to evade conscription.[75] The much-hated *consumos* tax on food, fuel and drink was partially abolished. His White Paper on local administration, allowing provinces to group together to take over a range of responsibilities from the state, was an intelligent response to the clamour for regional autonomy and indeed won the support of the Lliga. Above all, Canalejas took the first step towards tackling the issue which most divided Spaniards—that of clericalism. Shortly after he took office, a bill was published on the freedom of worship which allowed other religions besides Catholicism to publicize their activities. The consequent indignation of right-wing Catholics was further exacerbated by Canalejas's attempts to bring the expansion of the religious orders under governmental control through a Law of Associations. Relations between the government and the Vatican were broken off and Catholic reaction was mobilized throughout Spain.[76]

---

[72] For Canalejas's own justification of this decision see his speech in parliament on 19 Oct. 1912, *DSC* no. 161, 4630–40.

[73] For popular reactions against the Moroccan War see Andrée Bachoud, *Los españoles ante las campañas de Marruecos* (Madrid, 1988). Figures for *El Pueblo* from Reig (*Obrers*), 308.

[74] Canalejas (*El Partido*), 45.

[75] The payment of money to evade military service had already been abolished under Maura's government by a decree of August 1909.

[76] For a typical expression of Catholic 'fundamentalism', see P. Antonio Viladevall S.J., *La voluntad nacional en frente del jacobinismo afrancesado de Romanones y Canalejas*

The resulting compromise between Conservatives and the Liberal government allowed the passage of the so-called Padlock Law, which gave the government a measure of control over the religious orders pending a future Law of Associations.[77]

By the autumn of 1911, however, Canalejas felt besieged on all sides. The war in Morocco had flared up once again, complicated by the fact that French forces were pushing into the Spanish sphere in the North. Despite a ferocious campaign by Socialists and Republicans to abandon Morocco, Canalejas ordered the occupation of extensive territory within this sphere. However, the army was pinned down by costly skirmishes with the highly mobile guerrilla forces of the Rif tribes. Canalejas had also begun negotiations with the French to establish a clear demarcation line between their respective areas of control. At home, he had had to deal with a mutiny on board a Spanish warship and suppress a bloody uprising in a small Valencian town. The spiral of strikes in September had led him to suspend constitutional guarantees. His use of troops to quell disorder had strengthened the army's political clout and there was no longer any possibility of repealing the Law of Jurisdictions. Meanwhile, he had neither pacified the right nor won over the left, except for a handful of left-leaning intellectuals.[78] The Conservative politician Eduardo Dato reported in a letter to Maura on 29 September that Canalejas had told him that his policies had failed and that

[h]is fitness for office, his weariness, his health, a thousand circumstances counselled that he should drop everything now but that that would be to cede the prerogative to the promoters of strikes.[79]

When in January 1912 parliament resumed after a long break of six months, Canalejas's bitterness broke through. In a long and frank ex-

(Barcelona, 1907), in which the Liberals' plans are described as a Masonic plot (8) and the work of Lucifer (222).

[77] For more on this issue, see Fernando García de Cortázar, 'La Iglesia en la crisis del estado español (1898–1923)' in Tuñón de Lara (*La crisis*), 343–77. The outwardly devout king was deeply unhappy with Canalejas's law and insisted that the whole government turn out for the closing event of the International Eucharistic Congress in Madrid in June 1911: José Luis Vila-San-Juan (*Alfonso*), 256.

[78] Among them, the Republican deputy and journalist Luis Morote and the Oviedo Professor Rafael Altamira, both of whom joined the Liberal Party, while the Nobel prize-winning scientist, Santiago Ramón y Cajal, accepted a life senatorship: Francos (*La vida*), 500–1. Canalejas complained to the moderate Republican Melquíades Alvarez that he would have expected the left, if not to have supported him, at least to have displayed some benevolence towards his efforts to introduce reforms. Instead they had merely attacked him as reactionary: 601–2.

[79] Maura and Fernández Almagro (*¿Por qué?*), 210.

change with Maura, he complained that there was a radical, even insoluble contradiction between the two of them and that Maura's offer to collaborate with the government had been made 'in such a disdainful and arrogant way that it could be neither respected nor appreciated'. After complaining of his own exhaustion, Canalejas went on to declare that the problem they all faced was not the usual governmental crisis but 'a profound crisis of national life'.[80]

Canalejas's assassination later that year allowed his hagiographers to claim that had it not been for this fateful event, he would have solved Spain's crisis. The very fortuitousness of his assassination reinforced the tragic view of Spanish history whereby progress and stability were repeatedly denied by acts of irrational violence that seemed to spring from nowhere. Canalejas was shot dead on 12 November 1912 as he paused to look at the shop window of a book store in the Puerta del Sol, the central square of Madrid. The assassin, an anarchist wanted by the police and known to be plotting a violent deed, had been waiting for the passage of the royal carriage and had intended to assassinate the king. Recognizing Canalejas because he had seen him give a speech the day before from the spectators' gallery in parliament, the anarchist seized the opportunity and killed the premier instead, turning the gun on himself immediately afterwards.[81] The circumstances of Canalejas's assassination were remarkably similar to the attempt on Maura's life in 1904 when another anarchist, armed with a dagger and waiting for the arrival of the king, had plunged it instead into Maura, narrowly missing his heart.[82]

Canalejas's death robbed the Liberals of the man who had become their undisputed leader. Now they divided once again into factions. Convinced that it was still not sensible to recall Maura, the king turned to the leader of one of the Liberal factions, Count Romanones, to form a new government. Maura, believing the Liberals to have broken the implicit rules of the Restoration pact by toying with the devil, the Republicans and the left in general, renounced his leadership of the Conservatives. His official note repeated the position he had adopted since October 1909. He was not prepared to alternate in power with the Liberals and he gave Alfonso the option of forcing them to rectify their policies or of seeking a new Conservative leader or Party prepared to collaborate with them. By giving in to the pressure of forces outside the Restoration system, he argued, the king had destroyed its very foundation.[83]

When Romanones's government fell in 1913, Maura stood aloof and it

---

[80] *DSC*, 1912, no. 77, 2061–5.   [81] Francos (*La vida*), 666–77.
[82] Maura and Fernández Almagro (*¿Por qué?*), 229.   [83] Ibid. 233–4.

was left to one of his colleagues, Eduardo Dato, to form a new Conservative government. Dato's reluctant decision to serve as premier signalled the impatience of many Conservative politicians with Maura's stand. Most of the Conservatives followed Dato's lead. A minority, made up largely of young Conservatives, split from the Party and launched a vociferous and dynamic movement which claimed Maura as its leader and baptised itself with his name. Maura, however, had not given up the hope of recovering the leadership of the Conservatives in the long run and remained somewhat distant from a movement clamouring for his leadership.[84] The political crisis of 1913 shattered the fiction of the two-party system. Like the Liberals, the Conservatives were once more and perhaps now irrevocably split.

The strategy of the revolution from above was not abandoned. Attempts would be made once again to renew the regime from within. But the political system was now almost fatally weakened by internal divisions and external pressures. Without an organized base amongst traditional groups nor functional links with the new economic élites and relying on patronage and bureaucracy, the two parties of the establishment were increasingly out of touch with society. Speaking at a conference in 1913, the Lliga leader Francesc Cambó declared:

Spanish politics is monopolized by two pulverized parties and neither one has a leader at its head. They are no longer parties; they are gangs. They are no longer leaders but bosses of gangs.[85]

The failure of the revolution from above, whether that of Maura or of Canalejas, was due above all to the intractable problems of early twentieth-century Spain, which were summed up earlier as the dual crisis of legitimacy and modernization—the legacy of the wars of 1895–8, the rise of mass politics, the contradictions between modernity and tradition and the ideological polarization which all this encouraged. These interrelated factors combined to disable attempts to regenerate the regime from within or from above and made the stately *pas de deux* between the two parties impossible to sustain for much longer.

---

[84] See his letter to Ossorio, 4 July 1915 in María Jesús González Hernández, *Ciudadanía y acción. El conservadurismo maurista, 1907–1923* (Madrid, 1990), 59.
[85] Jesús Pabón, *Cambó* (Barcelona, 1952), 412.

8

The Fall of the Restoration System, 1914–1923

THE Restoration system did not survive the effects of the First World War. Although she did not enter the war, Spain was transformed by it. Under its impact, the prolonged crisis of legitimacy of the political regime became a crisis of the state itself as in 1917 the labour movement, the army, and the parliamentary opposition led by representatives of the Catalan bourgeoisie staged separate challenges against the ruling political order. In an effort to maintain the *status quo*, the king and the political élites formed coalition and national governments. These, however, failed to cope with the economic and social problems thrown up by the war and its aftermath. When, finally, the army seized power in 1923 with the approval or acquiescence of Spain's élites, they merely toppled a crumbling edifice long abandoned by most Spaniards.

The repercussions of the First World War on Spain were most dramatic and immediate in her economy. The shift to a war economy of much of Europe between 1914 and 1918 enabled Spanish industry and commerce to expand at an extraordinary pace to fill the gap. Textiles, leather goods, mining, iron, shipping, and chemicals boomed as demand rose from the war-torn economies to the north. Electrical capacity almost doubled between 1913 and 1918, marking a significant shift in the technological base of Spanish industry. In Bilbao alone, investments in new companies rose from 14.5 million pesetas in 1913 to 427.5 million in 1918.[1] Economic growth, in turn, stimulated banking and commerce. The number of Spanish banks rose from fifty at the beginning of the war to eighty by the end, while the number of current accounts quadrupled in the same period.[2] War-time speculation gave rise to a layer of *parvenu*

---

[1] Santiago Roldán and José Luis García Delgado, *La formación de la sociedad capitalista en España, 1914–1920* (Madrid, 1973), vol. 1, 70 and 77.

[2] Pedro Gual Villalbi, *Memorias de un industrial de nuestro tiempo* (Barcelona, 1923), 212.

bourgeois who displayed their wealth ostentatiously in the fashionable venues of the cities.[3]

The boom also dislocated the economy. Rapid growth fuelled severe inflation and by 1920 the price of basic necessities was as much as 120 per cent higher than in 1914. It heightened socio-economic and regional differences. The scarcity of goods in the interior and falling living standards led to renewed food riots and popular uprisings. Many rural workers left the countryside for the industrial cities where work was easier to obtain. By 1918 the number of industrial workers was 60 per cent higher than in 1910.[4] Inflation led workers to strike repeatedly to compensate for the fall in their real wages and in the conditions of boom employers were more prepared to concede wages rises than lose orders. As a result, there was a spectacular growth in union membership. The anarchist union, the CNT, created in 1911, claimed to have almost 800,000 members by 1919, of which half were in Catalonia alone, equivalent to the total working population of that region.[5] As industry grew and the nature of work and the shape of cities changed, the urban rioters of the early years of the century were increasingly drawn into the organized labour movement.

Indeed, so dramatic were the structural effects of the First World War on Spanish society that many historians have been tempted to see it as the starting-point of the decline of the regime and the rise of mass politics.[6] As we have argued throughout, both processes were present since at least the beginning of the century; the war merely accelerated their pace. The repercussions of the conflict, therefore, served to exacerbate an already existing crisis of modernization in Spain, widening the gap between city and countryside, industry and agriculture, workers and employers, and between the industrial bourgeoisie and the landowning oligarchy who controlled the political system.

The European conflict also sharpened the ideological differences within the country. The divisions between the democracies and the Central Powers were transmuted into the chronic Spanish dichotomies— modernization, democracy, and devolution versus tradition, order, and

---

[3] For a vivid portrait of the times, see ibid. 101–55.

[4] Roldán and García Delgado (*La formación*), 128–43.

[5] Pere Gabriel, 'Eren temps de sindicats. Reconsideracions a l'entorn de 1917–1923', in 'Els Sindicats del crim. Pistolerisme a Barcelona, 1917–1923', *L'Avenç*, no. 192 (May 1995), 14.

[6] Juan Antonio Lacomba, for example, writes that in that period, '[T]he mass of the population were brusquely awakened from their almost secular lethargy . . .' in *La crisis española de 1917* (Madrid, 1970), 51.

centralization. Events in Europe challenged many Spaniards' perceptions about the social and political order in their own country. As a Republican paper asserted,

The subversive power of the war, which is sinking emperors, throwing out kings, making all the old hierarchies tremble, is now reaching us.[7]

The bitter polemic over whether Spain should remain neutral or intervene and whether that neutrality should favour the democracies or the Central Powers sharply divided public opinion. The issue became so volatile that many cinemas refused to show newsreels in case fights broke out amongst the audience.[8] The problem was exacerbated by the German blockade of Spanish ports and the mounting attacks by German submarines on Spanish merchant ships suspected of carrying cargoes to or from France or Britain.

The social and political crisis of 1917 in Spain was part of the more general upheaval throughout Europe caused by the war which saw the emergence of the Soviet Union and of new states out of the fragments of the Austrian–Hungarian Empire. Indeed, the components of this upheaval were broadly similar in Spain and elsewhere—peasant uprisings, officers' revolts, proletarian revolution, and nationalist movements for independence. Clearly, the social and economic problems underlying the crisis in Spain were not of the same magnitude as in those parts of Europe devastated by the war. Nevertheless, so fragile was Spain's political system that she was fatally weakened by them.

Of all the challenges, none was as powerful as that of the labour movement. The wave of agitation that spread across Spain in 1916—almost two and a half million working days were lost that year compared to under 400,000 in the previous year—was impelled by the severe hardship resulting from war-induced inflation. Pressure from their rank and file forced the reformist leadership of the Socialist Union, the Unión General de Trabajadores (UGT), to form a common front with the revolutionary CNT in July 1916 to compel the government to take action over the economic crisis. Their ability to mobilize large numbers of workers was confirmed by a one-day general stoppage in December against the government's policies. The success of the strike emboldened the left to believe that they could gather together the multiple agitation amongst workers throughout Spain into a revolutionary general strike.

---

[7] Paradox, 'Fe', *La Campana de Gracia*, 16 June 1917.
[8] Francisco J. Romero Salvadó, 'Spain and the First World War: Neutrality and Crisis' (Ph.D. Thesis, University of London, 1994), 20.

The two unions were separated by fundamentally different strategies, however. For the CNT, the coming general strike was meant to sweep away the monarchy and instal a system of dual power, only vaguely defined in their documents, shared by trade unions and the radical bourgeoisie, whose identity was even less clear.[9] Unlike the Socialists, the anarchists had no time for the parliamentary road to socialism, which was mere 'games and deceits'.[10] For the Socialist leadership, on the other hand, the general strike was a means of bringing about a bourgeois republic as the first stage in the 'inexorable' march towards socialism. While the anarchists saw the Catalan bourgeoisie and the army as their natural class enemies, the Socialist leaders saw them as potential partners in the creation of a new capitalist republic. Their revolutionary rhetoric was tempered by a cautious, legalistic reformism in practice.[11] The divisions between the two movements were exacerbated by a regional split; while the CNT controlled union organization in Catalonia, the Levante and Andalusia, the UGT was dominant in Madrid, Asturias, and the Basque Country.

This ferment of social agitation throughout Spain and the consequent erosion of the government's credibility encouraged disgruntled officers to stage their own revolt against the political system. It was no coincidence that their rebellion began in Barcelona where the most powerful labour movement in the country was located. The origin of army discontent in 1917 lay in professional grievances over pay and promotion. As we saw in Chapter 6, the Moroccan war provided ample opportunities for officers on active service to rise in the ranks. Those stationed on the peninsula, on the other hand, found themselves rapidly overtaken in rank by younger officers.[12] The resulting grievance led to the formation of the Juntas, akin to trade union committees of officers of the rank of Colonel and below, which sprang up in garrisons throughout Spain. The men who led the Juntas couched their appeal in the fashionable language of regenerationism. Heavily tinged with nationalist and populist rhetoric and imbued with a deep resentment over the Spanish–American War, it

---

[9] See for example 'Programa Sindicalista del 17 de julio', in Lacomba (*La crisis*), Appendix 2, 472–5.

[10] 'Parlamentarismo, no; revolución, sí', *Solidaridad Obrera*, 3 Aug. 1917.

[11] For the Socialists' reformism, see Paul Heywood, *Marxism and the Failure of Organized Socialism in Spain, 1879–1936* (Cambridge, 1990).

[12] 'Cambio de orientación', *La Correspondencia de España*, 14 Aug. 1913, reproduced in *Los sucesos de agosto ante el Parlamento* (Madrid, 1918), 321–4.

called on the king to sweep aside the oligarchy which had presided over the Disaster and to launch a new democratic Spain.[13]

From the political feelers the Junteros put out, however, it was clear that the kind of regeneration they envisaged had more to do with the Conservative revolution from above than the radical revolution from below. The leader of the Juntas, the self-important Colonel Benito Márquez, let Maura know through an intermediary that he considered him the only possible solution to the crisis. In contrast, the attempt by the Radical leader, Alejandro Lerroux, to woo the Junta officers was contemptuously rebuffed.[14] Nor could the regenerationist discourse disguise the fundamentally corporatist nature of the officers' protest. The core of the Juntas' demands concerned professional grievances: on one hand, the unfair system of promotion, and on the other, the deterioration in officers' pay as a result of rampant inflation.

The creation of the Juntas in Barcelona and their subsequent spread throughout Spain alarmed the king and the government, in whose minds no doubt the recent example of the Russian military soviets loomed large. The Juntas were ordered to dissolve and their leaders were arrested. On 1 June, in an action not far short of a *coup d'état*, the Juntas issued an ultimatum to the government to release their fellow-officers and recognize the Junta movement; should it not do so, the document implied, the army would seize power.[15] The capitulation of the government and its resignation shortly afterwards was greeted with enthusiasm by all those wishing to see an end to the old politics. The vaccuum of power created by the revolt of the military gave rise to exaggerated hopes that the regime might be easily overthrown; indeed, the Republicans and Socialists immediately set up a provisional government. The officers' victory, however, was not the beginning of a democratic transition but the intensification of the process of army intervention in politics which had begun with the *¡Cucut!* affair in 1905 and would end in dictatorship in 1923.

The third challenge to the Restoration system came from the Lliga, led

---

[13] Márquez, Ex-Coronel, and Capó, J. M., *Las Juntas Militares de Defensa* (Barcelona, 1923), 204–8; n.a., *Renovación o Revolución. Historia documentada de un período (junio a octubre 1917)* (Barcelona, 1917), 92–116. At least among infantry officers, there was a tradition of setting up Juntas over professional grievances; thus the 1904 Junta in Barcelona (ibid.), 118–19.

[14] Fernando Soldevilla, *Tres revoluciones (Apuntes y notas). La junta de reforma. La asamblea parlamentaria. La huelga general* (Madrid, 1917), 17. For contacts between the Juntas and Maura: Maura and Fernández Almagro (*¿Por qué*), 303–4.

[15] Lacomba (*La crisis*), 128–30; for preparations for a military coup, see 134–5.

by the shrewd Francesc Cambó. Despite their powerful electoral base in Catalonia, the Lliga had gained little from their involvement in Restoration politics besides the *Mancomunitat*, a limited form of regional government conceded in 1914. The extraordinary growth of Catalan industry during the First World War had exposed even more clearly the gap between the region's economic and its political power, strengthening the Lliga's belief that they had a historic mission to wrest political control from the landed oligarchy that ran the state.[16] This ambition had been renewed by the factional disintegration of their traditional patrons, the Conservatives, in the aftermath of the Tragic Week. Without Maura at its helm, the Conservative Party offered little hope of the modernization sought by the Catalan Regionalists. Moreover, the growth of labour agitation during the war made political reform a matter of extreme urgency. The Lliga leader, Francesc Cambó, declared that the most conservative thing to be at that time was a revolutionary.[17]

The revolt of the Lliga had been provoked by the attempt of the Liberal government in 1916 to tax the extraordinary war profits of industry and commerce. The fact that the Minister responsible for drawing up the White Paper, Santiago Alba, a representative of the Castilian wheat-growing oligarchy and former leader of the National Union, was not going to apply the same tax to the agrarian sector only intensified their anger.[18] In the midst of the crisis created by the revolt of the Juntas, Cambó sought to create an alternative political bloc to the Restoration parties by mobilizing a wide range of allies. He had already tried to woo the Socialists, declaring to them a year earlier in their headquarters in Madrid that the only forces truly representative of the country were the Catalan Regionalists and the Socialists.[19]

Assured of considerable support amongst left-leaning parliamentary deputies, Cambó demanded the re-opening of the Cortes which had remained closed in the exceptional circumstances of the army revolt. The government's refusal led him to organize an alternative Assembly of Parliamentarians, which met in Barcelona on 19 July after an elaborate cat-and-mouse chase with the authorities, who had orders to dissolve any such subversive meeting. The meeting ended when the Governor of Catalonia,

---

[16] The Lliga leader Francesc Cambó declared, 'Catalonia, at a time in Spain's history that can be epic and can be tragic, feels all the grandeur and all the generosity of a mission of salvation of Spain which everyone attributed to it . . .': Pabón (*Cambó*), vol. 2, 511. See also the editorial in *La Veu* (*Baluart de Sitges*), 16 July 1917.

[17] Manuel Burgos y Mazo, *Páginas históricas de 1917* (Madrid, 1918), 110.

[18] For details, see Roldán and García Delgado (*La formación*), 255–322 and 459–77.

[19] 'La Conferencia del Sr. Cambó', *ABC*, 3 July 1916.

having traced the venue, entered and made a symbolic arrest of all the deputies present. As they left the building, the rebellious deputies were cheered by a crowd of supporters who had gathered outside.[20]

The Assembly of Parliamentarians was an extraordinary event in many senses. It represented the culmination of efforts since the Disaster to create a modernizing and democratic alternative to the ruling political order. Embracing all political forces opposed to the Restoration system except the anarchists—Catalanists, Republicans, Reformists, and Socialists—the Assembly called for the formation of a national government excluding the ruling parties, and for the preparation of a new constitution. In the feverish atmosphere of the summer of 1917, it appeared to mark the beginning of a stable, modern, bourgeois polity. The Catalan newspaper, *La Veu de Catalunya*, reflecting the widespread feeling of intoxication created by the Assembly, declared,

The powerful and invincible alliance of Catalonia and the renovating forces of Spain has been created. The two great rivers have joined their waters.[21]

Meanwhile, in their efforts to neutralize the military threat and the Catalan challenge, the king and his premier, Eduardo Dato, had shown a determination lacking in their dealings with the Restoration party factions. The Juntas were granted most of their corporate demands and the ageing General Weyler, hero in military eyes of the struggle to preserve Spanish Cuba, was dispatched on a placatory tour of the garrisons. Dato built a 'cordon sanitaire' around Catalonia, as Cambó complained, composed of censorship, anti-separatist propaganda and bribery.[22] Unknown to the premier, a secret meeting had been apparently held in a Barcelona convent between Cambó, Colonel Márquez, leader of the Barcelona Juntas, and two priests, shady emissaries of the king. During this meeting, as Márquez himself later claimed, a compromise over the forthcoming Assembly was reached whereby it would be held, as indeed it was, at a secret location to avoid a showdown with the authorities which might have raised its political impact.[23]

Cambó's apparent ambiguity about the Assembly may have been connected with its increasingly radical complexion. His hopes of winning

[20] Pabón (*Cambó*), vol. I, 512–19; Lacomba (*La crisis*), 200–4; Soldevilla (*Tres*), 120–9; *Los sucesos*, 365–80; Magi Morena i Galicia, 'L'Assemblea el 19', *La Veu*, 28–29 July 1917.
[21] 'Catalunya autónoma dins l'Espanya nova', *La Veu de Catalunya* (*Baluart de Sitges*), 16 July 1917.
[22] Pabón (*Cambó*), 511; José (Josep) Pla, *Francesc Cambó. Materials per a una historia*, vol. XXV of *Obra Completa* (Barcelona, 1973).
[23] Márquez and Capó (*Las Juntas*), 48–50.

over dissident conservative forces had been dashed when, in the first place, Maura had refused to entertain any idea of supporting an anti-constitutional movement, describing the Assembly as a 'professional flea-market'.[24] Despite intense pressure from some of his supporters, Maura had rejected Cambó's overtures as he had those of the Juntas, confident that his loyalty to the king and his prestige as a politician would eventually persuade Alfonso to call on him to save the regime.[25] In the second place, the Juntas had declined Cambó's invitation to support the Assembly because it was led by Catalanists, whom the military regarded with deep hostility as little more than separatists.[26] Thus the Assembly took on a markedly left-wing character and Cambó would have no problem in abandoning it when it no longer suited his purpose. What hastened his decision and that of the Juntas above all was the revolutionary challenge of the labour movement.

Since the one-day stoppage against the government in December 1916, the CNT and the UGT had been preparing for a more decisive general strike to topple the regime. They had the support of the Republican parties including the newly constituted Reformist Party. The Socialists also counted on the backing of the Lliga and the Juntas, though neither had expressed any support for such an action; after all, the Socialists believed, it was partly on their behalf that the general strike would eventually be launched.[27] The government undoubtedly read the situation more accurately. It was only eleven years since the Lliga and the Catalan bourgeoisie had recoiled in horror from the events of the Tragic Week and had abandoned their efforts to change the political establishment. A paralysis of industry at a time of boom combined with renewed violence in Catalonia might help to concentrate their minds on which side they really belonged. The army, on the other hand, would regard an upsurge of revolutionary 'insurgency' as a threat to their own institution and in those circumstances would respond more easily to the defence of the ruling order.

Though there is no conclusive proof, it is therefore likely that the government provoked the premature declaration of the general strike by secretly encouraging the rail company at the centre of a bitter and prolonged labour dispute to stand firm against any concessions to its work-

[24]   Maura and Fernández Almagro (*¿Por qué?*), 488.

[25]   Tusell (*Antonio Maura*), 173–4.

[26]   Looking back on events a few years later, the exiled Benito Márquez would consider this to have been a fundamental error: Márquez and Capó (*Las Juntas*), 46–7.

[27]   Lacomba (*La crisis*), 245–7.

ers.[28] The growing movement of solidarity for the rail-workers and the revolutionary impatience of the CNT forced a reluctant Socialist leadership to agree to a general strike in their support beginning on 13 August. Whether the government was involved or not, the outbreak of the general strike, merely three days before the next meeting of the Assembly was due to take place, could not have been better timed for its purposes.

The general strike of August 1917 was a disaster for the labour movement. As the authorities had calculated, the army remained loyal to the system while the Lliga remained aloof.[29] Hastily prepared, the stoppages occurred only in the main industrial centres and failed to spread to the countryside. A well-prepared government was able to mobilize the troops and crush the strike bloodily. In several days of street fighting, scores of strikers were killed, hundreds injured, and thousands arrested. Army repression was particularly savage in the Asturian mining valleys, where the troops went on the rampage against defenceless miners.[30]

The defeat of the general strike, however, was only a pyrrhic victory for the establishment. Far from shifting the political balance in the government's direction, it strengthened the hand of the Juntas and the Assembly. The army was able to claim that it had been used once again by a discredited system against the people.[31] Amidst almost universal condemnation of the government, the Juntas issued a new ultimatum to the king on 26 October; he was to dismiss the Premier and form a national government representing forces outside the Restoration parties. Alfonso bowed immediately to the first of their demands and sacked Dato.

Four days later, the Assembly met for a second time and reiterated its demand for a new constitution. In the course of the meeting, Cambó received a message from the king, calling him to a private meeting in the Palace. The purpose of this meeting was obvious to all politicians and political commentators; the king was sounding out members of a possible national government. Faced with the choice of persisting in his opposition

---

[28] This was a general assumption amongst all the spokesmen of the anti-Restoration movement of 1917, including Cambó. See his speech 'Una conferencia histórica', *La Veu de Catalunya*, 24 Oct. 1917 and 'Después de la huelga general'. *Solidaridad Obrera*, 25 Oct. 1917 and the parliamentary speeches on the events by the opposition in *Los sucesos*. For a brief review of the evidence see Romero (*Spain*), 403 nn. 79 and 83.

[29] For Márquez' position, see 'La qüestió militar', *La Veu de Catalunya*, 25 Oct. 1917; for the Lliga's view, 'Vaga general', ibid., 17 Aug. 1917.

[30] Enrique Moradiellos, *El Sindicato de los Obreros Mineros Asturianos, 1910–1930* (Oviedo, 1986), 58–9.

[31] See Márquez' statement to *El Heraldo de Madrid* in Soldevilla (*Tres*), 210–13; also 'Comunicación de la Junta Superior de defensa a los presidentes de las Regionales', in *Los sucesos*, 336–8.

to the political system or collaborating in a coalition government, Cambó chose the latter, believing that in the new political circumstances it was possible to transform the system from within.

Cambó's decision excited heated polemic in the Assembly. The left accused him of betraying the movement. Lerroux' paper *La Publicidad* scornfully proclaimed the end of hopes of constitutional reform:

Republicans, reformists and Socialists will return to their tents . . . and the regionalists will not get regional autonomy and will have to return to the politics of realism and 'possibilism' which consist of dragging out of the local authorities . . . the right to extend a telephone cable between two mountain villages.[32]

With a fine sense of irony, a Catalan Republican paper suggested that the Lliga had chosen to play the role of Calabria when they might have played that of Piedmont.[33]

Cambó insisted that by supporting the new government he was carrying out the Assembly's programme. With two Catalanists and other independents, the cabinet was no longer dominated by the political representatives of the oligarchy. Moreover, the government had promised to take on board the Assembly's demands.[34] His real motives may have been more complex. Having failed to convince the Juntas and Maura and his supporters to join the Assembly, the Lliga risked being swamped by the left within the movement; this, in turn, might result in the loss of the Lliga's more conservative supporters.[35] In a parallel situation some eight years previously, the Lliga had deserted the left-wing dominated Solidaritat Catalana in order to support Maura's revolution from above.[36] The perception of the threat posed by the left was magnified by events taking place in Russia, while the danger of a military coup also counselled a return to the Restoration fold.

Yet there could be little doubt that Cambó and his colleagues had underestimated the difficulty of transforming the political system from within. The editorial in *La Veu de Catalunya* greeting the new govern-

---

[32] 'De la crisis', 3 Nov. 1917.

[33] Paradox, 'El Govern de la desllealtad', *La Campana de Gracia*, 10 Nov. 1917.

[34] 'Declaracions d'en Cambó' *La Veu de Catalunya*, 3 Nov. 1917; 'IMPORTANTISSIMES DECLARACIONS D'EN CAMBÓ', ibid., 6 Nov. 1917.

[35] Cambó (*Memorias*), 254. For Cambó's attempt to woo the Juntas see 'En Cambó als coronels', *La Veu de Catalunya*, 30 July 1917 and the mauristas, 'Parlant amb en Cambó', ibid., 7 Aug. 1917.

[36] As Giner de los Ríos pointed out in *La Publicidad*, 6 Nov. 1917.

ment with the headlines, 'Catalonia triumphant. Victory!', and Cambó's own statement in the same issue that it represented a 'profound revolution' in relations between politicians and voters were wishful hyperboles.[37] Similarly, the Lliga's hopes of convincing the Spanish electorate in their programme of national renovation, encapsulated by the slogan 'Per Catalunya i per l'Espanya gran', were somewhat ambitious. Conversely, Cambó overestimated the danger of revolution from below. He refused to play the role of Kerensky when there was no threat of a Spanish Lenin.[38]

Indeed, in the new government of 'concentration', in which both the Lliga and the Juntas were represented, Cambó's hopes of a renovation of Spanish politics were immediately set back. Despite his intense campaigning, the elections of February 1918 proved that the oligarchy were still able to command or fix votes in vast swathes of backward Spain.[39] Within the cabinet, the two Catalan Ministers were unable to assert themselves, not so much out of weakness of character, as Cambó later claimed, but because the government was still dominated by the old political élite.[40] The government's authority was further enfeebled by external events such as the continued sinking by German submarines of Spanish cargo ships. It finally fell as a result of a strike by postal and telegraph workers who, following the example of the officers, had set up their own Juntas. The king, despairing of finding a stable government after failing to persuade any of the Restoration leaders to form a new cabinet, summoned them to the Palace where he was reported to have announced,

if here . . . this very night, a government is not formed which will save the situation . . . I will be across the frontier by dawn tomorrow morning.[41]

Maura's hour seemed finally to have arrived after almost nine years in the wilderness. In the dying years of the Restoration system, Maura had become the repository of a range of contradictory illusions amongst the right. For the military and for restless sections of the conservative middle classes, he was the strong man who would stamp out social unrest and sweep away the old politics. Maura's devoutness fooled many traditional-

[37] *La Veu de Catalunya*, 4 Nov. 1917.

[38] Romero ('Spain'), 295.

[39] For details, see Soldevila (*El año, 1918*), 37–48, and José Pla, *Francesc Cambó. Materials per a una historia*, vol. XXV of *Obra Completa* (Barcelona, 1973), 506–9.

[40] Cambó (*Memorias*), 264. Cierva for example, as Minister of War, obstructed the work of the cabinet: Maura and Fernández Almagro (*¿Por qué?*), 310.

[41] Soldevila (*El año, 1918*), 105.

ists into believing him a defender of the Church above the constitution. The politician who might have united the protest of the military Juntas and the Catalan bourgeoisie, had he not refused to challenge the Restoration system, now accepted the king's invitation to head a national government of salvation in March 1918. He did so with few illusions. After receiving the acclaim of his supporters outside his home in Madrid, Maura took his elder son into the privacy of his study, and, pointing to his desk, told him bitterly,

They kept me glued there for almost ten years, which could have been the most profitable [years] of my life, without allowing me to do anything useful, and now they ask me to preside over the whole lot. Let's see how long this balderdash lasts.[42]

Embracing four previous Premiers and three party leaders, Maura's cabinet was greeted with enormous enthusiasm by the press and the conservative public. With the energetic participation of Cambó as Minister of Public Works, Maura renewed the regenerationist policies of state intervention and economic nationalism that he had attempted to carry out during his government of 1907–9.[43] In reality, however, his national government was subject to the same pressures as its predecessor. The German submarine campaign against Spanish and French ships intensified; by the summer of 1918, some 20 per cent of the Spanish merchant marine had been sunk without any vigorous protest from successive Spanish governments, fearful of upsetting the delicate balance of neutrality within the country and under duress from the Germanophile king not to declare against the Central Powers. To this were added a rash of scandals about the network of spies, suborned officials, and newspaper editors funded by the Germans. The climate of instability was heightened by a wave of strikes against rising prices.

Maura's government was also undermined by the failure of the different political interests represented within it to agree on policy. The old élite viewed with intense suspicion the plans of the modernizers, amongst whom Cambó was the most outstanding, and the modernizers themselves clashed with each other. On 6 November, a few days before the Armistice in Europe, the national government fell. A grim-faced Maura emerged from the Palace announcing, 'Let's see which smart-arse now takes over power.'[44] For the first time, Maura appeared privately to consider that

[42] The word he used was 'monserga'; Maura and Fernández Almagro (*¿Por qué?*), 311.
[43] Tusell (*Antonio Maura*), 182–3. For Cambó's activities as Minister, see José Pla (*Francesc*), 513–19.
[44] Fernández Almagro (*Historia política*), 267.

the only solution to Spain's problems lay in military dictatorship.[45]

The end of the First World War brought severe problems to the Spanish economy, intensifying the climate of political and social crisis. As normal international trade resumed, the period of industrial expansion of the war years came to an end. The adjustment to a peace economy led employers to reduce wages and lay off workers. The unions responded with strikes and demonstrations which turned violent when the troops were called in.[46] Between 1919 and 1923 collective bargaining gave way to social war in which government, parliament, and the political system in general became increasingly marginalized. In the south, the hungry and semi-employed labourers rose in revolt against landlords, seizing their lands and clashing bloodily with the Civil Guard and troops sent to suppress them.

The inability of the state to ensure industrial or agrarian peace at a time of economic crisis led employers to bypass democratic institutions. In Catalonia, where the challenge of the labour movement was strongest, employers set up their own parallel bosses' union to organize lock-outs; they also mobilized vigilante squads and right-wing unions whose members were drawn from Catholic and Carlist organizations.[47] Their campaign to destroy the CNT was closely backed by the military authorities and the Juntas. In the process, the Catalan bourgeoisie drew closer to the army, shelving their support for the Lliga's policies, and abandoning the idea of political reform for the seductions of military dictatorship.[48]

Similarly, the simple attractions of revolutionary syndicalism, the belief that the unions could take over and run society, eroded the appeal of the Republican parties for many workers who had previously voted for them. The anarchists responded to the employers' campaign by setting up their armed gangs; one of their victims was Eduardo Dato himself. This erosion of faith in the parliamentary road to reform on the part of the bourgeoisie and workers was part of a wider crisis of liberal democracy in post-war Europe. The Spanish case can be regarded as a regional variant of the upheaval that occurred throughout the Continent which led to revolution in Russia and fascism in Italy and Germany.

---

[45] Tusell (*Antonio Maura*), 190.

[46] The number of strikes rose from an average of around 210 annually during the war to over 1,000 in 1920 while in the same period, the number of workers on strike rose fivefold (Roldán and García Delgado (*La formación*), vol. 1, 243.

[47] For an account of the right-wing workers' organizations see Colin Winston, *Workers and the Right in Spain, 1900–1936* (Princeton, 1985) and 'Els Sindicats' (*L'Avenç*).

[48] Bengoechea, Soledad, *Organització patronal i conflictivitat social a Catalunya. Tradició i corporativisme entre finals del segle i la dictadura de Primo de Rivera* (Montserrat, 1994).

The post-war crisis in Spain tilted the balance of power among the élites towards the military and those forces advocating an authoritarian solution to Spain's problems. The attractiveness of a military dictatorship was not simply that it would destroy the class-based unions. Amongst the military and many businessmen there was a growing conviction that mere repression was insufficient and that a corporatist model of labour organization on the lines of that advocated by the Italian fascists was necessary to ensure social peace.[49] Moreover, army leaders, such as Miguel Primo de Rivera, were known also to favour an intensification of state intervention and protection of industry.

What finally tipped the balance were the repercussions of a new disaster in Morocco in August 1921. We need to consider briefly developments in Spanish policy towards North Africa since the earlier disaster in 1909, before returning to the crisis of the Restoration system.

We have already seen how Canalejas set out to negotiate a demarcation between French and Spanish spheres of influence in Morocco. His efforts were rewarded, though not before he was assassinated, by a Franco-Spanish agreement towards the end of 1912 to create two respective Protectorates. The territory over which Spain was awarded jurisdiction was considerably smaller than that which had been negotiated in 1903–4. Nevertheless, Spain's renewed role in Morocco had been warmly embraced by the Liberals, by the king and most of his high command and the neo-colonial lobby, including representatives of the Catalan bourgeoisie and moderate Republicans. It was roundly condemned by the left and failed to arouse any popular enthusiasm, markedly absent in the Melilla campaign of 1909 and in the troubles of the following two years.

When a new war flared up in northern Morocco in 1919, Spain was almost as ill-prepared as it had been a decade previously. Most of the troops on active service continued to be poorly trained, housed, and clothed. The government and the military were chronically divided over policy towards the Protectorate; the high command wished to extend effective control over the whole area while the government, following traditional defensive strategy in Morocco, preferred to limit action to the immediate hinterland of the two coastal enclaves of Ceuta and Melilla.[50] Successive governments had also been reluctant to raise more funds for an unreconstructed army which had failed so badly in the past and was unpopular amongst many Spaniards.

---

[49] Bengoechea, *Soledad*, 32–3.
[50] For Maura's view, see Maura and Fernández Almagro (*¿Por qué?*), 350.

For these reasons, the Spanish high command in Morocco was unwisely divided between two generals who disagreed fundamentally about strategy. The first was the High Commissioner, Dámaso Berenguer, directly responsible to the government and a strong advocate of pacification through negotiation. His rival was the bellicose Commander-in-Chief, Fernández Silvestre, known to be in close touch with the king with whom he was rumoured to share expansionist ambitions.[51] By July 1921 Silvestre had rashly moved troops and positions deep into Moroccan territory. The Moroccan tribes under the able leadership of Abd-el-Krim gathered together their forces and fell on the Spanish troops led by Silvestre at the outpost of Annual. Deserted by their Moroccan regulars, the demoralized and outnumbered Spanish conscripts fled into the countryside. Silvestre himself was reported to have committed suicide. During the following days, 10,000 Spanish soldiers were massacred as the Moroccans fell on the fleeing troops and on the soldiers manning the string of isolated blockhouses and garrisons, until they reached the outskirts of Melilla itself.

The disaster of Annual deepened the crisis of the Restoration system. The army blamed the government and parliament for lacking the will and refusing the funds to wage war. Sections of public opinion blamed the army for a new demonstration of incompetence. The king was accused of complicity in the disaster in allegedly encouraging Silvestre to advance. Over the next two years, the question of the responsibility for the disaster hung over politicians, generals, and the regime itself, just as it had in the aftermath of the 1898 Disaster. Now, however, twenty-three years later, the problems facing the political system were much greater. By far the most serious was the labour agitation which had swept across many parts of Spain and had led to repeated and violent clashes between workers and the forces of law and order. Moreover, the dynastic parties were hopelessly fragmented, the army was deeply alienated from the government and opposition to the political system had grown and developed a mass basis on both left and right. Amongst the most influential voices on the left was the so-called Generation of 1914, heirs and survivors of the earlier generation, who were grouped around the periodical *España*.

For a brief moment, nevertheless, the Annual Disaster awakened hopes among Restoration politicians that some measure of unity could be created around a fresh programme of renovation. Once again, Maura was called on to form another coalition government with Cambó as Minister of

⁵¹ Carr (*Spain*), 520.

Finance. The new circumstances, however, made such a government even more prone to political crises. Maura's ministers, drawn from different parties and factions, could not agree on economic policy nor on Moroccan strategy nor even on when to lift the suspension of constitutional guarantees imposed as a result of the Disaster. Cambó's ambitious financial programme was rejected by Maura on the grounds that although he considered it 'perfect and the most lucid of all that have been presented to Parliament over the last few years, [it was] . . . in the present circumstances of time and place completely unrealizable'.[52] This was nothing less that an admission of the government's impotence and the failure of Maura's revolution from above. If Cambó could not accept this rejection, Maura added, the government would collapse. 'Personally,' he wrote, 'that would be the ideal solution; the government falling together, united by a financial programme of austerity and energy.'[53]

The continued activity of the military Juntas further destabilized the shaky coalition. Since their disbandment in 1917, the Juntas had regrouped under a new name and new leaders. In 1918 and 1920, their campaign to reform the promotion system had forced two Liberal cabinets out of office. Maura's government set out determinedly to dissolve them, since their continued existence as a *de facto* power outside the constitution was an intolerable threat to the Restoration system. His Minister of War, Cierva, once a champion of the Juntas, now squared up to them in his characteristically aggressive fashion. However, the king evidently felt great sympathy towards the officers; it even appeared from a Junta document that they had had private contacts with him behind the government's back.[54] The deal that was struck finally, whereby the Juntas were brought under the control of the Ministry of War, did nothing in reality to lessen their power to challenge the constitution.[55]

Maura's last government fell finally in March 1922 when the coalition on which it was based collapsed under the combined weight of external pressures and its own internal contradictions. Deeply disillusioned with the possibility of change, Maura resigned, refusing the king's suggestion, relayed to him by Cambó, that he should form a new government with the Catalan politician which would dispense with parliament and rule by decree.[56] Maura was too closely wedded to the liberal constitution to

---

[52] Maura's letter to Cambó, AM, Legajo 278, no. 8.   [53] Ibid.

[54] AM, Legajo 277, no. 12. At the very least, Alfonso did not wish to undermine his position as intermediary between government and army by signing a decree dissolving the Juntas: Tusell (*Antonio Maura*), 233.

[55] Soldevilla (*El año, 1922*), 33–5.

[56] Pabón (*Cambó*), vol. 2, Pt. 1, 355.

consider backing any authoritarian solution. He refused to be seduced by the popular movement which bore his name and which, under his leadership, might have presented a right-wing populist challenge to the Restoration parties. Happy to rouse the 'mauristas' in bullring speeches, Maura was loath to lead them anywhere. In any case, their challenge fell away when the movement divided into a small Christian-Democrat wing and a regenerationist, authoritarian wing.[57]

The last government of the Restoration system under the veteran Liberal García Prieto, Marquis of Alhucemas, who took over as Premier from Maura's successor, the Conservative Sánchez Guerra, was yet a new attempt to co-opt moderate Republicans prepared to work within the system. The leader of the Reformist Party, Melquíades Álvarez, became President of the Congress and a colleague of his Minister of Finance. Again, attempts to introduce reforms were foiled; a proposal to alter Article 11 of the Constitution to allow a limited degree of freedom of worship was repulsed by Catholic mobilization.[58] Moreover, the approaching publication of a report on the responsibility for the Annual disaster which was expected to implicate many officers and politicians, threatened to bring the government down. High-ranking officers were known to be discussing a coup and were in close touch with Catalan industrialists and other capitalists who had lost faith in the ability of the political regime to defend their interests in the midst of the social war raging in many parts of Spain.[59]

In a conversation between the king and Maura's son, Gabriel, Alfonso gave voice to his own disillusion with Restoration politics. 'The Liberals were shattered', he was reported as saying, 'the Conservatives were good for nothing and the other parties could not assume power either.' Instead, Alfonso was considering setting up a *de facto* dictatorship with leading politicians, backed by the army and run by a government of technocrats.[60] Evidently, the king's natural inclination towards intervention had finally got the better of his constitutional role as mediator. Within the narrow limits of the liberal monarchy, Alfonso had actively sought to encourage the creation of governments reflecting the widest possible range of opin-

[57] José Gutiérrez Ravé, *Yo fui un joven maurista* (Madrid, 1944); González Hernández (*Ciudadanía*).

[58] The Archbishop of Zaragoza, a leading opponent of Canalejas' attempts to reform State-Church relations, threatened severe sanctions against the government if it went ahead. He was assassinated by gunmen two months later: Soldevilla (*El año, 1923*), 79–81 and 181–2.

[59] Bengoechea (*Organització*), 257–83.

[60] Tusell (*Antonio Maura*), 250.

ion amongst the traditional élites. A dapper, affable young man who liked to think of himself as a most modern monarch, he was also instinctively closer to the military and clerical advisers who surrounded him in the Palace than to the complex and frustrating machinations of party politics.[61]

In reply to the king's suggestion of a semi-dictatorship, Antonio Maura agreed that there seemed to be no solution to the political crisis left within the framework of the constitution. He implied that it would be better for the king to let the military take over. The generals would not succeed in solving the problems nor remain in power for long; through the 'convalescence' of a military dictatorship, Spaniards might learn finally to participate in the political life of the country.[62]

When in September 1923 General Primo de Rivera seized power, waving the banner of regenerationism, few informed people were taken by surprise. Indeed, what was more surprising was that the liberal Restoration regime had lasted so long. For a quarter of a century since the fall of the Empire, it had surmounted countless challenges. Its protracted crisis was framed by two military disasters with a second disaster in 1909 situated roughly at the half-way point. At the root of this crisis lay the Disaster of 1898, to which the new dictator referred in the first sentence of his manifesto to the people on seizing power. From that moment, the hegemony of the landed oligarchy began to be defied by new forces seeking the modernization of Spain. Faced by their mounting challenge, the liberal monarchy attempted to broaden its appeal by attracting those on the right and the left willing to work within its parameters. This framework remained too narrow, however. The Restoration parties were unable to change in tune with an evolving society because they depended structurally on patronage rather than mobilization; their leaders' careers, prestige and, in many cases, wealth were tied to the perpetuation of the political system.

The Restoration state survived for twenty-five years principally because Spain remained a largely unmodernized society for most of that time. The residual strength of the regime lay in the fact that the potential

---

[61] For Alfonso's 'modernity', see Soldevilla (*Tres*), 975. His role in the crisis of the Restoration state has been the subject of much polemic. For two contrasting views, see Carlos Seco Serrano, *Alfonso XIII y la crisis de la restauración* (Barcelona, 1969) and Antonio Elorza, 'Nacionalización y corporativismo: el papel de la corona' in José Luis García Delgado (ed.), *La crisis de la Restauración: España entre la primera guerra mundial y la segunda República* (Madrid, 1986).

[62] AM, Legajo 277, nos. 12. and 259 n. 7; Tusell (*Antonio Maura*), 251–2; Gabriel Maura (*Bosquejo*), 20–1.

base for political change was largely confined to the cities amongst a relatively small number of middle and working classes, while huge areas of Spain remained in the thrall of traditional social relations dominated by the Church, the landlord, and the cacique. No pluralist, modernizing alternative emerged either because political culture in Spain became increasingly drawn towards the opposite poles of revolution and reaction. Symptomatic of this polarization was the relative failure of the Reformist Party, a social-democratic offspring of the Republican family which had attracted a new layer of regenerationist intellectuals.

While there had been opportunities for those movements seeking change to combine—in the aftermath of the Disaster, between 1907 and 1909, and especially during the crisis of 1917—their differences had been greater than their mutual opposition to the regime. These were above all class differences, intensified after 1917 by the hopes and fears created by the Russian Revolution. The wave of labour agitation from 1919 finally impelled the more conservative anti-Restoration forces into seeking an authoritarian rather than a democratic solution to Spain's crisis. Many others, because they feared revolution and hated Restoration politics, swallowed their distaste for military rule and succumbed to the false dawn of the new 'iron surgeon'.

Antonio Maura, whose own revolution from above was unjustly invoked to legitimize the dictatorship, did not live to see the fulfilment of his prediction that it would fail. Had he still been alive in 1931, however, he would have been dismayed by the outcome of that democratic 'convalescence' on which he had placed his hopes: the fall of the monarchy and the proclamation of the Second Republic.

Epilogue

The imperial myth

THE Disaster of 1898 and the loss of the remnants of the Spanish Empire cast a long shadow over the history of twentieth-century Spain. For several decades after the event, the Disaster remained the archetype of military grievances and a mythical reference-point for the right in general. In the first sentence of his manifesto to the Spanish people on seizing power, Primo de Rivera referred to 'the picture of misfortunes and immorality which began in '98 and threaten Spain with an early, tragic and dishonourable end'.[1] General Franco, in his wishful semi-autobiographical novel and film-script, *Raza*, implicitly established a link between the naval defeat in Santiago Bay and his own victory in 1939. In his text, he portrays Admiral Cervera declaring heroically as he sets sail from the harbour, 'History will judge us. No sacrifice is sterile; out of ours will arise the glorious events of tomorrow.'[2]

Yet both generals rebelled in response to more immediate concerns than historical resentment. Primo's list of grievances was a hotch potch of clichés that could be heard every day in the officers' mess or in right-wing café conversations: the waste of public money, the rise of crime and corruption, the decline of social standards and the increase of separatism, impiety and communism.[3] Such prosaic grudges were the stock-in-trade of a growing right-wing nationalism in Spain which was part of a wider counter-revolutionary movement in Europe in the wake of the First World War. Primo's military directorate was one of several authoritarian governments in Europe which supplanted old liberal establishments in the post-war period. They were successful largely because they were backed by economic élites fearful of social revolution. Their objectives were to crush the burgeoning left-wing challenge of the post-war period and to

---

[1] From *La Vanguardia*, 13 Sept. 1923, reproduced in Genoveva García Queipo, 'Primo de Rivera', *Cuadernos de Historia 16*, no. 269 (1985).

[2] Ramón Gubern, *Raza: un ensueño del General Franco* (Madrid, 1977), 30. Writing in the 1940s also, General Kindelán stated, 'At least up to the year 1936, everything that happened was a consequence of the year 98': Teniente General Kindelán Duany, *Ejército y política* (Madrid, 1946), 176.

[3] Ibid., p. ii.

regenerate their shell-shocked economy. The most influential model for Primo's Dictatorship was Mussolini's Italy, whose economy and society most closely resembled that of Spain.

Nevertheless, the supporters of military rule in Spain also sought to legitimize dictatorship by appealing to indigenous traditions dating back to the late nineteenth century. Amongst these the most influential was that of the regenerators, from whom right-wing apologists drew selectively, adopting the residual authoritarianism of some and ignoring the long-term democratic aspirations of the movement as a whole. Primo's supporters, for example, claimed he was the iron surgeon that Costa had called for in vain.[4] The Dictator's massive programme of intervention in the economy took up many of the regenerators' demands, notably the state plan to extend irrigation schemes to the parched lands of Spain's interior. And in his economic nationalism, characterized by the intensified protection of the Spanish economy and the corporative organization of business and labour, Primo was acting within a long-standing conservative tradition whose most recent exponent had been Antonio Maura.

At the heart of ideological justifications for authoritarian rule lay a distorted interpretation of the Spanish Empire and the manner of its loss. The 1898 Disaster was seen as the tragic culmination of misguided policies and philosophical currents fundamentally alien to Spain's historical identity. Amongst these were liberalism, democracy and regionalism. In this view, the rot of the Spanish state began not just with the liberal revolution of the early nineteenth century but with its source, the Enlightenment itself. The former regenerationist, Ramiro de Maeztu, one of Primo's house intellectuals, later described the ideologies spawned by the Enlightenment as the ivy choking the Spanish tree.[5] This interpretation of Spain's history since 1700 as a deviation from an authentic tradition symbolized by the Catholic monarchs had been common currency among nineteenth-century traditionalists and it had been given intellectual respectability towards the end of the century by conservative writers and politicians such as the historian Menéndez Pelayo and the Carlist Vázquez de Mella.[6]

---

[4] Ernesto Giménez Caballero, 'Interpretación de dos profetas: Joaquín Costa y Alfredo Oriani', *La Conquista del Estado*, no. 2, 21 Mar. 1931. See also Santiago Galindo Herrero, *El 98 de los que fueron a la guerra* (Madrid, 1952).

[5] *Defensa de la Hispanidad* (Madrid, 1934), 7–8. A more extremist interpretation saw liberalism and its offspring as the work of the devil: Zacarías García Villada, *El destino de España en la Historia Universal* (Madrid, 1936).

[6] Angel Ganivet, *Ideárium Español y el Porvenir de España* (Madrid, 1957, 5th edn., 1st edn., 1897); for Marcelino Menéndez Pelayo see in particular his *Historia de los Heterodoxos españoles* (Madrid, 1882).

What constituted this largely invented 'essential' Spain? Its core was an imperial myth, the belief that Spain had a divinely ordained mission in the world that had led her to discover and Christianize most of the American subcontinent. This was, as a textbook for military conscripts proclaimed in 1924, 'the most transcendental deed in the History of humanity'.[7] During the Empire, bonds had been created between Spain and her colonies that were indissoluble, despite their secession from the mother country. These bonds were not merely cultural and linguistic but spiritual as well. They were condensed into the concept of Hispanism or *hispanidad*, an ill-defined system of values—honour, centralism, spirituality, hierarchy, and so on—which were supposed to represent the antithesis of the divisive and materialist ideologies of the capitalist and communist worlds.[8]

Whatever its ambitions, the new imperialism of the Spanish right could not pretend to any new and significant territorial acquisitions. There were voices clamouring for a new empire in Africa but the mere pacification of Spain's Moroccan Protectorate by 1927 absorbed most of Spain's military energies.[9] A reconquest of any part of the old Empire was inconceivable even to its lunatic fringe. Instead, the neo-imperial vocation was couched in the vaguest terms as the right to establish the moral and spiritual hegemony of the 'true' Spain over Spanish America if not over the rest of the world.[10]

This distorted picture of the past and the nebulous vision of future greatness which accompanied it, was used to validate both the military coup of Primo in 1923 and Franco's insurrection of 1936. Only by returning to those qualities which had supposedly made Spain great in the past, as the Dictators' propaganda machines insisted, could the nation recover from its present prostration. The victorious regime of Franco, in particu-

---

[7] Teodoro de Iradier, *Catecismo del ciudadano* in Carlos Navajas Zubeldia, *Ejército, Estado y Sociedad en España (1923–1930)* (Logroño, 1991), 263.

[8] García Villada (*El destino*); José María Pemán, *Obras Completas* (Madrid, 1964), vol. 1. For a critical interpretation of Hispanismo, see Pike (*Hispanismo*).

[9] 'El momento español', *La Conquista del Estado*, no. 8, 2 May 1931, 77; these calls were taken up at the beginning of the Second World War by the Spanish fascist party, the Falange, when it was hoped to acquire some of France's North African territories as crumbs off Germany's table: José María de Areilza and Fernando María Castiella, *Reivindicaciones de España* (Madrid, 1941).

[10] 'Spain's imperial aspiration', an early Francoist text reads, 'could not be an imperialism in the pejorative sense of the word; that is, . . . land, money, domination. It . . . can only take the form of action in support of a demand, an imperious (rather than imperial) claim for restitution, an imperative of justice' Ricardo del Arco y Garay, *Grandez y destino de España* (Madrid, 1942), 290. For an earlier, equally amorphous statement see 'España, Sangre de Imperio', *La Conquista del Estado*, 30 May 1931, 134–40.

lar, set out to instil this historical myth through education, religion, and the media.[11] Its seductiveness rested not on any rational discourse but on its crude poetry, on the incantatory effect of repeated abstractions such as 'unity' and 'destiny' and on all the accompanying fascist-style iconography of images, banners, and uniforms that attempted to establish a continuity between the present and the medieval past.

The appeal of the imperial myth and the myth of an 'essential' Spain was not just that they were an ideal compensation for real inferiorities. Their attraction lay above all in their denial of modernity. For those social groups who felt threatened by the effects of modernization, the myths offered the comforting vision of an unchanging, traditional society in which the modern divisions of class and region were banished; it was indeed from these layers of society that the military uprising of 1936 derived much of its support. Yet, paradoxically, the Spanish right also embraced notions of modernity. This was not the same modernity as the 'Europeanization' envisaged by the regenerators, who had looked to Republican France as their model. On the contrary, right-wing modernity in Spain was an effort to reconcile economic development with the preservation of tradition and hierarchy. The autarky adopted by the Franco dictatorship in the first two decades after the Civil War was, on one hand, a fascist-inspired economic policy whereby modernization was to be accomplished by the intervention of an authoritarian state in isolation from the rest of the world; on the other, it was an ideological strategy by which the nation would be redeemed through the inculcation of those principles which had supposedly made it great in the past.[12] The Spanish right had learnt profoundly negative lessons from Spain's involvement on the international stage—from her abortive attempt to become a major exporter of cereals in the mid-nineteenth century and of wine during France's phylloxera crisis to the Disaster of 1898 and later, Spain's sterile intervention in Morocco. These experiences nourished the fatal illusion that the nation could achieve self-sufficiency by isolating itself from the rest of the world.

The end of the Spanish Empire as an organizing myth can be said to have occurred only when the dictatorship abandoned its bankrupt policy of autarky and Spain completed her long cycle of modernization in an

[11] Martin Blinkhorn, 'Spain: the "Spanish Problem" and the Imperial Myth', *Journal of Contemporary History*, vol. 15 (1980), 5–23; Eduardo González Calleja and Fredes Limon Nevado, *La Hispanidad como instrumento de combate. Raza e imperio en la prensa franquista durante la guerra civil española* (Madrid, 1988).

[12] Michael Robert Richards, 'Autarky and the Franco Dictatorship in Spain, 1936–1945', Ph.D. Thesis, University of London, 1995.

accelerated burst of development in the 1960s and early 1970s. The death of imperial nostalgia was concomitant with the almost universal spread of democratic and secular values that accompanied this modernization. It was then that Spain shed her last colony, the Spanish Sahara, in 1973, embraced democracy in 1976 and joined the European Community in 1986.

Sources and Bibliography

A. PRIMARY SOURCES

Abbreviations of sources referred to frequently in footnotes to the text are given in brackets.

1. ARCHIVES
1.1 Official
Archivo del Ayuntamiento de Zaragoza
Archivo General de la Administración (Alcalá de Henares), (AGA)
Archivo General del Ministerio de Asuntos Exteriores
Archivo Histórico Nacional, Serie A (AHN)
Arxiu Històric de la Ciutat de Barcelona (Casa de L'Ardiaca) (AHCB), Castellví papers
Arxiu Històric Comarcal de Montblanc
Biblioteca de Catalunya
Biblioteca Nacional de Madrid, Diario de las Sesiones de las Cortes (1898–1923) (DSC)
Public Record Office, Foreign Office (PRO FO)

1.2 Private
Arxiu Històric, Cambra de Comercio, Industria i Navegació de Barcelona
Archivo de la Fundación Maura (AM)

2. OFFICIAL PUBLICATIONS

Documentos presentados a las Cortes en la legislatura de 1898 por el Ministro de Estado (Madrid, 1898–1899)
Documentos presentados a las Cortes en la legislatura de 1905–6 por el Ministro de Estado (Madrid, 1906)
Ministerio de la Marina, *Correspondencia oficial referente a las operaciones navales durante la guerra con los Estados Unidos en 1898* (Madrid, 1899)
Ministerio del Ejército—Servicio Histórico Militar, *Acción de España en Africa*, vol. III (Madrid, 1941)
Historia de las Campañas de Marruecos (3 vols.) (Madrid, 1947–1981)
(British) Parliamentary Papers, Accounts and Papers, Commercial Reports, 1899–1903
Spanish Diplomatic Correspondence and Documents, 1896–1900, Presented to the Cortes by the Minister of State (Washington, DC, 1905)

U.S. Senate, Office of Naval Intelligence. 56th Congress, 1st Session, Doc. no. 388, *Notes on the Spanish-American War* (Washington, 1900)

3. NEWSPAPERS AND PERIODICALS

ABC
La Actualidad de la Provincias
Almanaque de Gedeón
Almanaque de las Provincias
Blanco y Negro
La Campana de Gracia
El Cardo
Lo Catalanista
El Clamor Zaragozano
La Conca de Barbará
El Correo Militar
La Correspondencia Militar
¡Cu-cut!
Diario Mercantil
Diario de Zaragoza
El Diluvio
El Diluvio (Suplemento ilustrado)
El Economista
El Ejército Español
El Enano
La Epoca
España
La Esquella de la Torratxa
El Gato Negro
El Globo
El Heraldo de Aragón
El Heraldo de Madrid
La Ilustración Española y Americana
El Imparcial
La Industria Harinera
La Industria Papelera
Instantáneas
El Liberal
Lucha de Clases
Madrid Cómico
El Madrid Taurino
Memorial de Artillería
El Mercantil de Aragón
El Nacional

El Noroeste
El Norte de Castilla
Nuevo Mundo
El Nuevo Régimen
El País
La Patria
El Poble Català
El Progreso
Progreso Militar
La Publicidad
El Pueblo
La Renaixensa
Revista Nacional
Revista Nueva
El Socialista
Solidaridad Obrera
Solidaritat
El Trabajo Nacional
La Tralla
La Vanguardia
La Veu de Catalunya

4. MEMORIES, DIARIES AND WORKS BY PROTAGONISTS

A. + B., *Apuntes en defensa del honor del Ejército* (Madrid, 1898).
ALAS, LEOPOLDO (CLARÍN), 'Un jornalero', *Narraciones breves* (Barcelona, 1989), 173–82.
ALBA, SANTIAGO, *Problemas de España* (Madrid, 1916).
ALGER, R. A., *The Spanish–American War* (New York, 1901).
ALMIRALL, VALENTÍ, *España tal como es (La España de la Restauración)* (Madrid, 1972). Originally published in 1886 under the title, *L'Espagne telle qu'elle est.*
——, *Lo Catalanisme* (Barcelona, 1886).
ALTAMIRA Y CREVEA, RAFAEL, *Cuestiones obreras* (Valencia, 1914).
——, *Psicología del pueblo español* (Madrid, 1902).
ALVAREZ ANGULO, TOMÁS, *Memorias de un hombre sin importancia (1878–1961)* (Madrid, 1962).
ALZOLA Y MINONDO, PABLO DE, *El problema cubano* (Bilbao, 1898).
——, *Relaciones comerciales entre la Península y las Antillas* (Madrid, 1895).
n.a. *The American–Spanish War. A history by the War Leaders* (Norwich, Connecticut, 1899).
AMETLLA, CLAUDÍ, *Memóries Polítiques 1890–1917* (Barcelona, 1963).
ARCO Y GARAY, RICARDO DEL, *Grandeza y destino de España* (Madrid, 1942).
AREILZA, JOSÉ MARIA DE, and CASTIELLA, FERNANDO MARIA, *Reivindicaciones de España* (Madrid, 1941).

ARROW, CHARLES, *Rogues and Others* (London, 1926).

ATENEO DE MADRID, *Discursos pronunciados en el Ateneo de Madrid durante las Conferencias Marítimas por los señores D. Damián Isern, D. Joaquín Sánchez de Toca y D. Antonio Maura* (Madrid, 1902).

AZAÑA, MANUEL, '¡Todavía el 98!', *Plumas y palabras* (Barcelona, 1976), 179–95.

AZCÁRATE, GUMERSINDO DE, *El régimen parlamentario en la práctica*, 2nd edn. (Madrid, 1892).

AZORÍN (J. MARTÍNEZ RUIZ), *El Alma castellana*, vol. I of *Obras Completas* (Madrid, 1919).

——, *Clásicos y Modernos*, vol. XII of *Obras Completas* (Madrid, 1919).

——, *Obras Selectas* (Madrid, 1982).

——, *Parlamentarismo español (1904–1916)* 2nd edn. (Madrid, 1916).

——, *La Voluntad* (Madrid, 1968).

BAROJA, PÍO, *Aurora Roja (la lucha por la vida)* (Barcelona, 1965).

——, *La Busca* (Barcelona, 1966).

——, *Cuentos*. 12th edn. (Madrid, 1983).

——, *Desde la última vuelta del camino. Memorias. Final del siglo XIX y principios del XX*, vol. III (Madrid, 1982).

BLASCO IBAÑEZ, VICENTE, *Contra la Restauración. Periodismo político, 1895–1904* (Madrid, 1978).

——, *La Horda* (Barcelona, 1948).

BRISSA, JOSÉ, *La Revolución de Julio en Barcelona* (Barcelona, 1910).

BUCKLE, GEORGE EARLE (ed.), *The letters of Queen Victoria*. 3 vols. (London, 1932).

BUENO Y JAVALOYES, MANUEL, *El primer batallón de María Cristina en el Camagüey* (Matanzas, 1897).

BUGALLAL Y ARAUJO, ISIDORO, *Notas políticas. Antes y después del desastre* (Madrid, 1908).

BURGOS Y MAZO, Manuel de, *Páginas historicas de 1917* (Madrid, n.d.).

BURGUETE, RICARDO, *¡La Guerra! Cuba (Diario de un testigo)* (Barcelona, 1902).

——, *¡La Guerra! Filipinas. (Memorias de un herido)* (Barcelona, 1902).

BUYLLA, ADOLFO, POSADA, ADOLFO, and MOROTE, LUIS, *El Instituto de Trabajo. Datos para la historia de la reforma social en España* (Madrid, 1902).

CABOT LODGE, HENRY, *The War with Spain* (New York and London, 1899, repr. New York, 1970).

CABRERA, MERCEDES, 'Testamento político de Antonio Maura', *Estudios de Historia Social*, no. 32–3.

CAMBÓ I BATTLE, FRANCESC, 'Catalunya y la Solidaritat'. *Conferencia donada al Teatre Principal el día 26 de Maig de 1910* (Barcelona, 1910).

——, *Memorias (1876–1936)* (Madrid, 1987).

——, *Memòries (1876–1936)* (Barcelona, 1981).

——, *El pesimismo español* (Madrid, 1917).

CANALEJAS Y MENÉNDEZ, JOSÉ, *Canalejas gobernante. Discursos parlamentarios. Cortes de 1910* (Valencia, n.d.).

——, *El Partido Liberal. Conversaciones con D. José Canalejas* (Madrid, 1912).

CANALEJAS FERNÁNDEZ, JOSÉ, *Reflexiones sobre la vida de mi padre* (Madrid, 1928).

CANALS, SANTIAGO, *La Solidaridad Catalana. Apuntes para su estudio* (Madrid, 1907).

CANALS Y VILARÓ, SALVADOR, *Los sucesos de España en 1909*, 2 vols. (Madrid, 1910).

CAPITÁN VERDADES, El, *Historia Negra. Relato de los escándalos occurridos en nuestras ex-colonias durante las últimas guerras* (Barcelona, 1899).

CASES-CARBÓ, J, *Catalonia. Assaigs nacionalistes* (Barcelona, 1908).

CASTELAR, E, *Crónica internacional* (Madrid, 1982).

CASTILLO-PUCHE, J. L., *Diario íntimo de Alfonso XIII* (Madrid, 1960).

CERVERA Y TOPETE, PASCUAL, *Guerra Hispano-Americana. Colección de documentos referentes a la Escuadra de Operaciones de las Antillas* (El Ferrol, 1899).

——, *The Spanish–American War. A Collection of Documents relative to the Squadron Operations in the West Indies* (Washington, 1899).

CHADWICK, FRENCH ENSOR, *The Relations of the United States and Spain*, 3 vols. (New York, 1909–11).

CHEYNE, G. J. G., *El renacimiento ideal: epistolario de Joaquín Costa y Rafael Altamira (1888–1911)* (Alicante, 1992).

——, 'La intervención de Costa en el proceso de Montjuich: correspondencia inédita con Pere Corominas y otros', *Bulletin Hispanique*, vol. LXVIII (1966), 69–85.

CIERVA Y PEÑAFIEL, JUAN DE LA, *Notas de mi vida*, 2nd edn. (Madrid, 1955).

CIGES APARICIO, MANUEL, *El libro de la vida trágica. Del Cautiverio* (Alicante, 1985).

COLL Y ASTRELL, JOAQUÍN, *Monografía histórica del Centro del Ejército y de la Armada* (Madrid, 1902).

COMAPOSADA, JOSÉ, *La revolución de Barcelona* (Barcelona, 1909).

——, *La revolución en Cataluña. Segunda parte de la revolución en Barcelona* (Barcelona, 1910).

Comisión de Reformas Sociales, *La clase obrera española a fines del siglo XIX* (Madrid, 1970).

CONCAS Y PALAU, VICTOR M., *La Escuadra del Almirante Cervera*, 2nd edn. (Madrid, 1900).

Congreso Africanista, *Primer Congreso Africanista* (Barcelona, 1907).

La Conquista del Estado, *Antología* (prólogo de Juan Aparicio) (n.p., 1939).

COROMINES, PERE, *De la Solidaritat al catorze d'Abril*, vol. II, *Diaris i records* (Barcelona, 1974).

CORRAL, MANUEL, *¡El Desastre! Memorias de un voluntario en la campaña de Cuba* (Barcelona, 1899).

CORTÉS CAVANILLAS, JULIÁN, *Alfonso XIII. Vida, confesiones y muerte* (Madrid, 1956).

CORTIJO, VICENTE DE, *Apuntes para la historia de la pérdida de nuestras colonias por un testigo presencial* (Madrid, 1899).

COSTA MARTÍNEZ, JOAQUÍN, *El comercio español y la cuestión de Africa* (Madrid, 1882).

——, 'Los intereses de España y Marruecos son armónicos', supplement to *España en Africa*, 15 Jan. 1906.

——, *Política hidráulica (Misión social de los riegos en España)* vol. 11, Biblioteca Económica (Madrid, 1911).

——, *Oligarquía y caciquismo como la fórmula de gobierno en España: urgencia y modo de cambiarla* (Madrid, 1902).

——, *Política Quirúrgica*, vol. VIII, Biblioteca económica. (Madrid, 1914).

——, *Reconstitución y europeización de España* (Huesca, 1924).

——, *Los siete criterios de gobierno* (Madrid, 1914).

——, *Colectivismo agrarion en España. Partes I y II. Doctrinas y hechos* (Madrid, 1898).

——, *Crisis Política de España. Discurso leído en los juegos Florales de Salamanca 15 septiembre de 1901* (Madrid, 1901).

——, *El problema de la ignorancia del derecho y sus relaciones con el status individual, el referéndum y la costumbre* (Barcelona, 1901).

C.P., *Ante la opinión y ante la historia. El Almirante Montojo* (Madrid, 1900).

DARÍO, RUBEN, *España Contemporánea* (Barcelona, 1987).

DOMÈNECH I MONTANER, LLUÍS, *Estudis Polítics* (Barcelona, 1905).

DOMINGO IBARRA, RAMÓN, *Cuentos históricos, recuerdos de la primera campaña de Cuba, 1868–1878* (Santa Cruz de Tenerife, 1905).

DUARTE, ANGEL, *El Republicanisme catalá a la fi del segle XIX* (Barcelona, 1987).

DURAN Y VENTOSA, LLUÍS, *Regionalisme y federalisme* (Barcelona, 1905).

ECHEGARAY, MIGUEL, *Gigantes y Cabezudos. Reseña y explicación de la Zarzuela Cómica en un acto y tres cuadros* (San Sebastián, 1899).

EFEELE, *El Desastre nacional y los vicios de nuestras instituciones militares* (Madrid, 1901).

FABIÉ Y ESCUDERO, ANTONIO MARÍA, *Mi gestión ministerial respecto a la isla de Cuba* (1898).

FELIZ, VICTORIANO, *Misión social del ejército* (1907).

FEUER, A. B., *The Santiago Campaign of 1898. A Soldier's view of the Spanish–American War* (Westport, Connecticut, 1993).

FIGUEROA Y TORRES, ALVARO DE, CONDE DE ROMANONES, *Doña María Cristina Hapsburgo Lorena. La discreta regente de España*, 2nd edn. (Madrid, 1934).

——, *Notas de una vida (1868–1901)* (Madrid, 1934).

——, *Las responsabilidades políticas del antiguo régimen de 1875 a 1923* (Madrid, 1925).

FITÉ, VITAL, *Las desdichas de la patria* (Madrid, 1899).

FLACK, HORACE EDGAR, *Spanish-American Diplomatic Relations Preceding the War of 1898*, 'Johns Hopkins University Studies in Historical and Political Science', vol. XXIV, (Baltimore, Jan.–Feb., 1906), 5–95.

FLINT, GROVER, *Marching with Gomez. A War Correspondent's field Note-Book kept during four months with the Cuban army* (Boston and New York, 1898).

Fomento del Trabajo Nacional, *Informe sobre el Projeto de ley de Administración Local* (Barcelona, 1907).

——, *Exposición elevada al presidente del Congreso de los Diputados* (Barcelona, 1899).

FORCADELL, CARLOS, *Parlamentarismo y bolchevización* (Barcelona, 1978).

FRANCOS RODRÍGUEZ, José, *El año de la derrota 1898. De las memorias de gacetillero* (Madrid, 1936).

GALLEGO, TESIFONTE, *La insurrección cubana. Crónicas de la Campaña* (Madrid, 1897).

GANIVET, ANGEL, *Ideárium español y El Porvenir de España*. 5th edn. (Madrid, 1957).

GARCÍA BARRON, CARLOS, *Cancionero del 98* (Madrid, 1974).

GARCÍA NIETO, MARÍA CARMEN; DONÉZAR, JAVIER M.; and LÓPEZ PUERTA, LUIS, *Bases documentales de la España contemporánea*, vols. V and VI (Madrid, 1972).

GARCÍA VILLADA, ZACARÍAS, *El destino de España en la Historia Universal* (Madrid, 1936).

GAZIEL (pseudonym CALVET), *Tots els camins duen a Roma. Història d'un destí 1893–1914* (Barcelona, 1958).

GENER, POMPEYO, *Heregías. Estudios de crítica inductiva sobre asuntos españoles*, 2nd edn. (Barcelona, 1888).

GIMÉNEZ CABALLERO, ERNESTO, 'Interpretación de dos profetas: Joaquín Costa y Alfredo Oriani', *La Conquista del Estado*, no. 2 (21 Mar. 1931), 223–7.

——, *Memorias de un dictador* (Barcelona, 1979).

——, *Los toros, Las Castañuelas y la Virgen* (Madrid, 1927).

GOMÁ TOMÁS, ISIDRO (Archbishop of Toledo), *El Caso de España. Instrucción a sus diocesanos y respuesta a unas consultas sobre la guerra actual* (Pamplona, 1936).

GÓMEZ MOLLEDA, D., *Unamuno 'agitador de espíritus' y Giner (Correspondencia inédita)* (Madrid, 1977).

GÓMEZ NÚÑEZ, SEVERO, 'La catástrofe del *Maine*', *Memorial de Artillería*, Serie IV, vol. IX, (Jan.–June 1898), 281–91.

——, *La Guerra Hispano-Americana*, 5 vols. (Madrid, 1899).

GONZÁLEZ DE CELLORIGO, *Memorial de la política necesaria y útil restauración a la república de España y Estado de ella y del desempeño universal de estos Reinos* (Valladolid, 1600).

GOOCH, G. P. and TEMPERLEY, HAROLD, *British Documents on the Origins of the War, 1898–1914*, vol. I: *The End of British Isolation* (London, 1927).

GRAELL, GUILLERMO, *La cuestión catalana* (Barcelona, 1902).

——, *Hacia la Nacionalización de la Economía. Discurso inaugural del curso 1908–*

9, leído por D. Guillermo Graell en el Salón de Actos del Foment del Trabajo Nacional en la noche del 10 Octubre de 1908 (Barcelona, 1908).

——, *Historia del Fomento del Trabajo Nacional* (Barcelona, n.d.).

GUAL VILLALBÍ, PEDRO, *Memorias de un industrial de nuestro tiempo* (Barcelona, 1923).

GUTIÉRREZ-GAMERO, E., *Mis primeros ochenta años (memorias)* (Barcelona, 1934).

GUTIÉRREZ RAVÉ, JOSÉ, *Habla el Rey. Discursos de Don Alfonso XIII, recopilados y anotados por* (Madrid, 1936).

——, *Yo fui un joven maurista* (Madrid, 1944).

HURTADO, AMEDEU, *Quaranta anys d'advocat. Historia del meu temps*, vol. I (Barcelona, 1964).

ISERN, DAMIÁN, *Del Desastre nacional y sus causas* (Madrid, 1899)

KINDELÁN DUANY, TENIENTE GENERAL, *Ejército y Política* (Madrid, 1946).

LABRA, RAFAEL MARÍA DE, *El pesimismo de última hora* (Madrid, 1899).

——, *El problema hispano-americano* (n.p., 1906).

——, *Proletarios . . . ; Maura, No!* (Barcelona, 1914).

——, *Las relaciones internacionales de España* (Madrid, 1899).

LEDESMA RAMOS, RAMIRO, *Discurso a las juventudes de España*, 3rd edn. (n.p., 1939).

LEÓN Y CASTILLO, F. DE, *Mis tiempos*. 2 vols. (Madrid, 1921).

LERROUX, ALEJANDRO, *De la lucha. Páginas de Alejandro Lerroux* (Barcelona and Madrid, 1909).

——, *Ferrer y su proceso en las Cortes* (Barcelona, 1911).

LLIGA CATALANA, *Història d'una política. Actuacions i documents de la Lliga Regionalista, 1901–1933* (Barcelona, 1933).

MACÍAS PICAVEA, RICARDO, *El problema nacional. Hechos, causas, remedios* (Madrid, 1899).

MADRAZO, DR., *¿El pueblo español ha muerto? Impresiones sobre el estado actual de la sociedad española* (Santander, 1903).

MAEZTU, RAMIRO DE, *Artículos desconocidos (1897–1904)* (Madrid, 1977).

——, *Defensa de la Hispanidad* (Madrid, 1934).

——, *Don Quijote, Don Juan y la Celestina. Ensayos en Simpatía* (Buenos Aires, 1952).

——, *Hacia otra España* (Madrid, 1899).

——, *Obreros e intelectuales* (Barcelona, 1911).

——, *La Revolución y los intelectuales* (Madrid, 1911).

MAHAN, ALFRED THAYER, *The Influence of Sea Power upon History, 1660–1783* (London and Cambridge, Massachussets, 1890).

——, *Lessons of the War with Spain and other articles* (London, 1899).

MALLADA, LUCAS, *Los males de la patria y la futura revolución española* (Madrid, 1969).

MARAGALL, JOAN, *Artículos (1893–1903)*, (Barcelona, 1904).

——, *De las Reyals Jornadas*, 2nd edn. (Barcelona, n.d.).

——, *Poesies*, vol. I, *Obres Completes* (Barcelona, 1929).

——, *El sentiment de pátria. Articles*, vol. XIII, *Obres Completes* (Barcelona, 1931).

MÁRQUEZ, E., CORONEL Y CAPÓ, J. M., *Las Juntas Militares de Defensa* (Barcelona, 1923).

MAURA GAMAZO, GABRIEL, *La cuestión de Marruecos desde el punto de vista español* (Madrid, 1905).

MAURA GAMAZO, GABRIEL, *Bosquejo histórico de la Dictadura*, 5th edn. (Madrid, 1930).

——, *Historia crítica del reinado de Don Alfonso XIII bajo la regencia de doña María Cristina de Austria* (Barcelona, 1919).

MAURA Y MONTANER, ANTONIO, *Antonio Maura: treinta y cinco años de vida pública. Ideas políticas recopiladas por J. Ruiz-Castillo* (Madrid, 1953).

MAURICIO, *La gran traición* (Barcelona, 1899).

MENÉNDEZ Y PELAYO, MARCELINO, *Historia de los Heterodoxes españoles* (Madrid, 1882).

MOLA VIDAL, EMILIO, *Obras Completas* (Valladolid, 1940).

MONEVA Y PUYOL, J., *La Asamblea Nacional de Productores (Zaragoza, 1899)* (Zaragoza, 1899).

MONTERO RÍOS, EUGENIO, *El Tratado de París* (Madrid, 1904).

MORERA Y BORÉS, J., *Quinze días á la presó. Impresions, notas y records dels nous que voluntariament varen constituirse presos en lo moviment gremial de 1899* (Barcelona, 1901).

MOROTE, LUIS, *El Pulso de España. Confesiones Políticas* (Madrid, 1904).

——, *Sagasta, Melilla. Cuba* (Paris, 1908).

——, *La Moral de la Derrota* (Madrid, 1900).

MUGUETA, JUAN, *Los Valores de la Raza* (San Sebastian, 1938).

MÜLLER Y TEJEIRO, LIEUTENANT JOSÉ, *Battles and Capitulation of Santiago de Cuba* (Washington, 1899).

NAVARRO, EMILIO (JUAN DE LA PURRIA), *Separatismo solidario (la Política en Cataluña)* (Barcelona, 1907).

OLIVÁN, FRANCISCO ANDRÉS, *Por España y para España* (Zaragoza, 1899).

OLIVER, MIQUEL S., *El caso Maura. Edición de homenaje popular* (Barcelona, 1914).

ORTEGA Y GASSET, JOSÉ, *España Invertebrada. Bosquejo de algunos pensamientos históricos* (Madrid, 1967, 15th edn.).

——, *Cartas de un joven español (1891–1908)* (Madrid, 1991).

——, *Obras Completas* (Madrid, 1983–87).

——, *Ensayos sobre la Generación del 98 y otros escritores españoles contemporáneos* (Madrid, 1981).

OSSORIO, ANGEL, *Barcelona. Julio de 1909. (Declaración de un testigo)* (Madrid, 1910).

OSSORIO Y GALLARDO, ANGEL, *Mis Memorias* (Buenos Aires, 1946).

PARDO BAZÁN, EMILIA, *Cuentos de la Patria* in *Obras Completas*. 4th edn., vol. I. (Madrid, 1973).

PARDO BAZÁN, EMILIA, *La Vida Contemporánea (1896–1915)* (Madrid, 1972).

PAULIS, J. and SOREL, F. DE, *Maura ante el pueblo* (Madrid, 1915).

PELLA Y FORGAS, J., *La crisi del catalanisme*, 2nd edn. (Barcelona, 1906).

PEMÁN, JOSÉ MARÍA, *Obras Completas*. 10 vols. (Madrid, 1964).

PÉREZ GALDOS, BENITO, *Cánovas* (Madrid, 1943).

PETRIE CHARLES, B. T. Sir, *King Alfonso XIII and His Age* (London, 1963).

PLÜDDEMAN, REAR-ADMIRAL, *Comments of Real-Admiral Plüddeman, German Navy, on the Main Features of the War with Spain* (Washington, 1899).

PI I MARGALL, FRANCISCO, *Artícoles* (Barcelona, 1908).

——, and PI Y ARSUAGA, FRANCISCO, *Historia de España en el siglo XIX*. vol. VII (Barcelona, 1902).

PICHARDO, HORTENSIA, *Documentos para la historia de Cuba*, 5 vols. (La Habana, 1977).

PIRALA, ANTONIO, *Anales de la Guerra de Cuba*. 3 vols. (Madrid, 1895).

——, *España y la Regencia. Anales de diez y seis años (1885–1902)*. 3 vols. (Madrid/Havana, 1904).

PIRRETAS, J. MARIAN, *El Tancament de Caixes. Descripció del Moviment Germinal de 1899* (Barcelona, 1899).

PLA, JOSÉ, *Francesc Cambó. Materials per a una historia*, vol. XXV, *Obra Completa* (Barcelona, 1973).

POLAVIEJA, MARQUÉS DE, *Mi política en Cuba. Lo que vi, lo que hice, lo que anuncié* (Madrid, 1898).

POSADA, ADOLFO, *Ideas e Ideales* (Madrid, 1903).

——, *España en crisis. La política* (Madrid, 1923).

——, 'Adolfo Posada décrit la situation de l'Espagne. (1899) Mouvement social. Espagne (1898)' in Serrano, Carlos, *Le Tour*. Appendix 3, (Paris, 1899), 324–38.

PRADERA, VICTOR, *Obra Completa*, 2 vols. (Madrid, 1945).

PRAT DE LA RIBA, ENRICH and MUNTANYOLA, PERE, *Compendi de la Doctrina Catalanista* (Sabadell, Barcelona, 1894).

PRAT DE LA RIBA, ENRICH, *La Nacionalitat Catalana* (Barcelona, 1910).

PRIMO DE RIVERA, FERNANDO, *Memoria del Teniente General Primo de Rivera acerca de su gestión en Filipinas* (Madrid, 1898).

PRIMO DE RIVERA, JOSÉ ANTONIO, *Selected Writings* (ed. by Hugh Thomas) (London, 1972).

RAMÓN Y CAJAL, SANTIAGO, *Mi infancia y juventud* (Madrid, 1955).

——, *El mundo visto a los ochenta años. Impresiones de un arteriosclerótico*, 5th edn. (Buenos Aires, 1948).

RECIO FERRARAS, ELOY, 'Diario inédito escrito por un soldado español en la Guerra de Cuba, 1896–1899' , *Revista de Historia de América*, no. 112, (July–Dec. 1991), 21–42.

REIG Y CASANOVA, ENRIQUE, *Sacrilegios y traidores, ó la masonería contra la Iglesia y contra España* (Palma, 1897).

n.a. *Renovación o Revolución. Historia política documentada de un período (junio a octubre 1917)* (Barcelona, 1917).

REPARAZ, GONZALO DE, *Política de España en Africa*, 2nd edn. (Madrid, 1924).

RÍA-BAJA, CARLOS, *El Desastre filipino. Memorias de un prisinero* (Barcelona, 1899).

RIERA, AUGUSTO, *La Semana Trágica. Relato de las sediciones e incendios en Barcelona y Catalunya* (Barcelona, 1909).

RIVERO Y MIRANDA, Conde de Limpias, *Las alianzas y la política exterior de España a principios del siglo XX. (Apuntes para un estudio)* (Madrid, 1914).

ROBERT, DR BARTOLOMEU, *Legislatura de 1901. Discursos del Dr. Robert* (Barcelona, 1902).

RODRÍGUEZ MARTÍNEZ, J., *Los desastres y la regeneración de España. Relatos e impresiones* (La Coruña, 1899).

ROOSEVELT, THEODORE, *The Rough Riders* (New York, 1903).

ROSAL Y VÁZQUEZ, ANTONIO DEL, *Los mambises, memorias de un prisonero* (Madrid, 1874).

——, *En la manigua, diario de mi cautiverio* (Madrid, 1876).

ROVIRA Y VIRGILI, ANTONI, *El nacionalismo catalán. Su aspecto político, los hechos, las ideas y los hombres* (Barcelona, 1917).

——, *Els polítics catalans* (Barcelona, 1929).

ROUTIER, GASTON, *L'Espagne en 1897* (Paris, 1897).

ROYO VILLANOVA, ANTONIO, *Treinta años de política antiespañola* (Valladolid, 1940).

SABORIT, ANDRÉS, *La Huelga de agosto de 1917* (Mexico, 1917).

——, *Joaquín Costa y el socialismo* (Algorta, 1970).

SALILLAS, RAFAEL, *Hampa* (Madrid, 1898).

SÁNCHEZ DE TOCA, JOAQUÍN, *Del Poder naval en España y su política económica para la nacionalidad ibero-americana* (Madrid, 1898).

——, *La crisis agraria europea y sus remedios en España* (Madrid, 1887).

n.a., *La Semana Sangrienta. Sucesos de Barcelona: Historia, descripciones, documentos, relatos, vista etc.* (Barcelona, n.d.).

SÁNCHEZ DE LOS SANTOS, MODESTO, *Las Cortes españolas: las de 1907, las de 1910, las de 1914*, 3 vols. (Madrid, 1908, 1910, 1914).

SERRA ORTS, ANTONIO, *Recuerdos de las guerras de Cuba, 1868–1898* (Santa Cruz de Tenerife, 1906).

SILIÓ Y CORTÉS, CÉSAR, *Maura. Vida y empresas de un gran español* (Madrid, 1934).

——, *Problemas de día* (Madrid, 1900).

SILVELA, FRANCISCO, *Artículos, Discursos, Conferencias y Cartas.* 3 vols. (Madrid, 1922–3).

SIÓN, *La Farándula. Sátira en defensa de los elementos armados* (Barbastro, 1900).

SOLDADO, JUAN (ed.), *Maura y el Anarquismo. Enseñanzas* (Durango, 1909).

SOLDEVILLA, FERNANDO, *El año polític. 1909* (Madrid, 1910).

——, *El año político 1910* (Madrid, 1911).

——, *El año político 1917* (Madrid, 1918).

——, *El año político 1918* (Madrid, 1919).

——, *El año político 1919* (Madrid, 1920).

SOLDEVILLA, FERNANDO, *El año político 1920* (Madrid, 1921).

——, *Tres revoluciones* (Madrid, 1917).

n.a., *The Spanish-American War. The Events of the War Described by Eye Witnesses* (Chicago and New York, 1899).

n.a., *Los sucesos de agosto ante el Parlamento* (Madrid, 1918).

TETUÁN, DUQUE DE, *Apuntes para la defensa de la política internacional y gestión diplomática del Gobierno Liberal-Conservador desde el 28 de marzo de 1895 al 29 de septiembre de 1897* (Madrid, 1902).

TORRAS I BAGES, JOSEP, *La tradició catalana*, in *Obres Completes*, vol. I (Montserrat, 1984), 225–716.

Un español, *Pequeñeces de la Guerra de Cuba* (Madrid, 1897).

UNAMUNO, MIGUEL DE, *Paz en la Guerra* in *Obras Completas*, vol. II, (Madrid, 1951), 13–327.

——, *Obras Completas* (Madrid, 1951).

——, *En torno al casticismo* (Madrid, 1961, 5th edn.).

LA VANGUARDIA, *La vida barcelonesa a través de la Vanguardia (1900–1917)* (Barcelona, 1977).

VÁZQUEZ DE MELLA Y FANJUL, JUAN, *Temas Internacionales*, vol. XXII, *Obras Completas* (Madrid, 1934).

——, *Política General*, 2 vols., vols. XIII and XIV, *Obras Completas* (Madrid, 1932).

VESA Y FILLART, ANTONIO, *Voluntarios de la Isla de Cuba. Historial del Regimiento Caballería de Jaruco y de su estandarte* (Barcelona, 1908).

VERHAEREN, EMILE and REGOYOS, DARÍO DE, *España negra* (Barcelona, 1899).

VILADEVALL, P. ANTONIO S. J., *La voluntad nacional en frente del jacobinismo afrancesado de Romanones y Canalejas* (Barcelona, 1907).

WEYLER Y NICOLAU, VALERIANO, *Mi mando en Cuba (10 Febrero 1896 a 31 Octubre 1897). Historia militar y política de la última guerra separatista durante dicho mando,* 5 vols. (Madrid, 1910–11).

WOLFF, SIR HENRY DRUMMOND, *Rambling Recollections,* 2 vols. (London, 1908).

B. SECONDARY SOURCES: BOOKS AND ARTICLES

ABELLA, RAFAEL, 'Los españoles de principios de siglo', *Historia*, vol. III, 'Los imperios frente a frente' (Madrid, 1983), 39–50.

ABELLÁN, J. L. *et al.*, *La crisis de fin de siglo: ideología y literatura. Estudios en memoria de R. Pérez de la Dehesa* (Barcelona, 1975).

ABELLÁN, JOSÉ LUIS, *Sociología del 98* (Barcelona, 1973).

AKEN, M. J., *Pan-Hispanism* (Berkeley, 1959).

ALLENDESALAZAR, JOSÉ MANUEL, *La diplomacia española y Marruecos, 1907–1909.*

——, *El 98 de los americanos* (Madrid, 1974).

ALMAGRO SAN MARTÍN, MELCHOR DE, *Biografía del 1900*, 2nd edn. (Madrid, 1944).

ALONSO, JOSÉ RAMÓN, *Historia política del ejército español* (Madrid, 1974).

ALONSO ALVAREZ, LUIS, 'Crecimiento de la demanda, insuficiencia de la producción tradicional e industrialización del sector tabaquero en España, 1800–1935', in Nadal and Catalán (La cara oculta), 163–97.

ALVAREZ JUNCO, JOSÉ, *El Emperador del Paralelo. Lerroux y la demagogia populista* (Madrid, 1990).

——, 'Cultura popular y protesta política' in Maurice, Magnien, and Bussy (eds.) (*Peuple*), 157–168.

——, *La ideología política del anarquismo español (1868–1910)* (Madrid, 1976).

ANDREW, C. M. and KANYA-FORSTNER, A. S., 'The French Colonial Party: its composition, aims and influence 1885–1914', *Historical Journal*, vol. XIV, I, (1971), 99–128.

ANNA, TIMOTHY E., *Spain and the loss of America* (Nebraska, 1983).

ARBOR, 'Numero extraordinario commemorativo de 1898', no. 36, Dec. 1948.

ARRIERO, MARÍA-LUZ, 'Los motines de subsistencias en España, 1865–1905', *Estudios de Historia Social*, no. 30 (July–Sept. 1984), 193–250.

ARTOLA, MIGUEL, *Partidos y programas políticos, 1808–1936*, vol. I, Los partidos políticos (Madrid, 1991).

AZCÁRATE, PABLO DE, *La Guerra del 98* (Madrid, 1968).

BACHOUD, ANDRÉE, *Los españoles ante las campañas de Marruecos* (Madrid, 1988).

BAHAMONDE, ANGEL and CAYUELA, JOSÉ, *Hacer las Américas. Las elites coloniales españoles en el siglo XIX* (Madrid, 1992).

BALBÉ, MANUEL, *Orden público y militarismo en la España constitucional (1812– 1983)* (Madrid, 1983).

BALFOUR, SEBASTIAN, 'The Lion and the Pig. Nationalism and National Identity in Fin de Siècle Spain', in Clare Mar-Molinero and Angel Smith, *Nationalism and National Identity in the Iberian Peninsula* (London, 1996).

——, 'The Loss of Empire, Regenerationism and the Forging of a Myth of National Identity', in Helen Graham and Jo Labanyi (eds.), *An Introduction to Spanish Cultural Studies* (Cambridge, 1995).

——, 'Riot, Regeneration and Reaction: Spain in the Aftermath of the 1898 Disaster', *The Historical Journal*, June 1995.

——, 'The Solitary Peak and the Dense Valley. Intellectuals and Masses in *fin de siècle* Spain', *Tesserae* no. 1, Dec. 1994.

BAÑÓN, RAFAEL and BARKER, THOMAS, *Armed Forces and Society in Spain, Past and Present* (New York, 1988).

BARBAT, GUSTAU and ESTIVILL, JORDI, 'L'anticlericalisme en la revolta popular del 1909', *L'Avenç*, n. 2 (May 1977), 28–37.

BARÓN FERNÁNDEZ, JOSÉ, *La Guerra Hispano-Norteamericana de 1898* (La Coruña, 1993).

BARR CHIDSEY, DONALD, *The Spanish American War. A Behind-the-Scenes Account of the War in Cuba* (New York, 1971).

BAUMGART, WINFRIED, *Imperialism. The Idea and Reality of British and French*

Colonial Expansion, 1880–1914 (Oxford, 1982).

BECK, EARL R., 'The Martínez Campos Government of 1879: Spain's Last Chance in Cuba', *Hispanic American Historical Review*, vol. LVI (1976), 268–89.

BENET, JOSEP, *Maragall i la setmana trágica* 4th edn. (Barcelona, 1968).

BENGOECHEA, SOLEDAD, *Organització patronal i conflictivitat social a Catalunya. Tradició i corporativisme entre finals del segle i la dictadura de Primo de Rivera* (Montserrat, 1994).

——, 'Les organitzacions patronals catalanes en el tombant de segle', *Afers*, 13 (1992), 104–20.

BERNAD ROYO, ENRIQUE, *Regeneracionismo, industrialización e 'instrucción popular'. Zaragoza, 1894–1914* (Zaragoza, 1986).

BLANCO AGUINAGA, CARLOS, *Juventud del 98*, 2nd edn. (Barcelona, 1978).

BLINKHORN, MARTIN, 'Spain: the "Spanish Problem" and the Imperial Myth', *Journal of Contemporary History*, vol. XV (1980), 5–25.

BONAFULLA, LEOPOLDO (pseudonym, JUAN BAUTISTA ESTEVE), *La Revolución de Julio en Barcelona*. 2nd edn. (Barcelona, 1923).

BOYD, CAROLYN P., *Praetorian Politics in Liberal Spain* (Chapel Hill, 1979).

BUSQUETS, JULIO, *El militar de carrera en España. Estudio de sociología militar*, 2nd edn. (Barcelona, 1971).

CABRERA, MERCEDES, 'El conservadurismo maurista en la restauración. Los límites de la "revolución desde arriba"', in García Delgado (ed.) (*La España*), 55–69.

CABRERA, M., COMÍN, F., and GARCÍA DELGADO, J. L., *Un programa de reforma económica en la España de la primera mitad del siglo XX* (Madrid, 1989).

CACHINERO, JORGE, 'Intervencionismo y reformas militares in España a comienzos del siglo XX', *Cuadernos de Historia Contemporánea*, no. 10 (1988), 155–84.

CACHO VIU, VICENTE, *La Institución Libre de Enseñanza*, vol. I: Orígenes y etapa universitaria (1860–1881) (Madrid, 1962).

CAJA DE AHORROS DE LA INMACULADA, *Aragón en su historia* (Zaragoza).

CALERO AMOR, ANTONIO MARÍA, *Movimientos sociales en Andalucía (1820–1936)* (Madrid, 1976).

——, 'El papel político de la Corona en el reinado de Alfonso XIII: criterios para una revisión' in García Delgado (ed.) (*España*), 271–84.

CALLEJA, LEAL and GUILLERMO, G., 'La voladura del Maine. Nuevas luces sobre un enigma histórico que terminó con el Imperio español', *Historia*, no. 176 (Dec. 1990), 12–32.

CAMPS I ARBOIX, JOAQUIM DE, *El tancament de caixes* (Barcelona, 1961).

——, *História de la Solidaritat Catalana (1905–1910)* (Barcelona, 1970).

CANELLAS LOPEZ, ANGEL, *Aragón en su historia* (Zaragoza, 1980).

CARDONA, GABRIEL, *El poder militar en la España contemporánea hasta la guerra civil* (Madrid, 1983).

CARO BAROJA, JULIO, *Introducción a una historia contemporánea del anticlericalismo español* (Madrid, 1980).

——, *El Carnaval (Análisis histórico-cultural)* (Madrid, 1965).

——, *El mito del carácter nacional. Meditaciones a contrapelo* (Madrid, 1970).

CARR, RAYMOND, *Spain, 1808–1975*, 2nd edn. (Oxford, 1982).

CARRERAS, ALBERT, *Industrialización española: estudios de historia cuantitativa* (Madrid, 1990).

CASTRO ALFÍN, DEMETRIO, 'Protesta popular y orden público: los motines de consumo', in García Delgado, J. L. (ed.) (*España*) 109–23.

CEPEDA ADÁN, JOSÉ, *Sagasta en la Regencia de María Cristina: Las horas amargas del 'Desastre'* (Madrid, 1994).

CHANDLER, JAMES A., 'Spain and the Moroccan Protectorate, 1898–1927', *Journal of Contemporary History*, no. 10 (Apr. 1975), 301–23.

CHEYNE, GEORGE J. G., *Joaquín Costa, el gran desconocido. Esbozo biográfico* (Barcelona, 1972).

CIPLIJAUSKAITÉ, BIRUTÉ, *Los Noventayochistas y la historia* (Madrid, 1981).

CIPRIANO VENZON, ANNE, *The Spanish–American War. An Annotated Bibliography* (New York, 1990).

COMALADA, ANGEL, *El ocaso de un parlamento* (Barcelona, 1985).

COMÍN COMÍN, FRANCISCO, *Hacienda y economía en la España contemporánea (1800–1936)*, 2 vols. (Madrid, 1988).

——, 'Estado y crecimiento económico en España: lecciones de la historia', *Papeles de Economía Española*, no. 57 (1993), 55.

COMPANYS MONCLÚS, JULIAN, *España en 1898: entre la diplomacia y la guerra* (Madrid, 1992).

CONNELLY ULLMAN, JOAN, *The Tragic Week. A study of anticlericalism in Spain, 1875–1912* (Cambridge, Mass. 1968).

CORTADA, JAMES W. (ed.), *Spain in the Twentieth-Century World. Essays on Spanish Diplomacy, 1898–1978* (London, 1980).

COSMAS, GRAHAM A., *An Army for Empire. The United States Army in the Spanish–American War* (Columbia, 1971).

COSTELOE, MICHAEL P., *Response to Revolution. Imperial Spain and the Spanish American revolutions, 1810–1840* (Cambridge, 1986).

n.a. *Cuba, les étapes d'une libération* (Toulouse, 1979).

CUADRAT, XAVIER, 'La Setmana Tràgica i el moviment obrer a Catalunya, *L'Avenç*, n. 2 (May 1977), 44–8.

CUCÓ, ALFONS, *Republicáns i camperols revoltats* (Valencia, 1975).

——, *El valencianismo político, 1874–1939* (Barcelona, 1977).

CULLA I CLARA, JOAN B., *El Republicanisme lerronxista a Catalunya (1901–1923)* (Barcelona, 1986).

DALMAU, ANTONIO R., *Tipos populares de Barcelona. Siglos XIX y XX* (Barcelona, 1945).

DAVIS, RICHARD HARDING, *The Cuban and Porto Rican Campaigns* (New York, 1898).

DELGADO, JAIME, *La Independencia hispanoamericana* (Madrid, 1960).

——, *La independencia de América en la prensa española* (Madrid, 1949).

DELEITO Y PIÑUELA, JOSÉ, *Origen y apogeo del 'Genero Chico'* (Madrid, 1949).

DEU I BAIGUAL, ESTEVE, *La indústria tèxtil llanera de Sabadell, 1896–1925* (Sabadell, 1990).

DÍAZ, ELÍAS, *La filosofía social del krausismo español* (Madrid, 1973).

DÍAZ DEL MORAL, JUAN, *Historia de las agitaciones campesinas andaluzas-Córdoba (Antecedentes para una reforma agraria)* (Madrid, 1967).

DICENTA, JOSÉ FERNANDO, *Luis Bonafoux, la 'víbora de Asnieres'* (Madrid, 1974).

DOMÍNGUEZ, JORGE I., *Insurrection or Loyalty. The Breakdown of the Spanish American Empire* (Cambridge, Mass., 1980).

DOYLE, MICHAEL W., *Empires* (Ithaca, 1986).

DURÁN, J. A., *Agrarismo y movilización campesina en el país gallego (1875–1912)* (Mexico, 1977).

DURNERIN, JAMES, *Maura et Cuba. Politique coloniale d'un ministre libéral* (Paris, 1978).

ELIZALDE PÉREZ-GRUESO, MARÍA DOLORES, *España en el Pacífico: la colonia de las Islas Carolinas, 1885–1899. Un modelo colonial en el contexto internacional del imperialismo* (Madrid, 1992).

——, 'La venta de las Islas Carolinas, un nuevo hito en el 98 español', (*Estudios Históricos*), vol. I, 361–80.

——, 'Una visión historiográfica de las coordenadas internacionales del Pacífico español, 1875–1899', in *Revista de Indias*, no. 49, (Jan.–Apr. 1989), 845–69.

ELORZA, ANTONIO, *La modernización política en España* (Madrid, 1990).

——, 'Nacionalización y corporativismo: el papel de la corona', in García Delgado, J. L. (ed.) (*La crisis*).

ENCISO RECIO, LUIS MIGUEL, 'La opinión pública española y la independencia hispanoamericana, 1819–1820', *Estudios y Documentos* no. 23, Departamento de Historia Moderna, Universidad de Valladolid, 1967.

Escuela Diplomática, *Corona y diplomacia. La monarquía española en la historia de las relaciones internacionales* (Madrid, 1988).

ESPADAS BURGOS, MANUEL, 'La Institución Libre de Enseñaza y la formación del militar durante la Restauración', *Estudios de Historia Militar*, vol. I. (Madrid, 1983), 495–514.

——, 'Orden social en la mentalidad militar española a comienzos del siglo XX', in García Delgado, J. L. (ed.) (*España, 1989–1936*), 345–59.

ESTRADE, PAUL, 'Cuba à la veille de l'indépendence: le mouvement économique (1890–1893)', 1 + 2 in *Melanges de la Casa de Velázquez* (Paris, 1977–8).

n.a. *Estudios Históricos. Homenaje a Los Profesores José María Jover Zamora y Vicente Palacio Atard.* 2 vols. (Madrid, 1990).

FABRA RIVAS, ANTONIO, *La Semana Trágica. El caso Maura* (Madrid, 1975).

FERNÁNDEZ ALMAGRO, MELCHOR, *Cánovas. Su vida y su política* (Madrid, 1972).

——, *Historia Política de la España Contempóranea.* 3 vols. (Madrid, 1956).

——, *La emancipación de América y su reflejo en la conciencia española*, 2nd edn. (Madrid, 1957).

——, *Historia del reinado de Don Alfonso XIII* (Barcelona, 1931).

——, 'Reacción popular ante el Desastre', *Arbor*, no. extraordinario (Dec. 1948), 379–97.

FERRARA, ORESTES, *The Last Spanish War. Revelations in 'Diplomacy'* (New York, 1937).

FLOOD, P. J., *France, 1914–18. Public opinion and the War Effort* (London and Basingstoke, 1990).

FONER, PHILIP S., *The Spanish–Cuban–American War and the Birth of American Imperialism, 1895–1902*, 2 vols. (New York, 1972).

FONTANA LÁZARO, JOSEP, *Cambio económico y actitudes políticas en la España del Siglo XIX* (Barcelona, 1973).

——, 'Colapso y transformación del comercio exterior español entre 1792 y 1827', *Moneda y Crédito* (Dec. 1970), 3–23.

——, 'Comercio colonial e industrialización: una reflexión sobre los orígenes de la industria moderna en Cataluña', in Nadal and Tortella (eds.) (*Agricultura*), 358–63.

FORNER MUÑOZ, SALVADOR, *Canalejas y el Partido Liberal Democrático (1900–1910)* (Madrid, 1993).

FRADERA, JOSEP M., 'Catalunya i Cuba en el segle XIX: el comerç d'esclaus', *L'Avenç*, no. 75 (Oct. 1984), 42–7.

FRANCOS RODRÍGUEZ, JOSÉ, *La vida de Canalejas* (Madrid, 1918).

FRIEDE, JUAN, *La otra verdad, la independencia americana vista por los españoles* (Bogotá, 1972).

FRIEDEL, FRANK, *The Splendid Little War* (Little, Brown, 1958).

FUSI, JUAN PABLO, *Política obrera en el país vasco (1880–1923)* (Madrid, 1975).

GABRIEL, PERE, 'Eren temps de sindicats. Reconsideracions a l'entorn de 1917–1923', in 'Els sindicats del crim: pistolerisme a Barcelona, 1917–1923', *L'Avenç*, no. 192 (May 1995), 14–17.

GALINDO HERRERO, SANTIAGO, *El 98 de los que fueron a la guerra* (Madrid, 1952).

GALLEGO, JOSÉ ANDRÉS, *La política religiosa en España, 1889–1913* (Madrid, 1975).

GAMBÓN PLANA, MARCELINO, *Biografía y bibliografía de D. Joaquín Costa* (Graus/Huesca, 1911).

GARCÍA DE CORTÁZAR, FERNANDO, 'La Iglesia en la crisis del estado español (1898–1923)', in Tuñón de Lara (*La Crisis*), 343–77.

GARCÍA DE CORTÁZAR, 'La Iglesia Española de la Restauración: definición de objetivos y prácticas religiosas', *Letras de Deusto*, (July–Dec. 1978).

GARCÍA DELGADO, JOSÉ LUIS (ed.), *La España de la Restauración. Política, economía, legislación y cultura* (Madrid, 1985).

——, *España entre dos siglos (1875–1931). Continuidad y cambio* (Madrid, 1991).

——, *La crisis de la Restauración: España, entre la primera guerra mundial y la segunda República* (Madrid, 1986).

——, *España, 1898–1936: estructuras y cambio* (Madrid, 1984).

——, 'Nacionalismo económico e intervención estatal 1900–1930', in Sánchez-

Albornoz (comp.) (*La modernizacion*), 176–93.

GARCÍA ESCUDERO, JOSÉ MARÍA, 'El Parlamento ante el Desastre', *Arbor*, no. extraordinario (Dec. 1948), 399–416.

GARCÍA FIGUERAS, TOMÁS, *La acción africana de España en torno al 98 (1860–1912)*, 2 vols. (Madrid, 1966).

GARCÍA LASAOSA, JOSÉ, *Basilio Paraíso. Industrial y político aragonés de la Restauración* (Zaragoza, 1984).

GARCÍA VENERO, MAXIMILIANO, *Antonio Maura, 1907–1909* (Madrid, 1953).

——, *Santiago Alba. Monárquico de razón* (Madrid, 1963).

GARRABOU, RAMÓN (ed.), *La crisis agraria de fines del siglo XIX* (Barcelona, 1988).

GARRIGA, RAMÓN, *Juan March y su tiempo* (Barcelona, 1976).

GAY DE MONTELLA, R., *Valoración hispánica en el Mediterráneo* (Madrid, 1952).

GIBSON, IAN, *En busca de José Antonio* (Barcelona, 1980).

GIL CREMADES, J. J., *El reformismo español* (Barcelona, 1969).

GIL PECHARROMÁN, JESÚS, 'Maura al poder', *Historia 16* (1989).

GÓMEZ MENDOZA, ANTONIO, 'De la harina al automóvil: un siglo de cambio económico en Castilla y León', in Nadal y Carreras (*Pautas regionales*), 159–86.

GONZÁLEZ CALLEJAS, EDUARDO and LIMON NEVADO, FREDES, *La Hispanidad como instrumento de combate. Raza e imperio en la prensa franquista durante la guerra civil española* (Madrid, 1988).

GONZÁLEZ CASANOVA, J. A., *Federalisme i autonomía a Catalunya (1868–1938). Documents* (Barcelona, 1974).

GONZÁLEZ HERNÁNDEZ, MARÍA JESÚS, 'Sobre Antonio Maura: el político, el mito y su política', *Revista de Occidente*, no. 77 (1987).

——, *Ciudadanía y Acción: el conservadurismo maurista, 1907–1923* (Madrid, 1990).

GROTTANELLI, CRISTIANO, 'Archaic Forms of Rebellion and their Religious Background', in Lincoln, Bruce (ed.) (*Religion*), 15–45.

GRENVILLE, J. A. S., *Lord Salisbury and Foreign Policy. The Close of the Nineteenth Century* (London, 1964).

GUBERN, RAMÓN, *Raza: un ensueño del General Franco* (Madrid, 1977).

GULLÓN, RICARDO, *La invención del 98 y otros ensayos* (Madrid, 1969).

HARRIS, WALTER B., *France, Spain, and the Rif* (London, 1927).

HARRISON, JOSEPH, 'Big Business and the Failure of Right-Wing Catalan Nationalism, 1901–1923', *The Historical Journal* no. 19 (1976), 901–18.

——, 'The Regenerationist Movement in Spain after the Disaster of 1898' in *European Studies Review*, vol. 9 (1979), 1–27.

——, 'Catalan Business and the loss of Cuba, 1898–1914', *Economic History Review*, vol. 27 (1974).

HEADRICK, DANIEL R., *Ejército y política en España (1866–1898)* (Madrid, 1981).

HEIBERG, MARIANNE, *The Making of the Basque Nation* (Cambridge, 1989).

HERNÁNDEZ SANDOICA, ELENA, and MANCEBO, MARCÍA FERNANDA, 'El Empréstito de 1896 y la política financiera en la guerra de Cuba', in *Cuadernos de Historia*

Moderna y Contemporánea, no. 1 (1980), 141–69.

HERNÁNDEZ SANDOICA, ELENA, 'Higiene y sociedad en la guerra de Cuba (1895–1898). Notas sobre soldados y proletarios', *Estudios de Historia Social*, no. 5–6 (Apr.–Sept. 1978), 361–84.

——, 'Pensamiento burgués y problemas coloniales en la España de la Restauración (1875–1887)', 2 vols. Ph.D. thesis, Universidad Complutense de Madrid (1982).

HERNÁNDEZ SÁNCHEZ-BARBA, MARIO, MALAGÓN, JAVIER, and LEAL SPENGLER, EUSEBIO, 'Presencia, conflictos y relaciones con los Estados Unidos de América. La crisis del 98. La Institución Libre de Enseñanza' in *Iberoamérica, una comunidad*, 2 vols., vol. II (Madrid, 1989), 713–25.

HERRICK, WALTER R. JR., *The American Naval Revolution* (Louisiana, 1966).

HEYWOOD, PAUL, *Marxism and the failure of Organised Socialism in Spain, 1879–1936* (Cambridge, 1990).

HILTON, SYLVIA L., 'Democracy goes Imperial: Spanish Views of American Policy in 1898', in Adams, David K. and Minnen, Cornelius A. van (eds.), *Reflections on American Exceptionalism* (Keele, 1994), 97–128.

——, 'The Spanish–American War of 1898: queries into the relationship between the press, public opinion and politics', *REDEN* (Revista Española de Estudios Norteamericanos), no. 7 (1994), 73–87.

HOBSBAWM, ERIC, *Labouring Men* (London, 1964).

HOLBO, PAUL S., 'The Convergence of Moods and the Cuban Bond "Conspiracy of 1898"', *Journal of American History*, vol. 55, no. 1 (June 1968), 54–72.

IBAÑEZ DE IBERO, CARLOS, MARQUIS DE MULHACÉN, *Política mediterránea de España, 1704–1951* (Madrid, 1952).

INMAN FOX, E., *Ideología y política en las letras de fin de siglo (1898)* (Barcelona, 1988).

——, 'El año de 1898 y el origen de los "intelectuales"', in Abellán, J. L. *et al.* (*La crisis*), 17–24.

——, 'Estudios preliminares: Ramiro de Maetzu y Whitney ante España (1897–1904)', in Ramiro de Maeztu, *Artículos desconocidos (1897–1904)*, 7–47.

——, *La crisis intelectual del 98* (Madrid, 1976).

JARDÍ, ENRIC, *El Doctor Robert i el seu temps* (Barcelona, 1969).

JIMÉNEZ CAMPO, JAVIER, 'La articulación política de las burguesías españolas', in García Delgado (ed.) (*España, 1898–1936*), 285–92.

JOVER ZAMORA, JOSÉ MARÍA, '1898: Teoría y prática de la redistribución colonial', *Fundación Universitaria Española* (Madrid, 1979).

——, *Política, diplomacia y humanismo popular en la España del siglo XIX* (Madrid, 1976).

——, (ed.), *El siglo XIX en España: doce estudios* (Barcelona 1974).

JUTGLAR, ANTONI, *Actitudes conservadores ante la realidad obrera en la etapa de la Restauración* (Madrid, 1970).

——, *Els burgesos catalans* (Barcelona 1966).

JUTGLAR, ANTONI, *Ideologías y clases en la España contemporánea*. 2 vols. (Madrid, 1968–9).

KERN, ROBERT W., *Liberals, Reformers and Caciques in Restoration Spain, 1875–1909* (Alburquerque, 1974).

LACOMBA, JUAN ANTONIO, *La crisis española de 1917* (Madrid, 1970).

LAÍN ENTRALGO, PEDRO, *La generación del noventa y ocho* (Madrid, 1945).

——, *Menéndez Pelayo. Historia de sus problemas intelectuales* (Madrid, 1944).

LAMBERT, FRANCIS J. D., 'The Cuban Question in Spanish Restoration Politics, 1878–1898', D.Phil. Thesis Oxford University, 1969.

LANNON, FRANCES, *Privilege, Persecution, and Prophesy. The Catholic Church in Spain, 1875–1975* (Oxford, 1987).

LÉCUYER, M. C. and SERRANO, C., *La Guerre d'Afrique et ses répercussions en Espagne (1839–1904)* (Paris, 1976).

LINCOLN, BRUCE, 'Notes Toward a Theory of Religion and Revolution', in Lincoln, Bruce (ed.) (*Religion*), 266–92.

—— (ed.), *Religion, Rebellion, Revolution. An interdisciplinary and cross-cultural collection of essays* (London, 1985).

LISSORGUES, YVAN, 'España ante la guerra colonial de 1895 a 1898: Leopoldo Alas (Clarín), periodista, y el problema cubano', in *Cuba, les étapes d'une libération* (Toulouse, 1979).

——, *Clarín Político*, 2 vols. (Barcelona, 1980).

LITVAK, LILY, *Transformación industrial y literatura en España (1895–1905)* (Madrid, 1980).

——, *España 1900. Modernismo, anarquismo y fin de siglo* (Barcelona, 1990).

LLADONOSA, MANUEL, 'Algunes consideracions entorn de Solidaritat Catalana i Solidaritat Obrera', *Recerques*, no. 14 (Barcelona, 1983), 61–7.

LLORENS I VILA, JORDI, *La Unió Catalanista (1891–1904)* (Barcelona, 1991).

LONBÈS, JEAN-NOËL and LEÓN ROSA, JOSÉ LUIS, *Vicente Blasco Ibañez. Deputado y novelista. Estudio e ilustración de su vida política 1898–1908* (Toulouse, 1972).

LÓPEZ, CARMEN and ELORZA, ANTONIO, *El Hierro y el Oro. Pensamiento político en España, siglos XVII–XVIII* (Madrid, 1989).

LÓPEZ-CORDÓN CORTEZO, MARÍA VICTORIA, 'La mentalidad conservadora durante la Restauración', in García Delgado, J. L. (ed.) (*La España*), 71–109.

LÓPEZ-MORILLAS, JUAN, *Hacia el 98. Literatura, sociedad, ideología* (Barcelona, 1972).

MAGNIEN, BRIGITTE, 'Culture urbaine', in Serrano, C. and Salaün, S. (eds.) (*1900*), 85–103.

MAINER, JOSÉ CARLOS, 'La Redención de los Paraninfos. Asambleas y regeneracionismo universitarios' in Tuñón de Lara, M. *et al.* (*La crisis*), 213–44.

MALUQUER DE MOTES BERNET, JORDI, 'El mercado colonial antillano en el siglo XIX', in Nadal, J. and Tortella, G. (eds.) (*Agricultura*), 322–57.

MARFANY, JOAN-LLUÍS, *La cultura del catalanisme* (Barcelona, 1995).

MARICHAL, JUAN, *El intelectual y la política en España (1898–1936). Cuatro conferencias* (Madrid, 1990).

MARIÑAS OTERO, LUIS, *La herencia del 98* (Madrid, 1967).

MARQUINA, RAFAEL, *Francesc Cambó* (Barcelona, n.d.).

MARRERO, VICENTE, *Maeztu* (Madrid, 1955).

MARTIN, BENJAMIN, *The Agony of Modernisation. Labor and Industrialization in Spain* (Ithaca, New York, 1990).

MARTÍN, MIGUEL, *El colonialismo español en Marruecos (1860–1956)* (Paris, 1973).

MARTÍN MARTÍNEZ, ISIDORO, 'Pedro Poveda, pedagogo innovador y divergente en la generación del 98', *Cuadernos de Investigación Historica*, no. 12 (Madrid, 1989), 45–62.

MARTÍN RODRÍGUEZ, MANUEL, 'Del trapiche a la fábrica de azúcar, 1779–1904', in Nadal and Catalán (*La cosa oculta*), 43–97.

MARTÍNEZ DE CAMPOS Y SERRANO, CARLOS, DUQUE DE LA TORRE, *La Reina Cristina y el Desastre* (Madrid, 1959).

MARTÍNEZ CUADRADO, MIGUEL, *La burguesía conservadora (1874–1931)*. 6th edn. (Barcelona, 1980).

——, *Restauración y crisis de la monarquía (1874–1931)* (Barcelona, 1991).

MARVAUD, ANGEL, *L'Espagne au XX siècle. Étude politique et économique* (Paris, 1913).

——, *La question sociale en Espagne* (Paris, 1910).

MAURA GAMAZO, G., DUQUE DE, and FERNANDEZ ALMAGRO, MELCHOR, *Por qué cayó Alfonso XIII. Evolución y disolución de los partidos históricos durante su reinado*, 2nd edn. (Madrid, 1948).

MAURICE, JACQUES and SERRANO, CARLOS, *J. Costa: Crisis de la Restauración y populismo (1875–1911)* (Madrid, 1977).

MAURICE, JACQUES, MAGNIEN, BRIGITTE and BUSSY GENEVOIS, DANIÈLE, *Peuple, mouvement ouvrièr, culture dans l'Espagne contemporaine. Cultures populaires, cultures souvrières en Espagne de 1840 à 1936* (Paris, 1990).

MAY, ERNEST R., *Imperial Democracy. The Emergence of America as a Great Power* (New York, 1961).

MESA, ROBERTO, *El Colonialismo en la crisis del XIX español* (Madrid, 1967).

MILLIS, WALTER, *The Martial Spirit: A Study of Our War with Spain* (Boston, 1931).

MOLAS, ISIDRE, *Lliga Catalana. Un estudi d'Estasiologia.* 2 vols. (Barcelona, 1971).

MOORE, BARRINGTON JR., *Injustice. The Social Bases of Obedience and Revolt* (London and Basingstoke, 1978).

MORADIELLOS, ENRIQUE, *El Sindicato de los Obreros Mineros Asturianos, 1910–1930* (Oviedo, 1986).

MORAL RUIZ, CARMEN DEL, *La sociedad madrileña fin de siglo y Baroja* (Madrid, 1974).

MORALES LEZCANO, VICTOR, *El Colonialism Hispano-francés en Marruecos (1898–1927)* (Madrid, 1976).

MORALES LEZCANO, VICTOR, *León y Castillo, Embajador (1887–1918). Un estudio sobre la política exterior de España* (Las Palmas, 1975).

MORALES PADRÓN, FRANCISCO, *Historia de unas relaciones difíciles (EEUU–América española)* (Seville, 1987).

MORENO FRAGINALS, MANUEL, *El Ingenio. Complejo económico social cubano del azúcar*, 3 vols. (Havana, 1978).

MORENO, FRANK JAY, 'The Spanish Colonial System: A Functional Approach', *Western Political Quarterly*, no. 20 part 1 (20 June 1967), 308–20.

MORGAN, WAYNE H., *America's Road to Empire: the War with Spain and Overseas Expansion* (New York, 1965).

MORRIS, EDMUND, *The Rise of Theodore Roosevelt* (New York, 1979).

MORSE, RICHARD M., 'The Heritage of Latin America' in Wiarda, Howard J., *Politics and Social Change in Los Angeles: The Distinct Tradition* (Amherst, 1974).

MOUSSET, ALBERT, *La Política Exterior de España, 1873–1918* (Madrid, 1918).

NADAL, JOAQUIM MARÍA DE, *Cromos de la vida vuitcentista* (Barcelona, 1946).

NADAL, JORDI, *El fracaso de la Revolución industrial en España, 1814–1913* (Barcelona, 1975).

——, 'Spain, 1830–1914' in Cipolla, Carlo M. (ed.), *The Emergence of Industrial Societies*, vol. II (London, 1973), 532–627.

NADAL, S., CARRERAS, A., and SUDRIÀ, N. (comps.), *La economía española en el siglo XX* (Madrid, 1987).

NADAL, JORDI and CARRERAS, ALBERT (eds.), *Pautas regionales de la industrialización española (siglos XIX y XX)* (Barcelona, 1990).

—— and CATALÁN, JORDI (eds.), *La cara oculta de la industrialización española. La modernización de los sectores no líderes (siglos XIX y XX)* (Madrid, 1994).

—— and TORTELLA, GABRIEL (eds.), *Agricultura, comercio colonial y crecimiento económico en la España contemporánea* (Barcelona, 1974).

NADAL I OLLER, JORDI, 'La industria cotonera' in Nadal i Oller, Jordi, *et al.*, *Història Econòmica de la Catalunya contemporània* (Barcelona, 1991), vol. III.

—— and CARLES SUDRIÀ, 'La controversia en torno al atraso español en la segunda mitad del siglo XIX (1860–1913)', *Revista de Historia Industrial*, 3 (1993).

NAVAJAS ZUBELDIA, CARLOS, *Ejército, Estado y Sociedad en España (1923–1930)* (Logroño, 1991)

NEALE, R. G., *Great Britain and United States Expansion: 1898–1900* (Michigan, 1966).

NOEL, GERARD, *Ena: Spain's English Queen* (London, 1984)

NUÑEZ, INDALECIO, 'Remember the "Maine"!', *Arbor*, no. extraordinario (Dec. 1948), 369–78.

NUÑEZ FLORENCIO, RAFAEL, 'La mentalidad militar en el marco de la Restauración canovista', *Cuadernos de Historia Contemporánea*, no. 14 (1992), 31–53.

——, *Militarismo y antimilitarismo en España (1888–1906)* (Madrid, 1990).

——, *El terrorismo anarquista, 1888–1909* (Madrid, 1983).

OLIVER, MIQUEL S., *La literatura del Desastre* (Barcelona, 1974).

OLIVIÉ, FERNANDO, *La herencia de un imperio roto. Dos siglos de política exterior española* (Madrid, 1992).

PABÓN, JESÚS, *Cambó*, 2 vols. (Barcelona, 1952).

——, *Días de ayer. Historias e historiadores contemporáneos* (Barcelona, 1963).

PARRY, J. H., *The Spanish Seaborne Empire* (Berkeley, 1966).

PARSONS, F. V., *The Origins of the Moroccan Question, 1880–1900* (London, 1976).

PAYNE, STANLEY G., 'Spanish Conservatism, 1834–1923', *Journal of Contemporary History*, vol. 13 (1978), 765–89.

——, *Politics and the Military in Modern Spain* (Stanford, 1967).

PÉREZ JR., LOUIS A., *Cuba. Between Reform and Revolution* (New York, 1988).

——, 'The Meaning of the Maine: Causation and the Historiography of the Spanish–American War', *Pacific Historical Review*. vol. 58 (1989), 293–322.

——, *Cuba Between Empires, 1878–1902* (Pittsburgh, 1983).

PÉREZ DE LA DEHESA, RAFAEL, *El grupo 'Germinal': una clase del 98* (Madrid, 1970).

——, *El Pensamiento de Costa y su influencia en el 98* (Madrid, 1966).

——, *Política y sociedad en el primer Unamuno* (Barcelona, 1973).

PÉREZ DELGADO, RAFAEL, *Antonio Maura* (Madrid, 1974).

——, *1898. El año del Desastre* (Madrid, 1976).

PÉREZ GARZÓN, JUAN SISINIO, *Luis Morote. La problemática de un Republicano (1863–1913)* (Madrid, 1976).

PIKE, FREDERICK B., *Hispanismo, 1898–1936* (London, 1971).

PIQUERAS ARENAS, JOSÉ ANTONIO, *La Revolución democrática, 1868–1874. Cuestión social, colonialismo y grupos de presión* (Madrid, 1992).

PLAZA ESCUDERO, LORENZO DE LA, 'España y la guerra anglo-boer (1899–1902)', *Cuadernos de Historia Contemporánea*, no. 10 (1988), 121–37.

PRADOS DE LA ESCOSURA, LEANDRO, *De imperio a nación. Crecimiento y atraso económico en España (1780–1930)* (Madrid, 1988).

PRIETO, ANTONIO, 'La generación del 98', *Cuadernos historia 16*, no. 285 (Madrid, 1985).

PUNSET, RAMÓN, 'Maura y el Maurismo. Perspectiva histórica de la revolución desde arriba', *Sistema*, no. 233 (Nov. 1979).

RAMOS, GEMMA and BENGOECHEA, SOLEDAD, 'La Patronal Catalana y la Huelga de 1902', *Historia Social*, no. 5 (Otoño, 1989), 77–95.

RAMSDEN, H., *The 1898 Movement in Spain. Towards a Reinterpretation with Special Reference to En torno al casticismo and Idearium español* (Manchester, 1974).

RANSON, E., 'British Military and Naval Observers in the Spanish–American War', *Journal of American Studies* (G.B.), 3.1. (July 1969).

RANZATO, GABRIELE, *La aventura de una ciudad industrial. Sabadell entre el antiguo régimen y la modernidad* (Barcelona, 1987).

REIG ARMERO, RAMIR, *Blasquistas y clericales. La lucha por la ciudad en la Valencia de 1900* (Valencia, 1986).

——, *Obrers i ciutadans. Blasquisme i moviment obrer. Valéncia, 1898–1906*

(Valencia, 1982).

REUTER, BERTHA ANN, *Anglo-American Relations during the Spanish–American War* (New York, 1924).

RICHARDS, MICHAEL ROBERT, 'Autarky and the Franco Dictatorship in Spain, 1936–1945', Ph.D. Thesis, University of London, 1995.

RICHARDSON, JOHN, *A Life of Picasso*, vol. I: 1881–1906 (London, 1991).

RIQUER, BORJA DE, 'Les eleccions de la Solidaritat Catalana a Barcelona', *Recerques*, no. 2 (Barcelona, 1972).

——, *Lliga regionalista: la burguesía catalana i el nacionalisme (1898–1904)* (Barcelona, 1977).

ROBLES EGEA, A., 'Formación de la conjunción republicano-socialista de 1909', *Revista de Estudios Políticos*, no. 29 (1982), 145–61.

ROBLES MUÑOZ, CRISTÓBAL, *Antonio Maura. Un político liberal* (Madrid, 1995).

——, *1898: Diplomacia y opinión* (Madrid, 1991).

——, '1898: La batalla por la paz. La mediación de Leon XIII entre España y Estados Unidos', *Revista de Indias*, vol. XLVI, no. 177 (1986), 247–89.

RODRÍGUEZ GONZÁLEZ, AUGUSTÍN R., 'Balances navales, estrategias y decisiones políticas en la guerra de 1898' in *Estudios Históricos*, vol. I (Madrid, 1990), 633–53.

ROLDÁN, SANTIAGO and GARCÍA DELGADO, J. L., *La formación de la sociedad capitalista en España, 1914–1920*, 2 vols. (Madrid, 1973).

ROLDÁN DE MONTAUD, INÉS, 'La Unión Constitucional y la política colonial de España en Cuba (1868–1898)', Ph.D. Thesis, Universidad Complutense de Madrid (1991).

ROMANO, JULIO, *Weyler. El Hombre de Hierro* (Madrid, 1934).

ROMERO-MAURA, JOAQUÍN, *'La rosa de fuego'. El obrerismo barcelonés de 1899 a 1909*, 2nd edn. (Madrid, 1989).

——, *The Spanish Army and Catalonia. The '¡Cu-cut! Incident' and the Law of Jurisdictions, 1905–1906* (Beverly Hills, 1976).

——, 'Terrorism in Barcelona and its Impact on Spanish Politics, 1904–1909', *Past and Present*, no. 41 (1968), 130–83.

——, 'Il Novantotto Spagnolo. Note sulle Ripercussioni Ideologiche del Disastro Coloniale', *Rivista Storica Italiana*, vol. LXXXIV (1972), 32–52.

ROMERO SALVADÓ, FRANCISCO J., 'Spain and the First World War: Neutrality and Crisis', Ph.D. Thesis, University of London, 1994.

ROMERO TOBAR, LEONARDO, *La Novela Popular española del siglo XIX* (Madrid, 1976).

ROSAS LEDESMA, ENRIQUE, 'Las "Declaraciones de Cartagena" (1907): Significación en la política exterior de España y repercusiones internacionales', *Cuadernos de historia moderna y contemporánea*, no. 2 (1981), 213–29.

ROSSI, ROSA, *Da Unamuno a Lorca* (Catania, 1967).

RUBERT DE VENTOS, XAVIER, *The Hispanic Labyrinth. Tradition and modernity in the Colonization of the Americas* (New Brunswick, 1991).

RUÍZ ALBÉNIZ, VICTOR, *Ecce homo* (Madrid, 1922).

SALES, NÚRIA, 'Servei militar i societat a l'Espanya del segle XIX', *Recerques*, no. 1 (1970), 145–81.

SALOM COSTA, JULIO, *España en la Europa de Bismark; la política exterior de Cánovas (1871–1881)* (Madrid, 1967).

SÁNCHEZ-ALBORNOZ, CLAUDIO, *Dípticos de Historia de España* (Madrid, 1982).

SÁNCHEZ-ALBORNOZ, NICOLÁS, *Las crisis de subsistencias de España en el siglo XIX* (Rosario, 1963).

——, (comp.), *La modernización económica de España 1830–1930* (Madrid, 1985).

SANDERSON, G. N., 'The European Partition of Africa: Coincidence or Conjuncture?' in Penrose, E. F. (ed.), *European Imperialism and the Partition of Africa* (London, 1975), 1–54.

SCOTT, REBECCA J., 'Explaining Abolition: Contradiction, Adoption and Challenge in Cuban Slave Society, 1860–1886', *Comparative Studies in Society and History*, vol. 26 (Cambridge, 1984), 83–111.

SECO SERRANO, CARLOS, *Alfonso XIII y la crisis de la restauración* (Barcelona, 1969).

——, 'Alfonso XIII y la diplomacia española de su tiempo', in Escuela Diplomática *Corona y Diplomacia* (Madrid, 1988), 185–211.

——, *Militarismo y civilismo en la España contemporánea* (Madrid, 1984).

——, *Perfil político y humano de un político de la restauración. Eduardo Dato a través de su archivo* (Madrid, 1978).

SERRA I CENDRÓS, GABRIEL, 'Montblanc: de la "Febre d'or" a la Fil. Loxera (1880–1893)', *Aplec de Treballs*, no. 8 (Montblanc, 1987), 181–243.

SERRANO, CARLOS, *Final del Imperio. España, 1895–1898* (Madrid, 1984).

——, *Le Tour du Peuple. Crise nationale, mouvements populaires et populisme en Espagne (1890–1910)* (Madrid, 1987).

SERRANO, C. and SALAÜN, S. (eds.), *1900 en Espagne (essai d'histoire culturelle)* (Bordeaux, 1988).

SERRALLONGA I URQUIDI, JOAN, 'Mítines y revoluciones en España, 1917', in Bonamusa, Francesc, *La Huelga General* (Madrid, 1991).

SEVILLA ANDRÉS, DIEGO, *Africa en la política española del siglo XIX* (Madrid, 1960).

——, *Antonio Maura. La Revolución desde arriba* (Barcelona, 1954).

——, *Canalejas* (Barcelona, 1956).

'Els sindacts del crim. Pistolerisme a Barcelona, 1917–1923', *L'Avenç*, no. 192 (May 1995), 13–41.

SMITH, JOSEPH, *The Spanish–American War. Conflict in the Caribbean and the Pacific, 1895–1902* (Harlow, 1994).

——, 'The "Splendid Little War" of 1898: a Reappraisal', *History*, vol. 80, no. 258 (Feb. 1995), 22–37.

SOLÁ, LLUIS, *'¡Cu-cut!' (1902–1912)* (Barcelona, 1967).

SOLDEVILA, CARLES, *Rovira i Virgili* (Barcelona, n.d.).

SOLÉ I SABATÉ, JOSEP and VILLARROYA I FONT, JOAN, *L'Exèrcit i Catalunya (1898–1936)*. *La premsa militar espanyola i el fet català* (Barcelona, 1990).

SOLÉ-TURA, JORDI, *Catalanisme i revolució burguesa* (Barcelona, 1967).

SUÁREZ CORTINA, MANUEL, *El reformismo en España. Republicanos y reformistas bajo la Monarquía de Alfonso XIII* (Madrid, 1986).

TATO Y AMAT, MIGUEL, *Sol y Ortega y la política contemporánea* (Madrid, 1914).

THOMPSON, E. P., 'The Moral Economy of the English Crowd in the Eighteenth Century', *Past and Present*, 50 (1971), 76–136.

TIERNO GALVÁN, ENRIQUE, *Costa y el regeneracionismo* (Barcelona, 1961).

TOGORES SÁNCHEZ, LUIS EUGENIO, 'España y la expansión de los Estados Unidos en el Pacífico. (De la guerra hispano-americana de 1898 y la pérdida de Filipinas al pleito por Sibutú y Cagayám de Joló)', in *Estudios Históricos*, vol. I. 655–75.

TOMBS, ROBERT (ed.), *Nationhood and Nationalism in France. From Boulangism to the Great War, 1889–1918* (London, 1971).

TORRE DEL RIO, ROSARIO DE LA, *Inglaterra y España en 1898* (Madrid, 1988).

——, 'La prensa madrileña y el discursos de Lord Salisbury sobre "Las naciones moribundas" (Londres, Albert Hall, 4 mayo 1898)', *Cuadernos de Historia Moderna y Contemporánea*, no. 6 (1985), 163–80.

TORTELLA, GABRIEL, *El desarrollo de la España contemporánea. Historia económica de los siglos XIX y XX* (Madrid, 1994).

TOWNSON, NIGEL (ed.), *El Republicanismo en España (1830–1977)* (Madrid, 1994).

TRASK, DAVID F., *The War with Spain in 1898* (New York, 1981).

TUÑÓN DE LARA, MANUEL, *Costa y Unamuno en la crisis de fin de siglo* (Madrid, 1974).

——, *La España del siglo XIX* (Barcelona, 1974).

——, *España: la quiebra de 1898* (Madrid, 1986).

——, *Estudios sobre el siglo XIX español* (Madrid, 1972).

——, *Historia y realidad del poder. (El poder y las élites en el primer tercio de la España del siglo XX)* (Madrid, 1967).

——, *Medio siglo de cultura española (1885–1936)* (Madrid, 1970).

——, *El movimiento obrero en la historia de España* (Madrid, 1972).

——, *et al.*, *La crisis del estado español 1898–1936* (Madrid, 1978).

——, *Prensa y Sociedad en España (1820–1936)* (Madrid, 1975).

TUSELL, JAVIER, *Antonio Maura. Una biografía política* (Madrid, 1994).

TUSELL, JAVIER and AVILÉS, JUAN, *La derecha española contemporánea. Sus orígines: el maurismo* (Madrid, 1986).

TZITSIKAS, HELENE, *El pensamiento español (1898–1899)* (Mexico, 1967).

VALENCIA, ANTONIO, *El género chico. (Antología de textos completos)* (Madrid, 1962).

VALLEJO, RAFAEL, 'Pervivencia de las formas tradicionales de protesta: los motines de 1892', *Historia Social* no. 8, Autumn 1990, 3–27.

VARELA ORTEGA, JOSÉ, 'Aftermath of Splendid Disaster: Spanish Politics before and after the Spanish American War of 1898', *Journal of Contemporary History*, vol. 15 (1980), 317–44.

——, *Los amigos políticos. Partidos, elecciones y caciquismo en la Restauración (1875–1900)* (Madrid, 1977).

VÁZQUEZ MONTALBÁN, MANUEL, *Los demonios familiares de Franco* (Barcelona, 1987).

——, 'Franco i el regeneracionisme de dretes', *L'Avenç*, no. 165 (Dec. 1992), 8–15.

VELARDE FUERTES, JUAN, 'Los planteamientos socioeconómicos del Gobierno Largo Maura (1907–1909) o bien El inicio del populismo económico en España: el Gobierno Largo Maura (1907–1909) o bien El nacimiento del populismo económico en España: el Gobierno Largo Maura (1907–1909)', unpublished article (Madrid, 12 Oct. 1984).

——, 'Primera aproximación al estudio de la Universidad de Oviedo como enlace entre la Institución Libre de Enseñanza y el Instituto de Reformas Sociales' in Tuñón de Lara, Manuel and Botrel, Jean-François, *Movimiento Obrero, Partidos Políticos y Literatura en la España Contemporánea* (Madrid, 1974), 223–40.

VICENS I VIVES, JAIME and LLORENS, MONTSERRAT, *Industrials i polítics del segle XIX* (Barcelona, 1958).

VILA-SAN-JUAN, JOSÉ LUIS, *Alfonso XIII: un rey, una época* (Madrid, 1993).

VILAS, JUAN BANTISTA (ed.), *Las relaciones internacionales en la España contemporânea* (Murcia, 1989).

VILLACORTA BAÑOS, FRANCISCO, *Burguesía y cultura. Los intelectuales españoles en la sociedad liberal, 1808–1931* (Madrid, 1980).

——, *El Ateneo de Madrid (1885–1912)* (Madrid, 1985).

VOLTES BOU, PEDRO, 'Las dos huelgas de contribuyentes en la Barcelona de fin de siglo', *Cuadernos de Historia Económica de Cataluña*, vol. V (Barcelona, 1971), 43–66.

——, *La semana trágica* (Madrid, 1995).

——, *La política de fin de siglo, a través de la prensa barcelonesa de la época*, Documentos y estudios, vol. XXII, (Barcelona, 1978).

WEBER, EUGEN, *France, fin de siècle* (Cambridge, Mass., 1986).

——, *Peasants into Frenchmen. The modernization of rural France, 1870–1914* (London, 1979).

WILKERSON, MARCUS M., *Public opinion and the Spanish–American War. A study in war propaganda* (Louisiana, 1932).

WINSTON, COLIN, *Workers and the Right in Spain, 1900–1936* (Princeton, 1985).

WISAN, JOSEPH E., *The Cuban Crises as Reflected in the New York Press (1895–1898)* (New York, 1934).

WOOLMAN, DAVID S., *Rebels in the Rif. Abd el Krim and the Rif Rebellion* (London, 1969).

YANIZ, JUAN PEDRO, *La crisis del pequeño imperio español* (Barcelona, 1974).

ZANCADA, PRÁXEDES, *Canalejas, Político y Gobernante* (Madrid, 1913).

ZINN, HOWARD, *A People's History of the United States* (London, 1980).

Index

	DATE DUE		